D1000063

Yale Historical Publications, Miscellany, 131

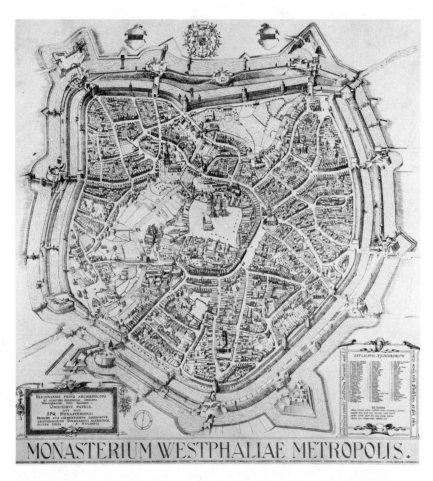

Aerial view of Münster, 1636; etching by Everhard Alerding. Westfälisches Landesmuseum für Kunst und Kulturgeschichte Münster; Westfalia Picta.

In the center of the city is the cathedral precinct. To its west across the Aa River is the parish of Überwasser; Saint Martin's is to its northeast; Saint Lambert's to the east; Saint Servatii, a tiny parish, to the southeast; and Aegidii parish to the south.

SOCIETY AND RELIGION IN MÜNSTER, 1535–1618

R. Po-chia Hsia

YALE UNIVERSITY PRESS
NEW HAVEN AND LONDON

BR858
M86
H77
1984

The thirty-first volume published under the direction of the Depart-
ment of History with assistance from the Kingsley Trust Association
Publication Fund established by the Scroll and Key Society of Yale
College

Copyright © 1984 by Yale University. All rights reserved. This
book may not be reproduced, in whole or in part, in any form
(beyond that copying permitted by Sections 107 and 108 of the U.S.
Copyright Law and except by reviewers for the public press), without written permission from the publishers.

Designed by Nancy Ovedovitz and set in Bembo type. Printed in
the United States of America by Edwards Brothers, Inc., Ann
Arbor, Michigan.

Library of Congress Cataloging in Publication Data

Hsia, R. Po-chia.
  Society and religion in Münster, 1535–1618.
  (Yale historical publications. Miscellany ; 131)
  Bibliography: pp. 273–95.
  Includes index.
  1. Münster in Westfalen (Germany)—Church history.
2. Sociology, Christian—Germany (West)—Münster in
Westfalen. I. Title. II. Series.
BR858.M86H77 1984   943'.56   83–14819
ISBN 0–300–03005–3

The paper in this book meets the guidelines for permanence and
durability of the Committee on Production Guidelines for Book
Longevity of the Council on Library Resources.

1   3   5   7   9   10   8   6   4   2

To my father, mother, and grandmother

FEB 3 1992

CONTENTS

TABLES AND FIGURES

ABBREVIATIONS

ADB	*Allgemeine Deutsche Biographie*
ARSJ	Archivum Romanum Societatis Jesu
BDAM	Bistums- und Diözesanarchiv Münster
Comp. Hist. Coll.	Compendium Historiae Collegii Monasteriensis Westphaliae
CTW	*Codex Traditionum Westfalicarum*
Duhr	Bernhard Duhr, *Geschichte der Jesuiten in den Ländern deutscher Zunge,* vols. 1 & 2
GG	*Geschichte und Gesellschaft*
GQBM	*Geschichtsquellen des Bistums Münster*
Hövel, *BB*	Ernst Hövel, ed., *Das Bürgerbuch der Stadt Münster 1538 bis 1660*
HZ	*Historische Zeitschrift*
JbWKG	*Jahrbuch des Vereins für Westfälische Kirchengeschichte*
JMH	*Journal of Modern History*
Keller	Ludwig Keller, *Die Gegenreformation in Westfalen und am Niederrhein. Aktenstücke und Erläuterungen*
	I. *1555–1585* (Leipzig, 1881)
	II. *1585–1609* (Leipzig, 1887)
	III. *1609–1623* (Leipzig, 1895)
Kerssenbroch	*Anabaptistici Furoris Monasteriensis . . . Hermanni Kerssenbroch,* ed., Heinrich Detmer, 2 vols.
Ketteler	Josef Ketteler, "Vom Geschlechterkreis des münsterschen Honoratiorentums," *Mitteilungen der Westdeutschen Gesellschaft für Familienkunde,* vol. 5, no. 9 (1928)
Krumbholtz	Robert Krumbholtz, *Die Gewerbe der Stadt Münster bis zum Jahre 1661*
Lethmate	Franz Lethmate, *Die Bevölkerung Münster i. W. in der zweiten Hälfte des 16. Jahrhunderts*
Litt. Ann.	*Litterae Annuae Societatis Jesu*
MSS.	Manuscripts
N	Unknown name
Niesert, *MUS*	Joseph Niesert, *Münsterische Urkundensammlung*
PfA	Pfarrarchiv
P & P	*Past and Present*
QFGSM (n.f.)	*Quellen und Forschungen zur Geschichte der Stadt Münster* (Neue Folge)

Ritter	Moritz Ritter, *Deutsche Geschichte im Zeitalter der Gegenreformation und des Dreissigjährigen Krieges,* 3 vols.
RKG	Günther Aders and Helmut Richtering, eds., *Gerichte des Alten Reiches. Reichskammer-Gericht. Reichshofrat,* 3 vols.
RWZfVK	*Rheinisch-Westfälische Zeitschrift für Volkskunde*
Röchell, *Chronik*	Johann Janssen, ed., *Die Münsterischen Chroniken von Röchell, Stevermann und Corfey*
SCJ	*Sixteenth Century Journal*
Schulte, KG	Eduard Schulte, "Die Kurgenossen des Rates 1520–1802," in *QFGSM,* vol. 3
Schwarz	*Die Akten der Visitation des Bistums Münster aus der Zeit Johanns von Hoya 1571–73*
StAM	Staatsarchiv Münster
StAM, AVM	—Altertumsverein Münster
StAM, FM	—Fürstentum Münster
StAM, FM, SFG	—Studienfonds Gymnasium Münster
StdAM	Stadtarchiv Münster
StdAM, GR	—Gruetamtsrechnungen
StdAM, KR	—Kämmereirechnungen
StdAM, RP	—Ratsprotokolle
StdAM, SP	—Schoehausprotokolle
StdAM, SR	—Schatzungsregister
Test. I & II	StdAM, B, Testamente I (sixteenth century) and Testamente II (seventeenth century)
UM	Universitätsmatrikel
Urk.	Urkunden
WF	*Westfälische Forschungen*
WZ	*Westfälische Zeitschrift*
ZfBLG	*Zeitschrift für Bayerische Landesgeschichte*

ACKNOWLEDGMENTS

During the course of research and writing, I have benefited from the encouragement and criticism of many scholars on both sides of the Atlantic; to two of them, I owe a special debt of gratitude. Steven Ozment has guided me along with judicious alternations of gentle nudges and penetrating criticisms; he has never let me forget that good history is more than just diligent research and that local historical studies must deal with wider issues of the age as well. Saving me from many confusing formulations, Harry Miskimin has directed me to write with lucidity and economy; his constant encouragements greatly sped me along in my writing. Jaroslav Pelikan gave me valuable suggestions on revising the thesis, while Thomas Brady and Robert Harding were kind enough to have read parts of the dissertation.

In Germany, Thomas Brady of the University of Oregon introduced me to scholars in Tübingen and shared with me his experiences of doing social history of the Reformation. Dr. Hans-Christoph Rublack and Dr. Ingrid Batori of the Sonderforschungsbereich "Spätmittelalter und Reformation" at Tübingen University discussed the preliminary findings of my research in a working session and kindly introduced me to the computer data-processing techniques of the Kitzingen Project.

In Münster, Dr. Karl-Heinz Kirchhoff welcomed me to the circle of local scholars, among whom he is the leading historian on the sixteenth century. Sharing with me his immense knowledge of the archives, he helped to make my stay in Münster a most productive year. Professor Heinz Stoob and Dr. Wilfried Ehbrecht of the Institut für Vergleichende Städtegeschichte offered me use of the facilities of the institute. With Dr. Ludwig Remling I spent many hours discussing the Jesuits and exchanging notes on the archives. To him and to the other scholars at the institute I express my warmest thanks. At the Stadtarchiv Dr. Helmut Lahrkamp and Herr Klaus Gimpel were most generous with their time and help. Dr. Peter Löffler of the Bistums- und Diözesanarchiv granted me permission to use fragile documents which awaited microfilming.

Father Edmund Lamalle, S.J., Prefect of the Roman Archives of the Society of Jesus, generously supplied me with microfilms when neither time nor money permitted me to visit the archives in person.

At Yale University Press, Charles Grench has been the ideal editor; and I have enjoyed working with Sally Serafim in preparing the manuscript. I must thank the anonymous reader for his valuable suggestions. My thanks also go to the Westfälisches Landesmuseum für Kunst und Kulturgeschichte Münster and Dr. Helmut Lahrkamp for providing me with photographs of the city, and to Robert Schnucker and the *Sixteenth Century Journal* for permission to include in the book materials from my article published in the journal.

Grants from the Social Science Research Council and the German Academic Exchange Service enabled me to carry out archival research in Germany during 1980–81; the generosity of the Whiting Foundation in the Humanities allowed me to finish writing the dissertation without interruption. Revisions for the manuscript were carried out at Columbia University, where I enjoyed the intellectual stimulation of the Society of Fellows in the Humanities.

October 1982
New Haven

INTRODUCTION

Günther Grass's allegorical novel, *Das Treffen in Telgte,* which describes
the attempt to revive German letters at the end of the Thirty Years' War,
brings together most of the prominent writers of the day, who were all
Protestants. Forced to convene in a desolate, war-torn little town, they
scoffed at the idea of meeting in proximity to the Catholic diplomats
who were haggling over the terms of peace in nearby "papist Münster."
One may be puzzled by Grass's summoning of writers only from Protestant Germany to deliberate on the revival of German literature. The
answer, however, is simple. In seventeenth century Germany, confessionalism dominated cultural life as strongly as it governed politics and
society. But even if Catholic writers were invited to participate in Grass's
fictitious meeting, very few would have actually turned up. Dominated
by Latin Jesuit drama, the literature of Catholic Germany made only a
modest contribution to the growth of a "national" vernacular tradition.
The most important Catholic writer of the Baroque, Johannes Scheffler,
better known as Angelus Silesius, was a convert; Jakob Balde and Friedrich von Spee, both Jesuits, gained literary fame primarily through their
Latin writings. This was especially true with Balde, one of the leading
neo-Latin poets of the seventeenth century. The existence of censorship
in Catholic territories further retarded cultural exchanges between the
"two Germanies."[1] Even in the eighteenth century, when a national
literature began to mature, it was essentially Lutheran in sentiment.
Many writers were Lutheran pastors or sons of pastors; Herder and
Lessing come readily to mind. The superiority of Lutherans over Catholics in German letters is just as unquestionable as the architectural sophistication of South Germany over austere North Germany. The ornate and
ostentatious Baroque and Rococo, particularly distinctive of Catholic
sacral buildings, are to be found mostly in Catholic Germany south of

---

1. On the cultural differences between Lutheran and Catholic Germany in the
realm of letters, see Dieter Breuer, "Zensur und Literaturpolitik in den deutschen Territorialstaaten des 17. Jahrhunderts am Beispiel Bayerns," in Albert Schöne, ed., *Stadt-
Schule-Universität. Buchwesen und die deutsche Literatur im 17. Jahrhundert* (Munich, 1976),
pp. 470–91.

the Main. The differences in culture between Catholic and Protestant suggest the central importance of confessionalism in German history, diminished but still present in contemporary Germany.

The confessional identity of the various German territories and cities crystallized in the century between the Interim (1548) and the Peace of Westphalia (1648). The study of the formation of confessions in Germany has so far focused on the two territories of Bavaria and the Palatinate. The former was the model of the Counter-Reformation absolutist state and the prime mover behind the League of Catholic princes; the latter was the most important Calvinist state, the mainstay of the Protestant Union, and the first opponent of Hapsburg Imperialist interest in the Thirty Years' War.[2]

Besides Bavaria, the Rhineland and Westphalia formed the second most important stronghold of Catholicism in sixteenth century Germany. The Bishopric of Münster, whose territory covered most of the extent of Westphalia, was the northernmost stronghold of Roman Catholicism in Germany and was almost completely surrounded by Protestant territories. To the west lay the Calvinist United Provinces; to the southwest, the largely Lutheran lands of the Duchy of Cleve-Mark-Berg; to the southeast, Calvinist Hesse-Kassel and Lutheran Hesse-Darmstadt; to the east, the Lutheran (later Calvinist) County of Lippe; to the northeast, Lutheran Osnabrück and Calvinist Bremen. In the midst of the diocese were the small Calvinist counties of Burgsteinfurt and Tecklenburg. The survival, indeed the vitality, of Catholicism in Münster in the Reformation era was truly remarkable. Not only did Catholicism withstand the advance of the Lutheran reform movement and the Anabaptist revolution, it managed to retain a distinctive confessional identity in the decades of religious confusion and ecclesiastical flexibility in the half century between the Anabaptist Kingdom (1534–35) and the election of a Wittelsbach Counter-Reformation bishop to the see (1585). Moreover, even before the arrival of the Society of Jesus, there was enough local strength to initiate the reinvigoration of the Catholic Church. The following pages will at-

2. For Bavaria, see Max Spindler, ed., *Handbuch der Bayerischen Geschichte,* vol. 2 (Munich, 1966) and Maximilian Lanzinner, *Fürst, Räte und Landstände: Die Entstehung der Zentralbehörden in Bayern 1511–1598* (Göttingen, 1980). For the Palatinate, see Volker Press, *Calvinismus und Territorialstaat. Regierung und Zentralbehörde der Kurpfalz* (Stuttgart, 1970) and Bernard Vogler, *Le Clergé Protestant Rhenan au Siècle de la Réforme 1555–1619* (Paris, 1976). The problem of confessionalization is the central theme of much of Ernst Walter Zeeden's writings; see his "Grundlagen und Wege der Konfessionsbildung in Deutschland im Zeitalter der Glaubenskämpfe," *Historische Zeitschrift (HZ)* 185 (1958), pp. 249–99 and other titles in the bibliography. See also Horst Rabe et al., eds., *Festgabe für Ernst Walter Zeeden* (Münster, 1976).

tempt to narrate this story of upheaval and continuity, of political and religious change. As the city of Münster dominated the bishopric, its spires and walls towering over the flat, extensive countryside, this work is essentially the history of the metropolitan city in the years when the lives of its burghers were profoundly shaped by the larger forces of religious change outside of their control.

In the spring of 1525, simultaneous with the great Peasants' War, many urban uprisings broke out in Northwest Germany: from Frankfurt, civic discontent spread northward, encouraging similar communal anti-clerical movements in Cologne, Münster, and Osnabrück. Once the revolutionary wave had subsided, the peasant armies defeated, the city councils rescinded concessions to disgruntled burghers made under duress. In Münster, the initial reform movement was suppressed when the magistrates regained full control in 1526. A new attempt at introducing evangelical reforms in Münster centered on an earnest young vicar, Bernhard Rothmann, who gained great popularity in 1531 by his fierce sermons attacking the abuses of the higher clergy. Supported by influential merchants, magistrates, and guild leaders, Rothmann broadened his critique to questioning the doctrines of the Old Church. The ideas of reform sparked civic excitement for renewal and mobilized the commune in its struggle to win religious liberty from the prince-bishop. At Christmas 1532, the civic militia captured most of Bishop Franz's councillors and the Catholic patricians in Telgte by surprise and forced the bishop to recognize the Reformation in Münster. In February 1533, the election of a solidly evangelical city council guaranteed the consolidation of the Reformation; Rothmann was appointed superintendent of the churches and he drew up an evangelical Church Ordinance.

In the summer of 1533, the paths of the magistrates and the reformer began to diverge. Influenced by radical sacramentalist preachers, Rothmann moved away from the Lutheran positions on the eucharist and on infant baptism. The colloquy of August 1533 marked the open break between the two Protestant factions. Rothmann carried with him the majority of the guild artisans and many burghers; the city council saw its members divided and its authority slipping away. In the winter of 1533, Anabaptist apostles heralding the ideas of Melchior Hoffmann and his disciple Jan Matthys arrived from the Netherlands. They preached the imminent end of the world and the need of the elect to purify and segregate themselves by re-baptism. Rothmann and his followers were baptized and the Anabaptists took power by capturing most council seats in the elections of 1534. Jan Matthys, the prophet of the movement, arrived in Münster; and all citizens had to choose between exile or re-baptism. Outside the city, Bishop Franz had gathered an army. Thus began the sixteen-month siege of the millenarian kingdom and the blood-iest episode in the early Reformation.[3]

Our story begins in June 1535, after the fall of the city to the siege army, and ends in 1618, on the eve of a much wider conflagration of arms from which Münster was to be spared. Three themes inform the history of Münster in these intervening years. The first theme of the book concerns the results of the Anabaptist revolution, and shows how the demographic losses and the sheer revulsion with the bloodshed helped to stabilize the rule of the restored civic elite and the position of the Catholic Church. Through family ties with the clerics of the various ecclesiastical institutions, through patterns of land- and fief-holding, through vicarial and mass endowments, the ruling elite in Münster was connected with the Catholic Church by material interest, family tradi-tions, and sentiments which transcended the immediately observable identity of interests. Far from being monolithic, the internal composition of the Catholic Church in Münster mirrored the myriad complexities in society. While a complete overlap between social groups and ecclesiasti-cal institutions never existed, the clerical hierarchy clearly corresponded to social divisions in society.

The second central theme of the book is the conflict between city and territorial state, between traditional political views inherent in the judi-cial and constitutional outlook of the medieval city commune and the self-assertion of the early modern, centralized territorial state. Compli-cating this conflict was the role confessions played in pitting the Counter-Reformation territorial state against the city which held on to traditional Catholicism and tolerance toward Lutherans. While the terri-torial officials were uncompromisingly committed to the goals of the Counter-Reformation, supporting the Jesuits and sweeping away local legal particularities which resisted the reform, the city magistrates were torn between commitment to defending the traditional rights of their city against the prince-bishop and supporting the work of the Society of

---

3. It is impossible here to give an adequate overview of the enormous body of literature on the Münster Anabaptist Kingdom. The following include the most important works. For Rothmann's writings, see the admirable edition by Robert Stupperich, *Die Schriften Bernhard Rothmanns* (= *Die Schriften des münsterischen Täufer und ihrer Gegner*, 1. Teil, Münster, 1970); for the theology of Melchior Hoffmann, the inspiration for the millenarian movement, see the definitive biography by Klaus Deppermann, *Melchior Hoff-mann: Soziale Unruhen und apokalyptische Visionen im Zeitalter der Reformation* (Göttingen, 1979); for a historiographic review, a Marxist interpretation, and a good narrative account, see Gerhard Brendler, *Das Täuferreich zu Münster 1534–35* (Berlin, 1966); for an opposing view by the leading scholar on the Anabaptist Kingdom and an exhaustive analysis of the social structure of the Anabaptist Kingdom, see Karl-Heinz Kirchhoff, *Die Täufer in Münster 1534/35. Untersuchungen zum Umfang und zur Sozialstruktur der Bewegung* (Münster, 1973).

Jesus and the Catholic Reformation. The years of increased tension between lord and city also saw heightened discord within the city walls as magistrates and citizens became divided into militant pro-Jesuit and Protestant factions. The moderate, traditional Catholic majority on the city council and among the populace came under greater and greater pressure to choose between confessional allegiance and loyalty to their civic ways. They solved the dilemma by removing confession as a matter of contention between city and lord, by endorsing the Counter-Reformation and suppressing Protestantism, but also by continuing to resist the territorial government's attempts to undermine civic liberties.

The third and final theme of the book deals with the impact of the Counter-Reformation on the Münsteraners. Through their devotion to educating the young, the Jesuits tapped a huge reservoir of youthful energies to transform the religious climate of the city. Tireless in their pedagogic, pastoral, and missionary work, the Society of Jesus succeeded in creating a new ideology to compete with the traditional world view of the burghers. By stressing doctrinal and ecclesiastical differences, they sharpened confessional consciousness and created divisions within the city, thus undermining traditional communal solidarities; by extolling the glory and the universality of the Catholic cause, they directed the attention of Catholic burghers away from preoccupation with their community to the wider horizons of Empire and Papacy, thus weakening the traditional, exclusive particularism of the medieval commune. The corporative, communal spirit of pre-Tridentine Catholicism, embodied in a multiple array of ecclesiastical institutions and forms of piety, gave way to the ordered, triumphant spirit of the Counter-Reformation. The following story is the history of the Münsteraners and those who helped to shape their lives in the years between the Reformation and the Counter-Reformation.

CHAPTER ONE

From Occupation to the Restoration of Civic Liberties

In the night of June 24, 1535, acting on information provided by a turncoat, the troops of Bishop Franz von Waldeck stole across the moat, scaled the city wall, and overpowered the nightwatch. Before the Anabaptists in Münster discovered the surprise assault, more than five hundred episcopal soldiers had made their way into the city. Street fighting continued into the first morning hours when the Saint Ludger's gate was thrown open and the besieging army poured in to finish off the defenders. Three hundred burghers threw up a wagon train (*Wagenburg*) and dug in at the main market; the rest of the defenders had been killed off or were in hiding. When they begged for mercy, the three hundred men were let out of the city, except for Jan van Leiden and other leaders of the Anabaptist Kingdom. After three more days of house-searching, slaughtering, and looting, the fifteen-month-long siege was finally over.[1]

Münster was in shambles. The iconoclasm of the Anabaptists and the bombardment of the city by the besieging army had inflicted severe damages; more devastating was the loss in life. The majority of the sixteen hundred defenders fell during the siege and the last battle; the five thousand women and fifteen hundred to two thousand old men and infants also suffered an extremely heavy toll because of starvation.[2] When the episcopal soldiers entered Münster they saw "mothers lying dead with dead infants in their arms" and corpses littering the streets.[3] The surviving women and children were driven out of Münster. The troops also looted everything they could lay hands on, regardless of whether the

1. For first-hand accounts of the fall of Münster, see the reports by the various commanders in the episcopal army in Carl A. Cornelius, ed., *Berichte der Augenzeugen über das Münsterische Wiedertäuferreich* (= GQBM II, Münster, 1853), pp. 358–69, 383–98.

2. On estimates of population in Münster under the Anabaptists and casualties of war, see Helmut Detmer, ed., *Hermanni a Kerssenbroch Anabaptistici Furoris Monasterium inclitam Westphaliae Metropolim evertentis historica narratio,* 2 vols. (= GQBM V & VI, Münster, 1899–1900), p. 700, n. 1; p. 736, n. 1. See also Karl-Heinz Kirchhoff, *Die Täufer in Münster 1534–35. Untersuchungen zum Umfang und zur Sozialstruktur der Bewegung* (Münster, 1973), p. 24 (hereafter cited as Kirchhoff, *Täufer*).

3. Cf. Chronicle of the Münster Bishopric, 1424–1557, in Johannes Ficker, ed., *Die Münsterischen Chroniken des Mittelalters* (= GQBM I, Münster, 1851), p. 338.

goods belonged to the fallen Anabaptists or to the Catholic citizens waiting to return. When Bishop Franz entered in triumph on June 28, Münster was an occupied city devoid of citizens and threatened by a possible outbreak of the plague.[4]

IN THE AFTERMATH OF THE ANABAPTIST KINGDOM

Revenge was the order of the day. The Anabaptist king, Jan van Leiden, and his two chief lieutenants, Bernd Knipperdolling and Bernd Krechting, were repeatedly interrogated under torture.[5] Sentenced to die on January 22, 1536, they were slowly tortured to death with red-hot pincers at the main city market in the presence of the bishop and the returned Catholic magistrates. Their mutilated bodies were then put into iron cages which hung from the spire of Saint Lambert to serve as a warning to future rebels.[6]

The fall of Münster, however, did not imply the destruction of the Anabaptist movement. Scattered by the fall of the godly city, the Anabaptists split into three main groups. Some remnants of the Münster defenders sought refuge with the duke of Oldenbourg, an enemy of Bishop Franz; there, they plotted a return to power. Another group followed the leadership of Jan van Batenburg and operated in the area between the bishopric and the Netherlands; they eventually degenerated into murderous and rapacious gangs of religious fanatics. These first two groups believed in the violent establishment of a new religio-social order; properties were to be shared by all believers and those who refused to join would be killed.[7] The third group followed a pacifist direction. Convinced by the error of the Münster Anabaptists and horrified by the violence of their coreligionists, Obbe Philips and his disciple Menno Simons led the Dutch Anabaptist movement away from bloody millenarian dreams to peaceful piety.[8] Anabaptist conventicles existed in secret

4. Cf. Kerssenbroch, p. 853.

5. For their confessions, see Cornelius, pp. 369–81, 398–410.

6. On the gruesome executions, see Kerssenbroch, pp. 873–75.

7. See the confession of Hermann von Pelkens, a locksmith from Hamm who was caught, interrogated, and executed in Münster in 1536. His confession (StdAM, B, causae criminales 174) has been published by Ernst Hövel as "Ein Beitrag zur Geschichte der wiedertäuferischen Bewegung nach 1535," *Quellen und Forschungen zur Geschichte der Stadt Münster (QFGSM)* IV (Münster, 1931). Pelkens proclaimed "dat de grundt der wederdope dyt in sick hebbe, dat alle gueden sollen gemeyne syn und alle de genne, sick an den handel nicht geven en wollen, umme to brengen, und in de doipe gelovet moeten hebn, der werlt entegen te syn" (p. 347).

8. For discussions of the various streams of Anabaptism in northwestern Europe after the demise of the Münster Anabaptist Kingdom, see Klaus Deppermann, *Melchior Hoffmann: soziale Unruhen und apokalyptische Visionen im Zeitalter der Reformation* (Göttingen,

after 1535, even in Münster, and maintained contact with one another through messengers and itinerant apostles. Through the capture of these messengers and the information they provided under interrogation, the authorities became aware of the existence of an extensive network of secret Anabaptist cells; the Anabaptist movement after 1536 not only affected the smaller towns and the countryside of the Bishopric of Münster but extended as far north as Groningen in East Friesland and as far south as Essen. Only in 1538 did the episcopal officials and city magistrates succeed in crushing these conventicles in Münsterland.[9] Between 1533 and 1546, excluding the Münsteraners, 150 men and 54 women were arrested as Anabaptists in the bishopric; and 73 of the men and 22 of the women received death sentences.[10] After 1540, the specter of another Anabaptist revolution finally vanished, although small bands of sectarians continued to commit occasional acts of terror.[11]

For the ruling class, religious innovations meant rebellion; the rooting out of Anabaptism also destroyed the initial advances made by the Lutheran Reformation in Münster. When Johann von der Wyck, syndic of Münster, leading supporter of the Lutheran Reformation and opponent of the Anabaptist, fled the city in February 1534, he received no mercy from Bishop Franz and was beheaded.[12] Other Lutherans were more fortunate. Of the eighty Münsteraners identified by contemporaries as leading Lutherans in 1532,[13] the majority joined the Anabaptist movement and perished; twenty men, however, fled the city in early 1534 and were allowed to return to Münster after June 1535.[14] Many of these

---

1979), pp. 312ff. and K.-H. Kirchhoff, "Die Täufer im Münsterland. Verbreitung und Verfolgung des Täufertums im Stift Münster 1533–1550," *Westfälische Zeitschrift (WZ)* 113 (1963), pp. 41–59, 83–91.

9. Cf. K.-H. Kirchhoff, "Täufer im Münsterland," pp. 60ff.

10. K.-H. Kirchhoff, "Exekutivorgane und Rechtspraxis der Täuferverfolgung in Münsterland 1533–1546," *Westfaelische Forschungen (WF)* 16 (1963), p. 178.

11. In 1547 Anabaptists, probably the Batenburgers, set fire to the village of Billerbeck, only twelve miles from the city of Münster; see the chronicle of Melchior Röchell, published in Johannes Janssen, ed., *Die Münsterischen Chroniken von Röchell, Stevermann und Corfey (= GQBM III, Münster, 1856)*, p. 237.

12. See the pamphlet *Warhafftige Historie/wie das Evangelium zu Münster angefangen/ und darnach durch die Wydderteuffer verstöret/wider auffgehört hat . . . fleyssig beschriben durch Henricum Dorpium Monasteriensem* (Wittenberg, 1536), sig. C3. The composer of this important pamphlet was undoubtedly a Lutheran; his exact identity, however, has yet to be determined. See also the debate between Robert Stupperich and Karl-Heinz Kirchhoff over the identity of the composer; their articles are published in *Jahrbuch des Vereins für Westfälische Kirchengeschichte (JbfWKG)* 51–52 (1958–59), pp. 150–60 and *JbfWKG,* 53–54 (1960–61), pp. 173–79.

13. Cf. Kirchhoff, *Täufer,* p. 17f.

14. See K.-H. Kirchhoff, "Eine münsterische Bürgerliste des Jahres 1535," *WZ* 111 (1961), pp. 75–94. The twenty men were Joh, Bastert, Peter Frese, Rotger Hulshorst,

Lutherans were community leaders, electors, guild elders, and magistrates; most returned to Münster as humbled men excluded from political office.[15] Politically disenfranchised, the Lutherans were also barred from openly expressing their beliefs. When a friend from Lübeck visited Jaspar Schroderken in 1536, the two sang Lutheran hymns in Schroderken's garden, whereupon they were reported to and fined by the city council.[16] Tainted by the odor of rebellion, the Lutheran Reformation was outlawed in Münster until 1555. Religious orthodoxy, to the authorities, remained the best guarantor of peace and order.

A massive transfer of properties within Münster followed the downfall of the Anabaptist Kingdom. In 1535, to help repay his huge war debts,[17] Bishop Franz ordered all properties of the Anabaptists confiscated. Estimated to be worth 98,697 guldens, the seized properties, however, were so overburdened with debts that buyers could not be found for many of the confiscated houses.[18] These were often given or sold back at a fraction of the estimated worth to pardoned Anabaptists or their kinsmen; others passed into the hands of buyers who agreed to assume the payments for the annuities for which the houses were put up as collateral by the burghers who became Anabaptists. Of the 631 properties confiscated (525 houses with adjoining gardens, 53 fields and gardens, 36 annuities, and 17 farm estates), 241 returned to the possession of pardoned Anabaptists and their kinsmen and 146 were sold to third parties.[19] Bishop Franz gave some of the houses to noblemen and cathedral canons in return for loans advanced during the siege; others he bestowed to com-

---

Jaspar Joddeveld, Joh. Langermann jun., Lubbert Lentinck, Joh. Mennemann, Peter Mensinck, Heinrich Modersohn, Ludger Mumme, Michael Nordinck (al. Hattinck), Joh. Rotermundt jun., Jaspar Schroderken, Reinert Stille, Rolef van Swolle, Gert Tunneken, Joh. Ummegrove, Joh. Wecheler, Claes Windemecker, and Wolter Westerhuis. The bellmaker Westerhuis was not included in the 1535 returnees; he probably came back to Münster in 1536; see K.-H. Kirchhoff, "Wolter Westerhuis (1497–1548) ein Glockengiesser in Westfalen," *WZ* 129 (1979), pp. 69–88.

15. The only exception was the merchant Johann Langermann junior, who served as magistrate between 1554 and 1584. His father, Johann senior, was one of Bernhard Rothmann's chief supporters in 1532 and dared not return to Münster. See appendix 1, no. 86.

16. Cf. Röchell, *Chronik,* p. 234.

17. The cost of the fifteen-month-long siege ran to over one million guldens; while the other Imperial princes and rulers contributed toward the upkeep of the siege army, the major share of the financial burden was borne by the bishop and the taxes levied by the territorial estates. See Ernst Müller, ed., *Die Abrechnungen des Johannes Hageboke über die Kosten der Belagerung der Stadt Münster 1534–1535* . . . (= *GQBM* VIII, Münster, 1937), p. vi.

18. Cf. Kirchhoff, *Täufer,* pp. 7ff.

19. The records of the commission in charge of the confiscation and sale of the Anabaptist houses do not indicate what happened to the other properties. See Kirchhoff, *Täufer,* p. 35.

manders, courtiers, and pages in reward for their service.[20] The Catholic families who constituted the ruling elite in Münster after 1535 also received or bought up houses, sometimes at a fraction of the estimated price—the Heerde, Plönies, Münstermann, Boland, Detten, Frie, Holtebuer, Huge, Joddeveld, Jonas, Körler, Mennemann, Modersohn, and Oeseden were among the buyers of Anabaptist houses.[21]

Efforts to restore the socio-economic structure of Münster prior to the millenarian revolution paralleled the redistribution of Anabaptist properties. While it was rather easy to prove ownership of houses, it was more difficult to reestablish the bonds of money. In July 1536, the city council asked holders of annuities to come forward and report honestly on rents in their name which had been destroyed by the Anabaptists; new bonds were to be drawn up and sealed.[22] The destruction of the property deeds of the ecclesiastical institutions did not alter the actual economic power of the Church. One of the first acts of the returned clerics was to reaffirm monetary obligations due the Church.[23]

Overburdened by debts and by exactions from the bishop, the city of Münster had the most trouble meeting interest payments. In 1536, the city council was able to pay only about one-quarter of the interest due on city debts; by 1542, the city met two-thirds of her interest obligations; and only in the late 1550s were the actual interest of city bonds paid according to their full value.[24] Loans forcibly raised from the cloisters by the Protestant magistrates in 1533 were simply not honored by the Catholic councillors after 1536.[25] Regarding citizens who held municipal debts, many of whom were magistrates or their kinsmen, the city council agreed in 1542 to render payment on interest due between February 1534 and June 1535, the period when Münster was under Anabaptist control.[26] The income of the city fell by about 60 percent between 1533 and 1536; revenues received by the *Gruetamt* did not reach the 1533 level until 1559 (see fig. 1.1).[27]

20. Cf. Kirchhoff, *Täufer,* nos. 74, 127, 146, 191, 254, 274, 275, 321, 443, 513, 638, 698, 741.

21. See Kirchhoff, *Täufer,* nos. 1, 11, 27, 88, 97, 165, 191, 194, 321, 443, 451, 468, 515, 555, 633, 668, 706, 729, 752.

22. StdAM, AII, 19a, fragment of council minutes and ordinances, 1536–43 (30 folio leaves), entry under July 3, 1536, fol. 30v.

23. Cf. StAM, FM, Minoriten-Münster, Urk. 5a (Dec. 7, 1540). The document is a receipt signed by Everhard von Büren, guardian of the Franciscan cloister in Münster, certifying the redemption of an annuity by certain burghers of Dülmen; the bond itself had been destroyed by the Anabaptists and should it turn up in the future it was to be invalid.

24. See StdAM, AVIII, 188, GR, vol. 3, fols. 17ff., 131ff.; vol. 4, fols. 149v ff.; and vol. 6, fols. 55ff.

25. See chap. 2, p. 51.

26. Cf. StdAM, AVIII, 188, GR, vol. 3, fols. 134v–135.

27. The Gruetamt was the major financial institution of the city in the sixteenth century,

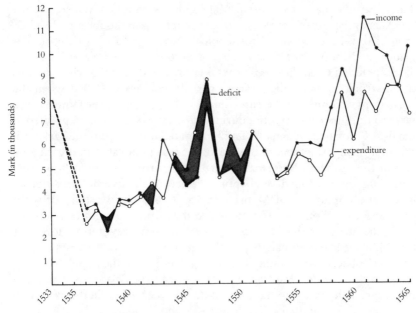

Figure 1.1 Budget of Münster, 1535–65
Source: StdAM, AVIII, 188, vols. 2–6

Underlying the financial troubles of the city and the depressed state of the economy was the enormous loss in population; the demographic growth of Münster after 1536 accompanied and stimulated economic recovery. The nature of that demographic recovery had important implications for changes in the social structure of Münster, changes crucial to the reordering of religion and the power distribution after 1536. With these questions in mind, we will now examine the pattern of population growth in post-Anabaptist Münster.

CHANGES IN DEMOGRAPHIC AND SOCIAL STRUCTURES

Shortly after they were exiled, the Anabaptist women and children started to drift back into Münster. Upon receiving a report from Wilkin Steding, the commander of the occupying force, Bishop Franz granted the women permission to reside, provided that they abjure Anabaptism

---

surpassing and incorporating many of the functions of the *Kämmerei*. The Gruetamt was established originally as an agency for the collection of beer-brewing tax; as beer-brewing became the most lucrative industry of Münster, the Gruetamt grew in importance and took on the function of raising loans and disbursing interest on bonds for the city government.

and swear allegiance to himself.[28] The citizens who fled Münster before the Anabaptists took power also began to return. In the summer of 1535, around five hundred male household heads swore a new oath of allegiance to Bishop Franz and were allowed to return to their native city.[29] They included Catholic families who left Münster in 1533 when the Lutherans took power and the leading guild families who fled when the Anabaptists dominated the city council in 1534; most of the families who were to dominate city politics during the next fifty years also appeared in the list of returned citizens. A few Lutheran families also came back with this first group; the men who were swept into political office by the success of the Lutheran Reformation in 1533 returned as political outcasts.

Adding the pardoned Anabaptist women to the five hundred households, the population of Münster in 1535–36 probably stood between three and four thousand. Compared to the estimated eight to ten thousand inhabitants of the city prior to the Anabaptist revolution, it is clear that Münster lost over half its population in the tumultuous years of 1534 and 1535. The siege accounted for the greater part of the population loss, but many citizens left Münster never to return. The Anabaptist Kingdom thus represented a demographic disaster unprecedented in the city's history, except for the Black Death of 1349–50.[30] Underpopulated Münster attracted villagers and townsmen from the surrounding countryside. As early as September 1536, Bishop Franz ordered the *Statthalter* and the magistrates to expel those who had come to the city in search of refuge and employment; Münsteraners were warned not to house outsiders for fear of possible Anabaptist infiltration.[31] Pressures to allow immigration, however, were too great to be legislated away. The city needed laborers and artisans for rebuilding; for the rustics and townsfolk outside of Münster, the capital city offered employment, cheap housing, and opportunities for getting ahead. After the 1538 success in destroying the clandestine Anabaptist cells in the bishopric, few hindrances were placed to prevent immigration. In 1538 (the only year in the immediate post-Anabaptist period for which demographic records are extant), 150 men and 47 women registered on the civic roll.[32] Most of the new citizens came from the surrounding towns and villages in Münsterland; others left homes in the Netherlands (Groningen, Amsterdam, Maastricht, and

28. Kerssenbroch, p. 861.

29. Cf. Kirchhoff, "Bürgerliste, 1535."

30. A medieval chronicle gave the figure of 11,000 for those who died of the plague in Münster; while the number is probably highly exaggerated, it still gives us a sense of the demographic disaster of 1350. See the chronicle of Florenz von Wevelinkhoven in *GQBM* I, p. 131.

31. See StdAM, AII, 19a, entry under Sept. 1, 1536, fol. 6v.

32. Cf. Ernst Hövel, ed., *Das Bürgerbuch der Stadt Münster 1538 bis 1660* (= QFGSM VIII, Münster 1936), pp. 59–63. Hereafter cited as Hövel, *BB*.

Roermund), in the Rhineland (Cologne, Xanten, Jülich), and in other parts of Westphalia (Dortmund, Hamm, Soest, Paderborn, Lippe, and Iserlohn) to come to Münster. Of the 50 men whose occupations are known, the majority lived from humble trades: 17 were day laborers, 10 shoemakers and tailors, and 3 former serfs. Only 4 men (2 goldsmiths, 1 shopkeeper, and 1 woolweaver) could be counted as well-to-do. Close to half of the 50 practiced building trades.

There is no reason to doubt that the flow of immigrants was very heavy in general in the decade after 1535. Men and women granted citizenship represented only a portion of the newcomers. The paucity of extant tax registers renders the estimation of population for the 1530s and 1540s difficult. For 1539, the first year for which tax records are available, only one of the six district (*Leischaften*) tax registers is extant (for Aegidius); for 1540, another (for Jodefeld) has survived. For the years 1548–50 registers exist for four of the six districts; and only in the 1590s do we have complete tax records for all six districts of the city.[33] Based on the population ratio between districts in the late sixteenth and early seventeenth century (see table 1.1), we can come up with rough population figures for the 1530s and 1540s, using only incomplete tax records.[34] Thus, I have estimated the population of Münster in 1540 at around 5,780 and that for 1550 to be roughly 7,570. Table 1.2 shows the distribution of population between the four districts for which records are available. In other words, demographic recovery advanced most rapidly between 1535 and 1540; thereafter the rate of population increase slowed. By the 1570s, population in Münster regained the pre-Anabaptist level; in the 1590s about ten thousand people lived in Münster, a figure little changed until the late seventeenth century.[35]

33. The tax registers are grouped under AVIII, 259 in the StdAM.

34. This method is reliable only because the area enclosed by the city walls remained essentially unchanged between the Middle Ages and the eighteenth century. The 1540 Jodefeld tax register entered 176 households (113 headed by men, 63 by women), 55 servants, 13 tenants and dependents. I have assumed the average household size headed by men to be five and that headed by women to be three. Households with female heads were overwhelmingly families headed by widows; we can thus assume that some of the children had grown up and no longer lived within those households. The tax rolls also indicate where households were headed by single men; judging from the tax assessments, those in the higher brackets were more likely to be widowers, well-established citizens who had lost their spouses; those in the lower brackets were likely to be single men in the first stage of their careers. Based on the above household sizes, I have estimated the 1540 Jodefeld district population to be around eight hundred souls. The 1539 tax register for Aegidii has been analyzed by Kirchhoff; see his *Täufer,* p. 40. He counted 306 households, 120 domestic servants, and 45 tenants, hence, a total district population of ca. 1,350.

35. Around the turn of the seventeenth century, there were about ten thousand souls in Münster, excluding the thousand or so students at the Jesuit College. For the late seven-

Table 1.1   *Distribution of Population between Districts*

Aegidii	Lamberti	Martini	Jodefeld	Liebfrauen	Ludgeri
1591					
24.03%	18.75%	16.25%	14.36%	12.99%	13.62% = 100
1603					
24.2%	20.1%	19.1%	11.9%	14.1%	10.6% = 100
Average					
24.1%	19.4%	17.7%	13.1%	13.6%	12.1% = 100

Sources: For 1591, Franz Lethmate, *Die Bevölkerung Münsters i. W. in der zweiten Hälfte des 16. Jahrhunderts,* p. 44; for 1603, StdAM, AVIII, 259, SR Aegidii, vol. 3, fols. 76–87; SR Lamberti, vol. 2; SR Martini, vol. 2; SR Jodefeld, vol. 2; SR Liebfrauen, vol. 2; SR Ludgeri, vol. 1 (all unpaginated).

Table 1.2   *Population Structure in Münster in 1548 and 1550*

	Households headed by		Servants		Tenants & others		
	M.	F.	M.	F.	M.	F.	?
Jodefeld 1548	167(10)★	65	38	50	5	41	9
Liebfrauen 1548	172(12)	56	12	16	2	6	—
Lamberti 1548	167(46)	69	40	48	10	33	69
Aegidii 1550	256(?)	86	81	121	8	12	8
Total	762(68+)	276	171	235	25	92	86

★The numbers in brackets refer to widowers and bachelors.

One factor in the demographic recovery of Münster helped to determine the political and religious structures of the city republic: the rapid turnover of the population between 1534 and 1554 was an event of immense significance. Including pardoned Anabaptists, the Münsteraners who returned to their native city in 1535 and 1536 could not have numbered more than five thousand; the Anabaptist movement had carried the major part of the citizenry with it, either through faith or coercion. After 1535, close to one-half of the inhabitants were immigrants new to the customs and history of the Westphalian metropole. In the normal course of urban demographic history, theoretically, one might

teenth century, see Helmut Lahrkamp, ed., *Münsters Bevölkerung um 1685* (= QFGSM, n.f. VI, Münster, 1972), p. 20.

expect a complete population turnover in premodern cities in a little over one century.[36] This process was gradual; old, established families died out in the course of generations and new names appeared to take their place. In Münster, however, the transition was abrupt. Many families were wiped out by the Anabaptist catastrophe; a casual comparison between family names in Münster before and after 1534–35 would indicate a drastic population turnover.

An analysis of the new citizens of 1538 shows that the majority of newcomers belonged to the middle and lower classes; day laborers, artisans of humbler trades, and former serfs constituted the bulk of the immigrants. In a normal process of social mobility and integration in the late medieval and early modern cities, many newcomers would quickly join the handicraft guilds and become politically active members of the civic community. Two factors, however, impeded the rapid political integration of the newcomers in Münster. For one, guilds did not exist after 1535. Blamed for instigating the Anabaptist rebellion, artisans were forbidden to organize; the *Gesamtgilde,* the political union of all guilds, was explicitly outlawed.[37] Furthermore, the Anabaptist revolution decimated the ranks of the guilds because many artisans fell defending the millenarian kingdom. The resulting weakness of the guilds thus vastly enhanced the authority of the magistracy; it took the artisans two decades after 1535 to regain the right of political representation and organization, and another sixty years to challenge the authority of the city council.[38]

Another characteristic of the demographic recovery also helped to enhance the power of the Catholic ruling elite in Münster. The majority of immigrants came from small towns in Münsterland where the Reformation movement did not make an important impact in the 1520s and 1530s. Both the Lutheran and the Anabaptist movements followed trade routes and affected initially the largest cities in the bishopric—Münster, Coesfeld, and Warendorf, in descending order of size. In Münster and Warendorf, where the Reformation movement succeeded at first in establishing itself, religious innovations and civic liberties were crushed by force.[39] In Coesfeld and Dülmen, Bishop Franz quickly suppressed the initial signs of Lutheran reform before religious sentiments could fuel

36. Cf. Harry A. Miskimin, "The Legacies of London: 1259–1330," in *The Medieval City,* ed. H. A. Miskimin et al. (New Haven, 1977), p. 217, n. 13.

37. Cf. Robert Krumbholtz, *Die Gewerbe der Stadt Münster bis zum Jahre 1661* (Leipzig, 1898), pp. 58f.

38. See chap. 5, pp. 136ff.

39. For the Reformation movement in Warendorf and the suppression of civic liberties by Bishop Franz in 1534, see K.-H. Kirchhoff, "Die Besetzung Warendorfs," *Westfalen* 40 (1962), pp. 117–22.

social movements.[40] A good part of the population in post-Anabaptist Münster had not seen the doctrines of the Catholic Church challenged, the clergy humiliated, and its authority undermined.

Perhaps the greatest challenge the Anabaptist Kingdom posed to existing social order was the threat it represented to family bonds. In medieval and early modern German cities, family power formed the basis of class domination; fundamental to the consciousness of townspeople in the sixteenth century was family consciousness.[41] When the Anabaptists in Münster pronounced all marriages dissolved and imitated Old Testament polygamy, they announced the most revolutionary aspects of their blueprint for salvation. Religious fervor destroyed the bonds of marriage and kinship: Lutheran husbands fled the city while their wives embraced Anabaptism; religious beliefs and city walls separated husbands from wives, parents from children, and brothers from brothers during the siege of Münster. The reports of the commission appointed by Bishop Franz to confiscate Anabaptist properties attest to the havoc the Anabaptist movement wrought on family ties. A considerable number of families perished; very few families emerged from the disaster without losing a member or kinsman.[42] Only the Catholic burgher elite remained intact; these families emerged from the experience with strengthened family ties and political power. When Borchard Heerde, a rich merchant and Catholic magistrate, drew up his will in 1539, he admonished his sons to keep harmony in the family and "to hold fast to the holy Catholic Christian Church and not to accept any other teachings or sects." Loyalty to the Catholic Church guaranteed family unity and political power in the eyes of the ruling elite.[43]

THE RULING ELITE

Between June 25, 1535, and May 4, 1536, Münster was under military rule. The exactions of the troops and the high-handed rule of the various military commanders embittered many citizens. Even in 1536, noblemen and commanders still used the pretext of confiscating Anabaptist properties to despoil Catholic citizens of their land outside Münster.[44] Only

40. Cf. K.-H. Kirchhoff, "Das Ende der lutherischen Bewegung in Coesfeld und Dülmen 1533," *JbfWKG* 62 (1969), pp. 43–68.

41. See Erich Maschke, *Die Familie in der deutschen Stadt des späten Mittelalters* (Heidelberg, 1980), esp. p. 97. For the importance of family and lineage in an early modern German city, see Christopher R. Friedrichs, *Urban Society in an Age of War: Nördlingen, 1580–1720* (Princeton, 1979), p. 185.

42. Cf. Kirchhoff, *Täufer*, pp. 25f.

43. See Borchard Heerde senior's will, StdAM, B, Test. I, no. 106, vol. 2, fols. 101ff. See also appendix 1, no. 57.

44. See copy of a letter from the city council to the cathedral chapter, dated Aug. 18, 1536, StdAM, AII, 19a, fol. 3.

when Bishop Franz appointed twenty-four magistrates in May 1536 to assist the *Statthalter* was the city republic on the way to recovering her lost liberties.

The twenty-four magistrates appointed for life consisted of twelve patricians and twelve burghers. All belonged to the ruling elite in Münster before the Reformation and only one man, Jobst Smithues, did not seem to have held political office previously.[45] As vassals of the bishop, the patricians received commissions in the episcopal army and paid feudal levies to help defeat the Anabaptists.[46] The burgher elite also contributed to the siege through taxes and loans, and received commissions to provide for the army.[47] In the June 1534 territorial tax, the first of its kind levied to finance the siege warfare, Münsteraners in exile paid 762 guldens; three men alone—Wilbrand Plönies, named Bürgermeister in 1536, Heinrich Herding, and Johann Herding—paid 300 guldens.[48]

When the city fell, Bishop Franz rewarded the loyalty of the Catholic burghers with political office. Although named by him, the city council was by no means a subservient body. When the 1536 *Landtag* at Laerbrock adopted resolutions to abolish Münster's liberties, the majority of the magistrates refused to go along. Besides restoring full rights to the clergy, the articles of the Landtag provided for the construction of a citadel inside Münster,[49] the nomination of future magistrates by the bishops, the stationing of troops, and the joint governance of Münster by the castellan, the episcopal judge, and the magistrates.[50] In January 1537, the magistrates from burgher families refused to sign away civic liberties and asked Bishop Franz to release them from their oaths. At this point, some patrician magistrates withdrew and declined to participate in the city's struggle; they closed ranks with the knights, whose status they

45. The names of the twenty-four magistrates are given by Kerssenbroch, p. 889.

46. See appendix 1, nos. 10, 13, 25, 38, 40, 43, 45, 46, 118, 127, 133, 135, 147, 148, 154.

47. Wilbrand Plönies, Johann Heerde, and Hermann Heerde were the most prominent burghers to serve in the besieging army. Johann Heerde, for example, procured gunpowder from Amsterdam; Hermann Heerde and Wilbrand Plönies were also in the pay of the quartermaster of the army. See Müller, *Abrechnungen,* pp. 12, 28, 58, 61–62, 115, 117; and Kerssenbroch, p. 530.

48. Cf. Müller, *Abrechnungen,* p. 12. For the origins of the territorial tax, see K.-H. Kirchhoff, "Die landständischen Schatzungen des Stifts Münster im 16. Jahrhundert," *WF* 14 (1961), pp. 117–32.

49. See K.-H. Kirchhoff, "Zwinger und Neuwerk. Beiträge zur Geschichte der Befestigung der Stadt Münster im ausgehenden Mittelalter," in *QFGSM,* n.f. V (1970), pp. 77ff.

50. For the new constitution of Münster dictated to the citizens at the *Landtag,* see Kerssenbroch, pp. 897ff., Joseph Niesert, *Münsterische Urkundensammlung. I: Urkunden zur Geschichte der münsterischen Wiedertäufer* (Coesfeld, 1826), pp. 256ff. Hereafter cited as Niesert, *MUS,* I.

aspired to attain and were content to let Münster become a territorial town without political autonomy.[51]

Münster was saved from her fate only by the intervention of outside powers and by Bishop Franz's predicaments. The siege of the Anabaptist Kingdom represented more than a war between bishop and rebellious citizens; the Anabaptists, as religious outcasts in the Empire, mobilized the combined opposition of Catholic and Protestant princes. Bishop Franz's principal allies included Landgrave Philip of Hesse, the central figure of the Schmaldkaldic League, and the Catholic duke of Jülich-Cleve and the prince-bishop Hermann von der Wied of Cologne. A portion of the enormous cost of fielding an army for fifteen months was raised by the Imperial estates; the fate of Münster informed the discussions in the Imperial Diets and the Circle Diets (*Kreistage*) as well. After the fall of the city, the Reichstag at Worms (November 1535) reached a decision on the fate of Münster: Citizens not implicated in the uprising were to receive back their properties and the city was to regain all her previous rights and liberties.[52] An Imperial commission visited Münster in March 1537 and disapproved of Bishop Franz's plans to suppress civic liberties and to aggrandize power.[53]

External pressure added to Bishop Franz's political and financial predicament. He simply ran out of money to finance building an absolutist territorial state; construction on the citadel in Münster stopped in 1537 when funds dried up. Moreover, the prince-bishop became embroiled in expensive wars. The house of Waldeck, a feudal vassal of Philip of Hesse, joined the Landgrave in his feuds with the dukes of Brunswick and Oldenbourg.[54] In 1538, Oldenbourg, Brunswick, and Tecklenburg forces attacked the weakly defended northern borders of the bishopric; the invaders were bought off only with a large indemnity.[55] At home, Bishop Franz also lost political support in the territorial estates when he tried to secularize the bishopric and join the Protestant Schmalkaldic League. The burgher elite in Münster took advantage of the bishop's financial troubles and confusion in the territorial government to petition for the restoration of civic liberties. Persuaded by close advisers in the payment of the Münsteraners and worn down by troubles abroad, Bishop Franz restored civic liberties in 1541 under two conditions—the

51. Cf. Kerssenbroch, pp. 885f.

52. Cf. Kerssenbroch, pp. 863f.

53. Cf. Kerssenbroch, p. 890.

54. For the close relations between Bishop Franz von Waldeck and Philip of Hesse, see Robert Stupperich, "Hessens Anteil an der Reformation in Westfalen," *Hessisches Jahrbuch für Landesgeschichte* 18 (1968), pp. 146–59.

55. Cf. Kerssenbroch, pp. 897–99.

ban on the guilds continued and only Catholic Church services were allowed.[56] The terms of the restitution, ratified in August 1541, were confirmed a year later by the other towns of the bishopric.[57] In 1544, Emperor Charles V also acknowledged the restoration of civic rights.[58]

The men in power between 1536 and 1554 can be divided into the patriciate (*Erbmänner*) and the burgher elite. Unlike the patriciates of other Westphalian and north German cities where successful new mercantile families won acceptance, the Münster patricians formed a tightly defined group and closed ranks to outsiders probably in the fourteenth century.[59] After the War of the Münster Bishopric (1450–57), during which a guild revolution forced the patricians to concede equal seats on the city council to the merchants and master artisans, the political influence of the urban aristocracy declined. Some families withdrew from city politics to lives of leisure on their country estates; the loss of power in Münster prompted them to seek acceptance by the lower nobility as peers. In the early sixteenth century, patrician participation in city government was limited to thirteen families, compared to the more than twenty families around the middle of the fifteenth century.[60] Their numbers dwindled further toward the close of the sixteenth century when many patricians elected to magisterial office refused to serve.[61] Patrician withdrawal from civic service was evident in a 1548 magisterial ordinance which decreed that those elected to serve who had houses in Münster and were in good health could not refuse.[62] Wishing to be considered noblemen rather than citizens, the patricians demanded tax exemption and immunity from civic laws; the burgher elite refused to give in and the quarrel was resolved in 1552 when Bishop Franz intervened.[63] He instructed both patricians and burghers, as long as they had residences in Münster, to assume the burden of political office when named.[64]

56. Kerssenbroch, p. 920; Niesert, *MUS*, I, pp. 290ff.

57. Kerssenbroch, p. 920; Niesert, *MUS*, I, pp. 314ff.

58. Kerssenbroch, p. 920.

59. For a comparative overview of the patriciates in Westphalian cities, see Friedrich von Klocke, *Das Patriziatsproblem und die Werler Erbsälzer* (Münster, 1965), pp. 27ff., esp. 39–41. For Münster's *Erbmänner*, see Helmut Lahrkamp, "Das Patriziat in Münster," in Hellmuth Rössler, ed., *Deutsches Patriziat 1430–1740* (Limburg, 1968), pp. 195–207.

60. For the mid-fifteenth century, see K.-H. Kirchhoff, "Die Unruhen in Münster/Westfalen 1450–57," in Wilfried Ehbrecht, ed., *Städtische Führungsgruppen und Gemeinde in der werdenden Neuzeit* (Cologne, 1979), pp. 71ff. For the sixteenth century, see appendix 1.

61. See appendix 1, nos. 12, 44, 75, 76, 125, 126, 138, 146.

62. See StdAM, AII, 1, 1548, fols. 7–7v, 8–9v, 11–12; these are various magisterial ordinances concerning the duty to serve as city councillors when elected.

63. See Kerssenbroch, pp. 920f.

64. See letter of Bishop Franz to the city council, dated April 12, 1552, StdAM, AII, 1a.

The second group of magistrates represented the most prominent and richest families of the burgher elite; the Heerdes, Plönies, Herdings, Münstermanns, and Holtappels were the most powerful clans outside of the patriciate.[65] Without exception, these families accumulated their fortunes through long-distance trade, primarily in cloth and grain, the staple commodities of the Hansa. Some rose from the ranks of the mercantile guilds in the fifteenth century and eventually severed their ties with the guilds when family power alone sufficed to perpetuate the wealth and political influence of the lineage.[66] In the first half of the sixteenth century, the families of the burgher elite underwent a metamorphosis, turning from a mercantile into a rentier elite. They owned country estates and extensive real properties inside and outside Münster. A substantial portion of their income was derived from interest on loans lent to the nobility and the patriciate; commercial capital comprised an even smaller proportion of the family fortunes. Among the citizenry, these families came closest to resembling the patricians, both in the absolute amount and in the structure of their family fortunes. The crucial difference between the burgher elite and the patriciate, other than the distinction in legal status, was one of political attitude; while the latter withdrew from civic affairs, the former came to dominate the politics of Münster. We witness here the formation of a second urban patriciate: Members of the Plönies and Herding families received Imperial noble patents in the early sixteenth century; and most branches of the clans came to title themselves after their country estates at the beginning of the seventeenth century.[67] Steadfastly Catholic during the years of religious

65. There are few available studies of the families in the burgher elite. For the Herdings, see Josef Ketteler, *Das Münstersche Geschlecht Herding* (Münster, 1926); for the Münstermanns, see the genealogical reconstitution by Joseph Prinz, "Johannes Münstermann. Zu einem Bildnis von Hermann tom Ring," *Westfalen* 40 (1962), pp. 300–07, esp. the genealogical chart. A manuscript collection, "Sammlung Spiessen", in StAM holds relevant data for the Heerdes and the Plönies; Clemens Steinbicker of Münster has compiled the basic genealogical data for many Münsteraner families. I would like to thank Dr. Karl-Heinz Kirchhoff and Dr. Helmut Lahrkamp for introducing me to these manuscript sources.

66. The Plönies are a case in point. A Wilbrand Plönies was Alderman of the clothiers' guild in 1489. See Krumbholtz, p. 210.

67. Hermann Plönies, the brother of Bürgermeister Wilbrand P. of Münster (appendix 1, no. 112), was Bürgermeister in Lübeck and knighted in 1532 by Emperor Charles V. The son of the magistrate Johann Herding senior, Heinrich, raised a company of troops and fought in Charles V's army at Pavia; he was knighted after the battle (1525). Heinrich's son, Johann junior, served as *Rittmeister* in the Imperial army during the Schmalkaldic campaigns. See Ketteler, *Geschlecht Herding*, pp. 11–13. On the ennoblement of burghers by the emperors in early modern Germany, see Erwin Riedenauer, "Kaiserliche Standeserhebungen für reichsstädtische Bürger 1519–1740. Ein statistischer Vorbericht zum Thema 'Kaiser und Patriziat,' " in H. Rössler, *Deutsches Patriziat*. See also his "Kaiser und Patriziat.

turmoil, the burgher elite returned to dominate Münster after 1535; they extended their influence into the power vacuum created by the ban on guilds and by the withdrawal of many patrician families from city politics. Together with the mercantile and guild leaders who would rise to share power on the city council after 1554, these men constituted the ruling regime in Münster and comprised the notability (*Honoratiorentum*), in contradistinction to the patriciate.[68]

The three most influential families in the twenty-five years after the Anabaptist Kingdom, in fact, in the next eighty years of Münster's history, were the Heerdes, the Plönies, and the Herdings. In all except eleven years of the period between 1536 and 1618, someone from one of the three families occupied one of the two posts of Bürgermeister; and in every single year of the period under consideration, some or all of the three families were included in the ruling regime.

The Plönies represented a classic merchant-magistrate family of the Hansa.[69] Besides supplying eight magistrates for Münster between 1500 and 1618, branches of the clan settled in Lübeck, Reval, and other Baltic trading centers as merchants and city councillors. Sons of the family in Münster attended Cologne University; they went into business, law, and the Church. The Plönies in Münster married with other families of the burgher elite, including the Heerdes, and also with the patrician Clevorn and Bischopinck clans. Like the nobility and the patriciate, the Plönies also formed "dynasties"; the men usually married more than once in their lifetime to produce numerous children; bastards of the clan further enlarged the size of the lineage.[70] Among the ecclesiastical institutions,

---

Struktur und Funktion des reichsstädtischen Patriziats im Blickpunkt kaiserlicher Adelspolitik vom Karl IV bis Karl VI," *Zeitschrift für Bayerische Landesgeschichte (ZfBLG)* 30 (1967), pp. 526–653.

68. The term *Honoratiorentum* has been applied by Josef Ketteler to Münsteraner families of the sixteenth and seventeenth centuries and is commonly adopted by historians studying Münster. The drawback of Ketteler's schema is that he does not give chronological distinctions for the different families. Some, like the families named here, dissolved their ties to the guilds in the early sixteenth century; others, such as the tanner Detten family or the butcher Modersohn family, did not completely detach themselves from their guild origins until the mid-seventeenth century. It is important to bear in mind that great differences in family wealth and prestige existed among the notability. The term is useful in differentiating the burgher families represented on the city council from the patriciate and the common citizens; it must be pointed out that Ketteler's "group" included different family alliances or groups within the ruling elite. See his "Vom Geschlechterkreis des Münsterischen Honorationrentums," *Mitteilungen der Westdeutschen Gesellschaft für Familienkunde* 5 (1928), pp. 422–30.

69. See appendix 1, nos. 109–14.

70. In his will, Hilbrand Plönies named two illegitimate daughters; see StdAM, B, Test. I, no. 421. Members of the Heerde and Plönies clans occasionally bequeathed small sums to their bastard kinsmen.

Plönies men could be found in the collegiate chapters of Old Cathedral and Saint Mauritz, strongholds of the patriciate; Plönies women entered convents and beguinages in Münster and in the Westphalian countryside. In the city, they formed a cluster of power in the parish of Saint Lambert with different generations occupying houses on Salzstrasse. Three of the five richest persons listed in the 1548 district tax register were Plönies.[71]

Equally powerful were the Heerdes.[72] Also clothiers in the beginning, the Heerdes were found among the burgher elite of various Hanseatic cities. In Münster, the clan provided six magistrates between 1500 and 1618, of whom the most powerful was the Bürgermeister Hermann Heerde.[73] Already a magistrate in 1532, he was appointed by Bishop Franz in 1536 and sat on the city council for thirty-five years until his death in 1571, serving after 1545 as Bürgermeister. Whereas the Plönies were the prominent clan in Saint Lambert's parish, the Heerdes lived in the parish of Saint Martin, around the corner from the Franciscan cloister. Through marriage, the Heerdes were related to the other families of the burgher elite, to the ruling families of other Westphalian families, and to the patrician Boland and Bischopinck. The two main lines of the clan derived their lineage from Borchard and Hermann Heerde senior; the former, one of the magistrates named in 1536, the latter, the father of Bürgermeister Hermann Heerde. Known for their strong support of the Catholic Church, men and women of the Heerde family appeared among the churches and cloisters of Münster and Münsterland; both of Borchard Heerde's daughters, for example, entered the convent of Saint Anne in Coesfeld. Their combined family wealth included extensive holdings of land and houses inside and outside Münster, capital invested in commercial enterprises, and large sums lent to the city government and to the Westphalian nobility. Borchard Heerde junior, one of the two sons of the magistrate Borchard Heerde senior, mentioned nearly 10,000 dalers in his will.[74] One of Bürgermeister Hermann Heerde's daughters, Klara, possessed 3,600 dalers although she was a nun.[75]

The Herdings also began as clothiers; Johann Herding, one of the magistrates appointed by Bishop Franz in 1536, served as the guild master of the clothiers' guild in 1528.[76] Both his son and grandson fought in the army of Charles V; the former received a noble title in 1525. When

---

71. StdAM, AVIII, 259, SR Lamberti, vol. 1, fols. 5 & 6v: Wolter Plönies assessed at 10 guldens, Johann P. at 6 G., Wilbrand P. senior and junior at 6 G. and 3 G. respectively.

72. See appendix 1, nos. 57–61.

73. See appendix 1, no. 58.

74. StdAM, B, Test. I, no. 435.

75. StdAM, B, Test. II, no. 437.

76. Krumbholtz, p. 40. He was magistrate between 1518 and 1525; see appendix 1, no. 63.

Johann junior, the grandson, returned to Münster in 1546, he married Ursula, the daughter of Bürgermeister Hermann Heerde, received 2,000 guldens in annuities as dowry,[77] and took over his grandfather's place on the city council. At this time, the family gave up trade entirely and derived their income solely from land rents and interest on annuities. Johann's account book, which covered the years from 1546 until his death in 1572, recorded vast sums lent out to the nobility and the patriciate; his debtors included the Count of Tecklenburg and a host of prominent Westphalian noblemen.[78] The income from land rents and interest on annuities alone indicated Johann had more than 20,000 dalers; there was, furthermore, the worth of his houses in Münster. In 1548, he paid 14 guldens on his properties in the Liebfrauen district, making him the second richest man who appeared in the four extant tax registers (after the patrician Johann Boland).[79] In 1568, he was assessed for three houses in Saint Lambert's parish as well.[80] His last residence was a sumptuous house on Rothenburg in the parish of Saint Ludger; the beautiful Gothic house was the closest thing to the urban palaces built by the ruling families of Renaissance Italy in unostentatious sixteenth-century Westphalia.[81] He succeeded his father-in-law and became Bürgermeister in 1571 after Hermann Heerde's death. After he died in 1573, a son, Heinrich, became Bürgermeister of Bocholt, while two others stayed in Münster: Hermann served as magistrate from 1579 to 1598 and Johann Heerde III was a member of the ruling regime between 1599 and 1634, serving most of those years as Bürgermeister.

THE RESTORATION OF GUILDS

Between 1535 and 1550, the city council strictly regulated the activities of merchants and artisans; appointed supervisors ensured proper magisterial control over the artisans, who were forbidden to organize. Since the

---

77. Cf. the account book of Johann Herding junior, StdAM, MS. 120, fol. 70.

78. The manuscript, in 201 folios, records annuity payments by his debtors, the dowry he received from Hermann Heerde, inheritance from his mother, and rents from farmlands he held in the bishopric. Aside from the counts of Tecklenburg and Steinfurt, other noblemen in his debt included the Mallinckrodt, the von der Recke, and the von Raesfeld. The account book (StdAM, MS. 120) is perhaps the single most valuable source for the study of family investment of the burgher elite in Münster.

79. StdAM, VIII, 259, SR Liebfrauen 1548, vol. 1, fol. 3.

80. See the property tax collected in 1568 to help repair the church spire of Saint Lambert; Karl Utsch, ed., "Die Kultusabteilung des Stadtarchivs Münster. Urkunden und Regesten," in *QFGSM* IX (Münster, 1937), pp. 46–54.

81. Construction on the family house began in Johann's lifetime and was completed in 1577 by his son Heinrich; see Friedrich Philippi, "Das alte Herdingsche Haus in Münster," *Westfalen*, 12 (1922), pp. 77–81.

guildsmen strongly supported the Reformation and Anabaptist movements in 1533 and 1534, any tinge of "guild democracy" was highly suspect in post-Anabaptist Münster and the magistrates came to look upon themselves as an *Obrigkeit* ruling over subjects (*Untertanen*), rather than as the betters among citizens equal before the law.[82]

After fifteen years of economic recovery, however, the handicrafts began to regain their self-confidence; the debacle of 1534–35 had not crushed the corporative spirit of the guildsmen. Many immigrant artisans had been, by this time, integrated into the social circles of the trades. The movement to complete the restoration of civic liberties and revive the guilds gathered momentum in the winter of 1552; on Christmas Day, the artisans met at the old choir of the cathedral to discuss the restoration of ancient guild corporations and free councillor elections.[83] On January 9, 1553, they presented a supplication to the city council in which they asked for the right to congregate, organize, and manage their own affairs.[84] Another note was presented to the magistrates on the eighteenth. When the city council rejected the two supplications, representatives of the guilds that had existed in Münster before 1535 gathered at the Franciscan cloister and swore to defend their common cause against possible repression by the magistrates. Once again, they drew up a petition.[85] Commissioners named by Bishop Franz failed to bring the two parties together and the matter went before the bishop in March.[86]

Similar to the situation in 1541, the movement to restore full civic rights in 1553 benefited from the prince-bishop's defeat in war. After the downfall of Philip of Hesse and the Schmalkaldic League in the Battle of Mühlberg (1547), the Landgrave's former ally became an easy prey to his enemies. In early 1553, Philip of Brunswick renewed an old feud with the prince-bishop, attacked Osnabrück and Münster, plundered Iburg, the episcopal residence, and sent Franz fleeing for his life to Münster.[87] Upon his arrival, representatives of the crafts and the citizenry offered their life and property to defend the bishopric. Moved by their protestation of loyalty and a monetary contribution, Bishop Franz restored the rights of the city of Münster in its entirety. Magisterial resistance finally yielded when Bishop Franz confirmed the restitution in writing; the document, signed on May 17, 1553, was endorsed by an Imperial letter from Charles V and Ferdinand I.[88]

---

82. Cf. Krumbholtz, pp. 60ff.
83. Kerssenbroch, p. 923.
84. Kerssenbroch, pp. 924f.; Krumbholtz, p. 81.
85. Kerssenbroch, p. 928; Krumbholtz, p. 83.
86. Kerssenbroch, p. 929; Krumbholtz, pp. 84ff.
87. Kerssenbroch, pp. 929f.
88. Kerssenbroch, p. 937; Niesert, *MUS,* I, pp. 350ff.

In 1554, twenty years after the election of the Anabaptist city council, free elections again took place in Münster. On the surface a move toward greater civic participation in the politics of the republic, the restored constitution and councillor elections still allowed the ruling elite to retain their power. Whereas election to the city council before 1535 was relatively straightforward, involving a twofold process whereby all law-abiding citizens selected ten electors (*Kurgenossen*) who in turn chose the twenty-four magistrates, the democratic process after 1554 was much more manipulative. A fourfold electoral process enabled the magistrates in office to influence the selection of electors and eventually help to determine the makeup of the new city council.[89] Ten magistrates from the outgoing council named ten citizens from the burgher assembly; these citizens chose another twenty who then selected the final ten Kurgenossen, the real electors of the magistrates. While the names of the Kurgenossen are generally known to us,[90] only a single document names those who participated in the third round of selection in 1555.[91] A careful analysis of the list of twenty-one citizens (two of them exercised one vote) who participated in the third round of selection reveals that everyone concerned had close ties with the magistrates in office, as retired councillors, as kinsmen, or as close friends.[92] The guild leaders, on the other hand, were strongly represented among the Kurgenossen. This new, four-round electoral system reflected the distribution of power in post-Anabaptist Münster. Challenged by the restoration of the guilds, the Catholic burgher elite was able to keep power in their hands; through a modus vivendi agreed with the guild leaders,[93] the ruling elite conceded partial power to the guild leadership with the tacit understanding that the political preeminence of the civic elite remain uncontested.

One of the first acts of the reenfranchised civic community was to expel the Jews. In 1536, several Jewish families obtained permission from

89. For the electoral process, see "Polizeiordnung der Stadt Münster," StAM, AVM, MS. 110, fols. 1v–4.

90. The names of the electors have been published by Eduard Schulte; see his "Die Kurgenossen des Rates 1520–1802," in *QFGSM* III (Münster, 1927), pp. 117–204.

91. StdAM, AII, 16–17, "Aus Ratslisten 1350–1531, 1555–1660." Eight loose leaves written in 1554 gave directions for selecting the electors and the magistrates. Folio 8 contains a list of twenty-five patricians and burghers who were elected to select the ten *Kurgenossen*. Four patricians excused themselves from participation; of the twenty-one men left, the brothers Thomas and Christian v. d. Wyck, patricians, jointly cast one vote. The majority of these electors in the third round of selection were patricians.

92. For a transcription and a detailed analysis of the document, see R. Po-chia Hsia, "Die neue Form der Ratswahl in Münster 1554–55," *WZ* 131/132 (1981/1982), pp. 197–204.

93. See the notary Pancratius Volbert's copy of the police ordinance which opens with the preamble describing how the new electoral system was agreed on by the magistrates and the citizens through long negotiations (StdAM, AI, 32, fol. 7).

Bishop Franz to purchase houses and reside in Münster upon payment of annual fees.[94] The 1540 Jodefeld tax register shows an "Abraham de Jodde" who was assessed 3 guldens; two other Jews, Solomon and Smor, appear in the 1548 Liebfrauen tax register, each assessed 4 guldens.[95] As physicians and moneylenders, the handful of Jewish families in Münster belonged to the well-to-do; many citizens, however, hated their presence. After the Jews were expelled from Münster a second time in the late fifteenth century, they could only enter the city with a letter of safe-conduct from the magistrates until Bishop Franz abolished civic liberties and let in the families.[96] Anti-Semitism expressed the darker side of civic sentiments for self-government and religious conformity; Jews were not allowed to reside in Münster until the Napoleonic Wars.[97] It was the guildsmen who embodied the exclusive, xenophobic forces in urban society; they resented "alien elements" in their midst, be they Jews, beggars, or Jesuits.

Within the guilds and their political union, the Gesamtgilde, oligarchic domination was also the principle of power. Decisions in the Gesamtgilde rested with the thirty-four guild masters (*Mesterlude*) who represented the seventeen guilds incorporated in the overarching political organization of the artisans. From their own ranks, the guild masters annually elected two Aldermen (*Olderlude*). A sort of shadow guild gov-

94. See Diethard Aschoff, "Die Stadt Münster und die Juden im letzten Jahrhundert der städtischen Unabhängigkeit (1562–1662)," *WF* 27 (1975), pp. 84–113. In 1536, a Benedikt Jodde purchased an Anabaptist house on Bergstrasse; see Kirchhoff, *Täufer*, p. 85.

95. StdAM, AVIII, 259, SR Jodefeld, vol. 1, fol. 12; in 1548 Abraham paid 4 guldens in taxes, see SR Jodefeld, vol. 1, 1548, fol. 3. For the other two, see SR Liebfrauen, vol. 1, 1548, fols. 2 & 3v.

96. After the 1350 pogrom and expulsion, the Jews resettled in Münster during the 1420s; they were expelled a second time in the second half of the fifteenth century. See Diethard Aschoff, "Die Juden in Westfalen zwischen Schwarzen Tod und Reformation (1350–1530)," *WF* 30 (1980), pp. 78–106. Aschoff dates the second expulsion between 1448 and 1535. A letter requesting safe-conduct from the magistrates dates from the first years of the sixteenth century; hence, the second expulsion probably took place in the last decades of the fifteenth century, roughly contemporaneous with similar expulsions in many other German cities. The letter is in StdAM, AVI, Polizei.

97. There is a good body of literature on Jews in Westphalia; on the pogroms directed at Jews during the Black Death see Bernhard Brilling and Helmut Richtering, eds., *Westfalia Judaica. Urkunden und Regesten zur Geschichte der Juden in Westfalen und Lippe. I. 1005–1350* (Stuttgart, 1967), docs. 203, 207, 211; and Diethard Aschoff,"Das Pestjahr 1350 und die Juden in Westfalen," *WZ* 129 (1979), pp. 57–68. For Münster and Münsterland see his "Das Münsterländische Judentum bis zum Ende des 30jährigen Krieges," *Theokratia* 3 (1979), pp. 125–84. See also the older literature by Viktor Huyskens, "Zur Geschichte der Juden in Münster," *WZ* 57 (1899), pp. 124–36, *WZ* 64 (1906), pp. 260–66; Carl Rixen, *Geschichte und Organisation der Juden im ehemaligen Stift Münster* (Münster, 1906); and Paul Bahlmann,"Zur Geschichte der Juden im Münsterlande," *Zeitschrift für Kulturgeschichte* 2 (1895), pp. 380–409.

ernment complemented the city council and assisted the magistrates in carrying out various functions.[98]

A strict hierarchy governed the individual guilds. Through a process of co-optation by which the guild masters named their own electors, a small group of prominent guild families was able to perpetuate power from one generation to another. Sons usually succeeded fathers in positions of leadership in the guilds; for example, the glassmakers Heinrich and Thomas Egberts, father and son,[99] controlled the guild of glassmakers, painters, and saddlers together with the tom Ring painter family.[100] Substantial disparity in wealth existed among guilds and within each trade. The three most powerful guilds were the clothiers, the shopkeepers, and the goldsmiths, in descending order of influence; the different sums of taxes paid by masters of the same trade reflected the substantial differences in wealth within the guilds. An unambiguous sense of hierarchy governed relations between journeymen and master artisans and between artisans and guild masters. After 1554, a guild aristocracy carried considerable political weight in city politics through its domination of the politically organized handicrafts. The rivalry between guild leaders and the magistrates was not a struggle between the more democratically minded burghers and an oligarchy, but between two elites who relied on two forms of corporative power, the craft guild and the family.

The year 1555 marked a turning point for Münster: The city had just won back her traditional rights. It was also the year when the empire enjoyed a formal religious peace. Many cities in the Empire did not survive the tumult of the Reformation movement unscathed. In Thuringia, the Imperial city of Mühlhausen was punished for her support of the millenarian prophet, Thomas Müntzer; after the princes had crushed the peasant uprising under Müntzer in May 1525, Mühlhausen lost its traditional liberties and came under the joint rule of the two Saxon houses.[101] In Northwest Germany, Charles V pursued an anti-urban policy in consolidating the power of the House of Hapsburg; when he imposed Catholic worship in Protestant cities during the Interim of 1548, widespread unrest broke out in Minden, Soest, and Osnabrück.[102] Münster's emer-

98. For the statutes of the Gesamtgilde, see the "Red Book," published in Krumbholtz, pp. 28ff., 41ff.

99. See appendix 1, nos. 47–48.

100. For the names of guild masters, see Krumbholtz, pp. 347–51.

101. Cf. Manfred Bensing, *Thomas Müntzer und der Thüringer Aufstand 1525* (Berlin, 1966), pp. 234–43.

102. See Franz Petri, "Karl V und die Städte im Nordwestraum während des Ringens um die politisch-kirchliche Ordnung in Deutschland," *JbfWKG* 71 (1978), pp. 19–30.

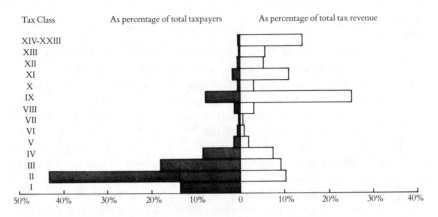

Figure 1.2 The Structure of Wealth in Münster, 1548–50

gence from religious turmoil, siege warfare, and the political subservience under the bishop was a remarkable story. What did urban society
look like at the time of the Peace of Augsburg? Here, we must turn to the
tax registers to come up with a better idea of the social structure of
Münster.

Figure 1.2 shows the wealth pyramid of Münster around 1548–50,
drawn according to the four district tax registers of 1548–50 (see table
1.3). The most significant fact was the large size of the lower stratum
which comprised about 57 percent of the population; the lower classes
included those described as "pauper" in the registers and those assessed at one or two schillings (tax class II). The vast majority of
domestic servants and apprentices fell under these two categories;
many were widows, presumably older women, who had troubles
making ends meet after the death of their husbands. Although occupations are not given in the tax registers of these years, based on later
records, we can assume that day laborers and the poorest artisans
predominated in these categories.

The lower middle class covered those who paid between 3 and 6
schillings in taxes (tax classes III and IV); numerically, they comprised
approximately 26 percent of the urban populace. These were usually
house owners, artisans for the most part, although eleven domestic servants also came under these tax brackets. The mainstay of the middle
stratum was significantly underrepresented in Münster during the 1550s.
Those paying between 7 schillings and one mark (= 12 s.) comprised
only 2.7 percent of the taxpayers, an abnormally low percentage when
we compare this wealth pyramid with the social structures of the well-

Table 1.3 Tax Groups in Münster, 1548–50

	Class	Houseowners	Residents	Servants
free		18	3	—
pauper	I	63	40	116
1–2 s.	II	328	104	274
3–4 s.	III	249	27	11
5–6 s.	IV	124	8	6
7–8 s.	V	23	2	—
9–10 s.	VI	11	—	—
11–12 s.	VII	8	—	—
16–18 s.	VIII	22	1	—
1 G.(= 22 s.)	IX	116	10	—
30–34 s.	X	8	—	—
2–2.5 G.	XI	27	1	—
3 G.	XII	9	—	—
4 G.	XIII	7	—	—
6 G.	XIV	3	—	—
8 G.	XV	1	—	—
9 G.	XVI	1	—	—
10 G.	XVII	1	—	—
14 G.	XVIII	1	—	—
15 G.	XIX	1	—	—

Note: In 1544, 1 gulden (G.) = 22 schillings (s.)
       1 daler = 21 s.
       1 Gelder Rider = 17 s.
       1 mark = 12 s.
       1 Hornsgulden = 9 s.
For purposes of comparison, I have converted all tax assessments into schillings; the exchange rates are published in J. Scotti, *Sammlung der Gesetze und Verordnungen . . . in . . . Münster . . .* (Münster, 1842), vol. 1, pp. 145–46.

researched South German cities.[103] The numerical weakness of the middle strata underscores the fact that many Anabaptists were recruited from this layer of urban society and the abnormality in 1550 reflected the severe impact of the rebellion on this segment of the citizenry.

103. Although historians have constructed different tax classes to measure wealth distribution of medieval and early modern German cities, a basic similarity in urban social structure still allows us to compare Münster in 1550 to other cities of the period. There existed a rough threefold division of urban society according to all tax records; the wealth pyramid normally had a broad base and narrowed drastically toward the pinnacle. Most German historians have adopted the term strata (*Schichten*) to describe wealth stratification. Those citizens who possessed less than 100 guldens were generally considered poor and members of the lower strata; those who owned goods worth between 100 and 1,000 guldens can be described as the middle strata, the solid ranks of the citizenry; those who had

The structural abnormality of civic society also highlights the unchallenged prominence of the upper strata; in Münster the upper reaches of society consisted of a lower, more numerical stratum (those assessed one daler = class IX) and the very small number of families at the pinnacle of society, the actual burgher elite. While they comprised less than 11 percent of the population, house owners in the upper strata gave more than 65 percent of the tax money collected. At the very top, eight persons alone paid more than 14 percent of all taxes. Between the poorest taxpaying burgher and the richest man was a difference in wealth of 330 times. From these upper reaches of society were recruited all the magistrates and guild leaders of Münster, not only for the 1550s but for the entire sixteenth century. Politics in Münster after the Anabaptist rebellion was clearly dominated by the very rich. A combination of family prestige, the tradition of political service on the city council, and enormous wealth cemented the preeminence of the Catholic ruling elite in Münster. These families, moreover, bolstered their position through the Catholic Church, from which they held fiefs, leased land, and to which they sent sons and daughters. In the next chapter, we shall examine the power of the Church in Münster and uncover the ties between clerics and magistrates.

---

more than 1,000 guldens belonged to the upper strata of urban society. The difficulty in comparing Münster with the other cities is that we do not know the rate of taxation; the division of taxpayers into classes or categories, nevertheless, allows for a rough comparison with other cities, even when the rates of taxation are different. What is being compared is not so much the absolute amount of wealth as the relative proportion of the three strata in different German cities. I have selected three samples: Hildesheim in 1525, Esslingen in 1458, and Nördlingen in 1579. The latter two Imperial cities are in South Germany; Hildesheim is in Lower Saxony. In all three cases, the lower strata comprised between 43 and 53 percent of the total population, a proportion similar to the social structure of Münster in 1550.

	Hildesheim 1525	Esslingen 1458	Nördlingen 1579
Lower	43.2%	48.7%	52.5%
Middle	51.0%	47.5%	43.1%
Upper	5.8%	3.8%	4.2%

The most striking difference is in the strength of the middle strata. While the three cities show that the middle strata comprised between 43 and 51 percent of all taxpayers, in Münster the citizens of middling wealth formed only 28 percent, with 26 percent grouped near the bottom of the range. Sources: Karl Uthmann, *Sozialstruktur und Vermögensbildung in Hildesheim des 15. und 16. Jahrhunderts* (Bremen, 1957), p. 33; Friedrichs, *Nördlingen*, p. 104; Bernhard Kirchgässer, "Probleme quantitativer Erfassung städtischer Unterschichten im Spätmittelalter, besonders in den Reichsstädten Konstanz und Esslingen," in Erich Maschke and Jürgen Sydow, eds., *Gesellschaftliche Unterschichten in den südwestdeutschen Städten* (Stuttgart, 1967), p. 83.

CHAPTER TWO

Church and City

Viewed from the air, Münster resembles two concentric circles radiating out from the cathedral—the smaller one the ecclesiastical immunity, the larger, the town area which surrounded it—representing a classic development of the city which grew around an episcopal see.[1] Many ecclesiastical immunities dotted the larger urban "ring" and further carved up the spatial unity of the city of the burghers. In the sixteenth century, prior to the coming of the Jesuits, Münster accommodated within its walls a cathedral, four parish churches, two Benedictine convents, one Augustinian nunnery, four beguinages, and four male cloisters. The collegiate Church of Saint Mauritz was located just outside of the walls.[2] At the end of the sixteenth century, these institutions supported almost five hundred clerics; in terms of the density of cleric-lay ratio, Münster was not far behind Cologne, the "German Rome."[3]

"THE MANY-HEADED MONSTER"

In Reformation pamphlets, the pope is often depicted as the Antichrist, and the Roman Church as the many-headed monster described in Apocalypse 13.[4] The second metaphor, at least, fits well. In the diversity of its social composition and in the multitude of interests it represented, the body of Roman clergy did resemble the eschatological beast. The Catholic clergy in the sixteenth century embodied every class across the social

1. For urbanization around ecclesiastical centers in the Middle Ages, see Henri Pirenne, *The Medieval City* (Princeton, 1969), trans. Frank Halsey, pp. 60ff.; and Franz Petri, ed., *Bischofs- und Kathedralstädte des Mittelalters und der frühen Neuzeit* (Cologne, 1976).

2. For a list of churches and cloisters in Münster with dates of foundation and brief bibliographic notes, see Ludwig Schmitz-Kallenberg, *Monasticon Westfaliae. Verzeichnis der im Gebiet der Provinz Westfalen bis zum Jahre 1815 gegründeten Stiften, Klöster, und sonstigen Ordensniederlassungen* (Münster, 1909). This useful handbook, however, is incomplete; the parish churches of Saint Lambert and Saint Servatius are not mentioned; moreover, the literature after 1909 has to be consulted.

3. Lethmate estimates that there were 586 clerics and servants in the 1590s, of whom 146 belonged to the secular clergy. See Lethmate, *Bevölkerung*, p. 34.

4. Cf. Hans Preuss, *Die Vorstellungen vom Antichrist im späteren Mittelalter, bei Luther und in der konfessionellen Polemik* (Leipzig, 1906), Teil II, esp. pp. 134–48.

spectrum, unlike the Protestant ministers, who were mainly recruited from the ranks of the solid burghers. It was the Roman Church's numerous entanglements with the mundane world which provided the ammunition for Protestant satires in the early Reformation years. From afar, the Catholic Church seemed like a unified monument, a magnificent cathedral rising above the surrounding secular burgher dwellings, a symbol of the contradistinction between the clerical and lay estates of society. Up close, the architectural unity dissolved into its many separate, often incongruous, aspects, each bearing the style of an age and betraying the centrifugal pulls of different social forces. A Münsteraner of the sixteenth century, who literally lived under the cathedral spires, was more aware of the separate components of the Church than he was of the silhouette of the Church towers which dazzle a visitor approaching the city.

The single most important factor in determining the attitude of burghers toward ecclesiastical institutions was the latter's responsiveness to the spiritual needs of the citizens. The more a particular group of clergy contributed to the salvation of the city, the more popular they were, while the clergy whose work was considered irrelevant or inimical to the city's salvation and whose leisurely privileges mocked the toils of the burghers naturally bore the brunt of hostilities. Anti-clericalism did not necessarily express doubts of the efficacy of Catholic doctrines and way of salvation, but rather the exasperation of laymen with a self-proclaimed professional elite who failed to live up to their vocation.[5]

Clerical institutions in Münster in the sixteenth century can be divided into three categories according to their susceptibility to lay control. The nature of the relationship between clerical groups and burghers coincided to a large extent with the variables of wealth and the spiritual state of the clergy. The richer, the more powerful the ecclesiastical institution, the less subject it was to lay control, and the more likely it was to be characterized by spiritual inertia.

At the pinnacle of the clerical hierarchy in Münster, other than the bishop, stood the canons of the cathedral chapter, who came from noble families of Westphalia. The list of canons reads like the roll call of the armigerous noble vassals of the Bishop of Münster.[6] Territorially the largest ecclesiastical principality in Northwest Germany, the Bishopric of Münster was the arena of many dynastic and political intrigues; the

---

5. The important distinction between anti-clericalism and anti-Catholicism is emphasized by Bernd Moeller, see his, "Bürger als Kleriker," in *Festschrift für Hermann Heimpel,* II (Göttingen, 1972), pp. 195–224.

6. For a list of the deans and provosts of the cathedral, see Friedrich Kiskemper, "Priesterverzeichnis," pp. 181–82; Kiskemper's typescript is deposited in BDAM. The list, however, is incomplete. See also *WZ,* Register zu Bd. 1–50, II, pp. 449–58; Register zu Bd. 51–75, II, pp. 148–52.

cathedral chapter, second only to the bishop in political power, became a corporation representing diverse, often conflicting familial interests among the nobility. Very few of the forty canons (twenty seniors and twenty juniors) resided in Münster, let alone attended chapter meetings and fulfilled the responsibilities of their benefice. Most took only the minimum clerical vows; some had benefices reserved for them while they were students or minors; a great many kept common-law wives, "whores" as the burghers scornfully called them; the majority bore arms, donned noble attire, and lived like their lay brothers and cousins. Collectively, they represented a bedrock of privilege, a last bulwark against the implementation of the Tridentine decrees and the Catholic reform.[7]

The death of Bishop Johann von Hoya in 1574 brought to a head the underlying conflict among the canons. Led by Johann von Westerholt, *scholasticus* of the chapter, the younger canons championed the candidacy of the Duke of Brunswick, a Protestant; the senior canons, under the leadership of Dean Gottfried von Raesfeld, opposed the Protestant candidacy, offered the see to Johann Wilhelm, son of the Duke of Jülich-Cleve, who administered the bishopric as interim *Statthalter*. The Catholic party also succeeded in having Westerholt removed and excommunicated.[8] The exercise of power was in the hands of a few senior canons, thanks to the general indifference and the high dropout rate below the senior ranks of the chapter. After 1588, when the two archbishops of Cologne, Ernst and Ferdinand, served simultaneously as the bishops of Münster, the senior canons assumed a greater role in the direct administration of the episcopal government, due to the long periods of absence of the prince-bishops. They presided at the head of the ruling council and were pivotal in supporting Archbishop Ferdinand's move to include Münster in the Catholic League just before the outbreak of the Thirty Years' War.[9]

7. There is a large body of literature on the Münster cathedral chapter; the major studies are: Heinrich Spieckermann, *Beiträge zur Geschichte des Domkapitels zu Münster im Mittelalter* (Emsdetten, 1935); Ulrich Herzog, *Untersuchungen zur Geschichte des Domkapitels zu Münster und seines Besitzes im Mittelalter* (Göttingen, 1961); Alois Schröer, "Das Münsterer Domkapitel im ausgehenden Mittelalter. Ein Beitrag zur Kirchengeschichte Westfalens," in *Monasterium. Festschrift zum 700jährigen Weihegedächtnis des Paules- Domes zu Münster* (Münster, 1966), pp. 471–510; and Franz Darpe, ed., *Die ältesten Verzeichnisse der Einkünfte des Münsterschen Domkapitels* (= *CTW* II, Münster, 1886/1960).

8. On the so-called Westerholt Strife, see Augustin Hüsing, *Der Kampf um die Katholische Religion im Bisthum Münster nach Vertreibung der Wiedertäufer 1535–1585. Aktenstücke und Erläuterungen* (Münster, 1883), pp. 92–146 and appended documents. See also Keller, *Gegenreformation, I, passim.* Hüsing's treatment, influenced by the *Kulturkampf,* was biased in stressing the Catholicism of the bishopric.

9. Münster joined the League on October 23, 1613; see Franziska Neuer-Landfried, *Die Katholische Liga 1608–1620* (Kallmünz, 1968), p. 232.

Also situated within the immunity of the cathedral were the residences of the canons and the vicars, quarters of their servants, and the small Church of Saint Jacob, which served as a parish church for the lesser inhabitants of the immunity.[10]

Two male orders in Münster were also of exclusively noble character. The Knights of Saint John and the Teutonic Order both settled in Münster in the thirteenth century. The latter played an important role in the eastward expansion of the Germanic peoples, Westphalia being one of the most important starting points of the *Ostkolonisation*. By the sixteenth century, however, their numbers had dwindled down to a handful, and the Münster house was dissolved in 1579.[11]

The Benedictine convents of Überwasser and Aegidii also belonged to the first category of ecclesiastical institutions where the civic community exerted no direct influence. Founded in 1040, the convent of Überwasser claimed independence from episcopal authority and thwarted Bishop Franz's attempt to dissolve it in 1536.[12] Drawn from all over Westphalia, the inmates of Überwasser were the daughters of noble and patrician families; their patrimonies and the substantial income of the convent enabled them to lead a life appropriate to their social standing. Aegidii cloister was founded in 1181 as a Cistercian convent and adopted the Rules of Saint Benedict in 1468. In the social hierarchy of the clerical establishment, it stood one rung below Überwasser. Daughters from the Münster patriciate were prominent among the nuns—three Bischopings, one Steveninck, and one Kerckerinck served as abbesses for the greater part of the sixteenth century.[13] Both convents, especially Überwasser, were big landlords in the diocese and derived the lion's share of their income from tithes and land rents.[14] In the late fifteenth century, the

10. On Saint Jacob's, see Adolph Tibus, *Die Jakobipfarre in Münster* (Münster, 1885); a list of feastdays and their manner of celebration are given on pp. 14–31.

11. The Teutonic Knights came to Münster in 1237 and their house, the *Georgskommende,* was located next to the Bispinghof in Überwasser parish. See Kerssenbroch, pp. 59ff.; and *CTW* V, pp. 119–46. The Knights of Saint John settled in Münster in 1282; the *Johanniterkommende* was situated on Bergstrasse. See Kerssenbroch, pp. 63ff.

12. Cf. Rudolf Schulze, *Das adelige Frauen- (Kanonissen-) Stift der Hl. Maria (1040–1773) und die Pfarre Liebfrauen-Überwasser zu Münster Westfalen (1040). Ihre Verhältnisse und Schicksale* (Münster, 1952, 2nd rev. ed.), pp. 168–69.

13. The mother superiors were Alheid Bischoping (+1503), Hildegund Bischoping (1503–40), Elizabeth Bischoping (1540–65), Anna Kerckerinck (1565–91), Lucia Warendorp (served 6 days before her death in 1591), Agnes von Averhagen (1591–?), Margaretha von Cassem (1602), Agnes Steveninck (1607). Kiskemper's "Priesterverzeichnis" names only the first three mother superiors, p. 184; the names and dates of the others are extracted from *Urkunden* of the convent. See StAM, FM, Saint Aegidii, Urk. 310a, 310b, 327a, 327c, 328 and BDAM, PfA Aegidii, Urk. 235.

14. For published records of the wealth of Aegidii convent, see Wilhelm Kohl, ed., *Urkundenregesten und Einkünfteregister des Aegidii-Klosters (1184–1533) (= QFGSM,* n.f. III,

convent of Überwasser owned 465 pieces of land scattered in no less than 47 parishes; in addition, some 350 peasant households paid tithe to the noble cloister.[15] The convents controlled hundreds of serfs and the nuns regularly exchanged serfs with noble and patrician landlords, often their relatives, to round out their properties.[16]

The four collegiate churches (Old Cathedral, Saint Ludger's, Saint Martin's, and Saint Mauritz's), the Augustinian nunnery of Niesing (Marienthal), and the Brethren of the Common Life comprised a second group of institutions. Their wealth, though substantial, was not comparable with that of the noble ecclesiastical institutions, and they were more open to lay influences through the interpenetration of their personnel and the civic elite. Niesing convent accepted women "from both noble and non-noble families"; it was markedly less exclusive and more open to the civic community, compared to Überwasser and Saint Aegidii.[17] The civic elite dominated the leadership: Four of the five mother superiors between 1472 and 1620 stemmed from patrician families; the sisters in the century after 1517 included women from patrician and notable Münsteraner families and a handful of noble inmates.[18] Many sisters were of humbler social origins; their family names correspond to the many house-owning and taxpaying burghers who appear in tax books and civic rolls.

The Brethren of the Common Life (*Fraterherren*) served as confessors to the Niesing sisters.[19] In fact, Niesing was founded in 1440 on statutes drawn up by the Brethren and the two institutions were very similar in their religious practices, devotional styles, and the social composition of

---

Münster, 1966), pp. 7–285. The rents of 1521 and the tithes collected in 1545 are published in Franz Darpe, ed., *Verzeichnisse der Güter, Einkünfte, und Einnahme des Aegidii-Klosters, des Kapitel an Saint Ludgeri und Martini sowie der Saint Georgs-Kommende in Münster . . .* (= *CTW* V, Münster, 1900/1958). For Überwasser convent, see Rudolf Schulze, op. cit., and Franz Darpe, ed., *Die Heberegister des Klosters Überwasser und des Stiftes St. Mauritz* (= *CTW* III, Münster 1888/1964).

15. Schulze, *Überwasser,* pp. 57ff. and *CTW* III, pp. 55–80.

16. Cf. StAM, FM, Saint Aegidii, Urk. 267b, 267c, 271d, 278d, 293d, 298a, 301a, 303a.

17. Kerssenbroch, p. 72.

18. The mother superiors were Jutte Kerckerinck (1472–91), Stenske v. Schonebeck (1491–1500), Elseke v. Drolshagen (1500–41), Katherina Schenckinck (1541–76), Christine v. d. Ruhr (1576–1620); see Wilhelm E. Schwarz, "Studien zur Geschichte des Klosters der Augustinerinnen Marienthal genannt Niesing zu Münster," in *WZ* 72 (1914), p. 81. See also Wilhelm Kohl, ed., *Das Bistum Münster I. Die Schwesterhäuser nach der Augustinerregel* (= *Germania Sacra,* n.f. III, *Die Bistümer des Kirchenprovinz Köln,* Berlin, 1968), pp. 16–21. A list of sisters of Niesing can be found in Schwarz, "Niesing," pp. 128–34 and in Kohl, *Bistum Münster,* I, pp. 186ff.

19. Names of Fraterherren who had served as rectors and confessors in Niesing can be found in Schwarz, "Niesing," pp. 134ff.; and in Kohl, *Bistum Münster, I* pp. 178–86.

their membership.[20] Founded in 1400, the house of the Brethren was the
first German congregation of the *Devotio Moderna*. The majority of the
Brethren came from burgher families, both in Münster and in other
Westphalian towns; the patriciate and the magistracy were seldom represented among the brothers.[21]

The four collegiate churches represented male counterparts to cloister
Niesing; the civic elite, the patrician and magisterial families, dominated
these institutions.[22] The one exception was Saint Mauritz, located outside
of the city where it owned much land in the parish of the same name;
here, many noblemen rubbed shoulders with their patrician brothers.[23]
Clergymen of humbler social origins seldom rose to the level of canonate
and were commonly found as chaplains and vicars in the collegiate
churches.

Through patronage, through the rights of presentation and collation,
and through financial support, the city council exercised considerable
influence over a third group of clerical institutions. The power of the
magistrates over the clerics ranged from traditions of collaboration with
the mendicant friars to the right of appointment and dismissal over many
vicarages. The four beguinages (Rosenthal, Ringe, Hofringe, Reine), the

20. The constitution of Niesing convent was drawn up by the Brethren of the Common Life in Münster, see Schwarz, "Niesing," pp. 86ff. It was not unusual to find sisters at
Niesing and Fraterherren who were related: Hermann Hanse and Anna Alters, burghers in
Münster, had a daughter, Richtmot, in Niesing, and a son, Dietrich, in the congregration
of the Brethren in Wesel. Cf. StdAM, B, Test. I, 242, vol. 7, fol. 8.

21. Cf. Kerssenbroch, pp. 61ff. The necrology of the congregation in Münster is
published by Heinrich A. Erhard, see his "Gedächtnissbuch des Frater-Hauses zu
Münster," *WZ* 6 (1843), pp. 89–126. The 29 brethren between 1500 and 1620 included one
Rembert von Guelich, son of the Guild Alderman and magistrate, Arnold v. Guelich.

22. For the personnel of the collegiate chapter of the Old Cathedral, see Kiskemper in
BDAM and Klaus Scholz, ed., *Die Urkunden des Kollegiatstifts Alter Dom in Münster 1129–
1534* (= *Westfälische Urkunden* II, Münster, 1978). Scholz is also editing the extant holdings
of the collegiate archive (deposited in StAM) for publication in the series *Germania Sacra*.
See his remarks on clerical wills in the archives "Einige Bemerkungen zu den Testamenten
münsterischer kanoniker," *Westfalen* 58 (1980), pp. 117–20. For the personnel at Saint
Ludger's, see the list of deans appended in *800 Jahre Sankt Ludgeri* (Münster, 1973), pp.
105–06. For the collegiate chapter of Saint Martin, see BDAM, PfA Martini, A101a,
"Canoniker an St. Martini 1100–1800." The provosts were all noblemen and the deans
included two patricians. Among the canons, many patrician and magisterial families were
represented. The 1571 diocesan visitation records the names of the clergy of most institutions; see Wilhelm E. Schwarz, ed., *Die Akten der Visitation des Bistums Münster aus der Zeit
Johanns von Hoya (1571–73)* (= *GQBM* VII, Münster, 1912).

23. For an incomplete list of the canons at Saint Mauritz's, see Kiskemper, "Priesterverzeichnis," p. 198; see also Schwarz, *Visitation*. After the cathedral chapter and Überwasser convent, the chapter of Saint Mauritz was the biggest collegiate landlord in the bishopric; in 1500, its landed estate comprised 196 lots and 25 cottages. See Werner Dobelmann,
Kirchspiel und Stift St. Mauritz in Münster (Münster, 1971), pp. 25f.

non-collegiate parish churches, (especially Saint Lambert's and Saint Servatii), the Franciscan cloister, and the many vicarages in the hospitals and poorhouses all fall under this category. Whenever lay initiative spearheaded the quest for eternal life, such as in the endowment of vicaries and in the foundation of beguinages and poorhouses, the magistrates automatically extended their authority into these new clerical spheres by virtue of their position as the *Obrigkeit* of the civic patrons.[24]

Magisterial patronage over twenty-four civic benefices gave the city council a means to dispense favors and to enforce discipline directly over a group of clergymen.[25] Competitions for openings were fierce; no less than fourteen candidates applied for a vicary in 1579.[26] The clergymen also had to maintain a high standard of morality. When the magistrates discovered in 1564 that Johann Suttorp, vicar at the Poorhouse "zur Aa," was living with a nun from Coesfeld, they promptly dismissed him.[27] Most of these "civic clergymen" came from the middling ranks of the urban community; when sons of patrician and magisterial families appeared among the list of holders, they often used these benefices as stepping stones which provided income while they were studying or waiting for fatter livings in the ecclesiastical hierarchy.[28] Of the eighty-

24. Three works deserve mention as exemplary studies of the relationships between Church and city. Foremost is Rolf Kiessling's *Bürgerliche Gesellschaft und Kirche in Augsburg im Spätmittelalter* (Augsburg, 1971). The others are Karl Trüdinger, *Stadt und Kirche im spätmittelalterlichen Würzburg* (Stuttgart, 1978) and Dieter Demandt, Han-Christoph Rublack, *Stadt und Kirche in Kitzingen* (Stuttgart, 1978). For an overview of recent scholarship and for bibliographical orientation, see Bernd Moeller, ed., *Stadt und Kirche im 16. Jahrhundert* (Gütersloh, 1978), especially the report by Hans-Christoph Rublack.

25. Cf. Helmut Lahrkamp, "Vom Patronatsrecht des münsterschen Rates," in *Studia Westfalica. Beiträge zur Kirchengeschichte und religiösen Volkskunde Westfalens. Festschrift für Alois Schröer*, ed. Max Bierbaum (Münster, 1973), pp. 214–39. For sources, see StdAM, AXIII, 51, "Liber Beneficiarorum Senatus Civitatis Monasteriensis 1550–1821"; and AXIII, 52, "Einkünfteregister der städtischen Benefizien." In Würzburg, an episcopal city roughly the same size as Münster, the magistrates exercised patronage over only seven vicarages around the year 1500; see Trüdinger, *Würzburg,* pp. 98–103.

26. StdAM, AII, 20, RP, 1580, Jan. 15, vol. 11, fol. 59v.

27. StdAM, AII, 20, RP, 1564, April 12, April 28, and May 15, vol. 1, fols. 19, 22, 23v–24.

28. Cf. Lahrkamp, "Patronatsrecht," pp. 225–26. A few more examples would suffice to show the patronage and favoritism shown by the magistrates in choosing candidates. Melchior v. d. Wyck, son of the city syndic Christian, was given a benefice on his father's intercession. Melchior, however, pursued legal studies at the university and had to return the collation to the city council, see StdAM, AII, 20, RP, 1564, vol. 1, fols. 1–1v, 3–3v. Philip Wesselinck, son of Johann Wesselinck, the personal physician to Bishop Franz, was granted a vicary in Saint Magdelena's Hospital as a minor and was allowed to draw income from the living although he was mentally ill and could not perform the services required of him. For more examples of favoritism on the part of the magistrates, see the council minutes regarding the appointments of the sons of Bürgermeister Hilbrandt Plönies and Alderman Christian Wedemhove, StdAM, AII, 20, RP, 1583, vol. 15, fols. 25v, 30v–31.

nine holders of these civic benefices in the period between 1535 and 1618, the magisterial-judicial elite supplied twelve members, the patriciate three, and the rest belonged to the solid *Bürgertum*.[29]

Saint Lambert's was traditionally the church of the merchant community; the parish, the richest in the city, supplied many magistrates, and the church enjoyed the support of the civic elite.[30] It was from Saint Lambert's that the Reformation movement was launched in 1532, when evangelically minded merchants and magistrates raised the lowly vicar at Saint Mauritz's, Bernhard Rothmann, to serve as preacher of the influential parish church.[31] Here, prominent burghers purchased family pews, buried relatives, endowed masses, and managed the substantial income of the parish.[32] If the cathedral represented the citadel of noble privilege, Saint Lambert's symbolized the confidence of the mercantile elite. Of the other parish churches, Saint Servatii was the smallest and many of its sixteen vicars also held livings in the other parishes.[33] The other four parish churches were subject to partial or total control of the cloisters or collegiate chapters and lay influences were greatly diminished.

The Franciscan cloister of Saint Catherine, located on Neubrückenstrasse in the parish of Saint Martin, was founded in 1247.[34] The mendicant friars were the first religious order which attended to the particular spiritual needs of the burgeoning medieval cities. As an order founded by the son of a merchant who renounced material possessions the minor friars enjoyed enthusiastic support among both rich and poor urban dwellers. Schism within the order in the early fourteenth century was

29. Analysis is based on "Liber Beneficiarorum," StdAM, AXIII, 51.

30. Cf. *Stadt- und Marktkirche St. Lamberti Münster (Westf.) Festschrift zur Feier der Wiedererrichtung am 31. Januar 1960* (Münster, 1960).

31. Kerssenbroch, p. 192.

32. On the sale of pews in Saint Lambert's, see BDAM, PfA Lamberti, Urk. 39 (1567), which records the purchase by Arnold v. Guelich, shopkeeper and Alderman and magistrate to be; see also Kart. 51, A18, "Acta specialia betr. die Nachweise welchen die Kirchensitze in S. Lamberti gehören 1560–1726." Many prominent families had also endowed vicaries, memorial masses, and prayer hours in Saint Lambert's: The Herdings endowed masses and a family vicary (Kart. 91 and Urk. 44); the Smithueses, Wedemhoves, and Bucks also endowed masses (Notata bursae Lambertinae, sig. XIXc la, fol. 78vff., Urk. 20, 49, 61). The bursary account books also list all benefactors, see Kart. 71, no. 70; Kart. 72, nos. 71a, 71b, 72; and Kart. 73, no. 73.

33. The parish archive of Saint Servatius in BDAM holds very few documents; only one document, a notarial instrument, pertains to the period before 1600. A list of the clergymen named in the 1571 visitation records can be found in Kiskemper, "Priesterverzeichnis," p. 201.

34. The former archive of the Franciscan cloister, now part of the StAM, contains only three Urkunden for the years prior to 1630. The only source for the study of the cloister in the sixteenth century is a Latin chronicle compiled in the mid-eighteenth century by the cloister archivist; see StdAM, MS. 4.

reflected in conflicts within the cities; the *fraticelli* championed the cause of the *popolo minuto* and of the lower classes, while the Franciscans were supported by the merchants and guild elite in Italian cities.[35] In Münster, the burghers saw the friars as their own religious order, a civic counterpart to the traditional religious orders, where aristocratic elements predominated.[36] The magistrates extended protection and patronage to the Franciscans, granted them the use of real properties, honored them with periodic alms. In turn, the friars cared for the sick and poor and opened their cloister to secular use.[37] The magistrates often conducted business at Saint Catherine's, the Franciscan cloister.[38] They and their families found final resting places in the Franciscan churchyard.[39] Magisterial families that had risen from the guilds cherished the strongest ties with the friars. Bürgermeister Hermann Heerde, the most forceful leader in Münster in the three decades after the Catholic restoration, lived on Vossgasse, around the corner from the cloister. He and the Heerde clan were among the most consistent supporters of the friars.[40] Many of the magisterial families that remained Catholic in the Reformation years originated from the ranks of the guilds in the fifteenth century; their ties to the Franciscans dated back to at least the mid-fifteenth century during the time of the War of the Münster Bishopric (1450–57).[41] The struggle

35. On the relationship between the Franciscans and urban movements in Italy during the Middle Ages, see Marvin B. Becker, "Florentine Politics and the Diffusion of Heresy in the Trecento: A socioeconomic Inquiry," *Speculum,* 34 (1959), pp. 60–74; and Hans Baron, "Franciscan Poverty and Civic Wealth as Factors in the Rise of Humanistic Thought," *Speculum* 13 (1938), pp. 1–37. For similar relationships in France and in Germany, see Jacques Le Goff, "Ordres mendients et urbanisation dans la France médiévale," *Annales* (1970), pp. 924–46; and John Freed, *The Friars and German Society in the Thirteenth Century* (Cambridge, Mass., 1977).

36. There are two short studies of the Franciscans in Münster; see J. Nordhoff, "Die Minoritenkirche zu Münster," in *Organ für Christliche Kunst* 18 (1868), and Bernhard Bockholt, *Die Orden des heiligen Franziskus in Münster* (Münster, 1917).

37. The best study of the interdependence between the Franciscan Order and cities is Bernhard E. J. Stüdeli's research on Franciscans in the cities of the German-speaking cantons of the Swiss Confederation. See his *Minoritenniederlassungen und mittelalterliche Stadt* (Werl, 1969).

38. StdAM, AII, 20, RP, 1566, May 10, vol. 3, fol. 16; for Swiss examples, see Stüdeli, pp. 87–101.

39. Among others, the patrician Kerckerincks and Schenckincks were buried in the Franciscan churchyard. See StdAM, B, Test. I, 297 and 337.

40. The Franciscan churchyard provided the traditional burial ground for the Heerde clan; see wills of some Heerdes in StdAM, B, Test. I, 106; Test. II, 435, 676, 679.

41. On the War of the Münster Bishopric, see the older narrative study of Ursula Meckstroth, "Das Verhältnis der Stadt Münster zu ihrem Landesherrn bis zum Ende der Stiftsfehde 1457," in *QFGSM* n.f. II (Münster, 1962), pp. 3–196, and the recent structural analysis by Kirchhoff, "Die Unruhen in Münster/Westf. 1450–1457," in Ehrecht, ed., *Städtische Führungsgruppen*.

between rival candidates for the episcopal see sparked a guild revolution in Münster which propelled the leading guild families into sharing power equally with the patriciate. At the time of the urban unrest, the Franciscan cloister served as the meeting place of the guildsmen.[42] Similarly, when the guild leaders agitated for the restoration of guilds and councillor elections in 1552 and 1553, they met in the cloister of the friars.[43] While anti-clericalism was a sentiment shared by many artisans, the Franciscans continued to enjoy the patronage of the guild masters throughout the sixteenth century; it was only with the coming of the Counter-Reformation that relations between burghers and friars were strained.[44]

Of the many beguinages established in Münster between 1240 and 1340, only four remained in the sixteenth century.[45] In the late fifteenth century, Rosenthal beguinage adopted the Augustinian Rule; Reine, Ringe, and Hofringe followed the Third Rule of Saint Francis.[46] The beguinages were founded by city women, burghers who lacked the social distinction to enter the noble convents; in no way can they be understood as institutions for poor women. The non-patrician civic elite was the most prominent social group in the beguinages. Between 1500 and 1618, six of the eight mother superiors at Rosenthal came from magisterial families; the other two were daughters of judges. Of the twenty-five sisters, fifteen belonged to families of the guild elite who also sent at least one family member to the city council in the same period; the other ten beguines were women from guild, notarial, and judicial families.[47]

Founded in 1248 for "honorable burgher children," Ringe beguinage was equally popular among women of the civic elite.[48] An incomplete list of nineteen sisters compiled for the years between 1540 and 1618 shows that the vast majority (fifteen sisters) came from magisterial or guild elite

42. Kirchhoff, "Unruhnen 1450–57," p. 208.

43. Kerssenbroch, pp. 926f.

44. The chronicle of the Franciscan cloister mentions the warm support of the guilds in the second half of the sixteenth century; see StdAM, MS. 4, fol. 44.

45. For a comprehensive discussion of the origins and development of the beguinages in Münster, see Karl Zuhorn, "Die Beginen in Münster," *WZ* 91 (1935), pp. 1–149.

46. Zuhorn, "Beginen," p. 83.

47. On Rosenthal beguinage, see August Bahlmann, *Das Kloster Rosenthal* (Münster, 1857), an older, not always reliable study, and Kohl, ed., *Bistum Münster,* pp. 296–318, which corrects inaccuracies in Bahlmann. The mother superiors between 1520 and 1620 were, in chronological order, Anna Holtappel, Kunneke Modersohn, Anna v. Averhagen, Maria Rodde, Elisabeth Wesselinck, Anna Voss, Klara v. Averhagen, and Anna Torck. The Torcks and the Wesselincks were families of lawyers, judges, and physicians; the other families were all represented on the city council.

48. The description comes from the letter of guild Aldermen and masters to the city council, dated May 14, 1613, in StdAM, AXIII, 426.

families.[49] Whereas the magisterial families who had left the guilds and abandoned trade preferred to send their daughters to the more prestigious convents of Aegidii, Niesing, and to other cloisters in Münsterland, the guild elite cultivated close ties with the beguinages. Dowries given to daughters often ended up as part of the endowment when they joined the beguinages; some women dedicated themselves to the religious life in widowhood, after their children had grown up to take care of the family trade; just as in guild households, maids, too, were found in the beguinages.[50] Hofringe and Reine represented "lesser" beguinages where fewer magisterial families were represented.[51] The beguines attended church services and mixed freely with their fellow burghers. Leading a life that was pious but not cloistered, the beguines were nevertheless recognized by their fellow citizens as religious women who expressed the piety of the city in their own particular way.

Last of all, there was the "infantry" of the levitical army—the many vicars who sang daily masses for the salvation of their donors and shouldered the responsibilities of the canons for a fraction of the latter's income.[52] Although at the bottom of the ecclesiastical hierarchy, the

---

49. There is no published list of sisters at Ringe beguinage. I have compiled a partial personnel list from wills, Urkunden, and other sources: (A) Mother Superiors: 1544 Christina Rodde (StdAM, B, Test. I, 160); 1613 Engela Tünneken (StdAM, AXIII, 426). (B) Sisters: 1540 Elisabeth Bisping (Test. I, 393); 1541 +Elisabeth Holthaus, Gertrud Plate (StAM, FM, Aegidii, Urk. 257); 1539–89 Elisabeth Mumme (Test. I, 240 & 632); 1549 Wennake Iserman (Test. I, 520); 1575 Katherina Jonas (Test. I, 560; Test. II, 1794); 1580 Gertrud Grüter (Test. I, 691); Trignehe Jonas (Test. I, 247); 1595 Enneken Wedemhove (Test. I, 427); Clara Boland (Test. II, 847); 1609 Richtmot Münstermann (Test. II, 334); 1613 Elseke Glandorp, Gertrud Münstermann, Gertrud Jonas (StdAM, AXIII, 426); Anna tom Ring and Anneken Boland, late sixteenth century (Test. I, 160).

50. Cf. the will of Hilde Beckers, a maid in Rosenthal, StdAM, B, Test. I, 363.

51. There are no published lists of beguines at Reine and Hofringe; the following lists have been compiled mainly from extant wills in the StdAM.

I. Reine
A. Mother Superiors: 1540 Steyneke Rodde (BDAM, PfA Lamberti, Kart. 16, A5, 16) 1572 Anna Raemers (StdAM, B, Test. I, 17).
B. Sisters: 1549 Elske Olierleger (Test. I, 520); 1572 Barbara [Raestrup?] Test. I, 287); 1605 Elske Einen (Test. I, 647; Test. II, 1856); N. Meiler (Test. I, 717); 1616 Elisabeth Vogdinck and Katherina Stille (Test. II, 1500).

II. Hofringe
1556 Anna Rybbeker (Test. I, 620); 1559 Gatake Langermann (Test. I, 572); 1566 Elske Husman and N. Mersman (Test. I, 491); 1590 N. Hosen (Test. I, 247); 1597 Margaretha Langermann+ (Test. I, 292); 1607 Katherina Wittover (Test. II, 1079); 1616 Stina Lodde (Test. II, 1021).

52. At the end of the sixteenth century, there were forty-one vicarages in the cathedral, eight in the Old Cathedral, seven in Saint Ludger's, six in Saint Martin's, sixteen in Saint Servatii, six in Überwasser, ten in Saint Mauritz's, and another ten to twelve in the hospitals

vicars did not constitute a clerical proletariat. Some were sons of the civic elite and bastards of patricians and noblemen; they could supplement the meager income of their livings with comfortable patrimonies. Others, not blessed with rich parents, managed on income not much more than that of a day laborer. The low income of the vicaries forced some to hold several benefices simultaneously; their best hope was to rise to the position of chaplain or pastor in the parish churches, where more substantial income would relieve them of constant money worries. It was from this stratum of the clergy that many advocates of the Reformation were recruited. Vicars who were often better educated than the pastors and canons were enthusiastic about the new Reformation message, a sentiment further fueled by personal experiences of the corruption of the higher clergy. In the quarter of a century after the Religious Peace of Augsburg, there still existed strong discontent among the vicars with the corrupted lifestyles of many canons. The dean and provost of Saint Martin explicitly warned the vicars in 1571 not to incite lay hostility toward the higher clergy.[53]

While the personnel and income of the different ecclesiastical institutions give us an idea about their social composition, the records of the 1571 diocesan visitation leave behind a picture of their spiritual state.[54] A visitation team was appointed by Bishop Johann von Hoya to investigate the condition of all clerical institutions as a preliminary step to the eventual implementation of the Tridentine decrees. In the city of Münster itself, the commission passed over the cathedral chapter and Überwasser convent, which cited traditional privileges. Extensive and detailed questionnaires, however, were prepared for the parish churches, monasteries, and nunneries; the commissioners scrutinized all aspects of religious life, from probing into heresy, concubinage, the adherence to monastic dis-

---

and poorhouses. Taking into consideration clerical pluralism, there must still have been close to 100 vicars; see Lethmate, *Bevölkerung,* pp. 31–33.

53. The warning reads: "Nostro sacellano in virtute sanctae obedientiae precipiendo mandamus . . . neve nostros, . . . in concionibus virulentia ac detractoria lingua carpant. . . . Multoque minus ferendum, ut quis auram popularem venando in ecclesiasticos magistratas aliosque clericos tenere ad populum invehatur, quo nihil aliud efficitur, quam ut plebem, alioqui satis in clerum irritatam, irritationem reddat, ac gliscenti seditionum igni oleum subministret." The document, deposited in StAM, FM, Martini, is published in full in Viktor Huyskens, *Everwin von Droste, Dechant an der Kollegiatkirche Saint Martini zu Münster (1567–1604), und die Stiftsschule seiner Zeit. Teil I: Vom Leben und Wirken Everwin von Droste* (Münster, 1907), pp.21–22.

54. See Schwarz, *Visitation* (= GQBM VII), full citation in n. 22. The revised edition of *Die Visitation im Dienst der kirchlichen Reform* (Münster, 1977), ed. Ernst W. Zeeden and Hansgeorg Molitor, gives exhaustive information on visitation records, both published and archival, for all German territories and cities in the sixteenth and seventeenth centuries.

cipline, and the fulfillment of divine offices, to investigating the relations between cloistered inmates and the finances of the institutions.[55]

A general picture of the spirituality of the clergy emerges from the answers to these visitation questionnaires. Although all clerical institutions protested their loyalty to the Roman Church and denied having heretics in their midst, some were clearly far from moral and disciplinary rigor. The collegiate churches (Old Cathedral, Saint Martin's, Saint Ludger's, and Saint Mauritz's), strongholds of clerical privileges, scored badly. Many canons lived with wives and children, donned ostentatious, expensive attire, bore arms, drank to excess, and neglected the performance of divine offices.[56] In other words, they were hardly distinguishable from their noble and patrician relatives. The convents did somewhat better. No scandalous behavior defamed Aegidii and Niesing, but the letter and spirit of cloistered life were violated by many minor transgressions. The nuns did not keep silence, neglected matins and vespers, and mixed freely with their maids. The picture we have is one of generally pious women from the upper class who lived in a relaxed and comfortable environment, eschewing the extreme rigors of cloistered life.[57] The *Fraterherren* and the Franciscans seemed to have been characterized by a spiritual tepidity which was pious but devoid of dedication and distinction.[58] The parochial clergy in Münster came out as the most conscientious and dedicated of all clerical groups; pastors, chaplains, and vicars, especially at Überwasser and Saint Lambert's, dutifully said mass, vigilantly kept prayer hours, regularly read the Scriptures, and all but a few adhered strictly to celibacy.[59] They were the ones who stood closest to the burghers through pastoral care and were named as confessors and friends in many wills.

One thing unified these disparate ecclesiastical bodies—the recourse to clerical privileges. Exempted from taxation and civic duties, the clergy was also immune from prosecution in the city's court. Churches and cloisters provided sanctuary for all who sought it. The wealth and privileges of the Church embittered many burghers who saw the clergy as economic competitors and indolent parasites. Artisans of the craft guilds were especially hostile to the clergy. Opposition between clergy and laity, however, cannot obstruct the fact that the Church played an important role in Münster's economy; land and capital wove a thousand threads that entangled *ecclesia* and *civitas*. What were the patterns of entwinement?

55. For the questionnaires, see Schwarz, *Visitation,* pp. 6–38.
56. Cf. Schwarz, *Visitation,* pp. 43–70.
57. Ibid., pp. 83–84, 86–87.
58. Ibid., pp. 77–80.
59. Ibid., pp. 70–77, 80–85.

LAND AND CAPITAL

In an episcopal principality, it was only obvious that the Catholic Church would be the largest landowner, but it would be a mistake to overemphasize the necessary opposition between a feudal agrarian ecclesiastical regime and commercially minded urban communities. A great deal of recent scholarship is devoted to elucidating the interdependence between city and country, between commerce and agriculture in the Middle Ages and in the sixteenth and seventeenth centuries.[60] In Münster, a clear-cut opposition between commercial urban elites and landowning churchmen never existed; until the early fifteenth century, municipal government in Münster was monopolized by the patriciate, many of whom originated as *ministeriales* of the bishops and all owned estates in the environs of the city.[61] By the sixteenth century, the non-patrician urban elites were also increasingly sinking investment in land. Both magisterial and leading guild families bought up farms, pastures, and gardens around Münster.[62] The pursuit of landownership inevitably brought the urban elite into contact with the Church, and it is in landholding that the pattern of interpenetration between segments of urban society and the rural clerical regime is most visible.

As the largest landlord in the diocese, the Bishop of Münster dispensed favor and patronage through the grant of numerous fiefs to noblemen and patricians.[63] The roll of fiefholders (*Lehensbuch*) under Bishop Franz von Waldeck, compiled between 1548 and 1554, lists close to two hundred fiefs. Half of them were granted to patricians and burghers and the other half were held by noblemen.[64] Most of the ruling patrician families in Münster held at least one, some as many as thirty fiefs. A few non-patrician magisterial families in Münster also appeared in the roll—the Vendts, the Smithues, and the Voss were represented. These families also served in the episcopal officialdom as judges and bailiffs (*Amtmann*). The core magisterial families of Münster, whether engaged in trade or living on invested capital, were absent. The vast majority of these fiefs

60. See the bibliographic essay of Rolf Kiessling, "Stadt-Land-Beziehungen im Spätmittelalter. Überlegungen zur Problemstellung und Methode anhand neuerer Arbeiten vorwiegend zur süddeutschen Beispielen," in *ZfBLG,* 40 (1977), pp. 829–67; see also Erich Maschke and Jürgen Sydow, eds., *Stadt und Umland* (Stuttgart, 1974).

61. See Karl Roth, *Die Ministerialität der Bischöfe von Münster* (Münster, 1912).

62. A good example is the substantial landholding of the magistrate Johann Herding around Münster; see his account book, StdAM, MS. 120, fols. 50–64.

63. The urban elites in Augsburg and in Strasbourg also held fiefs from their bishops; see Kiessling, *Augsburg,* pp. 197–201; and Thomas A. Brady, *Ruling Class, Regime and Reformation at Strasbourg 1520–1555* (Leiden, 1978), pp. 76–92, 127–40.

64. StAM, AVM, MS. 51, "Münsterisches Lehenbuch, aus der Zeit des Bischofs Franz von Waldeck."

held by the urban elite were concentrated in a circle centered on Münster with a radius of less than twenty miles; very few lay near the rim of the bishopric, especially near the Dutch border, where poor peat soil predominated. Lordship over these fiefs sometimes entailed the exercise of feudal jurisdiction over serfs; it always enriched the holders with agricultural products which could be sold in Münster for a handsome profit. Some fiefs stipulated military service from their holders and were held by patricians, whose names were also entered in the roll call of the armigerous vassals of the bishop.[65] Most of the twelve patricians appointed by Bishop Franz to the Münster city council in 1536 had been called up as vassals by the prince-bishop to help crush the Anabaptist rebellion.[66] In addition to their own allodial estates, these fiefs enabled the Münster patriciate to live nobly. Hence, as landowner, the Church accelerated the absorption of a part of the urban elite into the ranks of the lower nobility.

Close relations between bishop and patriciate were duplicated on a smaller scale between noble ecclesiastical institutions and the urban elite. Several patrician families—the Warendorps zum Emshaus, the Stevenincks, and the Bischopincks—also held fiefs from the cathedral chapter and from Überwasser cloister.[67] The Joddevelts, a magisterial family resident in Überwasser parish, had been fiefholders of the noble Benedictine convent from the late fifteenth century.[68] Through landownership, the Münster patricians came into possession of serfs living on their estates and often exchanged them with those subject to the aristocratic-patrician Benedictine convents of Überwasser and Aegidii in order to round out their properties.

Another way the feudal agrarian regime penetrated urban society was through the presence of serfs in the city of Münster itself. Bondsmen of the cathedral chapter (*Wachszinsige*) lived within the compounds of the cathedral where they served as maids and servants of the noble canons. A few were able to save up enough money to purchase their manumission and to obtain citizenship in Münster.[69]

65. Entered in the vassal roll were the following patricians: five Bischopincks, three Bucks, three Kerckerincks, and three Stevenincks, two Drostes, two Schenckincks, two Clevorns, two Warendorps, two Wycks, and one each from the Travelmann, Tilbeck, Grael, Drolshagen, and Tinnen. See StAM, AVM, MS. 145d, "Registrum Militarium des Stiffts Münster Anno Domini 1584."

66. Cf. Müller, *Abrechnungen,* pp. 11–12, 16, 92–93, 95, 101–02, 108.

67. Cf. BDAM, PfA Martini, Urk. 19, 20, 23, 25, 26, 28, 30, 35, A174.

68. BDAM, PfA Martini, Urk. 30.

69. The considerable number of serfs residing in clerical immunities necessitated a clause in the police-ordinance (constitution) of the city which prohibited them from taking up a civic trade; see StAM, AVM, MS. 110, "Polizei-Ordnung der Stadt Münster 1558," fols. 50v–52v. For serfs who were sworn in as burghers after manumission, see Hövel, *BB,* under 1538, nos. 55, 65, 75, 108–09; under 1575, nos. 254, 256. See also StdAM, B, Test. I,

Immediately outside the city walls, the Church owned much land, some of which was donated by pious burghers. In the course of the sixteenth century, more and more of these camps, pastures, and gardens passed into burgher hands either through sale or lease. The passion for land was not exclusive to the urban patriciate and magistracy, most of the well-to-do burghers, the richer guildsmen included, eagerly grabbed up land outside of the city walls.[70]

Within the walls of Münster the Church was still a substantial, though somewhat diminished, landlord. The bulk of clerical properties lay within the immunities; outside of these, the concentration of houses owned by clerics was highest in Überwasser parish where almost 20 percent of all houses were exempted from taxes because of clerical ownership.[71] The parish churches also owned a few houses which were rented out to sextons, church wardens, and other tenants.[72]

The major economic role played by the Church inside the city of Münster was not that of a landlord, but that of a creditor. Both institutions and individual clerics lent out large sums through the purchase of promissory notes or annuities (*Renten*). These credit instruments generally entitled the bearer to annual interest payment of 5 percent on the principal, the highest rate approved by the theologians, unless they were specified as life annuities (*Leibrente, Lyffrente*) which entitled the holder to receive 10 percent annual interest during his lifetime. Most promissory notes could be redeemed, but there were some which gave the bearer the right to collect interest and pass on the annuities from generation to generation. The seller or debtor had to put up a collateral, generally land or house, to guarantee that the buyer or creditor would retrieve his invested capital.[73] Princes, bishops, noblemen, merchants, artisans, peas-

---

230 and 346 for wills of serfs residing in Münster. In the Middle Ages, the cities offered serfs an opportunity to win their freedom; if the serfs resided in the cities for more than one year they automatically won manumission, hence the proverb, "Stadtluft macht frei." Cf. Hans Planitz, *Die Deutsche Stadt im Mittelalter* (Graz, 1954), p. 254.

70. The income of the Pastorate of Saint Lambert in the late sixteenth century included land rents from six burghers: One was the magistrate Christoph Höfflinger; one, Aleke Droste, belonged to the patriciate; one, Johann Joddevelt, was a member of the notability; the other three, a Konning, a Nunninck, and a Hardlandt, were not represented among the magistracy or the guild elite. See BDAM, PfA Lamberti, Kart. 65, no sig., "Registrum der Aufkünfte welche zu pastorie S. Lamberti binnen Münster gehoren."

71. Schulze, *Überwasser*, p. 137.

72. Cf. BDAM, PfA Lamberti, Kart. 16, "Kirchenrechnungen: Belege 16.–18. Jh.," no. 15, accounts, 1546–50, fols. 10v–12v; seven houses belonging to the church were rented "for one life" to church wardens and other tenants. Saint Ludger's also owned a small house and garden; both were rented out. See PfA Ludgeri, Kart. 19, "Reckenschup der upborunge und vthgyffte der kerkern Ludgeri . . . 1565" (unpaginated).

73. On the development of Renten as credit instruments, see Wilfried Trusen, "Zum Rentenkauf im Spätmittelalter," in *Festschrift für Hermann Heimpel, II*, pp. 140–58. For

ants, and governments all raised capital through the sale of annuities. This ubiquitous financial instrument helped to define social relations in the cities, where relationship to land was not the sole determinant in the assignment of individuals in the social hierarchy.[74]

All ecclesiastical institutions kept careful records of their loans. The copybooks compiled in the late fifteenth and sixteenth centuries record transactions of earlier centuries; since very few of the original notarial instruments have survived, the copybooks provide the best available sources for studying the Church as creditor. For the period 1535–1618, copybooks are extant for only a few churches.[75] Account books of cloisters and churches furnish another source, although mere sums rather than details of the transactions are given.[76] As far as individual clerics are concerned, only a handful left behind wills detailing their annuities, and few of these have survived. From these fragmentary pieces we can only draw a very rough sketch of the role of the Church in the capital market, but it is one which permits an assessment of the economic importance of the Catholic Church in Münster.

Noble ecclesiastical institutions with huge tracts of land, such as the cathedral chapter and the Benedictine convents, derived only a small part of their income from annuities. The greater part of their income came from tithes and rents; often collected in kind, these were directly consumed by the clergy or sold on the market for a handsome price. The paucity of records allows only a few brief remarks to be made on the other ecclesiastical institutions. The beguinages and the collegiate

---

problems posed by credit instruments for the Catholic Church, see Julius Kirschner, "The Moral Problem of Discounting Genoese Paghe 1450–1550," *Archivum Fratrum Praedicatorum*, 47 (1977), pp. 109–67; and his "The Moral Theology of Public Finance: A Study and Edition of Nicholas de Anglia's 'Quaestio Disputata' on the public debt of Venice," also in the *AFP*, 40 (1970), pp. 47–72. For theological discussions on taking interests in Germany on the eve of the Reformation, see Heiko A. Oberman, *Werden und Wertung der Reformation* (Tübingen, 1977), pp. 161–77.

74. Some annuities yielded so-called "eternal interests" (*Ewigszinsen*). An annuity drawn up in 1588, secured against a farm in Billerbeck, passed into the possession of the chaplainry of Saint Aegidius in 1606; it was still yielding interest in the mid-nineteenth century; see BDAM, PfA Aegidii, A75.

75. Extant copybooks and rent-registers exist for the pastorate of Saint Lambert (BDAM, PfA, Kart. 64); for the *Speckpfründen* of Saint Ludger (PfA Ludgeri, Kart. 35); for the Church and poorfund of Saint Aegidius (PfA Aegidii, A8, A97; Kopiar I & V).

76. Many of the account books of cloisters and churches now deposited in the StAM have been published in the series, *CTW*, in *QFGSM*, and in *Germania Sacra*. In the BDAM, see PfA Lamberti, Kart. 71 (registers 70, 72); Kart. 72 (registers 71a and b); Kart. 73 (register 73); Kart. 81 (A28); PfA Ludgeri, Kart. 19; PfA Martini, A60, A61, A113; PfA Aegidii, A27, A34–38, A75. The archive of Saint Servatius contains no documents pertaining to the period and the archive of Überwasser was largely destroyed during the Second World War.

churches where the urban elite prevailed invested most of their income in annuities.[77] Most of the credit held by the Church belonged to individual clerics, who often inherited large sums of money from their noble or patrician parents. Vicars also bought annuities with personal savings to supplement the meager income of their benefices. Only a few clerical wills are extant, but they show some patterns of investment. The sisters Elizabeth and Maria von der Berswordt, nuns in Überwasser and Marienfeld, and daughters of the Bürgermeister Johann von der Berswordt, each held annuities worth 3,000 dalers, subscribed by noblemen, patricians, cloisters, and the territorial government (*Landschaft*) of Münster.[78] The Dean of Saint Ludger and canon at Saint Martin's, Dr. Gerhard Krane, listed fourteen annuities worth 860 dalers in his will.[79] Anton Tünneken, vicar at the cathedral, was creditor to no less than thirty-six parties in fifteen towns and villages in Münsterland; his total capital amounted to 1,427 guldens in 1539, which would qualify him as a rich artisan in the social structure of Münster.[80] While it is impossible to calculate the exact amount of capital in the hands of the clergy in Münster, the sum would definitely be well over 100,000 dalers for any period in the sixteenth century. The actual size of the capital in clerical hands may well have amounted to several times the estimated minimum.

To appreciate the enormity of this sum, one has only to look at the debt and income of the city of Münster. At the height of civic indebtedness in the 1590s, interest payments on the municipal debt amounted to 750 dalers; except for a handful of liferents at 10 percent, the bulk of the municipal debt was contracted at 5 percent interest, rendering the total actual debt roughly 15,000 dalers.[81] At the end of the sixteenth century,

77. In 1687, Rosenthal beguinage owned annuities whose capital totaled 29,325 Reichstaler, an enormous sum even taking into consideration the inflation of the sixteenth century. See Kohl, *Bistum Münster,* I, p. 307.

78. In 1610, Elizabeth had annuities worth 2,150 dalers: 600 d. were lent out to the Paderborn cathedral chapter, 500 d. to Überwasser convent, 700 guldens to the nobleman Georg Nagel; see StAM, FM, SFG, II Loc. 7, no. 4:3, fols. 26–27v. Maria received 245 dalers 9 schillings in 1619 from interest on her annuities; the money was lent out to patricians (Buck, Bischopinck, Schenckinck), to the Münster Estates, to Überwasser convent, and to the nobility (Schedelich v. Osthoff, Count of Bentheim, v. Loe). Her will (1606) is in StAM, FM, SFG, II, Loc. 7, no. 4:4, fols. 51–52v; her account book and receipts are fols. 55–56v and fol. 100 in the same signature.

79. Of the fourteen annuities at 6 percent interest worth 860 dalers capital, 300 d. were lent out to burghers, 360 d. to serfs and peasants, and 100 d. to noblemen and patricians; see StdAM, B, Test. II, 1997 (1622), fol. 169.

80. Interest on twenty-two of the thirty-six annuities was paid for with grain. Among his debtors were two noblemen (v. d. Recke and v. Lintelo), two patricians (Steveninck, v. d. Tinnen), and three burghers of Münster; see StdAM, B, Test. I, 494, fols. 64–68.

81. Figures based on accounts of the Gruetamt; StdAM, AVIII, 188, vol. 10 (1591–99).

city income totaled 6,000–7,000 dalers annually; even in the best days of municipal finances, the years before 1618, an average of only 25,000 dalers rolled into Münster's coffers per year.[82] In other words, the amount of credit given out by the Church could pay the civic debt many times over and exceeded municipal revenues manyfold.

Since all promissory notes drawn up in the sixteenth and early seventeenth centuries are not extant, we cannot calculate the credit in clerical hands as a proportion of the entire capital market. The available information, however fragmentary, still allows certain generalizations. Money lent out by the Church must have constituted a good part, if not actually the major part, of the capital raised and borrowed in Münster. While the Church remained on balance a major creditor, only a small part of urban society came out on the plus side of the credit scale.[83]

Who borrowed from the clergy? Almost everyone. Governments, noblemen, merchants, artisans, peasants—even other clerics—borrowed money to finance wars, trade, marriages, to pay for expenses in times of sickness, or just to keep up an expensive way of life. Both burghers and peasants contracted heavy debts; among the former, the dwellers of the smaller semi-agricultural towns were heavily indebted to the clerics and burghers of Münster. Rural indebtedness to the clergy and to Münsteraners was common,[84] although the situation was not as grave as the plight of many peasants in the wine-growing regions of the South, in Alsace, for example.[85] Enjoying little economic freedom due to their servile status, many peasants were bypassed by the money economy. They farmed for their lords, not for the markets in the cities, and had to obtain written permission from their masters before they could contract loans.[86]

---

82. In 1614, income of the city totaled 51,454 marks, in 1615, 52,624 m., in 1616, 55,276 m., in 1617, 54,927 m., in 1618, 58,081 m. Figures from StdAM, AVIII, 188, vol. 13 (1614–20).

83. The Urkunden deposited in Pfarrarchiv Aegidii, by far the richest collection of all the parish archives, provide a sample for closer analysis. Altogether, 143 Urkunden record transactions of the sixteenth century; of these, the clergy were creditors or recipients of donations in 69 transactions; another 10 represent transactions between clerics; 39 pertain to the purchase of annuities by overseers of the parish and poorfunds from lay debtors. If this sample is at all representative, the prominent role played by clerics in the capital market is manifest.

84. On rural indebtedness to Münster clergy and burghers, see BDAM, PfA Aegidii, Urk. 206a, 236a, 241, 242, 243, 243a.

85. Engaged in the highly commercialized viticulture, the peasants of Lower Alsace depended heavily on townsmen and clergy for capital; see Francis Rapp, "Die soziale und wirtschaftliche Vorgeschichte des Bauernkrieges in Unterelsass," in Bernd Moeller, ed., *Bauernkriegstudien* (Gütersloh, 1975), pp. 29–45.

86. Cf. BDAM, PfA Lamberti, Urk. 30; PfA Martini, Urk. 60 (A123); PfA Aegidii, Urk. 241, 256, 206a.

A good many Münsteraners had probably borrowed from the Church at one time or another. The Anabaptist movement in 1534–35 had a strong undercurrent of a rebellion against the bondage of money. Rich burghers who joined the movement burnt annuities in their possession to show solidarity with their coreligionists.[87] When the Anabaptists took power, they destroyed most municipal documents, including nearly all the annuities, and prohibited the use of money in the city of the saints.[88] After the collapse of the rebellion, episcopal officials found out that heavy debts burdened most of the confiscated Anabaptist houses.[89] The Roman Church must have generated much resentment when ecclesiastical measures were applied to enforce the payment of interest—in 1562, the sentence of excommunication was passed on a couple, burghers of Überwasser Parish, for failure to pay 2 guldens in interest to a cathedral vicar.[90]

Another big borrower was the municipal government of Münster. Clerical holding of the municipal debt grew substantially between 1535 and 1618, both in absolute sums and in relative proportions to the other creditors. In 1537, about 40 percent of the municipal debt was held by the clergy; eighty years later, the proportion had risen to 60 percent (see fig. 2.1). Among the various clerical groups, the lower secular clergy, many holding civic benefices, possessed the vast majority of annuities. A few nuns also held liferents, but no ecclesiastical institution, except for the Franciscan cloister, was represented in the list of creditors at the end of the sixteenth century.[91] Endowments for civic vicaries were often entrusted to the magistrates; thus the heavy annuity payments to the civic clergy did not signify the city's growing dependence. In fact, after 1535, the city council consistently pursued a policy of eradicating debts owed to churches and cloisters in order to free the city of potential ecclesiastical pressure. At the same time, the cloisters in Münster considered the pur-

87. Cf. Heinrich Detmer, *Bilder aus den religiösen und sozialen Unruhen in Münster während des 16. Jahrhunderts. II. Bernhard Rothmann* (Münster, 1904), p. 88.

88. Kerssenbroch, p. 558.

89. Cf. K.-H. Kirchhoff, *Täufer,* pp. 80–82.

90. The excommunicated couple were Johann Stoltenkamp and Anna Demmer; see BDAM, PfA Lamberti, Urk. 37.

91. The pattern of clerical holding of the municipal debt in the late sixteenth century contrasts strongly with that of the previous century. For the years before 1533, only one account book of the Gruetamt has survived; in it are entered annuity payments for the years 1480–82 (StdAM, AVIII, 188, vol. 1). In 1480, the clergy held 41.6 percent of the municipal debt, a proportion which fluctuated little for the greater part of the sixteenth century. However, almost one-third of all debt in 1480 was held by clerics outside of Münster; for the clergy residing within Münster, the cloisters and the canons of the cathedral and the collegiate churches represented major creditors. The civic clergy, the only ecclesiastical group under the control of the city council, were not prominent among the creditors.

Mark

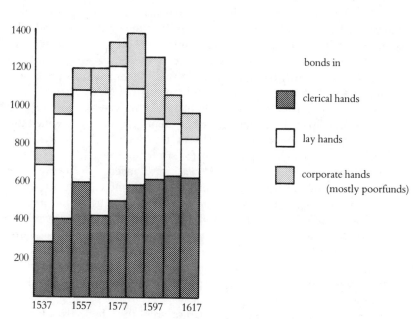

Figure 2.1 Clerical Holdings of the City Debt

chase of municipal annuities a bad investment because the Catholic magistrates staunchly refused to honor debts contracted by the Protestant city council in 1533, money which was borrowed from the convents.[92]

The Church played a paradoxical economic role in Münster. When she flexed her economic muscles, the burghers feared and resented her strength; but without the Church, the livelihood of many artisans would be threatened. Wine merchants in the confidence of cloisters enjoyed a secure and comfortable income; ecclesiastical orders for reliquaries created work for goldsmiths, sculptors, painters, woodcutters, to men-

92. In 1533, the Protestant city council borrowed 160 guldens from Aegidii convent, 200 G. from Überwasser, 100 G. from Niesing, and 100 G. from the Brethren of the Common Life (StdAM, AVIII, 188, GR, vol. 2, fols. 3–3v). After the Catholic magistrates returned to power, the loans were recorded in the 1536 account book of the Gruetamt (vol. 3, fol. 21), but no records of interest payments or redemptions can be found in the subsequent account books. It seems that the magistrates simply refused to repay the loans, because in 1594 the abbess of Aegidii petitioned the magistrates for payment on two annuities which were sealed by the city council in 1533; the magistrates refused to honor the promissory notes, claiming (inaccurately) that the notes were drawn up under the Anabaptist regime (StdAM, AII, 20, RP, 1594, Nov. 18, vol. 26, fol. 83). In 1606, a similar request by the nuns of Überwasser to have their 1533 annuities honored by the city council was also denied (StdAM, AII, 20, RP, 1606, June 5, vol. 38, fol. 91v).

tion only some of the trades affected. The rebuilding and repair of churches after 1535 preoccupied stonemasons, glassmakers, carpenters, and many day laborers for years.[93] Thanks to the Church, a steady flow of income, either in the form of agricultural products or in cash, flowed into Münster from the surrounding countryside and small towns. As landlord and creditor, the Church drew wealth from all over the bishopric and redistributed part of that wealth among the Münsteraners. In the 1590s when numerous peasants sought refuge in Münster to escape the ravages of the Spanish and Dutch troops, many parish priests willed their annuities to help the swollen ranks of the poor.[94] The churches and cloisters also provided employment for some.

The flow of monies, however, was unbalanced. The clergy grew richer with growing lay piety, a direct result of the Counter-Reformation, which endowed the *sacerdotium* with a new dignity and purpose in the economy of salvation. The combined income of the vicaries of Saint Lambert, for example, increased almost sixfold between 1535 and 1618 (see fig. 2.2). A fundamental economic fact of the second half of the sixteenth century was the steady and continuous rise in grain prices, an increase which outstripped the rise in prices of manufactured goods and in wages.[95]

Firmly nestled in the feudal agrarian regime, the Church steadily augmented its income as the price of agricultural produces rose; by receiving part of their tithes and rents in kind, various ecclesiastical institutions and individual clerics were able to stay comfortably ahead of the price inflation, and, incidently, ahead of most merchants and artisans as well. Essentially relieved of the constant need to make ends meet, the clergy of the seventeenth century, richer and more learned than their brethren before the Reformation, could afford to devote themselves to moral and religious enhancement. The gradual improvement in the economic well-being of the Catholic clergy in the century after the Reformation was a significant factor that contributed to the success of the Counter-Reformation in Münster.

93. Among those who benefited greatly from the rebuilding of Überwasser cloister were the wine merchant Lambert Arkquart, the glassmaker Reinert Stelle, and the masters of the smiths' guild; see Schulze, *Überwasser,* pp. 172–74, 186–88, 385–86, 392.

94. Bernhard Bleicken, vicar of Saint Servatius, donated 1,000 dalers, the bulk of his estate, to the poorfund of Aegidii (BDAM, PfA Aegidii, A100, Fund 1, 8, 1593); Wilhelm Lübecke, vicar in the cathedral, donated 200 d. to Aegidii Elende in 1595 (PfA, Aegidii, Urk. 247); the provost of Aegidii, Wessel Huisman, a *Fraterherr,* endowed a poorfund in 1589 (PfA, Aegidii, Urk. 243a).

95. Cf. Wilhelm Abel, *Massenarmut und Hungerkrisen im vorindustriellen Deutschland* (Göttingen, 1977), pp. 21–29; and Harry A. Miskimin, *The Economy of Later Renaissance Europe, 1460–1600* (Cambridge, 1977), pp. 43–52.

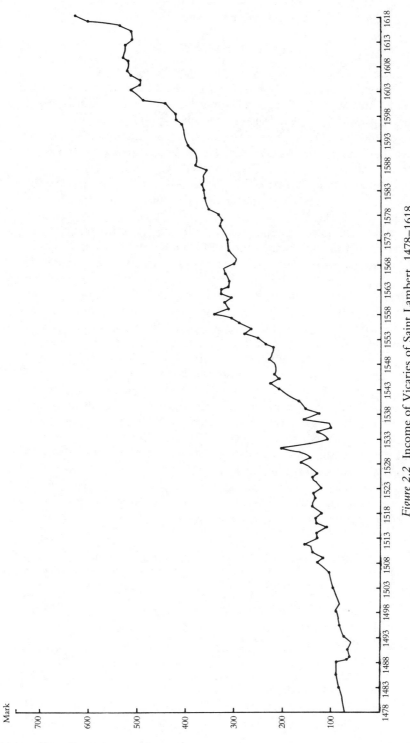

Figure 2.2 Income of Vicaries of Saint Lambert, 1478–1618

Source: BDAM, PfA Lamberti, Akten, Kart. 71, nos. 70–72, Kart. 72, nos. 71a–b, Kart. 73, no. 73.

CITY AND SALVATION

Catholic magistrates were no less eager than their Protestant colleagues to curb the power of the Church; loyalty to Rome did not mean subservience to the clergy. The sentiments which sparked the 1525 anti-clerical unrest in Münster, a prelude to the bloodier episode of 1534–35, were still present after the suppression of the Anabaptist rebellion.[96] Artisans resented economic competition from the clergy; the grievances presented by the rebellious burghers in 1525 included protest against the weaving of cloth and the manufacture of handicraft goods in the cloisters, and the demand that all clergy should share civic burdens.[97] While the ferocious hostility of the Anabaptists toward the clergy horrified the Catholic magistrates, the logic of civic political ideology dictated that the city council restrict the influence of the clergy and uphold the sovereignty of the commune. Above all, the salvation of the city depended on the collective piety of all inhabitants, an enterprise too critical to be entrusted solely to the often unreliable clerical professionals.

There were two aspects to the lay initiative to win salvation. On the negative side, the magistrates tried to contain the power of the Church and, where possible, to roll back her sphere of influence. On the positive side, the burghers took active measures to express their piety by endowing preacherships, vicarages, poorhouses, and hospitals.

The key to controlling clerical privileges was the eradication of abuses associated with clerical immunity to civil jurisdiction. Probably emboldened by the humiliation of the city after the Anabaptist debacle, a few clergymen openly flouted civic pride. Under Bishop Franz, before civic privileges were fully restored in 1554, Johann von Aken, preacher in the cathedral, committed adultery with the wife of a burgher. The woman, a repeated offender, was executed by the magistrates; after the death of Bishop Franz, the city fathers also threw the priest into prison.[98] Through the mediation of the new bishops, Wilhelm von Ketteler

96. The uprisings of the peasants in 1524 and 1525 encouraged urban unrest in many cities of the Empire; see Rudolf Endres, "Zünfte und Unterschichten als Elemente der Instabilität in den Städten," in Peter Blickle, ed., *Revolte und Revolution in Europa* (= *Historische Zeitschrift*, n.f., Beiheft, Munich, 1975), pp. 151–70. The grievances of the Münsteraners were influenced by the forty-six articles drawn up by discontented Frankfurt burghers; the articles are published in Adolf Laube and Hans W. Seiffert, eds., *Flugschriften der Bauernkriegszeit* (E. Berlin, 1975). For the general, structural conflicts between burghers and clergy, see Anton Störmann, *Die Städtischen Gravamina gegen den Klerus am Ausgange des Mittelalters und in der Reformationszeit* (Münster, 1912). On anti-clericalism during the Peasants' War, see Henry Cohn, "Anticlericalism in the German Peasants' War, 1525," in *P & P* 83 (1979), pp. 3–31.

97. The thirty-four articles of grievances are found in Kerssenbroch, pp. 133–38.

98. Röchell, *Chronik,* pp. 6–7, 12.

(1554–57) and Bernhard von Raesfeld (1557–66), the city council and the cathedral chapter negotiated an agreement which regulated jurisdiction over clerics who committed criminal offenses and adultery in Münster. The terms of the agreement, ratified on August 13, 1558, granted the magistrates the right to arrest delinquent clerics in Münster and to turn them over to the bishop for punishment. Clergymen who had done bodily harm to magistrates, their families, and servants were to be punished by the city fathers if swift and prompt sentences were not forthcoming from the Ecclesiastical Court.[99] The settlement represented a victory for the burghers, but another source of conflict was not discussed in 1558: Did the magistrates have the right to arrest criminals who fled to sanctuary in churches and cloisters? In 1557, Johann zum Klei, a barber, sought sanctuary in the Franciscan cloister to escape a murder trial. The magistrates arrested him and sentenced him to death, in spite of Bishop Bernhard's intercession.[100] Churches and cloisters provided subsequent lawbreakers no guarantee from prosecution; the magistrates did not hesitate to violate ecclesiastical sanctuary to bring criminals to face civic justice.[101]

If the full restoration of privileges in 1554 enabled the magistrates to reassert civic autonomy against clerical domination, the repair of churches allowed burghers to express their piety and independence in the face of the clergy. The money for rebuilding and repairing the parish churches came mainly from the piety and generosity of the parishioners. When the spire of Saint Lambert's threatened to collapse in 1568 (it was never properly repaired after 1535), the magistrates levied a parish tax to pay for a new spire.[102] Likewise, in 1581, the city council subsidized the repair of the spire of Saint Aegidius's, which had collapsed and damaged the choir.[103] The warfare of 1534–35 also destroyed the parish school of Saint Martin and damaged the church itself; the school was rebuilt in 1578 with money collected in the parish, and lay donations helped to repair damages to the church building. It is thus understandable that the parishioners regarded the church as their property and resented having to pay fees for the ringing of church bells and being told by the clergy that the church was not available for all community activities.[104] The magistrates in-

99. For the full text of the 1558 agreement, see Röchell, *Chronik,* pp. 13–18.

100. Röchell, *Chronik,* pp. 12–13.

101. In 1574, Bernt Boggelman, a barber, sought asylum in Überwasser convent after he had killed his wife; officers were instructed by the magistrates to enter the convent in spite of the protests of the nuns; see StdAM, AII, 20, RP, vol. 9, fols. 42v–43v.

102. See Karl Utsch, "Die Kulturabteilung des Stadtarchivs Münster. Urkunden und Regesten," in *QFGSM* IX (1937), pp. 48–54.

103. StdAM, AXIII, 43.

104. Cf. StdAM, AXIII, 39, fols. 6–8.

formed the canons in 1580 that sons of burghers could no longer be excluded from the school as before, and they came down on the side of the parishioners in 1590 when the latter presented a list of grievances against the canons of Saint Martin's.[105] Even in the case of the cathedral school, the magistrates extended their authority: They arrested students who had committed criminal offenses, even if they had been tonsured,[106] and helped the schoolmasters in disciplining the students.[107] Only after the Jesuits had taken over the gymnasium in 1588 did the magistrates cease to arrest and judge students, except in severe criminal cases.

Disagreements between burghers and clerics were not unusual in Catholic cities, and the magistrates' attempts to integrate the Church into urban society hardly aroused charges of anti-clericalism. While pursuing a consistent policy of asserting civic political authority over the Church in Münster, the magistrates never lost sight of the Anabaptist specter and suppressed overt acts of anti-clericalism among the burghers.[108] In the second half of the sixteenth century, the ruling elite of Münster could be described as both Erastian and Erasmian. The magistrates believed in the virtues of republicanism and the autonomy of civic politics; they were also some of the most pious men in the city republic, who thought Christianity was more than a matter of rites and doctrines, and best expressed itself in works of public charity.

In the founding of poorhouses and in the endowment of charity funds, the magistrates took the lead, either by virtue of their position as city fathers or as private citizens.[109] In 1590 or 1591, Bürgermeister Dr. Heinrich Vendt founded a poorhouse in Aegidii parish which quickly became a favorite recipient of civic donations.[110] In 1592, the councillor Johann Verendorp and his wife Margaretha Plate, a childless couple, founded an

---

105. For the magistrates' decision on admissions policy to the parish school, see the council minutes of Jan. 26, 1580, in StdAM, AII, 20, vol. 12, fol. 2v. For the grievances of the parish, see StdAM, AXIII, 39, fols. 4v–8.

106. Hermann v. Diepenbrock, *scholasticus* of the cathedral, protested the arrest and judicial torture of Johann Kreyenfenger, a student who had already received the first tonsure, as a violation of academic and clerical privileges (StdAM, AXIII, 47). Kreyenfenger was later executed after having been found guilty of sorcery; see Offenberg, *Bilder,* I, p. 85.

107. See StdAM, AII, 20, RP, 1581, Jan. 16, vol. 12, fol. 72v.

108. The council minutes of 1584 note that "item das etyliche Burgere widder die Geistlichen sich ungepuerlich verhalten sollen" (StdAM, AII, 20, June 8, vol. 16, fol. 29). In 1600, Johann v. Moers and his children were jailed for several days for having insulted the bailiff of Überwasser in public (StdAM, AII, 20, April 28, vol. 32, fol. 29v).

109. Cf. Trüdinger, *Würzburg,* pp. 123ff. and appendixes 2 and 6.

110. Cf. StdAM, B, Test. I, 180, fol. 60v; 181, fol. 77v; 523 (Pergament); and Test. II, 1200.

orphanage with 1,000 dalers, the first of its kind in Münster.[111] At the end of the decade, Bürgermeister Vendt and his son-in-law, councillor Lic. Heinrich Frie, endowed the poorhouse Frie-Vendt in memory of their late wives.[112] The Poorhouse "Buddenturm" in Überwasser parish was founded earlier in the century by the Joddevelts, a magisterial family and one of the most prominent clans in the parish.[113]

These charitable undertakings of the sixteenth century continued a long civic tradition. Poorhouses (*Armenhäuser*), poorfunds (*Almissenkorb, Armenfonds*), *Elende* (plague-houses for maids, servants, students, and travelers), and endowments of food and clothing for the poor (*Speckproven, Speckpfründen, Armenkleidung*) already existed in every parish in the High Middle Ages.[114] Founded and managed by laymen, these institutions represented an aspect of the collective piety of the urban community and the mutual reliance of the burghers in the search for succor, sanctity, and salvation. Some of the funds came under the direct supervision of the city council; others were managed by prominent residents of the parish who were usually magistrates, electors, guild masters, notaries, and lawyers. Similarly, funds for the upkeep of churches and for parish affairs and accounts for the purchase of candles were all controlled by laymen. The parish church account and the parish poorfund were the most important institutions of their kind. The overseers, the *Templerer* or *Kirchenprovisoren* for the former and the *Almissener* for the latter, often managed an investment portfolio of thousands of dalers.[115] Most of the lay overseers were close to the center of political power—magistrates, judges, and the guild leaders generally held these positions. Prior to the Reformation, the provisors were elected, probably by all burghers of the parish. The bloodshed of 1534–35 taught the magistrates that democracy and religious fanaticism often went hand in hand, and they were careful to keep the control of parish affairs under the close supervision of the city council. The 1563 ordinance for the Parish Church of Saint Martin gave detailed instructions on how the provisors should be elected: The outgoing provisors were to name two electors who then nominated the future

111. StdAM, B, Test. I, 41 and 307; cf. AII, 20, RP, 1592, July 20, vol. 24, fol. 70.

112. BDAM, PfA Aegidii, Urk. 107, endowment certificate of Frie-Vendt Poorhouse.

113. In her will (1608), Ursula Joddeveld mentioned that the poorhouse was founded by her grandparents; StdAM, B, Test. II, 563.

114. Account books of the charitable institutions are deposited in StdAM, C (Stiftungsarchiv) and in BDAM, PfA, Ludgeri, Kart. 35 (Speckpfründen); Kart. 48 (Almosenkorb); PfA Aegidii, A97, A100, A103–108 (Armenfonds). For comparisons with Würzburg and Augsburg, see Trüdinger, *Würzburg,* pp. 104–18; and Kiessling, *Augsburg,* pp. 159–74, 219–34.

115. In 1618, the *Speckpfründen* of Saint Lambert had an income of ca. 850 dalers, most of which represented interest on annuities; the endowment could not have been less than 5,000 to 6,000 dalers; see StdAM, C, Speckpfründen Lamberti, no. 13.

provisors; magistrates of the parish, already overburdened with the task of governance, were not to be elected as provisors, but they could serve as electors and thereby manipulate the elections.[116] The process of co-optation resembled the procedure of councillor election after 1554, which diminished the role of the community by abolishing direct elections and enhanced the influence of the magistracy through a fourfold electoral process.

When lay initiatives supplanted clerical efforts, when greater responsibilities for salvation came under the control of the burghers, the potential for conflicts between social groups also increased. The line that divided the clergy from the laity was but one of the many geological faults that scarred the landscape of the city; within each estate, class and familial divisions were just as important in explaining behavior. The Church and the city coexisted in a tense equilibrium; they needed one another, and yet each tried to extend its sphere of influence at the other's expense. The precarious balance established after the catastrophe of the Anabaptist Kingdom was not threatened until the 1580s, when the reinvigorated sacerdotal regime resolved to subjugate the laity once again. In the vanguard of the Catholic Reconquest fought the Society of Jesus; to these shock troops of the Counter-Reformation we will now turn our attention.

116. BDAM, PfA, Martini, A18, "Kirchenordnung 1563," fols. 1–1v.

CHAPTER THREE

Ad majorem Dei gloriam

"From those who live in Münster, not a few things have been accomplished for the greater glory of God and the salvation of men." Thus begins the 1596 *Litterae Annuae* of the Jesuit College in Münster.[1] Whereas in 1588 the Jesuits still complained that Catholic faith in Münster "was not pure and poisoned by the Lutherans,"[2] in 1596 they reported triumphantly: "How much have we strengthened the ruins of the Church in these places and restored it! Not only do we have the zeal of the young, the goodwill of all burghers towards us also grows day by day."[3] Behind this self-praise lay the labor of the Society in transforming the religious identity of the city and the fierce resistance they often encountered.

Dedicated, talented, erudite, the Jesuits were usually men of impeccable moral quality and vast energies; they were, however, self-righteous in their moral rectitude, intolerant of opposition, and all too ready to castigate their enemies as diabolical, and their presence in Münster caused a storm of protest. Their activities gained them many fervent adherents but also embittered many in the same civic republic. Putting "pure religion" above the toleration of a free republic, the Jesuits were mainly responsible for creating divisions in the body politic and for the formation of political parties based on confessional lines.

Their work was as multifaceted as their social origins. They served as the vanguard of the princely–episcopal territorial state; they advanced the boundaries of the visible (Roman) Kingdom of God in actual territorial terms; they taught and molded generations of youth, training them to become future rulers, councillors, prelates, and priests; they acted as clergy for the clergy, visiting cloisters, guiding priests, nuns, and monks; they played the roles of councillors and confessors to the territorial nobility and cultivated the friendship of the civic magistracy; they preached in

---

1. *Litt. Ann.*, 1596, p. 284.
2. *Litt. Ann.*, 1588, p. 183.
3. ". . . Et Ecclesiae ruinas in his locis quantum valemus, restaurare, non enim studia solum habemus iuventutis, sed universae etiam civitatis erga nos benevolentia in dies augetur . . ." *Litt. Ann.*, 1596, p. 290.

the parishes and administered the sacraments; they guided the spiritual elite of the Catholic laity organized in the various Marian sodalities; they contributed to civic culture by staging plays and organizing and leading magnificent religious processions; they exorcised demons, converted heretics, and castigated Protestants. To their supporters, they were the true soldiers of Christ, to their enemies, the praetorian guards of the imperialist Counter-Reformation Papacy.

THE COMING OF THE JESUITS

As early as 1582, the dean of the Cathedral and leader of the Catholic faction on the chapter, Gottfried von Raesfeld, wanted to turn the under-populated Franciscan cloister into a Jesuit college in order to check Protestant influences in the bishopric.[4] The *Statthalter* of the bishopric, Duke Johann Wilhelm of Jülich-Cleve, wrote to the magistrates in Münster regarding this plan. Pressured by the guild leaders and remembering the loyalty of the friars to the city, the magistrates resisted the plan, stressing in their reply to the duke the long-standing services performed by the friars.[5] Another reason, not mentioned in the letter to the duke, was the stiff opposition of the guild leaders. The protocol of the city council of October 12 contains the following entry:

> Since the Jesuits are unknown to this place and the citizenry is unfamiliar with them, moreover, in these extremely dangerous and worrisome times when in neighboring cities disunity among the burghers was introduced on account of religion and its divisions, the magistracy expresses its reservations to allow the Jesuits into the Franciscan cloister.[6]

The protocol of the Schoehaus reflected in even sharper terms the disapproval of the guild leaders: noting with satisfaction the decision of the city council, the guild leaders added they feared that admitting the Jesuits would eventually lead to the Inquisition.[7] The political pressure exerted

---

4. Duhr, *Jesuiten,* I, p. 144.

5. See letter of city council to Duke Johann Wilhelm, dated Oct. 26, 1582, StdAM, AXIII, 436, esp. fols. 8–10v. As examples of the close ties between city and Franciscan cloister, the letter mentions that the friars received and dined the magistrates, fulfilled their civic duties by helping the burghers in times of sickness and at marriages, threw open the cloister as a meeting place for burghers and the guilds, and buried many pious burghers in their cemetery. Moreover, quite a few magistrates had joined the cloister in past centuries. See also the council minutes of Oct. 5, 1582, StdAM, AII, 20, RP, vol. 14, fols. 49v–51v.

6. StdAM, AII, 20, RP, 1582, Oct. 12, vol. 14, fols. 54–54v, ". . . deweil die Jesuiten disser ort unbekant, und dye burgerschatt ihrer nit kendlich, auch die gantz geferliche und besorgsame zeiten in den nachburen stedden wegen der Religion und deren Speltung und uneinicheit zwisschen den Burgeren und Underthanen geffuret, als gehe es Einen Erb. Rat bedencken die Jesuiter zu der Minoriter Cloeser zugestatte. . . ."

7. StdAM, AXI, 76, SP, vol. 1, 1582, Oct. 12.

by the guilds forced the city council to adopt an openly recalcitrant position; there were, however, many councillors who privately favored the admission of the Jesuits. Duke Johann Wilhelm chided the magistrates for meddling in "a purely clerical affair" and insisted that Jesuit education was essential for the proper upbringing of Catholic children, for the common good, and for the maintenance of public order.[8] Shortly thereafter, the duke resigned from the position of Statthalter to take up rule in the duchy after the death of his elder brother. The whole question was dropped until after the election of Archbishop Ernst of Bavaria to the Münster See in 1585. A pupil of the Jesuits in Munich and a strong proponent of the Counter-Reformation, he vigorously supported the installation of the Society in Münster. When Dean Gottfried von Raesfeld died in 1586 he bequeathed 30,000 dalers for the founding of a Jesuit college.[9]

This time the city council quickly approved of the admission of the Jesuits. On January 15, 1588, in a session attended by only the eight magistrates holding the higher ranks within the city council, the motion to admit the Jesuits passed with just one dissenting voice. The dissenter, Rotger Ossenbrügge, merely suggested that the guild Aldermen should be consulted first.[10] Three days later, the guild leaders appeared before the magistrates, expressing their grave reservations and asking the council to delay its decision until after the new elections in February.[11] This time, the motion was put before the full session of the council; only two magistrates cast votes in favor of the Aldermen's proposal to delay the decision.[12] Not wishing to push the guilds into open opposition, the magistrates did agree to delaying the formal vote after the new councillor election. On February 19, the city council ruled that "after having pondered on the upmost necessity of a permanent good school in this city for the support of both the clergy and the laity . . . [it] has therefore decided by majority vote . . . to allow the Jesuits to take up the running and rule of the cathedral school."[13] They reached a compromise with the guild leaders agreeing to restrict the presence of the Fathers to the cathe-

8. Letter of Duke Johann Wilhelm to the city council, dated Nov. 27, 1582, StdAM, AXIII, 436. In the letter, the duke denounced that the Franciscan cloister was inhabited by "untügentlichen, ungelerten unnd in religions Sachen unerfarnen, auch eins unzimlichen unnd ungeburlichen Lebenns unnd Wandels, Ihrem Orden ungemess Personen. . . ."

9. Duhr, *Jesuiten,* I, pp. 145f. Gottfried von Raesfeld's will is deposited in StAM, SFG, I, Loc. 9, no. 1. Among the trustees of the endowment were the leading Catholic magistrates, Bürgermeister Dr. Heinrich Vendt, Dr. Hermann Heerde, Goddert Travelmann, and Heinrich Plönies.

10. StdAM, AII, 20, RP, 1588, Jan. 15, vol. 19, fol. 4.

11. StdAM, AII, 20, RP, 1588, Jan. 18, vol. 19, fol. 5.

12. Ibid.

13. StdAM, AII, 20, RP, 1588, Feb. 19, vol. 20, fol. 7.

dral immunity, to prohibit them from purchasing houses in the city, and to forbid them to preach in the parish churches.[14]

In October, the Jesuits began instructing at the cathedral school, having first dismissed the former teachers of the gymnasium.[15] They also preached in Saint Jacob's, a chapel within the cathedral immunity which served the spiritual needs of its inhabitants.[16] Both incidents caused alarm and resentment among the guildsmen who protested to the city council.[17] The Jesuits, on their part, regarded themselves in missionary territory and wanted to "lead the citizens to the proper religion and life."[18] In spite of the goodwill of the magistrates and the support of the senior cathedral canons, the Jesuits entered Münster in an atmosphere of tension and mutual suspicion between themselves and the leaders of the mercantile and craft guilds. Clashes were to follow. But in the years immediately after their arrival, the Jesuits concentrated on capturing the minds and souls of the young.

THE JESUITS AS EDUCATORS

Prior to the advent of the Jesuits, instruction of the young was in the hands of schoolmasters at the gymnasium, teachers at the parish schools, and private masters who drilled the rudiments of reading and writing into children whose parents could afford to give them a smattering of linguistic skills.[19] Still a regional center of learning between 1535 and 1588, the cathedral school had nonetheless lost the splendor it had had in

14. StdAM, AII, 20, RP, 1588, Feb. 19, vol. 20, fol. 7v.

15. In the summer of 1605, the schoolmaster Heinrich Brecker beseeched the magistrates to exempt him from watch-duties. He and other masters were dismissed from the gymnasium when the Jesuits took over the school. A dedicated teacher who had taught for twenty-six years in Münster prior to his dismissal, he was forced then to eke out a meager living teaching grammar privately to children. A workday of over twelve hours was the norm for the teachers because of their low pay. In 1583 the schoolmasters had already petitioned the magistrates to exempt them from watch-duties; after the arrival of the Jesuits their very livelihood was threatened. See StdAM, AXIII, 48 & 48a.

16. BDAM, MS. 180, "Spicilegium Ecclesiasticum," vol. 19, fols. 22–28.

17. StdAM, AXI, 76, SP, vol. 2, fol. 7.

18. *Litt. Ann.*, 1588, p. 184.

19. There is no comprehensive study of education in sixteenth-century Münster; existing works concentrate on the Gymnasium Paulinum, on which documentation is the most abundant. Information on the parochial schools and on private schoolmasters is scarce, fragmentary, and must be gleaned from a large variety of archival sources. The best studies of the gymnasium prior to the coming of the Jesuits are: Rudolf Schulze, ed., *Das Gymnasium Paulinum zu Münster 797–1947* (Münster, 1948); Joseph König, *Geschichtliche Nachrichten über das Gymnasium zu Münster in Westfalen seit Stiftung desselben durch Karl den Grossen bis auf die Jesuiten 791–1592* (Münster, 1821); and the collection of essays in *Königliches Paulinisches Gymnasium zu Münster. Festschrift zur Feier der Einweihung des neuen Gymnasialgebäudes am 27. IV 1898* (Münster, 1898).

the heyday of humanism, when Rudolf von Langen, Johann Murmellius, and Johann Glandorp expounded on the elegance of Latin and Greek grammar.[20] Except for Hermann von Kerssenbroch, composer of the *History of the Anabaptists* and a fervent Catholic, the teaching profession was not distinguished by loyalty to the Roman Church. A certain confessional indifference or outright adherence to Protestantism, in fact, characterized many schoolmasters before the Jesuit takeover.[21] The master of the parish school of Saint Martin, Johann Bloccius, was a Lutheran, a fact which did not prevent him from being hired in the first place.[22] Only in 1582 did Duke Johann Wilhelm instruct the dean of Saint Martin to discharge Bloccius because he did not follow the curriculum of the cathedral school and included "suspicious authors" on the reading list for his pupils.[23] The parishioners rallied to Bloccius's defense and the case quickly turned into a contest of jurisdiction between the clergy and the laity.[24] The city council pleaded Bloccius's case before the duke and eventually the hapless schoolmaster was pensioned off.[25] It is important thus to see the coming of the Jesuits not as an isolated incident, but in the context of the confessional struggle for the control of education, against the background of the strengthening of princely power at the expense of local, civic customs, and in terms of the traditional pattern of lay-clerical conflicts.[26]

20. Cf. J. B. Nordhoff, *Denkwürdigkeiten aus dem Münsterischen Humanismus. Mit einer Anlage über das frühere Press- und Bücherwesen Westfalens* (Münster, 1874); and D. Reichling, *Johannes Murmellius. Sein Leben und seine Werke. Nebst einem ausführlichen bibliographischen Verzeichnis sämtlicher Schriften und einer Auswahl von Gedichten* (Freiburg i. B., 1880; repr. Nieuwkoop, 1963).

21. In 1571, Master Johann Niehuis of the parish school at Saint Ludger's was questioned by the magistrates on account of the use of Lutheran texts; see StdAM, AII, 20, RP, 1571, Dec. 3, vol. 7, fol. 31v. Bernt Capellaen, master of the sixth class at the cathedral school died in 1587 without confessing and communicating at the hands of the clergy. Dean Everwin Droste of Saint Martin denounced him as a Lutheran and wanted to refuse him burial; see StdAM, AII, 20, RP, Nov. 16, vol. 19, fol. 94. In 1596, the Jesuits reported on the conversion of a number of Lutheran schoolmasters, *Litt. Ann.*, 1596, p. 287.

22. He is not to be confused with Lic. Johann Block (Bloccius), who was also a Protestant and a city councillor. Lic. Block matriculated at Marburg University in 1578 and later received his Licentiat in Canon and Civil Law at the University of Basel. See Hans Georg Wackernagel et al., eds., *Die Matrikel der Universität Basel,* 2 vols. (Basel, 1956), no. 409. See also appendix 1, no. 17.

23. Letter of Duke Johann Wilhelm to the dean and canons of Saint Martin, dated March 24, 1582, StdAM, AXIII, 39a.

24. The arbitrary dismissal of Bloccius was one of the grievances presented by the parishioners of Saint Martin against the collegiate chapter in 1591, StdAM, AXIII, 39, esp. fol. 4.

25. Letter of protest of city council to Duke Johann Wilhelm (1583) and two drafts, StdAM, AXIII, 39a, fols. 6–15v.

26. Another incident in this conflict was the 1591 mandate issued by Archbishop Ernst which prohibited the use of unauthorized texts in all primary schools (*triviale Scholen*) of the

The fall term of 1588 at the gymnasium opened with a series of public lectures, delivered by the Jesuit Fathers in Latin and Greek to impress the burghers; a solemn high mass was celebrated; and the pomp and trappings of academia completed the inauguration ceremonies.[27] The Fathers were masters at town-gown relations and invited all the civic dignitaries to attend. Remembering the former fame of the gymnasium and hoping for the spread of the renown of the civic republic through its school, the magistrates were duly impressed.

Not noticeably different from that of a Protestant gymnasium except when it came to theological training, the curriculum of the Jesuit College stressed classical learning. Boys of seven began with the rudiments of Latin, progressed to learning and memorizing the Latin, then the Greek, masters of antiquity. A liberal arts curriculum in the first years stressed the *trivium,* drilling the students thoroughly in grammar, logic, and rhetoric; later on in life, the students attended classes in philosophy and theology, when the Scriptures and the Church Fathers were digested. By his late teens, the student was ready to attend university or enter the Society itself.[28] Following the general educational principles of the time, the Jesuits relied on strict discipline, detailed in school rules and often enforced by flogging, to control the behavior of the students. Religious indoctrination was also indispensable to both Catholic and Protestant pedagogy; students at the college in Münster were required to attend mass, encouraged to communicate frequently, and enjoined to confess once a week.[29] Through a system of resident proctors, who were older and more reliable students, the Fathers kept watch over the moral rectitude of lodgers.[30] Almost all educators of the sixteenth century believed in disciplining a youth's mind as well as subjugating his bodily urges.[31]

The unique feature of Jesuit education was the total environment it created to shape the personality of its pupils. Unlike Protestant schools,

---

bishopric. The city council protested because the mandate infringed upon the judicial competence of the magistrates. See StdAM, AXIII, 39a, fols. 5–5v.

27. For descriptions of the ceremonies, see StAM, FM, SFG, "Comp. Hist. Coll.," fols. 1–1v; Bernard Sökeland, *Geschichte des Münsterschen Gymnasium von dem Übergange desselben an die Jesuiten im Jahre 1588 bis 1630* (Münster, 1826).

28. For the curriculum and ordinance of Jesuit colleges, see Bernhard Duhr, *Die Studienordnung der Gesellschaft Jesu* (Freiburg i.B., 1896), passim. The complete texts of the various pedagogic ordinances, as well as documents on the earliest Jesuit colleges in Germany, are printed in G. M. Pachtler, ed., *Ratio Studiorum et Institutiones Scholasticae Societatis Jesu,* 4 vols. (Berlin, 1887–94).

29. *Litt. Ann.,* 1589, p. 237.

30. Heinrich Tebbe, "'Pädagogen' und 'Praeceptoren' am Gymnasium zu Münster," *Königliches Paulinisches Gymnasium. Festschrift,* pp. 105–28.

31. On comparable views in Lutheran education, see the informative book by Gerald Strauss, *The Lutheran House of Learning* (Baltimore, 1978), chapter entitled "Pedagogic Principles."

where lay overseers had the power to appoint and dismiss teachers or to change the curriculum, the Jesuits had complete control over the learning process, subject only to the review of their superiors.[32] Also different from Lutheran pedagogic principles was the Jesuit emphasis on the active participation of the pupils in extracurricular activities, especially in various forms of religious devotion. Here, Lutheran and Catholic theologies diverged. When man's sinful nature and passivity in gaining salvation were stressed, as in Lutheranism, education aimed to curb the willfulness of man and to instill in him obedience and discipline.[33] When the active will and actions of the individual were seen as God's gifts to further the glory of his name, as the teachings of the Jesuits clearly spelled out, education encouraged the active development of the individual in conformity with the tenets of Catholic doctrine.[34] The Jesuits identified, encouraged, and rewarded talent without fail. A system of incentives complemented negative rules to prompt the individual student to develop in the path of the Fathers' expectations. Academically gifted students were singled out for praise; constant competitions within classes and between classes sharpened the keenness of the students. Those with good academic records and religious zeal were organized into Marian sodalities—they elected their own "officers," held meetings under the guidance of the Jesuits, sang at church services, and occupied a special place of honor during religious processions.[35] Through processions and particularly through school plays, the Jesuits offered the students a chance to distinguish themselves not only in front of their parents and peers, but also to appear as actors, as young recruits in the ranks of Christ's armies, and in the public arena.[36]

Unmistakable in Lutheran pedagogy was the supreme role of the father both in disciplining the children at home and as surrogate father in the person of the schoolmaster.[37] Lutheran teachings praised familial har-

32. On the power of Lutheran magistrates in the province of education, see Strauss, pp. 183–87. The case of Strasbourg provides an interesting example of the clash between orthodox Lutheran magistrates and Calvinist pedagogues; see the discussion of the gymnasium and the schoolmaster Johann Sturm in L. Jane Abray, "The Long Reformation: Magistrates, Clergy, and People in Strasbourg" (Ph.D. diss., Yale University, 1978), pp. 56–69.

33. Strauss, pp. 41ff.

34. In their teachings, Saint Ignatius and the Jesuits stressed the sense of calling and activism; see Ernst Walter Zeeden, *Deutschland im Zeitalter der Glaubenskämpfe* (Munich, 1977), pp. 132–34, 138ff.; and H. Outram Evennett, *The Spirit of the Counter-Reformation* (Cambridge, 1968), pp. 43ff.

35. On Marian sodalities, see Duhr, *Jesuiten,* I, pp. 357–71; II:2, pp. 81–122. For the description of one such procession organized by the Jesuits in Münster, see StAM, FM, SFG, "Comp. Hist. Coll.," fol. 63, entry under July 8, 1613.

36. For Jesuit school plays, see chap. 7, pp. 173–76.

37. Cf. Strauss, pp. 117–26.

mony and the obedience of wives and children to the *paterfamilias,* in many ways God's representative in every household. In an age of misogyny, Catholic pedagogues naturally also stressed paternal authority. Two points, however, sharply distinguished Jesuit from Lutheran education. Whereas lines of authority ran from father to son and from teacher to student in Lutheran communities, Jesuit education did not necessarily reinforce parental authority; often it ran contrary to the assertion of family discipline. This was most evident in cases where Catholic sons openly defied the authority of Protestant fathers. The *Litterae Annuae* of the Münster College cited many instances of boys and young men who ran away from Protestant households and who persisted, despite the objection of their parents, in attending the Jesuit College. Many students, indeed, came from the Protestant cities of Hamburg, Bremen, Lübeck, and from cities of Lower Saxony; they came either out of their own will or were sent by Catholic parents in these reformed areas. If need be, even maternal love could be spurned. The Jesuits noted how one student refused the pleas of his "heretical" mother to leave Münster and to return to Calvinist Burgsteinfurt.[38] At times, the Jesuits also acted as mediators and helped to alleviate the acerbity of generational conflict.[39]

The second difference stems from the image of the mother in Jesuit education. Obviously no women were actually involved in the instruction of the young, nor were girls admitted to the colleges, but Mary, the Mother of God, was a central focus of Jesuit piety. We have mentioned the role of the Marian sodalities; important also was the promotion of pilgrimages to Marian shrines in Münsterland in which the students in the sodalities took a central part.[40] The mediating role of a maternal figure alleviated the rigors of an all-male educational system. More important, it was through the mothers of many students that the Jesuits introduced or strengthened Catholic worship in their households. In 1602, a burgher who had not communicated in the Catholic Church for twenty years was moved by the example of his son in the sodality to read Peter Canisius's catechism; further encouraged by his wife, he finally returned to the fold of the Mother Church.[41] Many students urged their mothers to communicate and to confess more frequently.[42] The familial hierarchy was reversed when "parents were led by sons, grown-ups by young ones to go to the tribunal of the clergy: Now the young follow not the father, but the mother follows the young, and the father follows

38. *Litt. Ann.,* 1598, pp. 386–87.

39. *Litt. Ann.,* 1589, p. 237.

40. Pilgrimages to the nearby Marian shrine in Telgte were regularly undertaken by the sodalities; see StAM, FM, SFG, "Comp. Hist. Coll.," fol. 54.

41. *Litt. Ann.,* 1602, p. 560.

42. *Litt. Ann.,* 1602, p. 556.

the mother."[43] In place of the hierarchy of the natural family, the Jesuits offered the young the bosom of the Mother Church and the guidance of spiritual fathers.

What attracted young men to the Jesuits? If the *Litterae Annuae* are to be believed—and even taking into consideration the partisan stance and slight exaggerations, there is no reason to doubt the basic reported facts—the success of the Jesuits rode on the wave of a youth movement at the end of the sixteenth century.[44] Not only young men, but also many young women, ran away from home to seek sanctity and spiritual guidance with the Jesuits. We must remember that at the birth of the Society, the Reformation in Germany was already one generation old, and when the Jesuits started work in Münster, the initial fervor of the Reformation movement was already three generations away. While a recent study argues for the legitimacy of labeling reforms in the cities during the second half of the sixteenth century "late city reformations," the popular basis for the movements had partially died out and the emotional appeal had paled.[45] In contrast, the Society of Jesus was new and vigorous. The

43. *Litt. Ann.*, 1602, p. 558.

44. A note on the nature of Jesuit sources is in order here. The superiors of all Jesuit colleges and missions were required to send annual reports, the *Litterae Annuae,* to the provincials, who, after having compiled the reports of the different Jesuit congregations in their provinces, forwarded them to the general of the Society in Rome. The generals, especially Aquaviva and Vitelleschi, dictated detailed guidelines on how the *Litterae Annuae* were to be composed: they asked for numbers of personnel and students, statistics on communicants and income of the colleges, exact descriptions of missions undertaken, deeds of exemplary Fathers, and names of devotees and benefactors of great piety. Unverified miracles, information derived through confessions, and exaggerations of achievements and self-praise were to be avoided. Histories of colleges should contain dates of foundation, endowment figures, achievements of students, and a chronicle of major events. It is apparent that self-praise often found its way into the reports, especially when the Fathers were referring to the tricks of their opponents, but the *Litterae Annuae* and the histories of the colleges are often the only sources we have of the activities of the Jesuits in the crucial years before the beginning of the Thirty Years' War. In Rome the generals had the reports prepared for publication. Between 1583 and 1607, sixteen volumes of the *Litterae Annuae* covering the years 1581–99 were printed; in 1618 and 1619, fourteen additional volumes for the years 1600–14 were published. When publications resumed in 1658, the first volume was of the year 1650. *Litterae Annuae* of the years 1615–49 exist only in manuscripts in the Archives of the Society in Rome. Reports of the college in Münster between 1588 and 1618 are no longer extant in the former archive of the Lower Rhine Province, today part of the Historisches Archiv der Stadt Köln. Where available, I have used the published reports for the years between 1588 and 1614; in other cases, manuscripts from the Archivum Romanum Societatis Jesu have been consulted. For a detailed discussion of the nature of the *Litterae Annuae* see Duhr, *Jesuiten,* I, pp. 675–78; II:2, pp. 358–60.

45. Cf. Kaspar von Greyerz, *The Late City Reformation in Germany: The Case of Colmar 1522–1628* (Wiesbaden, 1980), pp. 196–205. Greyerz distinguishes between a popular Reformation in the 1520s which was accompanied by the Peasants' War and urban unrests and a late city Reformation imposed from above by the magistrates in the last third of the sixteenth century, which excited neither popular opposition nor agitation.

first rector of the Münster College, Peter Michael, was forty-six years old when he went to establish the congregation. Other Fathers who worked in the initial decades were men under forty; they belonged to the generations born in the 1550s and 1560s, men to whom the Reformation was an event which had occurred in the lifetimes of their fathers and grandfathers. To the students who attended the Jesuit colleges, the reform movement of the 1520s and 1530s belonged to another era. Lutheranism in the last decades of the sixteenth century had hardened into inflexible orthodoxy after the many bitter doctrinal battles between followers of the orthodox tradition and the more flexible Philippists. Although it still held the loyalty and affection of multitudes of German burghers, Lutheranism could neither compete with Calvinism on the international scene nor was it especially appealing for the young.[46]

Confessional conflict often took the form of generational conflict; the universal claims of the Counter-Reformation created strains within the family and elevated disagreements between children and parents to a higher plane. With the emphasis on family life and devotion, Lutheranism could not rival the fellowship of youth groups provided by the Jesuits. Through membership in Marian sodalities, young men broke away from the fetters of parental authority and came to know the wider horizons of the reinvigorated Catholic world, one which stretched from the Americas to remote, exotic Japan. Jesuit education offered a vision for the young: some joined the Society and spent the greater part of their adult lives away from their home towns, moving from one Jesuit college or mission to another; others remembered the excitement of fellowship in their student days after they had become rulers, officials, priests, or lawyers.

The advent of the Jesuits also gave a focus to various efforts to promote Catholic education in Münster. The suffragan bishop, Johann Krythen, had already endowed a scholarship fund in 1575 and in 1581 to enable Catholic boys who had finished their schooling in Münster to pursue theological studies in Cologne.[47] In 1599, four Dettens, three brothers and a sister, all children of the late councillor Bernd van Detten the Older, endowed a family scholarship fund to support study at the Jesuit College. They specified that only male relatives who had been certified by the Jesuits as unwavering Catholics could apply for the scholarships.[48] As the Jesuit College attracted more local sons, funds for

46. A case study of how village elders welcomed the Lutheran Church Ordinance, which gave family fathers greater power over the young, is the article by Thomas Robisheaux, "Peasants and Pastors: Rural Youth Control and the Reformation in Hohenlohe, 1540–1680," *Social History* 6 (1981), pp. 281–300.

47. StAM, AVM, MS. 168.

48. BDAM, PfA Lamberti, Kart. 112, "Copia Fundationis Collegii Detteniani," fol. 6.

the Society increased. Parents whose sons attended the college and subsequently entered the Society were generous in their donations. Supporting the educational enterprise of the Jesuits became for many Catholics another avenue toward salvation. In an entreaty to enlist support for the founding of a Catholic university in Münster under Jesuit control, Matthaeus Timpe described what the Fathers could do for their benefactors: They were required to say mass and recite the rosary for their patrons, thus generous giving to the college earned merits toward eternal salvation.[49]

The number of students at the college climbed from six hundred in 1588 to one thousand by 1598; the enrollment varied from year to year, depending on whether Münster was affected by the plague, but never fell far below the eight hundred figure after 1588.[50] Among the students were noblemen, including one future prince-bishop, Christoph Bernhard von Galen (who would go on to suppress civic liberties in 1661), many future city councillors and officials, and a good number of Jesuit recruits at the college. Sons of burghers who went through the Jesuit College and later entered the Society helped to increase civic support for the Fathers and alleviate the initial suspicions on the part of most citizens. The educational undertaking of the Jesuits was the single most important factor in changing the religious and cultural identity of the city of Münster.

THE POWER BROKERS

Who were the Jesuits? From the *Litterae Annuae,* from records of the former archive of the college, and from wills of burghers, 111 Jesuits—39 priests, 48 masters, and 24 novices—can be identified.[51] The place of origin of almost two-thirds of them can be identified or surmised with a reasonable degree of certainty. Of the 69 identified Jesuits, 29 were Münsteraners, 20 came from Münsterland or from other places in Westphalia, 5 were Rhinelanders (all except one native of Cologne), 9 originated from North Germany outside of Westphalia, 2 were South Germans, and one each came from Hesse, Franconia (the city of Nuremberg), Belgium, and Lorraine. A number of those without specific places of origin were most probably Rhinelanders or natives of the archdioceses

49. Matthaeus Timpius, *Erhebliche unnd wichtige Ursachen/ warumb weise unnd fürsichtige Leuth/ auss gottseligem eiffer/ bey sich beschlossen haben/ von dem so Gott ihnen gnadiglich verliehen/ hülff zu thun/ dass man in der wollöblichen Statt Münster/ welche die Hauptstatt ist inn Westphalen zu fundieren unnd zu Stifften: unnd warumb billich alle Vaterlands liebende hertzen zu solchem hochpreisslichen Werck unnd frewdenreichen anfang behülfflich seyn sollen/* (Münster: Lambert Raesfeldt, 1612), sig. B4–B4v.

50. *Litt. Ann.,* 1598, p. 386; Duhr, *Jesuiten,* I, p. 552, p. 726.

51. See appendix 2.

Table 3.1   *The Social Background of Münsteraner Jesuits*

Elite		Bürger	
Patriciate	1	Printer	1
Magisterial	9	Baker	1
Official	5	Butcher	1
		Others	11

of Mainz and Trier, judging from their overall career pattern within the Society of Jesus. The mobility of the Jesuits renders it very difficult to pin down their exact social and geographical origins; biographical data of the men who came to work in Münster are buried in several dozen archives scattered throughout Germany. Novices accepted in Münster were sent to Paderborn, Trier, or Mainz, making it most difficult to trace their subsequent careers; likewise, a number of recruits accepted in other cities of the Lower Rhine Province came to Münster for their probation and training. Rarely did a Father spend his entire career in one city. Even transfers between provinces were not uncommon. Several native sons of Münster reached positions of eminence within the Society: Hermann Bosendorf and Gottfried Otterstett later became provincials of the Lower Rhine Province, others served as rectors of Jesuit colleges throughout the Upper and Lower Rhine provinces. The 29 Münsteraners represented a variety of social backgrounds; the majority belonged to the solid *Bürgertum*. Table 3.1 presents a rough scheme of their social background.

If we look at the amount of inherited wealth they gave to the Society when they took their vows, the range of the wealth spectrum coincided pretty much with the larger wealth spectrum of the city, minus the extremes at both ends. Jesuit recruits from Münster came from a spectrum ranging from modest middle-class families to very rich and influential magisterial families. Significant was the absence of the laboring masses and the over-representation of magisterial families. The factor of mobility was of crucial importance in preventing the "domestication" of the Society, a development which characterized the settlement of the two mendicant orders in German cities in the thirteenth century.[52] Native Münsteraners served in their home town for a few years and many were

52. In his work, *The Friars and German Society in the Thirteenth Century,* John Freed demonstrates the concomitant expansion of the two mendicant orders and spreading urbanization. From the very beginning, the friars, especially the Franciscans, were involved in communal politics, mediating between bishops and burghers, and taking sides in struggles between burgher factions. The ministeriales, patricians, and knights provided the leadership of the two orders. While the Dominicans appeared to be a more exclusive religious order, many artisans and merchants joined the ranks of the Franciscans. See also Stüdeli, *Minoritenniederlassungen,* pp. 132–34, where he discusses the phenomenon in Switzerland.

sent away; some eventually returned to head the college but the personnel in Münster at any one time included Jesuits from different parts of Germany and Europe. The international and supra-regional character of the Society of Jesus in Münster stood out in sharp contrast to the Franciscan cloister, where the overwhelming majority of the inmates were born in the city or in the villages of the *Umland* of Münster.[53]

Power is inseparable from wealth. The spiritual vigor and activities of the Jesuits depended on a sound financial base. Since tuition was free, the success of the Jesuit College in Münster brought in its wake increasing financial burdens. Stipends had to be found for students who were poor but talented; the growing ranks of the faculty and support personnel had to be fed; the extensive missionary activities of the Fathers required travel expenses; the great number of communicants consumed large quantities of bread and wine.[54] Most important of all, new buildings had to be erected for study and worship. Construction on the Jesuit church in Münster, Saint Peter's, began in 1591, and a decade of work kept a constant drain on the finances of the college.[55] Surpassing the beauty of most parish churches in Münster, Saint Peter's stands as a monument to the power of the Jesuits. In this citadel of piety, the Jesuits stockpiled many objects of great sacral power—relics of saints, reliquaries, and icons from the isolated Catholic churches in Protestant North Germany, from Groningen and Catholic Netherlands, where they stood in danger of destruction and desecration.[56]

It seemed to many Fathers that the very success of their missionary efforts depended on a steady income of dalers. Hence, the Jesuits eagerly solicited financial support from the powerful; noblemen, patricians, officials, and city councillors were their potential benefactors.

Foremost among their patrons were the Cologne archbishops Ernst and Ferdinand of Bavaria, uncle and nephew, both students of the Jesuits

53. The chronicle of the Franciscan cloister in Münster laments the decline of the once-renowned congregation after the "tumult" of the Anabaptists thus: "Conventus nempe hic ante Anabaptisum tempora florentissimus habebat etiam incolas ex ditionibus imo nobilibus familii progenitas et in ordine nostro professos. . . . verum florido isto conventus statu per Anabaptistas turbate, et exinde variis ex causis magis, magisque deficiente vix nisi pauperiorum civium et vicinorum rusticorum filii pro assumendo ordine haberi potuerunt ut satis testantur Recepta et Exposita de eorumdem investitoria professionibus, parentibus etc. Pauperimo certi modo loquentia." StdAM, MS. 4, fols. 37–38.

54. In 1603, it cost 140 florins to support a priest and 90 florins to support a novice in Landsberg; expenses were probably comparable in Münster. The college in Münster received an income of 1,290 dalers in 1606, ranking it seventh in the wealth hierarchy of the Jesuit colleges of the Lower Rhine Province; in 1636, its income soared to 4,005 dalers, second only to the college in Cologne. See Duhr, *Jesuiten*, II:2, pp. 632, 647.

55. Cost for the construction of Saint Peter's was covered mainly by the 4,300 dalers given by Archbishop Ernst and the cathedral chapter. See *Litt. Ann.*, 1596, p. 290.

56. *Litt. Ann.*, 1598, pp. 388–89; 1600, p. 408.

in Munich. Aside from monetary gifts and political support, the archbishops also incorporated the income of a number of benefices under the funds of the college. By 1618, the Jesuits in Münster were receiving the income from seven vicaries in the bishopric and collecting tithes from the parish of Nienberge, three miles from the city walls. Although the incorporation of one of these benefices brought the Society into bitter conflict with entrenched clerical interests,[57] the college was able to draw its income from pastures, cottages, farms, and woodlands scattered over a wide area. The growing financial power of the Society in Münster not only extended the actual geographical control of the college, but also integrated it into the existing feudal agrarian regime. With the passage of time, the college accumulated huge tracts of land; many stemmed from the generosity of magisterial families whose sons entered the Society, others were acquired by purchase. By the middle of the seventeenth century, the Jesuit College had become one of the major landlords of the bishopric.[58] In the city of Münster itself, however, the legislation against the amortization of taxable properties (the so-called Dead Hand) prevented the Jesuits from owning more than a couple of houses.[59] Moreover, the legal possession of these donated real properties was secured only after long-drawn-out legal battles against burgher claimants and only against the protests of the guilds.

The Jesuits were clearly not a civic religious order in the way that the Franciscans were. Not only did the Society in Münster belong to the ruling class of the feudal agrarian regime, the Fathers also served more or less willingly as the instruments of the Counter-Reformation absolutist state. However, one should caution against categorically labeling the Society of Jesus a part of the absolutist forces which emerged at this time. Religion, not politics, remained the ultimate goal of the Jesuits. In France, the defense of Catholic religion meant, for some Jesuits, supporting the radical, anti-royalist, revolutionary League forces, and the endorsement of tyrannicide—the assassin of Henri IV was after all a fanati-

---

57. The Jesuits had a nasty run-in with Dr. Plate, holder of the benefice of Saint Anthony's Chapel at Emner in the parish of Albersloh. The dispute found its way to Rome, where Plate got a favorable hearing. In 1596, the Jesuits settled with Plate, pensioned him off with 300 dalers, and helped to gain a benefice at Saint Ludger's in Münster for his nephew. See Sökeland, pp. 47–49; StAM, FM, SFG, III Loc.2, nos. 6 & 7.

58. See the many land titles acquired by the Jesuits in StAM, FM, SFG, III Loc. 8b–9a, "Freie Gründe, Gärten, Kampen und Wiesen vor Münster."

59. When properties passed into clerical hands, they received exempted status and were removed from the tax base of the city; furthermore, canon law forbids the alienation of church properties. Thus a piece of property became "dead" for the purposes of taxation and business transactions after it came under the ownership of the clergy. For an explanation of the term "Dead Hand," see *Lexicon für Theologie und Kirche,* eds., Josef Höfer & Karl Rahner, (Freiburg i. B., 2nd rev. ed., 1965), vol. 10, pp. 262–63.

cal supporter of the Jesuits.[60] In Germany, the configuration of political forces was different. The emperors and Catholic princes were the most fervent supporters of the Catholic order and it was around them that forces of the Counter-Reformation rallied.[61] The political ideas which were later given expression by Adam Contzen, the Jesuit confessor of Duke Maximilian I of Bavaria, the prime mover behind the Catholic League in the Empire, were taking on concrete political shape in the activities of the Münster Fathers.[62]

Archbishop Ernst was on close personal terms with the Society; whenever he visited Münster he lodged with the Jesuits. The personnel at the college also served as special envoys in the archbishop's attempts to recatholicize the smaller towns of the Bishopric of Münster in the decades before the outbreak of the Thirty Years' War. Jesuit Fathers journeyed in pairs or alone to preach to Lutheran burghers in Meppen, Vechta, Vreden, Warendorf, Norwald, Lüdinghausen, Greven, to name just some of the places mentioned in the *Litterae Annuae* and the *Historia Collegii*. These missionary activities met with varying degrees of success; the Jesuits strengthened the resolve of Catholics, converted some "heretics," but ran up against the firm opposition of most Protestants.[63] Besides working within the boundaries of the diocese, the Jesuits also undertook long-distance missions into Protestant territories. They visited the eastern provinces of the Netherlands, the counties of Rietberg and Bentheim, and the largely Protestant Bishopric of Osnabrück.[64] It was also based in Münster that missions to Hamburg were launched.[65] The

60. Although the Society as a whole was divided over the question of whether to support the anti-royalist Leaguers, the Jesuits in Rouen and Paris clearly allied themselves with the League. See Philip Benedict, *Rouen during the Wars of Religion* (Cambridge, 1981), pp. 195–96; J. H. M. Salmon, "The Paris Sixteenth, 1584–94: The Social Analysis of a Revolutionary Movement," *JMH* 44 (1972). Ravillac, the assassin of Henri IV, dreamt of becoming a Jesuit and frequently sought the spiritual guidance of the Fathers. See Roland Mousnier, *L'Assassinat d'Henri IV* (Paris, 1964), p. 12.

61. Cf. Robert Bireley, *Religion and Politics in the Age of the Counterreformation* (Chapel Hill, 1981).

62. Cf. Ernst-Albert Seils, *Die Staatslehre des Jesuiten Adam Contzen, Beichtvater Kurfürst Maximilian I. von Bayern* (Lübeck, 1968), esp. pp. 54f., 81f., 101ff., 183ff. Contzen defined the essence of the (Catholic) state as the defender of Catholic religion, upholder of public morality, and suppressor of seditious Protestants. Hereditary monarchy, in his view, was the ideal form of government. See also Robert Bireley's study of Contzen's influence on Maximilian's foreign policy during the Thirty Years' War, *Maximilian von Bayern, Adam Contzen S.J. und die Gegenreformation in Deutschland 1624–1635* (Göttingen, 1975).

63. Cf. StAM, FM, SFG, "Comp. Hist. Coll.," 1616, fol. 79v: "P. Lemmius per Pasche Werne hasit, sed non placuit populo. . . ."

64. See, for examples, *Litt. Ann.*, 1597, pp. 250–52; StAM, FM, SFG, "Comp. Hist. Coll.," fols. 10v, 17v.

65. Father Heinrich Rotthausen, a member of the Jesuit college in Münster, was missionary in Hamburg prior to the outbreak of the Thirty Years' War. See Duhr, *Jesuiten*, II:1, p. 136; and appendix 2.

dedication of individual Fathers laid the groundwork for subsequent success; the full-scale recatholicization of the diocese came during the early years of the Thirty Years' War, when the troops of the Catholic League backed up the sermons of the Jesuits with pikes and muskets.[66]

Mediating between the princes and the people, the Jesuits can be described as power-brokers. The description can be understood in another sense as well. Fundamental to the meaning of the Society of Jesus was the attempt to reassert sacerdotal authority and to re-establish the cosmic hierarchy wherein the clergy stood superior above the laity, interceding on their behalf with the Almighty. Even the secular prince had to humble himself before the successors of the Apostles; in the words of Cardinal Bellarmine, "If a prince truly wants to be a Christian prince, he must acknowledge four superiors: Almighty God of the Highest, his pontiff, bishop, and confessor."[67] One of the most important results of the Reformation was the drastic transformation of lay-clerical relations. Even in Lutheran areas where a ministerial class (*Pfarrerstand*) began to consolidate, the supremacy of lay society over the *sacerdotium* had been irreversibly established.[68] The Jesuits, on the contrary, presented themselves as the elite of the clergy. Chaste, learned, and fired with a sense of mission, the Jesuits embodied all that the post-Reformation Catholic clergy was not. They carried within themselves the moral strength, the divine grace, and the learning to bring forth the fruits of salvation to all, to uphold the one, true, Catholic Church, and to purge the world of evils. The Jesuits came, literally, to enchant the world again.

What better proof of their prowess than to do battle with the Devil himself and win? Among the "victories" listed in their *Litterae Annuae*—these annual reports actually read like dispatches from the actual battle fields—the Jesuits in Münster mentioned at least eight cases of successful exorcism performed between 1588 and 1618.[69] A girl struck dumb re-

66. See Albert Weskamp, *Westfalen und der Liga* (Münster, 1891), pp. 187–202; Keller, *Gegenreformation*, III, pp. 354–64.

67. *De Officio Principis Christiani*, quoted in Seils, *Staatslehre*, p. 184.

68. Cf. Bernd Moeller, "Kleriker als Bürger," *Festschrift für Herman Heimpel*, II (Göttingen, 1972), pp. 195–224. The section on the impact of the Reformation on the clergy is reiterated in his *Pfarrer als Bürger* (Göttingen, 1972), pp. 15ff. Bernard Vogler's study of the Protestant clergy in the Palatinate, the best work of its kind, shows that the nobility, the patriciate, the high officialdom, and the mercantile elite, as well as the masses of peasants, were completely absent in the new, emerging ministerial class. Recruited overwhelmingly from the artisanal and burgher ranks, the Protestant clergy manifested "une docilité quasi-totale à l'égard du pouvoir politique et sortout d'orthodoxie. Rare sont ceux qui osent affirmer une certaine séparation entre les domaines temporels et spirituels." See his *Le clergé protestant rhenan au siècle de la reformé 1555–1619* (Paris, 1976), p. 145; see also pp. 18–21, 145–47, 351–55.

69. Litt. Ann., ARSJ, Rh. Inf. 48, fols. 29, 162, 204 (for the years 1593, 1610, 1616); *Litt. Ann.*, 1596, p. 286; 1601, p. 617; 1602, pp. 555–56.

covered her voice after the Jesuits expelled the demon; a boy of eight possessed by the Devil was delivered, thanks to the Fathers; a student at the college who was of great devotion suffered demonic possession and was cured after exorcism; a woman in the power of Satan was saved after the Jesuits prayed for her soul in Saint Peter's; still another female victim was snatched from the clutches of the Devil after the Fathers had sweated it out for three days engaging the evil spirit in numerous skirmishes before he finally conceded defeat. In addition to these spectacular feats of Catholic arms, the Jesuits also "cured" the mentally disturbed, people who suffered what contemporaries called "melancholia," by hearing confession and giving spiritual counseling.[70] These triumphs spread the renown of the Society far and wide. A man whose house was haunted came all the way from the Netherlands to seek advice, whereupon the Fathers told him to sprinkle holy water on the building to drive out the Poltergeist.[71] "To offer counsel to those who are vexed by frightful tricks and injuries caused by the Devil, and who often seek help from us, is, indeed, not a little charity." Thus commented the Jesuits themselves.[72]

While the practical-minded burghers might think little of these superstitions, the unschooled rustics were very impressed. Peasants who lived near Münster brought in the crippled, the mentally ill, and the sick, hoping to find cure with the Jesuits; Catholic maids and peasants ran away from their Calvinist lords to go to the Fathers.[73] The Society of Jesus succeeded where the medieval clergy failed: They offered a superior system of rituals and magic which vanquished the rivals of the clergy in the countryside, the cunning folk of the villages. But while the erudite Jesuits could walk the fine line between the divine and demonic worlds, discerning through their piety and learning the differences between madness and evil, the laity lacked such sophistication. The coming of the Jesuits in Münster also meant the creation of an atmosphere of intense fear of the Devil and the escalation of witchcraft accusations. Although the actual process of witchcraft accusations and trials has not been critically studied for Münster,[74] the Jesuits, no doubt, encouraged

70. *Litt. Ann.*, 1597, pp. 248–49; 1605, p. 725. On the phenomenon of madness and its treatment in the sixteenth century, see H. C. Erik Midelfort, "Madness and the Problems of Psychological History in the Sixteenth Century," *SCJ* 12 (1981), pp. 5–12.

71. *Litt. Ann.*, 1605, p. 725.

72. *Litt. Ann.*, 1602, p. 555.

73. *Litt. Ann.*, 1602, pp. 552–53.

74. Ludwig Humborg's dissertation on witchcraft trials in Münster, *Die Hexenprozesse in der Stadt Münster* (Münster, 1914), is hardly more than a compilation of archival sources on the subject. While the study provides useful information on the facts of the trials, there is no investigation into the social background of witchcraft accusations and witchcraft beliefs. What the dissertation does show is that most trials took place between 1600 and 1650, and that women comprised the majority of the accused.

witch-hunts by their teachings and exorcisms, as shown by the role played by young students in accusations.[75] It was no coincidence that the period of the most rapid expansion of the Society of Jesus in Westphalia overlapped with the height of witchcraft accusations and trials.[76]

THE SUPPORTERS

Since the Society supported the expansion of the Counter-Reformation state, the prince-bishops Ernst and Ferdinand became the most powerful patrons of the college in Münster. They sent gifts of wine, monetary donations of thousands of dalers, visited the college, lodged, dined, and conversed with the Fathers.[77] They stood by the Jesuits when conflicts arose between the city and the Society, and encouraged their own officials to emulate their own largess and piety.

The Jesuits also tried to strengthen the Catholic faith of the nobility and to convert Protestant noblemen. Jesuit Fathers in Münster served as confessors and advisers to the counts of Rietberg and Bentheim, as well as to the lesser nobility.[78] Noblemen who held official rank in the territorial administration also adhered strongly to the cause of the Society.[79] In 1614, Archbishop Ferdinand stipulated that all officials must obtain certificates from the clergy, proving they went regularly to confession and communicated at least once a year; they, in turn, would act as moral police supervising the life of the people.[80] Through their strong ties with the cathedral chapter and other noble cloisters, the Jesuits exerted another influence on the nobility. Opposition to the Society within the cathedral chapter collapsed when the two leading Protestant canons, Johann von Westerholt and Bernt von Oer, were arrested in 1588 for murdering Melchior Droste in a street brawl in Münster.[81] The Jesuits saw in this act

75. In 1599, a student at the college denounced to the Jesuits the patrician Justinus Schenckinck for casting a spell. StdAM, AII, 20, RP, 1599, Feb. 19, vol. 31, fol. 10v.

76. Gerhard Schormann has shown that Westphalia was the center of witch-hunts in Northwest Germany during the first half of the seventeenth century; see his *Hexenprozesse in Nordwestdeutschland* (Hildesheim, 1977), pp. 96–99, 112–14.

77. StAM, FM, SFG, "Comp. Hist. Coll.," fols. 8v, 36v, 37, 57, 61, 80v.

78. In 1610, the count of Bentheim and his family visited the Jesuit College in Münster; two sons of the count of Rietberg who studied in Münster entered the religious life. StAM, FM, SFG, "Comp. Hist. Coll.," fols. 50v, 62v; see also *Litt. Ann.,* 1600, pp. 404–06.

79. Cf. StAM, FM, SFG, "Comp. Hist. Coll.," fols. 37v, 43v, 52, 65.

80. Keller, *Gegenreformation,* III, pp. 314–17.

81. When the Jesuits first arrived in Münster, they complained of the moral laxity of the majority of the cathedral canons, most of whom were Lutherans and resided on their family estates. Of the forty canons, the Jesuits claimed that only six were good Catholics. The two young canons, Westerholt and Oer, led the anti-Jesuit faction. On March 23, 1588, the two got into an argument with Melchior Droste, a member of the Teutonic Knights, ambushed him after they left the dinner party, and were subsequently arrested.

the hand of God in furthering the work of the Society.[82] Among the cathedral canons the Jesuits singled out for praise were Gottfried von Raesfeld, his brothers, Heinrich and Johann, and Arnold von Büren.[83] The attitude of the chapter as a whole was one of benign neglect, approving of the work of the Society as long as it did not interfere with the personal life of the canons themselves.[84] The Fathers also enjoyed great success with the noble Benedictine convents—Überwasser, Freckenhorst, and Marienfeld—visiting the inmates, hearing confession, and administering communion.[85] They also aided the abbess of Essen in trying to rekindle Catholic faith in that Protestant city.[86]

As the northernmost stronghold of Catholicism in Germany, Münster became a "Little Rome" for the Catholic nobility of Protestant North Germany. Among the prominent visitors to the college were the sister of the count of Lippe, who had a Jesuit confessor,[87] and Countess Elizabeth von Mansfeld, who converted to Catholicism and spent her last years in Münster.[88] The Catholic nobility in the Netherlands and East Frisia also sent their sons to be educated in Münster; seven entered the religious life on the encouragement of the Jesuits in 1601.[89]

Although the Jesuits placed great importance on their work among the nobility and enjoyed support among many noble families, the nobility as a whole could not be counted as their most enthusiastic supporters, the reason being that the Reformation had won over many Westphalian noble families to its side. Calvinism, in particular, competed with the

---

For an assessment of the religious position of the cathedral chapter, see StAM, MSS. VII, 1026, 1, "Hist. Coll. Mon.," fols. 4, 5–5v. For a description of the crime, see Röchell, *Chronik,* pp. 99–102.

82. StAM, MSS. VII, 1026, 1, "Hist. Coll. Mon.," fol. 5v.

83. StAM, MSS. VII, 1026, 1, "Hist. Coll. Mon.," fol. 2.

84. Before 1600, concubinage was the rule rather than the exception among the canons, including Arnold von Büren, the bursar of the chapter. The few senior canons who regularly attended chapter meetings exercised power, which explains the strength of the Catholic faction in spite of their numerical inferiority. See Wilhlem Kohl, "Die Durchsetzung der tridentinischen Reform im Domkapitel zu Münster," in Remigius Bäumer, ed., *Reformatio Ecclesiae. Festgabe für Erwin Iserloh* (Paderborn, 1980), pp. 729–47; see also Alois Schröer, "Das Tridentinum in Münster," in Georg Schreiber, ed., *Das Weltkonzil von Trient,* vol. 2 (Freiburg i. B., 1951), pp. 295–370.

85. StAM, FM, SFG, "Comp. Hist. Coll.," fols. 30v, 31v, 52v, 53, 66, 75.

86. The Benedictine convent in Essen was the lord of the commune in the Middle Ages; the Reformation proved to be the final step in the liberation of the city from its ecclesiastical overlord. For the visits of the abbess to the Jesuit College in Münster, see StAM, FM, SFG, "Comp. Hist. Coll.," fols. 75v, 76.

87. StAM, FM, SFG, "Comp. Hist. Coll.," fol. 41.

88. *Litt. Ann.,* 1598, pp. 385–86; StAM, FM, SFG, "Comp. Hist. Coll.," fol. 57v.

89. Interestingly, none of them entered the Society itself: the two mendicant orders and the Carthusians each received one novice, the Benedictines, four. *Litt. Ann.,* 1601, p. 616.

Table 3.2 Benefactors of the Jesuit College in Münster* to 1618

Clergy		donations	Laity		donations
women	(19)	9,500d.	nobility	(10)	2,550d.
men	(22)	9,300d.	civic elite	(24)	5,800d.
			Bürger	(21)	3,000d.
	41	18,800d.		55	11,350d.

*These figures exclude donations by the archbishops and the cathedral chapter.

Counter-Reformation for the adherence of the nobility.[90] To some noblemen, Catholicism appeared too dangerously tied with the centralizing and absolutist policies of the prince-bishops.[91] The greatest enthusiasm for the work of the Society was found among a part of the civic elite. By this term is meant not only the magistrates on the city council in Münster, but also the patricians and territorial officials of burgher origins.

Table 3.2, donations from benefactors of the Jesuits, has been compiled from extant records of the college and from wills of burghers (for the list of donors see appendix 3). These ninety-six benefactors included forty-one clerics and fifty-five laymen; together they gave approximately 30,150 dalers to the college in thirty years.

There are several ways to interpret this data. First, the clergy as a whole supported the Jesuits more strongly than the laity did. This confirms the assertion that the Jesuits appeared as a clerical elite who administered to the spiritual needs of the "lesser" clergy. Noteworthy was the enthusiastic support given by a number of clergymen who were active in rejuvenating Catholicism either before the advent of the Jesuits or concomitant with the work of the Fathers. Everwin Droste, dean of Saint Martin, had served on the diocesan visitation commission under Bishop

90. Outside of the Palatinate, Northwest Germany was the stronghold of Calvinism in the Empire prior to the declaration for the reformed religion by the House of Brandenburg. The area's proximity to the Netherlands and the role many noble houses played in leading the revolt probably accounted for the prestige of the reformed faith. Calvinist territories in Northwest Germany included the County of Bentheim-Steinfurt-Tecklenburg, the counties of Diepholz, Nassau-Siegen, Wittgenstein, and Lippe. See Alois Schröer, *Die Reformation in Westfalen. Der Glaubenskampf einer Landschaft,* vol. 1 (Münster, 1979); see also Ritter, *Deutsche Geschichte* I, pp. 524ff. and II, pp. 363ff.

91. In 1607, the knights of the Bishopric of Münster protested Archbishop Ernst's edict which prohibited the burial of Protestants in Catholic churchyards. On November 24, 1608, in a stormy meeting of the Münster Estates, the nobleman Johann von der Recke shouted at the archbishop, accusing him of wanting to suppress the liberties of the nobility. See Keller, *Gegenreformation,* II, pp. 398–99, 411–12.

Johann von Hoya in 1571;[92] Johann van Detten composed a devotional tract in Low German and helped to found the Collegium Dettensiam;[93] Matthaeus Timpe had battled for the Catholic cause in Osnabrück before accepting the rectorship of the Collegium Dettensiam in Münster.[94] A number of them were illegitimate sons of clergymen and might have seen in their own fervor a way to atone for the sins of their fathers. Everwin Droste's illegitimate son, Franz Droste, and Matthaeus Timpe, also son of a clergyman,[95] were among the most generous benefactors of the Society of Jesus (see appendix 3, nos. 29 & 40). The relationship between the Jesuits and their female clerical supporters is of considerable interest and will be discussed below when we examine the general relations between women and the Society.

The second point to be made is that the strongest support for the Jesuits came from the civic elite. Among the laity, twenty-four benefactors from patrician, magisterial, and official families donated more than half of the total sum given by laymen. When we break down the social composition of the clergy according to social categories, the result is even more revealing: nine women and seven male clerics came from families of the civic elite and gave more than 12,900 dalers, or close to three-quarters of the entire clerical donations. In other words, almost two-thirds of all donations between 1588 and 1618 stemmed from the generosity and piety of lay and clerical members of the civic elite. Since this particular social stratum supplied the plurality of Jesuit recruits from Münster, the donation pattern resembles the general testamental bequests to the clergy in the city in that a good number of benefactors were giving to relatives or friends.[96]

A third vantage point is to look at the group of benefactors through familial lenses. Many were related: the three Missings were father and children; there were also Matthaeus and Katherina Timpe, brother and sister; Johann von der Berswordt and his two daughters; Anna Boland and Elizabeth Frie, mother and daughter; three Kerckerincks; two Kleinsorgens; two Vosses; and two Wittfelds. Of the more than eighty families represented in the universe of donors, eight family groups—Missing, Timpe, v.d. Berswordt, Detten, Droste, Frie-Vendt, Herding, Kercke-

---

92. See Schwarz, *Akten Visitation*, p. xli. Droste's will, now deposited in StAM, FM, Saint Martini, has been published by Viktor Huyskens in *Everwin von Droste*, pp. 49–51. In his will, Everwin called Franz Droste "naturalem meum filium."

93. See n. 48; Detten's will is deposited in StAM, FM, SFG, III Loc. 1, no. 8.

94. For a brief biography of Timpe, see Paul Bahlmann's article in *ADB* vol. 39, pp. 53–55.

95. His parents were Johann Timpe, pastor in Letten, and Alheid Holtmann; their wills are deposited in StAM, FM, SFG, III Loc. 1, no. 39, vol. 1, fols. 1–2, 25.

96. Cf. chap. 7, p. 183.

rinck—gave 18,300 dalers, or roughly 62 percent of the total contributions. Three families alone, the Missings, the Timpes, and the von der
Berswordts, endowed the Jesuit College with about one-third of the total
donated sum. Clearly, civic support of the Society of Jesus rested on a
very select social base.

The paramount importance of the civic elite among the benefactors
does not imply that the civic elite of Münster were among the Society's
earliest supporters. The families represented in this group came from a
wide geographical area and had looser ties or no ties at all with the city of
Münster itself. The von der Berswordts were an eminent patrician family
from the Imperial City of Dortmund, a city which had adopted Lutheranism in the second half of the sixteenth century.[97] Johann von der Berswordt, Bürgermeister of Münster (1579–83),[98] was the brother of Hil-
debrand von der Berswordt, Bürgermeister and one of the very few
Catholics left on the city council of Dortmund.[99] Johann's daughter,
Elizabeth, bequeathed 2,000 dalers to the Jesuits for the express purpose
of establishing a mission in her home town, a pious wish which was
never fulfilled.[100] The Kleinsorgens and Rahms belonged to the judicial-
official class in Werl, a small town on the southern boundary of the
Bishopric of Münster.[101] The Wittfelds originated from Coesfeld, the
second largest city in the bishopric.[102] The supra-regional support given
by the civic elite reflected an underlying transformation in the social
structure of Westphalian cities in the course of the sixteenth century. The
Reformation, often accompanied by a broadening of the basis of political
participation, deprived many Catholic elite families of their political
base, and accelerated the trend toward the integration of the civic elite
into the officialdom of the Counter-Reformation territorial state. Another development, meanwhile, ran contrary to the first. Where the
territorial prince succeeded in crushing civic liberties and reinstalling
Catholic worship in the small dependent towns, a new elite arose to serve
as judges, magistrates, and officials in these subjugated communities.
The careers of the von der Berswordts and the Kleinsorgens exemplified
these two opposite, yet complementary, developments.

97. Cf. G. Krippenberg, "Das Patriziergeschlecht der Berswordt und Dortmund," in
Beiträge zur Geschichte Dortmunds und der Grafschaft Mark, 52 (1955), pp. 102ff. and genealogical chart 6.

98. See appendix 1, no. 7.

99. See Krippenberg, geneal. chart 1.

100. See her will, dated March 3, 1611, in StAM, FM, SFG, II Loc. 7, no. 4, fols. 30ff.,
esp. fol. 30v.

101. See will of Lic. Gerhard Kleinsorgen, episcopal official in Werl, in StAM, FM,
SFG, III Loc. 1, no. 22, fol. 19; see also the will of Margareta Rahm, certified by Dr.
Christian Kleinsorgen, archiepiscopal vice-official in Werl, ibid., III Loc. 1, no. 25, fol. 32.

102. StAM, FM, SFG, "Comp. Hist. Coll.," fol. 59v.

Very often, a document reveals more by what it omits than by what it tells. In our list of benefactors, not a single guild Alderman or guild master honored the Jesuits with gifts; only one Modersohn, a long-standing butcher family notable for its ties to the magistracy and the Catholic Church, represented the guild elite. A number of guild leaders were Protestants, but the Aldermen Arnold von Guelich and Christian Wedemhove were definitely good Catholics.[103] Missing too were many magistrates. Although two Bürgermeisters, three city councillors, and the city syndic appeared on the list of benefactors, the *majority* of councillors who served between 1588 and 1618 withheld their support. The three most powerful magisterial families—the Herdings, Heerdes, and Plönies—were only represented by their womenfolk among the earlier benefactors, although they were to become firm supporters of the Society in the middle decades of the seventeenth century. In the conflicts between the city council and the archbishops over jurisdictional competence, between the city and the cathedral chapter over the minting of copper coins, the Jesuits too often ended up on the wrong side of the magistrates. The councillors who would otherwise have supported the Society were constrained by the demands of their office to defend civic liberties and to preserve the peace in the face of the religious fervor of the militant Catholics.

Concomitant with the success of the Jesuits arose what must be recognized as a new wave of religious mysticism among women. The support and patronage of noblewomen in Ignatius of Loyola's career is well known; likewise, the Jesuits in Münster taught and embodied a form of piety which appealed to the religious sentiments of many Catholic women. In the "purified" theology and worship of the Protestant Churches there was no place for Mariology. While women played significant roles in Anabaptism,[104] in the Calvinist Church in

103. Both men, the first a shopkeeper, *Kramer,* the latter a clothier, kept family chronicles in which their religious sentiments and loyalty to the Catholic Church were clearly manifest. See "Familienchronik Guelich," StAM, AVM, MS. 172; and Helmut Richtering, ed., "Die Familienchronik des Johann Wedemhove von 1610," *Westfalen* 40 (1962), pp. 133–49.

104. On the prominent role played by women in the Anabaptist movements in the Netherlands and in Münster, see Albert F. Mellink, *Amsterdam en de Wederdopers in de zeestiende Eeuw* (Nijmegen, 1978), pp. 46–48, 64–66; A. J. Jelsma, "De Koning en de Vrouwen; Münster 1534–1535," in *Gereformeerd Theologisch Tijdschrift,* 75 (1975), pp. 82–107. The relationship between Anabaptism and women is best summed up by George Williams in *The Radical Reformation* (Philadelphia, 1975), pp. 506f.: "Nowhere else in the Reformation Era were women so nearly the peers and companions in the faith, and mates in missionary enterprise and readiness for martyrdom, as among those for whom believers' baptism was an equalizing covenant, consummated in terms readily employing the language of betrothal and the marriage bed. The Anabaptist insistence on the covenantal principle of freedom of conscience for all adult believers and thereby the extension of the

France,[105] and in the sectarian movements in England during the Civil War,[106] in the actual social consequences of the Reformation in Germany they were relegated to the roles of obedient spouses and pious mothers. In an age when paternal authority and marital bonds held together the basic fabric of the social network, the full forces of social repression could be brought to bear on diffident women who stood outside of the family structure.[107] A recent study of marital litigation in the Diocese of Constance reveals that the majority of cases were presented in court by women, hinting at the enormous dissatisfaction with the married or amorous life on the part of the female partners.[108] When wives were expected to give birth to half a dozen or more babies and when maternal mortality at childbirth was shockingly high, the unattractiveness of married life must have been a sentiment shared by many women. The only socially respectable alternative to marriage and one of the few ways of self-fulfillment for women was the religious life, in the medieval sense of the word. The secluded life of a convent thus offered a haven and alternative to the possible tyranny of husbands and fathers, the companionship of other women, and the chance to pursue the more sublime goals in life. Young girls of noble families often had their future spouses chosen for them by parents who were more concerned with the political and dynastic aspects of the matrimonial union than with the actual wishes of their daughters. In 1612, three young noblewomen ran away from their Calvinist parents to escape arranged marriages; the Jesuits in Münster, to whom they went, successfully persuaded them to enter the religious life.[109] Nor were they the only ones. Two young women from noble Lutheran families went to the Jesuits "to still the inquietude of their souls."[110] Both lukewarm Catholic and Protestant noblewomen sought spiritual comfort and peace by confessing and communicating at the hands of the Fathers in Münster.[111]

---

priesthood of the Christophorous laity to women constituted a major breach in patriarchalism and a momentous step in the Western emancipation of women. Besides numerous patronesses, protectresses, and martyrs, the Radical Reformation acknowledged several prophetesses, at least two women apostles, and one redemptress."

105. See Nancy L. Roelker, "The Appeal of Calvinism to French Noblewomen in the Sixteenth Century," *Journal of Interdisciplinary History* 2 (1972).

106. See Keith Thomas, "Women and the Civil War Sects," *P & P* 13 (1958).

107. In his study of witch-hunts in Southwestern Germany, H. C. Erik Midelfort convincingly argues that the growing number of unmarried and single women would appear as a seditious element in society, viewed from the perspective of the patriarchal family. See his *Witchhunting in Southwestern Germany, 1562–1684: The Social and Intellectual Foundations* (Stanford, 1972), pp. 182–87.

108. See Thomas M. Safley, "Marital Litigation in the Diocese of Constance, 1551–1620," *SCJ*, 12 (1981), pp. 61–77.

109. *Litt. Ann.*, 1612, pp. 324–25.

110. Litt. Ann., ARSJ, Rh. Inf., 48, fol. 204.

111. Litt. Ann., ARSJ, Rh. Inf., 48, fol. 176.

Comfort and peace consoled some, others were inflamed by religious ecstasy. "A young noblewoman who was called to the Catholic faith," reported the Jesuits, "once she has absorbed the light of the true doctrine, the ardor of her piety was such that . . . she destined her soul for perpetual virginity."[112] Still others drove themselves to ever higher forms of religious ecstasy by various means of self-mortification.[113] These extreme women ascetics subsisted on meager diets of bread and water, and through self-flagellation, hair shirts, rough, knotty ropes, and iron fetters, "sought to contain the flames of their religious passions."[114] The parallel with late medieval mysticism of the beguines was evident; even the erotic images of religious passions can be discerned in the language of devotion.[115] The devotees bequeathed to the Society of Jesus all their earthly possessions and invoked, in their wills, Jesus as their spiritual and eternal bridegroom.[116] Matthaeus Timpe, who guided one such group of female Jesuit devotees, wrote a tract of edification in which he praised the "garden of pleasure of the virgin soul," and promised eternal salvation for women who kept perpetual chastity.[117] While the Jesuits rejoiced in the enthusiasm of their female devotees, the occasional excesses of the women brought embarrassment for the Society and aroused the suspicion and disapproval of the solid burghers. In 1615, the magistrates strongly rebuked Timpe and the devotees of the Society, among them both young women and students of the college, for holding an all-night vigil in open air, in the churchyard of Saint Martin, where "under the pretext of devotion bad examples were set," and forbade any future gatherings.[118]

New spiritual passion was accompanied by new objects of spiritual piety. The Rosary symbolized the renewed Marian devotion. Made in silver or gold, and often decorated with jewels, these symbols of spiritual sublimity and social status were mentioned in wills and passed on from one generation of female devotees to their friends and relatives.[119] We

112 *Litt. Ann.*, 1597, pp. 247–48.

113. *Litt. Ann.*, 1605, pp. 724–25.

114. *Litt. Ann.*, 1602, p. 553.

115. On the beguines, see the standard work by Herbert Grundmann, *Religiöse Bewegungen im Mittelalter,* (Hildesheim, 2nd rev. ed., 1961), chaps. 4–6. See also the succinct treatment by Brenda M. Bolton, "Mulieres Sanctae," in Susan M. Stuard, ed., *Women in Medieval Society* (Philadelphia, 1976), pp. 141–59, where she argues that the imbalance of sex ratio and the unattractiveness of married life chiefly accounted for the popularity of Beguine houses.

116. See will of Anna Hamelholte, StAM, FM, SFG, II Loc. 8, no. 17, fol. 2.

117. Matthaeus Timpe, *Lustgarten der Jungfraün . . . 26 Paradiesgärtlein und Predigten. . . .* (Münster: Lambert Raesfeld, 1611).

118. StdAM, AII, 20, RP, 1615, April 10, vol. 47, fol. 137.

119. Matthaeus Timpe constantly emphasized the great merits of reciting the rosary in his writings; see, for examples, *Theatrum Historicum, continens Vindictas Divinas et Praemia*

catch a glimpse of the spiritual world of these women through the books they left behind. Prominent among the readings were tracts of edification with titles such as "Little Garden of Souls," "Well for Thirsty Souls," "Imitation of the Virgin Mary," "Reflections on the Secrets of the Rosary," "The Life of Saint Ignatius," his *Spiritual Exercises,* Thomas von Kempis's *Imitatio Christi,* writings by Timpe, and vernacular catechisms.[120] These reading materials point to the continuation of female piety in the manner of the *Devotio Moderna* and the beguines, and the rejuvenation of that pietistic tradition by the Jesuits in Northwest Germany.

If chastity and virginity led to eternal life, sexual permissiveness opened the gates of Hell. The shadow image of the devout virgin was the woman of loose morals. The 1616 *Litterae Annuae* of the college reported that the Fathers urged three prostitutes to adhere to a life of virtue, which all of them promised to do. A few days later, one of the women was seen by the Fathers carousing in the company of men, whereupon, in the words of the Fathers, "she was struck dumb by the Devil" and suffered excruciating pain until her contrition and exorcism performed by the Jesuits relieved her of the physical torments.[121] Put upon the pedestal of a renewed Catholic piety on the one hand, women were also more likely to suffer a worse fate, sinners in the realm of sexual morality and victims of relentless witch-hunts.

THE SOCIETY OF JESUS AND THE CITY REPUBLIC

In 1602, Father Sebastian zum Kley, a native Münsteraner, willed his share of the paternal inheritance to the Society. It included a house on Aegidii Strasse, inhabited by his in-law, Dr. Dietrich Eickvordt, *Almissener* or poorfund overseer of the parish of Saint Aegidius, who disputed the partition of the inheritance.[122] On May 17, accompanied by notaries to prove their claim, several Jesuit Fathers entered Eickvordt's house and demanded he vacate it at once. The latter lodged a complaint with the magistrates, pointing out that the Jesuits had bypassed the authority of the city council, which held the right to arbitrate in all civil disputes. Obviously displeased with the Society's disregard for civic authority, the

---

Christianum Virtutum (Münster: Michael Dale, 1625), pp. 224–25; and *Der Ceremonien warumb/ das ist lautere unnd klare ursachen und ausslegungen der furnemmsten Ceremonien/ . . . sampt etlichen ungereimpten/widerspinnigen Ceremonien und Geberden der Sectischen* (Münster: Lambert Raesfeld, 1609), p. 50.

120. See inventories of the possessions of Elizabeth Missing and Anna Hamelholte, StAM, FM, SFG, II Loc. 9, no. 32, fols. 28–28v; II Loc. 8, no. 17, fol. 18.

121. *Litt. Ann.,* 1616, ARSJ. Rh. Inf., 48, fol. 203v.

122. StAM, FM, SFG, II Loc. 6, no. 110, notarial instrument of Jan. 24, 1602.

city council informed the Jesuits that the dispute must be settled by the magistrates and that their action "was unseemly in a free republic."[123] Rebuffed, the Fathers acquiesced, filed a lawsuit against Eickvordt, and a settlement was eventually negotiated.[124] The incident, nonetheless, revealed the constant tension between the Society and the burghers, and the dilemma the magistrates faced as patrons of the Jesuits on the one hand, and as defenders of the rights and customs of the civic republic on the other.

The rashness of a few hotheads among the personnel of the Jesuit College wore thin the magistrates' goodwill, which the first Fathers had carefully cultivated after their arrival in Münster. The relationship between council and college was at its best under the rectorship of Father Peter Michael (1588–95). Influential magistrates like Johann v. d. Berswordt, Dr. Heinrich Vendt, and Dr. Hermann Heerde enjoyed the company of the erudite and pious men and honored the college with their presence during performances of school plays or dropped in occasionally to have lunch with the Fathers.[125] Favors shown by the city council, however, had their limits. In 1593, when incursions of Dutch troops into Westphalia became more menacing, the Jesuits agitated publicly to be allowed to form a company of militia and stockpile gunpowder within the compounds of the college; both requests were flatly turned down by the city council.[126] This example clearly demonstrates that in the minds of the magistrates there was no confusion between religion and politics, and that the constitution and peace of the urban commune was not to be compromised for the sake of confessional loyalty. As the *Obrigkeit* who extended patronage and protection, *Schutz und Schirm,* the city council expected respect and cooperation from the Jesuits. The goodwill turned sour when, on two occasions, the impertinent remarks of a certain Magister Johann Steil threatened to poison the good relations between council and college.

In August 1604, Magister Steil forbade his students to witness a public execution at the city market, saying that the city and Archbishop Ernst were contesting the right to impose capital punishments in Münster, and, in his opinion, the civic magistrates were clearly overstepping their jurisdictional competence and the execution would mean, in fact, homicide, and excommunication of the authorities as well as all spectators.

123. StdAM, AII, 20, RP, 1602, May 17, vol. 34, fols. 139–40.

124. See StdAM, AII, 20, RP, vol. 41, fols. 126, 141, 176, 181, 193, 211, 218, 223, 227.

125. Johann v. d. Berswordt, for example, invited Father Michael to retire to his country estate in the summer of 1588 to flee the plague in the city; see StAM, MSS. 1026, 1, "Hist. Coll. Mon.," fol. 8v. See also StdAM, AII, 20, RP, 1593, Oct. 11, vol. 25, fol. 83; StAM, FM, SFG, "Comp. Hist. Coll.," fols. 28v, 65.

126. StdAM, AII, 20, RP, 1593, July 8, vol. 25, fol. 55v.

Several students who did slip out to watch the execution were later flogged.

Incensed by this offense to the dignity of the commune, the guild Aldermen and masters urged the magistrates to investigate. At the meeting in the college between the delegates of the council and the Fathers, Lic. Wittfeld told the Jesuits that it was most painful to have a magister who could influence the minds of young boys to denigrate openly the authority of the city council. The right to impose capital punishment had been one of the privileges of the commune for over three hundred years, a custom confirmed by its reported usage in the chronicles and uncontested by emperors, kings, and princes in the past. If Magister Steil, a Nuremberger, was ignorant of local laws and customs, he should simply keep his mouth shut. The rector, Father Copper, tried to appease the displeasure of the councillors, claiming that the Society did not question the jurisdictional competence of the city council and that the words of Steil had not been properly understood in the right context. Magister Steil, in turn, explained he meant "death" by "homocidium," not murder, and exclaimed he would rather die than call the magistrates murderers. Satisfied with the answers, the councillors agreed to drop the matter, but before they left they reminded the Jesuits of the benevolence and piety of the magistrates, the favors the college had received, and warned that the Jesuits should not speak irreverently of the magistrates again.[127]

Only two years later, Magister Steil embarrassed the Society again when he called two members of the city council liars. The councillor Lic. Beifang and secretary Heinrich Holland had been sent to the Imperial Court in Prague to protest the actions of Archbishop Ernst in subverting civic liberties. On their return, they informed the council of the news they had heard in Prague of the expulsion of the Jesuits from the Republic of Venice.[128] When told by one of his students, Magister Steil exploded, called the story a lie. Then he uttered, moreover, various threats against "the seditious burghers" who had vituperated against the Society, remarking that they should reflect on the matter in front of the spire of Saint Lambert, where cages carrying the remains of the three executed Anabaptist leaders were still hanging. One of the students in the class

127. Cf. StAM, FM, SFG, "Comp. Hist. Coll.," fol. 30. The incident is also described in Sökeland, p. 49; and *quasi verbatim* in Offenberg, II, pp. 32–34.

128. The Jesuits in Venice were expelled as retaliation for the papal interdict of 1606; see the exhaustive study of the conflict between the Republic of Saint Mark and Pope Paul V by William J. Bouwsma, *Venice and the Defense of Republican Liberty* (Berkeley, 1968), pp. 253–54, 344–45, 386–87. See also StAM, FM, SFG, "Comp. Hist. Coll.," fol. 35v. Sökeland gives the wrong year for the incident, 1616 instead of 1606; and Offenberg, who follows his account, repeats the mistake. See Sökeland, pp, 49–51; Offenberg, II, pp. 34–35.

was the son of the guild Alderman Heinrich Otterstett and he told his father the threats of the magister; enraged, the Alderman and other guild leaders demanded that the magistrates take action against Magister Steil. This time, the Jesuits escaped the wrath of the magistrates by arguing that the student had twisted and falsified the words of Steil. In any case, the magister had proved too much of a liability and was soon dismissed from the Society, after which he went to Coesfeld, further working for the cause of the Jesuits.[129]

Present in both incidents are all the key factors in the relations between the Society and the city of Münster: the ambiguous position of the city council, caught between a favorable attitude toward the Jesuits and the responsibilities of defending civic dignities; the implacable hostility of the guild leadership toward the Society; the larger political context of struggles between princely power and republican liberties. Let us now examine how these three sets of factors interacted in the central controversy between the burghers and the Jesuits: the problem of exempting the Fathers from the wine excise.

The Treaty of Dülmen, concluded between the Bishop and the Estates in 1526, regulated many points of conflict between clergy and laity. One of the agreements reached stipulated that only the cathedral canons were to be exempted from wine excise.[130] In 1599, the Jesuits petitioned the city council for the extension of that privilege to themselves, which the magistrates turned down on January 7, 1600.[131] At stake was not so much the financial aspect of an excise on wine, which comprised, in any case, only a small part of the income of the city, but the privileged status that tax-free consumption of wine entailed. Münster belonged to beer-drinking North Germany, where Rhine and Mosel wines had to be imported via Cologne; the city council levied a tax on the general consumption of this "luxury drink;" and some of the wine-merchants ranked among the richest burghers in the city. On the other hand, the Jesuits—many of them Rhinelanders and South Germans, hence wine-drinkers—considered the privilege as rightfully belonging to such an esteemed religious order.

In January 1601, the Jesuits imported 9 ohms of wine.[132] Before a session of the council the guild Aldermen and masters demanded that

129. See Duhr, *Jesuiten,* II;1, pp. 102f.

130. For the Treaty of Dülmen, see Kerssenbroch, pp. 150–51.

131. StdAM, AII, 20, RP, vol. 31, fols. 117v–18.

132. An ohm, a unit of measuring the volume of liquids, equals 142.62 liters in the Rhineland, 148.63 liters in Lippe, and 144.95 liters in Bremen; no measurement for Münster is available but the figure is certainly not far from the above figures. See Fritz Verdenhalven, *Alte Masse, Münzen und Gewichte aus dem deutschen Sprachgebiet* (Neustadt a.d. Aisch, 1968), pp. 22, 38.

excise must be collected in spite of a motion of the council, which had been passed by majority vote, to grant tax exemption on 3 ohms of wine in favor of the Jesuits. Bürgermeister Vendt, leader of the pro-Jesuit magistrates, suggested exempting from taxation the amount of wine necessary for mass in Saint Peter's. Immediately, the guild leaders objected, fearing that the parish clergy would follow suit and that the terms of the Treaty of Dülmen might be jeopardized. Agreeing reluctantly with the guild leaders, the magistrates informed the Jesuits that although the council itself looked favorably on their request, the commune was opposed to it.[133] The Fathers, however, simply refused to pay because one year later they still owed tax on 10 ohms of wine.[134] The *Weinherr* pleaded the case of the Jesuits before the full council, citing the Fathers' pedagogic achievements and the large number of communicants at Saint Peter's. Knowing the guild elite would disagree and encouraged by the example of the city of Cologne, which also refused to grant exemption on the wine-tax to the Jesuits, the magistrates again handed down a negative decision.[135] Still another petition from the Fathers in January 1603 was rejected due to the fierce opposition of the guild leaders.[136]

Debate over the issue preoccupied the council for the next eight years, particularly between 1603 and 1606, when this local issue of clerical privilege versus civic customs turned into a contest between the forces of the Counter-Reformation and the defense of republican liberties. Frustrated in their attempts to gain a favorable hearing from the magistrates, the Jesuits simply pronounced they were de facto free of all civic burdens,[137] and wrote to Emperor Rudolf II to ask for support. A letter from the emperor arrived in Münster in July 1603, in which he admonished the magistrates to lift civic burdens from the eminent Society of Jesus.[138] The council decided to humor Imperial wishes and informed the guild leaders of their new position.[139]

Imperial intervention transformed a formerly lay-clerical disagreement into open confrontation between the predominantly Catholic city council and the guilds, where Protestants exerted a greater influence. In the councillor meeting of October 3, Bürgermeister Vendt proposed that the guild Aldermen be instructed to overcome expected opposition within the guilds and to ascertain that there were no Anabaptists in the craft

133. StdAM, AII, 20, RP, 1601, Jan. 22, vol. 33, fols. 14–16, 17.

134. StdAM, AII, 20, RP, 1602, Jan. 3, vol. 33, fol. 333.

135. Ibid.

136. StdAM, AII, 20, RP, 1603, Jan. 16, vol. 34, fol. 356; AXI, 76, SP, vol. 3, fols. 41–41v.

137. StdAM, AII, 20, RP, 1603, March 3, vol. 35, fol. 20.

138. StdAM, AII, 20, RP, 1603, July 24, vol. 35, fol. 76.

139. StdAM, AII, 20, RP, 1603, July 24, Aug. 8, vol. 35, fols. 76, 88, 96v.

guilds who might lead opposition to the Jesuits, thus clearing the city of the suspicion of harboring the odious sect and demonstrating its loyalty to Catholicism in honor of the "pious memory of Bishop Franz, who restored civic liberties in 1554." The other councillors readily agreed to pressure the guild leaders into favoring the grant of tax exemption on 9 or 10 ohms of wine for the Jesuits.[140] On the thirteenth, the magistrates summoned the two guild Aldermen, Thomas Egberts and Heinrich Otterstett, and the two guildmasters of the fullers, who were appointed by the city council, to appear in the town hall. Praising the Jesuits for their educational work and reminding the guildsmen of the emperor's wishes, the magistrates also admonished the four men to support the position of the city council before the assembly of all guildmasters. The Aldermen replied they must first consult with the masters; at the Schoehaus meeting on the same day, the guild leaders decided to resist the magistrates.[141]

One week later, the Aldermen returned with more than a dozen guildmasters and stated their regret that they could not agree with the magistrates. Furthermore, they asked the magistrates to appoint a deputation from among their ranks to visit the college and warn the Fathers to desist from further petitioning the emperor, lest they be compelled to bring the matter before the full assembly of all guildsmen. Lamenting the takeover of the gymnasium by the Jesuits and the dismissal of former teachers at the school, the guild leaders feared that the Jesuits were spying on burghers by questioning their students. A good number of burghers, the Aldermen added, wanted to contribute money for the founding of a school to counter the pernicious influence of the Society.[142]

The councillors met on the twenty-fourth to debate how to deal with the obstinacy of the guilds. Once more, Bürgermeister Vendt reminded his fellow councillors that they must obey the emperor and win over the guild leaders by persuasion. A reasonable amount of wine, 12 ohms or so, could be exempted from the excise. The motion passed without dissent.[143]

On November 21, the guild leaders returned to the council chamber for another meeting with the magistrates. Disagreeing outright with the position of the council, the guild leaders argued that the Jesuits were generally hated in the neighboring United Provinces and that many burghers resented their dismissal of the former teachers of the cathedral school. They repeated their suggestion of October 24 that they intimidate the Jesuits, adding that, if the council granted to the Fathers this one privilege, the latter would stop at nothing. Moreover,

140. StdAM, AII, 20, RP, 1603, Oct. 3, vol. 35, fols. 128–128v.
141. StdAM, AII, 20, RP, vol. 35, fol. 132v; AXI, 76, SP, vol. 3, fols. 56v, 69v.
142. StdAM, AII, 20, RP, 1603, Oct. 20, vol. 35, fol. 134.
143. StdAM, AII, 20, RP, vol. 35, fols. 138v–139.

the guild leaders desired that all past arrears and future wine taxes be collected promptly; otherwise, they would have to report the matter to the general guild assembly. The Aldermen also related how the Jesuits had misled (*verführt*) Hermann Huge, son of the shopkeeper Bernard and erstwhile canon in Xanten, into joining the Society, whereupon the Jesuits immediately pounced on the prebend, leaving Huge's nephew out in the cold, without a benefice. The councillor Bernard van Detten the Younger urged the guild leaders to consider the matter from the perspective of the city, which could ill afford to offend the highest political authority in the land. He added, moreover, that the cathedral chapter, waiting to subvert civic privileges for some time, might exploit any bad relations between emperor and city to undermine Münster. Taking up the issue of civic privileges, the guild leaders cited the terms of the Treaty of Dülmen and compromised by saying they would not object to giving a sum of money in secret to the college, if the Jesuits could not pay the tax. Faced with the recalcitrance of the guild leaders, the magistrates instructed secretary Holland and councillors Meinertz and Lennep to inform the Fathers of the goodwill of the city council, but to tell them that the matter must be dropped for the time being because of strong opposition in the commune.[144]

Having won the battle, the guild leaders pressed their advantage and reminded the *Weinherren* in early January 1604 to collect arrears in wine taxes from the Jesuits immediately, suspecting the magistrates of leniency toward the Society.[145] In March, they presented more grievances before the city council, complaining first of all that "the Jesuits were conducting their assemblies in the cathedral most vehemently and vulgarly," then reporting the Fathers' intention of visiting the parochial schools in order to lure away the students. The guild Aldermen and masters asked the council to put an end to this, because the Jesuits could otherwise spy on the household activities of the burghers. In closing, they also requested the council to forbid the Jesuits from visiting houses of burghers where private schoolmasters were lodging.[146]

Adamant to defend God's cause in the face of "heretical opponents," the Jesuits tried another tactic and enlisted the support of Archbishop Ernst, the nominal lord of the city of Münster. On February 10, 1604, Archbishop Ernst sent the college two barrels of wine as a gift. Hesitant at first to admit the wine untaxed, the gatekeepers finally allowed passage. The guild leaders saw right away another trick of the Fathers to circumvent civic laws, and demanded a written note by the arch-

144. StdAM, AII, 20, RP, 1603, Nov. 21, vol. 35, fols. 159–159v.
145. StdAM, AII, 20, RP, 1604, Jan. 9, vol. 35, fols. 184–184v.
146. StdAM, AII, 20, RP, 1604, March 26, vol. 36, fols. 22–23.

bishop from Kaspar Höfflinger, *Landrentmeister* of the bishopric who was supervising the delivery of the wine (he happened to be the brother of Father Balthasar Höfflinger, S.J.), before they would agree to turn over the wine to the college. In relating this episode to the magistrates, the Aldermen also expressed the displeasure of many burghers with Father Balthasar's Sunday sermons, which excoriated those who opposed the Society.[147]

Somewhat irritated by the stubbornness of the guildsmen, the magistrates wanted to settle the matter quickly, and when in December 1605, the Fathers again beseeched the council for tax exemption, the latter favored the college with 12 ohms of tax-free wine annually.[148] At the next meeting of the council, the Aldermen and guild masters protested the decision reached without their consent, and expressed their worry that such a move might create the impression that the presence of the Jesuits received official blessings. The guild leaders further voiced their grave reservations over the bequests of Everwin and Franz Droste to the Society, which amounted to the enormous sum of 3,500 dalers.[149] Since the craft guilds dominated the militia, the magistrates backed off from open confrontation. Meanwhile, the Catholic faction on the city council was working quietly to diminish the political strength of the guilds by encouraging dissatisfaction among burghers who were not organized into guilds and directing their grievances against the highhandedness of the guild elite.

In 1606 and 1607, the anti-Jesuit guildsmen extended their campaign by forcing the Fathers to pay custom dues and preventing them from teaching in the parish churches. One of the original conditions for the admission of the Society into Münster was that the Fathers could not administer in the parish churches, a ban still effective at least as late as 1599.[150] In April 1607 the guildsmen charged that the Jesuits were giving catechism lessons in Saint Lambert's and Saint Ludger's; the magistrates replied that they too were concerned, but since the parish clergy did not protest, they felt nothing could be done. Disgruntled, the guild leaders lost their temper; they said the Jesuits promised to stick to the cathedral school, "now they are teaching catechism, surely, the Inquisition will come next." As long as the city council protected Lutherans from religious persecution, the guild leaders declared, they would abide by the magistrates' decision.[151]

147. StdAM, AII, 20, Protocol Extraordinarium 1604, Feb. 10, vol. 36, fols. 164v–166.

148. StdAM, AII, 20, RP, 1605, Dec., 19, vol. 37, fol. 157v.

149. StdAM, AII, 20, RP, 1605, Dec., 16, vol. 37, fol. 161.

150. Litt. Ann., 1599, ARSJ, Rh. Inf., 48, fol. 95.

151. StdAM, AII, 20, RP, 1607, April 6, vol. 39, fols. 59–60. A year later, the Jesuits invaded the citadel of burgher piety, the Hospital of Saint Magdelena; by 1613, they were teaching catechism in four of Münster's six parishes. See StAM, FM, SFG, "Comp. Hist. Coll.," fols. 43, 44v, 65v.

Later in the year, in winter, the Jesuits passed on another letter from the emperor to the magistrates.[152] Led by Lic. Wittfeld, the syndic, the Catholic magistrates pushed through a motion to exempt the Jesuits from paying the wine excise, while specifying that this was done on account of their pedagogic services and that the terms of the Treaty of Dülmen were by no means annulled.[153] Even at this point, the Aldermen and guild masters refused to compromise, and haughtily responded that only after the Jesuits had paid their arrears in taxes could the question of exemption be discussed at all. The patience of the magistrates was at an end, and the guild leaders were told in no uncertain terms that any future injuries to the rights of the city or to its burghers were to be blamed on the stiff-necked guildsmen. The council had taken the interests of the city to heart and saw no other alternative but to write to the emperor, explicitly blaming the guilds for this impasse. Undaunted, the guild leaders merely replied, "the more time passes, the more the Fathers snatch things from around them; they must be frightened off now."[154] Still, the guildsmen did not want an open break with the magistracy. In January 1608, they grudgingly consented to granting tax exemption on 12 ohms of wine to the Jesuits on condition that the Fathers continue to be docile, that they keep on teaching, that they sign a note acknowledging their status as *clerus secondarius,* that they recognize this concession was in deference to Imperial wishes, and that they continue to uphold and respect all prerogatives and privileges of the city, as stipulated in the Treaty of Dülmen.[155] In June 1609, the Fathers signed and returned the note to the magistrates,[156] and in August 1610, a decade after the initial petition, the Aldermen and guild masters finally gave their consent to the granting of tax exemption.

The forces in defense of civic liberties and the freedom of worship had won the particular battle over wine excise, although it was a pyrrhic victory. The conflict, however, was but one of the many assaults mounted by the forces of the Counter-Reformation against the city republic of Münster. Meanwhile, confrontation over religion had spread to every member of the body social, to debates on the city council, to contests between various social and political groups. Who were the Catholics? Who were the Protestants? How did confessional tensions affect the political process in the city republic? It is to these questions that we must now turn in order to understand the underlying social process at work, which threatened to rupture the cohesion and harmony within the city walls.

152. StdAM, AII, 20, Protocol Extraordinarium 1607, Nov. 26, vol. 39, fol. 187.

153. StdAM, AII, 20, Protocol Extraordinarium 1607, Dec. 14, vol. 39, fols. 209v–210v.

154. StdAM, AII, 20, Protocol Extraordinarium 1607, Dec. 17, vol. 39, fols. 213–14.

155. StdAM, AII, 20, RP, 1608, Jan. 14 & 19, vol. 40, fols. 12v–13, 15.

156. StdAM, AII, 20, RP, 1609, June 19, vol. 41, fol. 105v.

CHAPTER FOUR

The Formation of Parties

The burghers who returned to Münster in 1535 after the suppression of the Anabaptist rebellion included those who were sympathetic to the Reformation movement before it took on a revolutionary and Anabaptist turn. Sentiments which underlay the Reformation were too strongly rooted in the discontent with the Roman Church to be immediately destroyed by the restoration of the Catholic ruling regime. After 1535, while Anabaptists were being relentlessly hunted down, burghers with Lutheran sympathies in Münster prudently kept their religious convictions to themselves. Since only Catholic worship was allowed—although the police ordinance of 1558 did not explicitly bar Protestants from obtaining citizenship—there is no evidence of the open existence of a Lutheran community in Münster. From time to time, however, the magistrates got wind of clandestine, nightly conventicles in burgher houses, where itinerant preachers brought godly word to those who were already unfavorably disposed toward the ungodly Roman Church.[1] The few incidents which came to light probably represent only a small part of the actual activities which continued to keep alive the Protestant message.

Some of the actual reforms in worship effected in 1533 persisted after the Catholic restoration, the most important being the administration of communion in both kinds. Clerical marriages, to cite another important vestige, were also common, at least until the 1570s.[2] When Emperor

---

1. In 1566, the shopkeeper Dietrich Körding was questioned by the city council because he challenged a priest to give Lutheran sermons; StdAM, AII, 20, RP, Sept. 19, vol. 3, fols. 39v–41. In 1604, the magistrates received report that two itinerant preachers were giving nightly sermons in a house on Vossgasse, occasions which a chaplain from Saint Lambert's also attended; RP, May 3, vol. 36, fol. 210v.

2. For clerical concubinages in Münster, see Schwarz, *Akten Visitation,* passim. For communion in both kinds by the laity, see the documents appended in Huyskens, *Everwin von Droste,* pp. 19–20. At Easter of 1571, the dean of Saint Martin reported on the enthusiasm of the parishioners to receive Holy Communion thus: "Custos apud venerabilem dominum thesaurarium curabit, ut mature in coena domini adferantur mille et sexcentae hostiae pro communicaturis. . . . Solent in feriis paschalibus communicentes in parochia nostra esse numero fere mille et quingenti, ad quod requiruntur *quindecim canthari vini.*" And again at Christmas: "Vigilia nativitatis Christi thom ersten seven ofte achte hundert kleine hostien tho halen vor die Kommunicarten in die nativitatis Christi, und *seven kanne wienes.*" The italics are mine.

Charles V conceded the right of worship to Lutherans in the 1555 Religious Peace of Augsburg, tensions in Münster gradually relaxed. Three factors contributed to the peaceful co-existence of Catholics and Protestants in the Westphalian metropole.

First, the Catholic magistrates who returned to Münster after 1535 identified the misfortunes of their city with the political unrest brought about by the Reformation. After they retired or died off, the younger men who took their place on the city council in the 1550s and 1560s did not harbor personal bitterness and were thus more tolerant of confessional differences.

Second, before the coming of the Jesuits and the election of a Wittelsbach bishop in the 1580s, sharp and exclusive confessional lines did not divide the civic community. Most burghers called themselves "good Christians" rather than "good Catholics" in their wills; members of the same family chose different confessions to suit personal conscience; Protestants and Catholics worked side by side in the mercantile and craft guilds. In church service, Catholic worship between 1535 and 1588 manifested a heavy admixture of Lutheran innovations and Catholic vestiges: beside *communio sub utraque specie,* Lutheran German hymns and ecclesiology also influenced the attitudes of Catholics in Münster.[3] There were expectations that a general council of the Church would eventually heal the temporary schism and that priests would be allowed to marry. Confrontations arose when it turned out that the Catholic Church had refused to compromise with the Protestants and when the new clergy sought to re-impose religious authority over the laity.

The last factor contributing to the atmosphere of toleration in the fifty years after 1535 was the economic revival of Münster after the devastations of war. The underpopulated city in 1535 presented unusual economic opportunities and social advancement for many. In 1538 alone, 197 men and women swore the burgher oath and took up new residences in Münster.[4] As a member of the Hansa and as the manufacturing and trading center of Westphalia, Münster attracted merchants and journeymen, many of whom married local women and settled. Quite a few came from Protestant cities—Hamburg, Lübeck, Bremen, and Nuremberg, to name just the most prominent examples; others emigrated from the Netherlands and from the Duchy of Jülich-Cleve, where the Reformation had made much headway. The burghers knew well that religious intolerance was the bane of civic prosperity, and they continued to foster economic growth through an open and pragmatic policy.

3. As late as 1595, the Jesuits still complained of the corruption of liturgy; they claimed that Lutheran manners of worship were adopted in most parishes and Lutheran hymns deformed Catholic liturgy. See ARSJ, Rh. Inf. 48, *Litt. Ann.,* 1595, fol. 49v.

4. Hövel, *BB,* pp. 59–63.

The 1580s were a crucial turning point. After his election to the Münster See in 1585, Archbishop Ernst of Cologne emulated the rule of his father and tried to enforce the twin policies of political centralization and confessional orthodoxy, measures crucial to the successful consolidation of the absolutist state in Bavaria.[5] The clergy began to assume the function of a moral police force denouncing burghers who did not confess and communicate. At the same time, the Jesuits slowly consolidated clerical leadership over a segment of the citizenry through education and through the Marian sodalities. While Protestants in Münster were forced to defend the rights of conscience and civic liberties, a militant Catholic nucleus, loyal to Rome, was emerging in the larger civic community.

THE PROTAGONISTS

Since no formal Protestant church organization existed in Münster, it is impossible to determine the size of their community. The only sources available are the names of burghers who were denounced by zealous Catholic priests for having refused to communicate, confess, or receive extreme unction. Likewise, the Jesuits also identified their most prominent opponents, several of whom sat on the city council. From these fragmentary references, essentially recorded between 1582 and 1618, forty-five men and women can be identified by name, and often by occupation.[6] They represented the more visible and articulate members of the Lutheran, the Calvinist, and the Anabaptist communities. Together with their family dependents, the identified group numbered almost two hundred souls. The fact that several were elected magistrates and guild leaders implied the existence of an even larger Protestant community. Table 4.1 shows the occupational distribution of the identified Protestants.

It is apparent that Protestantism was strongest in the guilds, a fact that is hardly surprising given the artisans' anti-clericalism and the prominent part guild masters played in the Anabaptist movement. More interesting are the trades represented. Almost one-third of our sample of Protestants were engaged in the clothing trades, with the fullers and the furriers ranking near the top of the list. These two guilds occupied a rather esteemed position in the hierarchy of the clothing trades, standing below the prestigious and powerful clothiers' guild, ranking equally with the

5. On the consolidation of the absolutist state and the accompanying measures of the Counter-Reformation, see the articles by Heinrich Lutz and Dieter Albrecht on "Das konfessionelle Zeitalter," in *Handbuch der Bayerischen Geschichte,* vol. 2 (Munich, 1966), ed. Max Spindler.

6. For the names of the identified Protestants and full documentary citations, see appendix 4.

Table 4.1   Occupations of Identified Protestants, 1566–1618

A. Lutherans and Calvinists

shopkeepers	5	clothiers	2	sculptors	1
jurists	3	tailors	2	bakers	1
fullers	3	peddlers	1	moneymen	1
furriers	3	painters	1	journeymen	1
schoolmasters	3	glassmakers	1	servants	1
merchants	3	goldsmiths	1	patricians	1
				unknown	3

Total: 37

B. Anabaptists

hawkers	2
bakers	1
unknown	5

Total: 8

tailors, and above the cloth-cutters and the linenweavers.[7] Another two Protestants belonged to the rich and powerful clothiers' guild, whose members traded with the Hanseatic cities and with the Netherlands. Here, merchants of different religious persuasions co-existed peacefully. With five members in the list, the shopkeepers' guild (*Kramergilde*) came out as the trade with the strongest pro-Protestant sentiments. The shopkeepers were merchants of middling wealth who traded in spices, clothes, paper, and a host of other products.[8] In the Gesamtgilde, the shopkeepers, together with the clothiers, the glassmakers, and the furriers, supplied most of the Aldermen between 1554 and 1618. The artistic trades were also strongly represented, and among the liberal professions which were not incorporated into guilds, Protestantism found support among some schoolmasters and jurists.[9]

Notably underrepresented were trades associated with food processing—the bakers appeared twice and the two exclusive butchers' guilds, which cherished strong ties with the magistracy and the Catholic Church, did not appear at all. Absent too were the barbers, the coopers, the bookbinders, the founders, the linenweavers, the smiths, the shoemakers, the stonemasons, the carpenters, the tanners, and the leather-

7. For the entry fees of the clothing guilds, a measure of their social prestige, see Krumbholtz, pp. 226, 357–61, 386ff., 472.

8. On the shopkeepers' guild, see Krumbholtz, pp. 254ff.

9. Many schoolteachers bitterly opposed the Jesuits because the latter lured away their students and thus threatened their livelihood; see *Litt. Ann.*, 1589 (Rome, 1591), p. 236: "Ita vacue factis haereticorum ludis, quibus abundat Vestphalia, vicinos magistellos ranunculosque in popinis clamantes, in nostri nominis invidiam atque obtrectationem egregie concitavimus."

makers. Some of these unrepresented trades were guilds that were comparatively new, founded only after 1535, whereas all of the guilds represented in the list of Protestants had been incorporated before 1535. Tradition and prestige went together: many of the unrepresented trades stood near the bottom of the guild hierarchy; their incorporation came only after years of petition and their autonomy was restricted by strict magisterial supervision. Conspicious also was the very limited influence of Protestantism outside of the Gesamtgilde, except for the teaching profession. Many occupations unrepresented in the union of guilds, such as the important brewers and innkeepers, as well as the majority of the liberal professions, do not appear in our list of Protestants. In sum, we can conclude tentatively that Protestant sympathies were strongest in the older, more prestigious craft guilds, where literacy was common, where the nature of the trades had little or nothing to do with agriculture, and where the guild brothers were also afforded a high degree of self-respect and individualism. By contrast, the trades which involved the handling of agricultural and animal products, such as baking, butchery, beer-brewing, leather-making, and tanning, did not seem to favor Protestantism. Occupations not organized into guilds, the patriciate, the merchant elite, and the lower classes in general hardly played a role, with the notable exception of the teaching profession.

The fact that eleven magistrates, five guild Aldermen, and seventeen electors[10] (Kurgenossen) are included in the list (with role overlaps) only highlights the social respectability of the Lutherans and Calvinists in Münster. Unlike the Anabaptists, who continued to suffer the stigma of rebels and who tended to be recruited from the humbler occupations, the Lutherans and Calvinists enjoyed enough community support to be elected to the city council.

Among the prominent Lutherans and Calvinists an informal alliance existed, cemented by marriage, friendship, and shared opposition to the Roman Church. Heinrich Dickman, Andreas Wilckinghoff, Lic. Johann Block, Heinrich Forckenbeck, Johann Greving, and Severin Stoltenkamp—guild Aldermen, magistrates, merchants, and leading Protestants—were all related by marriage.[11] Johann Block, magistrate, Licentiat, and Calvinist, was brother-in-law of the shopkeeper and guild Alderman, Heinrich Dickman; Block's wife and Dickman's third wife both came from the Hesseling family in Warendorf. Dickman's first two wives were Elsa Forckenbeck and Anna Wilckinghoff, linking him to another two prominent Protestants. Some of these men had settled in

---

10. The names of the electors have been published by Eduard Schulte, "Die Kurgenossen des Rates," *QFGSM* III (Münster, 1927), pp. 117–204.

11. See appendix 4, nos. 4, 11, 13, 14, 29, 35.

Münster from neighboring Calvinist territories: Heinrich Dickman was born in Burgsteinfurt; Lic. Johann Beifang's father served as judge in that nearby Calvinist county; and the widow of Melchior Steinhoff, Christina Stummel, later married Johann Köttich, the Bürgermeister of Burgsteinfurt, after the death of her first husband; the guild Alderman Christoph Hesse and his wife emigrated from Bremen in 1580. Others, Wilhelm Niehaus for one, came to Münster from the Netherlands.[12]

Most of the identified Protestants belonged to the generations born in the 1550s and the 1560s; at the time of heightened confessional tensions after 1600, these men were already well-established merchants and guild masters. In fact, some of them were old men who would soon die. Born and raised in years when Calvinism was ascendant in Northwest Germany, these men felt the challenge posed by the Counter-Reformation, which threatened to undermine the peaceful co-existence of the different confessions in Münster. They took up the defense of traditional civic privileges and the right of conscience against the new forces of the Catholic Reformation—a movement, as we shall see later, championed by men one generation younger than themselves.

More abundant are sources dealing with the Catholics. In a city where the majority of the inhabitants professed, at least nominally, the Roman faith, membership in confraternities offers a reliable criterion to differentiate the more pious from the larger multitudes. But here, it is important to choose the appropiate confraternities for closer analysis. From the fourteenth to the late seventeenth century there were no less than twenty-seven confraternities in Münster, each expressing a particular social and religious character.[13] While all confraternities can be understood as voluntary mutual-aid associations or cooperatives for salvation, some emphasized the convivial aspects of fellowship while others stressed the pursuit of salvation through collective piety.[14]

The confraternities in Münster before the advent of the Jesuits can be divided into three categories according to their primary function.[15] The first group was organized along occupational lines, such as the confraternity of the merchants, which resembled the craft guilds in that it repre-

---

12. See appendix 4.

13. For brief descriptions of the confraternities, see Augustin Hüsing, "Die alten Bruderschaften in der Stadt Münster," *WZ* 51 (1903), pp. 95–138.

14. Hüsing sees the confraternities founded before 1534 as more religious and clerical in character whereas those formed after 1535 bore a greater social and neighborly stamp; ibid., pp. 96 & 107.

15. For a typology of confraternities in late medieval and early modern Germany, see Ludwig Remling, "Bruderschaften in Franken. Kirchen- und sozialgeschichtliche Untersuchungen zum spätmittelalterlichen und frühneuzeitlichen Bruderschaftswesen" (Ph.D. diss., Würzburg University, 1981), pp. 1ff.

sented an integrated socio-religious corporation. The original clerical confraternities of the High Middle Ages, the Great Kaland of the cathedral canons and the confraternity of vicars, also fit into this category because membership was based on occupational status.[16]

A second type of confraternity was based on the neighborhood. These corporations all honored Saint Peter as their patron saint. They did not appear until after 1535.[17] They promoted neighborliness through mutual help and organized neighborhood festivities. The Saint Peter confraternities came into existence in the post-Anabaptist years and provided institutions for social integration in a city where the terrible loss in population was replenished with heavy immigration from the surrounding countryside and towns. These neighborhood confraternities offered a sense of continuity and social cohesion for the many new city dwellers who came from smaller towns and villages in Münsterland where neighborhood associations were common.[18]

Devotion to a particular saint characterized the third and most common type of confraternity. They were often based on a parish, and membership in them was open to both parishioners and other residents of the city. Aside from entry fees and regulations governing the lay/clerical and the male/female ratios, membership was normally open to all social classes. Brothers and sisters jointly attended mass in honor of their patron saints; they recited prayers, followed funeral processions, took communal meals, helping departed members and encouraging the still living brothers and sisters in the uncertain journey to paradise. Although the clergy served as spiritual advisers, laymen managed the confraternity funds and organized collective worship and feasts.[19] The mushrooming

16. The Great Kaland was founded around 1300 and the Small or Vicars' Kaland was formed in 1305. The lay confraternities of this type included the Merchants' Confraternity dedicated to the Virgin Mary (1408) and the Confraternity of Sextons.

17. By 1582, five Saint Peter's Confraternities had been founded; four more came into existence during the seventeenth century.

18. Neighborhoods were especially common in Münsterland, especially in the area west of Coesfeld. See Franz Krins, *Nachbarschaften im westfälischen Münsterland* (Münster, 1952).

19. Rich sources are still extant for the study of certain confraternities. A complete list of members and book of statutes exist for the Confraternity of Saint George, founded in 1511; now deposited in the StdAM as MS. 79. Lists of provisors and members of the Confraternity of Our Lady have also been published by Clemens Steinbicker (see n. 22). Partial lists of members, both in printed and manuscript forms, are extant for the following confraternities: (1) Confraternity of Saint Francis, founded in 1602; membership list from 1602–28 (StAM, MSS. I, 273); (2) Confraternity of Our Lady at Saint Ludger's, names of provisors between 1601 and 1640 (BDAM, PfA Ludgeri, Akten, Kart. 47); (3) Confraternity of Saint Catherine at Saint Lambert's, founded in 1330 and renewed in 1536 (BDAM, PfA Lamberti, Akten, Kart. 113); (4) Confraternity of Saint Anthony at the Hospital; names of provisors can be found in *Die 600jährige St. Antonii Erzbruderschaft Münster i.*

of this type of confraternity in the fifteenth century expressed a strong desire on the part of laymen to participate directly in religious life and might reflect latent discontent regarding the efficacy of purely clerical means of salvation.[20]

After 1588, when the Society of Jesus established its presence in Münster, still another type of confraternity came into being. Unlike the traditional confraternities, which were geographically confined to Münster itself, Jesuit sodalities formed an extensive network, linking Catholic devotees in many lands, subject to and supervised by the provincials and generals.[21] In contrast to the idiosyncratic, traditional confraternities in which local men honored local saints, Jesuit sodalities were dedicated to the more universal sacred entity of the Virgin Mary and encompassed fervent devotees in all parts of the Catholic world.

It is thus clear that only two of the four types of confraternities discussed above can properly be understood as strictly confessional in orientation. In the cases of confraternities organized on occupational and locational lines, the factor of religious voluntarism cannot be readily isolated from common professional interests or neighborhood solidarity. To examine the social basis of the Catholic renewal in Münster, I have chosen a confraternity from each of the other two types for closer analysis.

The confraternity in Aegidii parish dedicated to Our Lady was founded in 1441.[22] According to its statutes, membership in the confraternity was to comprise seventy-two men (forty-eight had to be from the parish itself; twelve were to be clergy and sixty to be laymen) and an unspecified number of women. Entry fee was set at one gulden and the provost of Saint Aegidius cloister was to serve as the spiritual guardian ex officio. Between 1540 and 1618, the confraternity enrolled almost four hundred men and an unknown number of women; occupations of around 86 percent of the brothers have been determined and table 4.2 shows the occupational breakdown. Three major occupational groups

---

Westfalen (Münster, 1969); (5) Confraternity of Merchants B.M.V. and Saint John; list of thirty-seven brothers in 1538, Hüsing, p. 131; (6) Confraternity of Our Lady at Überwasser; list of twelve members in 1536, Hüsing, p. 105. While the lists remain fragmentary, they still represent valuable sources for the study of the social basis of Catholicism in Münster. The major obstacle, however, is the uneven survival of tax records for the sixteenth century and the lack of occupational indications in the tax rolls. A systematic analysis comparing membership lists of the confraternities and tax records, similar to the one undertaken by Remling for Franconian cities, is impossible in this case.

20. Cf. Remling, pp. 19–21.

21. On Jesuit sodalities which originated as student organizations at the colleges, see Duhr, *Jesuiten,* I, pp. 357–71; II:2, pp. 81–122.

22. The membership list and statutes are published by Clemens Steinbicker as "Die Liebfrauen-Bruderschaften an der Pfarr- und Klosterkirche St. Aegidii (1441–1941)," in *QFGSM,* n.f. III (Münster, 1966), pp. 287–382.

Table 4.2   Occupations in the Confraternity B.M.V., Aegidii, ca. 1540–1618

Territorial Government:		Trades in the Gesamtgilde:	
chancellor	1	bakers	10
vice-chancellor	1	wine merchants	6
Hofrichter	1	goldsmiths	6
Rentmeister	2	clothiers	5
Gograf/Freigrafen	6	shopkeepers	5
Siegelkammer		smiths	5
(clerks, servants)	5	butchers	4
		tailors	2
City Government of Münster:		fullers	2
city councillors	12	furriers	1
clerks and		stonemasons	1
servants	9	glassmakers	1
		founders	1
Jurists:		coopers	1
doctors and			
licentiates	23	Trades not in Gesamtgilde:	
procurators	15	physicians	3
notaries	38	apothecaries	1
		printers	1
Clergy and Church Officials:		innkeepers	
clergymen	133	joiners	1
bailiffs	7		
sextons	1	Unspecified trades	8
		Unknown occupations	63
Others:			
nobles	4		
rentiers	1		

are clearly visible: the clergy were the most numerous (133), followed by the jurists, officials, and magistrates (113), while the merchants and artisans ran a distant third (65).

Among the clergy, almost all belonged to the ranks of the secular clergy. The illustrious list included two bishops and many canons of the cathedral chapter and the collegiate churches.[23] The most striking aspect in the pattern of occupational distribution among lay brothers was the preponderance of men in legal or official positions. With thirty-eight members, the notaries represented the single most numerous occupation in the confraternity; they were matched by the combined strength of the procurators and jurists with academic degrees. The majority of these men served in various governmental institutions, twenty-one primarily

23. The two bishops were Bernhard von Raesfeld and Christoph Bernhard von Galen, see Steinbicker, "Liebfrauen-Bruderschaft," p. 295.

in the courts of the territorial state. The group also included magistrates, of whom seven are listed in the table by their judicial-official ranks because of their much longer tenure of office in the territorial judiciary and bureaucracy. The traditional mercantile and artisanal trades were under-represented. Whereas the overall ratio of the number of guild craftsmen to jurists and officals in Münster was roughly five to one in 1600, the latter group outnumbered the former by almost two to one in the confraternity.[24]

The further breakdown of the trades demonstrates the greater strength of the wealthier guilds and the insignificant presence of the poorer crafts. All of the top seven guilds supplying the most confraternity brothers can be described as rich and powerful guilds. Many trades enjoyed close economic ties with the Catholic Church: the wine merchants found a ready market in the consumption of the ecclesiastical institutions and noble clerical lords; the goldsmiths and smiths benefited greatly from the many construction and artistic projects commissioned by the churches and cloisters. Also noteworthy is the strong representation of the food-processing trades. The fact that clothiers and shopkeepers were found in equal strength among both Catholics and Protestants argues against identifying confessional and occupational groupings in the merchant community too closely.

Families of the patrician and burgher elite show up frequently in the list of lay and clerical brothers. Many of the sixty-three brothers whose occupations have yet to be identified came from the burgher elite, whose ties to the Catholic Church were known to be close. While the patriciate was more strongly represented in the mid-sixteenth century, their withdrawal from city politics ceded preeminence within the confraternity to the burgher elite, the notability, who constituted the most important social sub-group around the turn of the century. Altogether 6 Holthauses, 5 Modersohns, 4 Dettens, 4 Vosses, 3 Münstermanns, 3 Vendts, 3 Fries, and 3 Mummes were represented.

To be sure, membership in the traditional Confraternity of Our Lady at Aegidii is an indication of Catholic piety. Nevertheless, specific support for Counter-Reformation militancy can be better measured by scrutinizing enrollment in the Jesuit sodalities. By the beginning of the Thirty Years' War, the Jesuits in Münster had already organized five sodalities; three of them comprised students at the college and the other two, one German- and one Latin-speaking, accepted burghers and resi-

---

24. In 1588, the Gesamtgilde presented 753 men for militia duty. Together with craftsmen not represented in guilds, the number of men engaged in a bourgeois trade in Münster could not have been less than 1,500. The number of notaries and jurists in Münster at the beginning of the seventeenth century has been estimated at about 300. See Krumbholtz, p. 120; and Hövel, *BB*, pp. 52ff.

dents as members.[25] The most important sodality was the Latin-speaking Sodalium Beatae Mariae Virginis Assumptionis.[26] Its statutes were confirmed by the general of the Society, Claudius Aquaviva, in 1610, when he imparted privileges and incorporated the Münster chapter into the arch-confraternity in Rome.[27] Membership of the sodality in Münster stood at about one hundred men; very few women joined the sodality until after the 1640s. Father Balthasar Höfflinger and other Jesuit patres served as spiritual advisers to the sodality, which included all of the leading clerical and lay supporters of the militant Counter-Reformation in Münster. Between 1614 and 1616, six magistrates belonged to the sodality: They were Bürgermeister Johann Herding, Hermann Heerde, Lic. Johann Alers, Dr. Heinrich Bockhorst, Dr. Heinrich Frie-Vendt, and Lic. Wilhelm Lageman.[28] Another, Christian Wedemhove, was the son of magistrate Johann Wedemhove.[29] The leading clerical supporters of the Counter-Reformation were also present: Dr. Johann Hartmann,[30] vicar-in-spiritualibus, was appointed by Archbishop Ferdinand to oversee the implementation of the Tridentine decrees in the Diocese of Münster; from the pen of Matthaeus Timpe, also a member, flowed voluminous tracts which fueled confessional passions; Johann van Detten, canon of the Old Cathedral, distinguished himself as one of the major native clergymen to support the Jesuits.

Almost two-thirds of the sodality brothers occupied positions in the

25. Cf. StAM, FM, SFG, "Comp. Hist. Coll.," fol. 65v.

26. The most important extant sources on the sodality are: (1) Protocol Book of the years 1614–16, "Liber Sodalitatis Civicae Monasteriensis, continens eius acta et administrationum ab anno 1614" (StAM, MSS. VII, 1034) and (2) Membership Roll for the seventeenth century, "Nahmenbuch der sonderlich zu Tothfällen vereinigten Sodalium Assumptae zu Münster in Collegio Paulino, S.J." (StAM, AVM, MS. 303). The first source is by far the more important one because it keeps a record of the activities of the sodality, including the role it played in city politics.

27. The document of confirmation is now deposited in the BDAM; see PfA Martini, Urk. 43.

28. Cf. StAM, MSS. VII, 1034, "Liber Sodalitatis," fols. 1, 15–15v; 1614, Jan. 19–26; 1615, Feb. 3 and 8. See also appendix 1, nos. 1, 19, 50, 60, 65, 85.

29. There were two Christian Wedemhoves at this time; one was the son of Johann, and the other was his nephew, son of Christian (+1595). The second Christian matriculated as notary in 1625 after having studied law in France and Italy; he must have been born around 1600 and hence was too young to belong to the Jesuit sodality in 1614. The other Christian, Johann's son, born in 1592, would have been the right age to join the sodality. He died in 1626. See Richtering, "Chronik Wedemhove," p. 143, n. 86, and p. 145, n. 108.

30. Johann Hartmann (1579?–1624), a native of Bonn, studied at the Collegium Germanicum and became canon in his native town in 1605. Called by Archbishop Ferdinand, he served as general vicar of the archbishop-elector in the Bishopric of Münster from 1613 to 1619. He later became a trusted councillor under the Archbishop Ferdinand. See H. Vogt, "Der Bonner Dechant Johannes Hartmann," *Bonner Geschichtsblätter,* vol. 18 (1964), pp. 45–53.

territorial state bureaucracy and the law courts; they served as judges, advocates, procurators, and notaries.[31] The most prominent ones were Dr. Christoph Clute (Cloet), learned councillor and assessor at the Ecclesiastical Court;[32] Lic. Arnold Tegeder,[33] assessor at the Chamber Court (*Weltlicher Hofgericht*); Dr. Theodor Niehaus, secretary of the sodality, procurator at the Ecclesiastical Court;[34] Dr. Johann Droste, syndic of the episcopal government;[35] and Dr. Johann Römer, prefect of the sodality in 1614, who was named episcopal judge by the archbishop in 1616.[36]

A handful of shopkeepers, clothiers, bookbinders, linenweavers, and church organists also appeared in the records of the sodality. Other brothers included students of theology at the Jesuit College, who were, by definition, the most senior students. Aside from the students, most brothers of the sodality were relatively young, with few over forty years old. Only one of the six magistrates mentioned above died before the 1630s.[37] Most of the notaries matriculated or registered with the Ecclesiastical Court in the first two decades of the seventeenth century, putting the years of their birth in the decades after 1570. In contrast to the identified Protestants, who were in their fifties and sixties in the first decade of the seventeenth century, these Jesuit supporters represented a younger group who belonged to the generations born in the 1570s and 1580s. In other words, these men came of age at the same time as the Jesuits consolidated their presence in Westphalia. Some may have been students at the college who later gave the Society their support as magistrates and officials in public life. Similar to the alliances discernible among the leading Protestant families, most of the prominent figures in the sodality were also linked by marriages; the connubial pattern, no doubt, was reinforced by intermarriages between families nurtured in the same judicial-academic milieu (see table 4.3).

Whereas some Protestant families in Münster had emigrated from

31. The conclusion is based on comparing the names mentioned in the protocol of the sodality and two published lists of notaries and procurators who served in the bishopric. The published lists are: Wilhelm Kohl, "Die Notariatsmatrikel des Fürstbistums Münster," and Josef Ketteler, "Katalog der münsterischen Notare und Prokuratoren," both in *Beiträge zur westfälischen Familienforschung* 20 (1962), pp. 3–163.

32. Cf. StAM, MSS. I, 38, "Bestallungsbuch der Bischöfe, 1590–1685," fols. 107v and 125; and appendix 1, no. 34.

33. Ibid., fol. 42.

34. Cf. Ketteler, "Katalog," p. 154.

35. Cf. StAM, MSS. I, 37, "Bestallungsbücher," fol. 127.

36. Cf. StAM, MSS. VII, 1034, "Liber Sodalitatis," fol. 22, 1616, Jan. 31. An older Dr. Johann Römer, probably the father of the man in question, had served as assessor in the Chamber Court and died in 1581. See StAM, MSS. I, 37, fol. 98; and his will, StdAM, B, Test. I, no. 687.

37. Lic. Wilhelm Lageman died sometime after 1624.

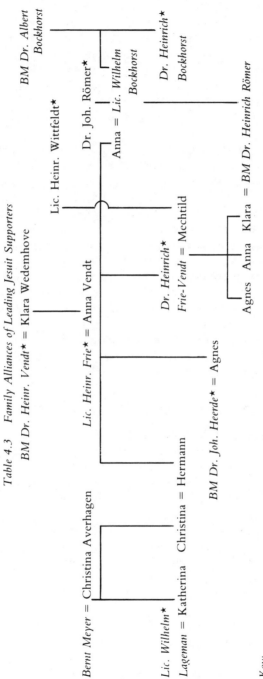

Table 4.3 Family Alliances of Leading Jesuit Supporters

Key:
★denotes membership in the sodality B.M.V. Assumptionis or donor to the Jesuit College
Italics denote membership on the city council

Burgsteinfurt, Bremen, Nuremberg, and the Netherlands, many of the sodality brothers had emigrated from the smaller towns in the bishopric. The notary Wilkuin Fustinck, who succeeded Dr. Johann Römer as prefect, was born in Dülmen and acquired Münster citizenship in 1613;[38] Wilhelm Lageman came to Münster from Ibbenbüren and became Bürger in 1610;[39] the linenweaver Heinrich tom Brinck emigrated from Havixbeck and swore Bürger oath in 1612;[40] Lic. Reinert Ketwich took citizenship in 1605;[41] and Dr. Johann Römer became a citizen only in 1610.[42]

The Protestants and the Catholic militants drew their strength from two distinct social groups. The crafts organized in the Gesamtgilde, especially the shopkeepers and the clothing trades, expressed the strongest sentiments for Protestantism. Unmistakable zealots in the cause of the Counter-Reformation and firm allies of the clergy in the restoration of orthodoxy were the officials, jurists, and notaries, most of whom served in the expanding judicial machinery of the territorial state. An important characteristic shared by the leaders of the Protestants and the militant Catholics was that overwhelmingly they were recent immigrants whose families had settled in Münster no more than two generations back. They were *homines novi* in another sense as well: many of them attained positions of honor within the guilds or on the city council only in their lifetime and did not benefit from the well-established familial prominence which the traditional civic elite enjoyed. What were the social milieux of these two opposing groups?

MERCANTILE AND JUDICIAL MÜNSTER

The major adherents of the Protestant and the militant Catholic parties belonged to two camps, two social milieux—the one traditional, mercantile, and artisanal and the other innovative, judicial, and official. Underlying the drama of confessional conflict and the formation of parties was the general transformation of the social structure and the function of the city of Münster in the half century after 1570. Fundamental to the process of change was the relative decline of the merchant community and the rise of a jurist-official class, a development which transformed the character of the burgher elite as well. Until the third quarter of the sixteenth century, the ruling elite in Münster came predominantly from mercantile families engaged in long-distance trade in cloth—a common

---

38. Cf. Ketteler, "Katalog," p. 147; Hövel, *BB*, p. 154, no. 2347.
39. See appendix 1, no. 85.
40. Cf. Hövel, *BB*, p. 151, no. 2289.
41. Cf. Hövel, *BB*, p. 127, no. 1781; his wife was Katherina Mennemann.
42. Cf. Hövel, *BB*, p. 141, no. 2070.

characteristic, in fact, of the political structure of most Hanseatic cities.[43] Both the patriciate and the burgher elite formed trading companies and partnerships, attended the *Hansatage* in Lübeck and the *Drittelstage* in Westphalian cities and in Cologne, set up businesses in the London Steelyard, in Antwerp, in Lübeck, and in the Baltic German ports.[44]

Although the Anabaptist revolt temporarily disrupted trade, commerce picked up soon after the traditional ruling elite regained power. Long-distance trade, primarily in the standard Hansa commodities of cloth and grain, flourished between the 1550s and 1570s. Several Münster merchants and magistrates formed companies and participated in the rapid expansion of the maritime commerce along the Atlantic seaboard, operating out of Antwerp, the richest city in northwestern Europe. In 1565, the patrician and magistrate Johann Grüter joined in the founding of a trading company based in Antwerp with over 10,000 dalers initial capital, handling cloth, linen, silk, damasks, satin, and wool.[45] Hillbrand Plönies, one of the richest merchants in Münster and a magistrate, went into partnership with his in-laws, Johann and Franz Brechte from Hamm, between the years 1567 and 1577; they marketed iron, steel, and armor produced by the mines and smitheries of the County of Mark.[46] The Bürgermeister Johann von der Berswordt traded with Flanders and England.[47] The magistrate Christoph Höfflinger was business partner with Borchard Heerde junior, a cousin of the Bürgermeister Hermann Heerde.[48] Many other families represented in the ruling elite were also leading merchant families; the Mennemanns, Münstermanns, Fries, Körlers, Langermanns, Oesedens, Roddes, Stöves, and Wedemhoves represented the most prominent of these mercantile-magisterial families.

When disagreement between estates and king flared into full-scale warfare in the Netherlands, the well-established patterns of trade were seriously disrupted. The pillage of Antwerp by unpaid, battle-worn, and

43. Cf. Philippe Dollinger, *Die Hanse* (Stuttgart, 1966; rev. German ed.), pp. 176ff.

44. Merchants from Münster who did business in the London Steelyard and represented their city in Hansa conferences during the sixteenth century included the patrician Bischopinck, Schenckinck, Droste, Grüter, and Boland, and the burgher Heerde, Plönies, Langermann, and Berswordt. See Eduard Schulte, "Eine Londoner Liste von Münsterschen Erbmännern," *QFGSM* IV (Münster, 1931), p. 335.

45. Cf. Helmut Lahrkamp, "Münsters wirtschaftliche Führungsschichten," *QFGSM* n.f. V (Münster, 1970), pp. 16ff.

46. Cf. Lahrkamp, "Führungsschichten," p. 18. For the development of mining, metallurgy, and urbanization in the County of Mark during the late medieval and early modern centuries, see Dieter Stievermann, *Städtewesen in Südwestfalen: Die Städte des Märkischen Sauerlandes im späten Mittelalter und in der frühen Neuzeit* (Stuttgart, 1978).

47. Cf. Lahrkamp, "Führungsschichten," pp. 26f.

48. Cf. Lahrkamp, "Führungsschichten," pp. 21, 28; see also the will of Borchard Heerde, StdAM, B, Test. I, no. 435.

murderous mercenaries in Spanish service in 1576 dealt the death blow to
that city's economic preeminence in northwestern Europe. At the same
time, competition between the English Merchant Adventurers and the
Hansa merchants and the erratic mercantilist policies of both the Empire
and England seriously undermined the well-established patterns of
trade.[49] Between the 1570s and the beginning of the seventeenth century,
merchants in Münster, as in all parts of the Empire, had to adjust to the
rapidly shifting patterns of trade in pursuit of substantial, albeit increasingly elusive and uncertain, profits. While Münster's trade with Cologne
and Lübeck continued to flourish, its traditionally strong ties with
Flanders, England, and the Hanseatic Baltic gradually disappeared. Amsterdam, Emden, and Hamburg rose to fill the gap left by the decline of
Antwerp and Lübeck and, in the scramble for opportunities, not everyone won.[50]

The second half of the sixteenth century saw the eclipse of many
trading companies, the most notable being the Fugger firm in Augsburg.
In Münster, judging from the estates described in the wills of several
merchants, such as that of Christoph Höfflinger, it appeared quite difficult for merchants to accumulate large profits from long-distance trade.[51]
In 1611, a Calvinist merchant named Höbbeling defaulted on loans
amounting to 23,000 dalers.[52] Clearly, the years after 1570 were hard
times for German long-distance trade, compared to the half century of
burgeoning growth between around 1470 and 1520. Many big merchants
lost interest in trade and turned to managing their landed estates, which

49. In spite of competition and armed conflict during the fifteenth century, the Merchant Adventurers represented not so much a threat as a nuisance to the Hansa, which still
dominated Baltic trade. After 1570, the rise of the Dutch Republic posed another threat to
the commerical domination of the Hansa, a position already undermined by the loss of
Hansa privileges in England. In 1597 Lübeck succeeded in persuading Emperor Rudolf II to
prohibit trade with the English; see Dollinger, *Hansa,* pp. 252–53, 391–401, 440–44. The
Imperial Edict was enforced by the city fathers of Münster; see StdAM, AII, 20, RP, 1598,
August 28, vol. 30, fols. 35–36.

50. Research in the past two decades has presented us with a clearer picture of the
economic conditions of northwestern Europe in the century of transition between 1550 and
1650. The notion of a general decline of the Hansa must be understood in conjunction with
the spectacular rise of Hamburg and Emden. Likewise, the decline in international trade
occurred in the context of the growth of regional markets in the Empire. On recent
literature on the German economy during this century of change, see Hermann Kellenbenz,
Deutsche Wirtschaftsgeschichte, vol. 1 (Munich, 1977), chap. 7. Kellenbenz's excellent treatment of trade and manufacture is complemented by the discussions of agriculture and social
change in the older volume edited by Hermann Aubin and Wolfgang Zorn, *Handbuch der
deutschen Wirtschafts- und Sozialgeschichte,* vol. 1 (Stuttgart, 1971). See also the new series
under the editorship of Kellenbenz which deals with the larger European context, *Handbuch
der europäischen Wirtschafts- und Sozialgeschichte,* vol. 3 (Stuttgart, 1980).

51. StAM, FM, SFG, II. Loc. 6, no. 37, fols. 101–103v.

52. Cf. StAM, FM, SFG, "Comp. Hist. Coll.," fol. 55v.

they had acquired, following earlier merchant practice, as protection for their mercantile profits. The laments of the clothier Johann Wedemhove probably echoed the sentiments of many.[53]

> Alas! Fortune has not smiled on me, although I have neither neglected opportunities nor have I sold out my inventories. It is daily experience which has made me aware that our times are no longer the same as in years past, and now there is a different, deceitful, and false world, one in which no trust exists between men. Thus, we have given up trade and are now taking up sowing and planting; and may God bless us well at all times with good harvest and healthy beasts.

Things were only slightly better for the merchants of middling rank. Without extensive trans-regional and international business associates, the shopkeepers in Münster usually operated in an economic region of limited radius, seldom beyond the confines of Westphalia and the neighboring Netherlands and Rhineland.[54] Protected from external competition by their guild, the shopkeepers, nevertheless, began to feel the adverse effect of the Dutch-Spanish warfare when the conflict spread to the Westphalian bishopric in the 1580s. The roads from the Rhineland to Münster were so unsafe that the papal nuncio in Cologne, Johann Franz Bonomi, broke off his journey from Cologne to Münster in the spring of 1585.[55] In 1589, Dutch troops overran the Greven Fair, the largest in the region; Münsteraners suffered a loss of more than 30,000 dalers, of which the bulk was borne by the shopkeepers.[56] The next year, five shopkeepers, including the Protestants Johann Uding and Heinrich Forckenbeck, petitioned the city council for compensation of monetary losses amounting to 1,476 dalers, which they had sustained due to the quartering of Spanish troops in the bishopric.[57]

Except for the food-processing trades, which benefited from the rapid rise in grain prices, the other crafts tightened ranks and tried to exclude newcomers and outside competition by exerting political pressure on the

53. Quoted from Richtering, "Chronik Wedemhove," p. 147.

54. The best overview of merchants and merchant life in the sixteenth century is Pierre Jeannin's, *Les Marchands au XVIe siècle* (Paris, 1969). He divides merchants into three main categories—the aristocrats of capital, such as the Fuggers, the businessmen or merchants of international trade, and the small merchants. The clothiers of Münster would fall into the second category, and the shopkeepers into the third.

55. See *Nuntiaturberichte aus Deutschland 1585–90. 1. Abt. Die Kölner Nuntiatur. 1. Hälfte* (Paderborn, 1895), ed. Stephan Ehses and Aloys Meister, pp. 75ff., letter of Bonomi to Cardinal Como, dated May 11, 1585. Bonomi was on a mission to persuade the Münster cathedral chapter to elect Archbishop Ernst of Cologne as the diocese's next bishop.

56. For details of the Dutch raid on Greven, see Röchell, *Chronik,* pp. 104–07. The shopkeepers lost 11,916 dalers' worth of goods; their loss was followed by the 4,750 dalers lost by the clothiers and the 1,600 dalers lost by the fullers.

57. Cf. StdAM, AXIV, 66, letter of petition.

city council. The clothing trades, where Protestant sentiments ran high, were especially hard pressed. Manufacturing and marketing the traditional, heavier draperies, the well-established clothing guilds faced unfavorable competition from the new, lighter, cheaper, and hence more popular, linen fabrics. The majority of linenweavers received wages; many did not belong to a guild; and a great deal of production went on in the rural areas, where the absence of rigid guild rules facilitated production and the application of the putting-out system.[58] It became commonplace in most of the older guilds to fill the overwhelming majority of positions with sons of masters and raise barriers for outsiders who wanted to join their guilds. The overall mood among the guilds was one of defensiveness, of suspicion of economic and religious novelties, and of stubborn efforts in city politics to ensure the retention of their economic and political privileges.[59]

While the defense of civic liberties and religious toleration fell upon the shoulders of merchants and artisans upholding the traditional economy against adverse tides, their opponents—the officials, jurists, and notaries—embodied the new force of the Counter-Reformation territorial state. The first Münster bishop who attempted to implement diocesan reforms was also the first prince to expand the territorial bureaucracy. Under Bishop Johann von Hoya (1567–74), a legal humanist himself, the chancery was expanded, the privy council institutionalized, the financial administration streamlined, and the courts reorganized. Both the Ecclesiastical Court (*Offizialat, Geistlicher Hofgericht*) and the newly created Chamber Court (*Weltlicher Hofgericht*), the highest secular judicial instance in the bishopric,[60] were located in Münster. The expansion of government, the introduction of Roman law, and the increased litigation associated with the canon law court created a great demand for academically trained lawyers. To facilitate political centralization, the provenance of the traditional common-law courts in the small towns and countryside (*Gogerichte*) was reduced, and the Chamber Court became the highest court of

58. On the importance of linen weaving in Westphalia, see Dollinger, *Hanse,* p. 299; Hermann Kellenbenz, *The Rise of the European Economy: An Economic History of Continental Europe from the Fifteenth to the Eighteenth Century,* revised and edited by Gerhard Benecke (London, 1976), p. 120; and Hermann Rothert, *Westfälische Geschichte. Bd. II. Das Zeitalter der Glaubenskämpfe* (Gütersloh, 1964), pp. 203–07.

59. Cf. Krumbholtz, pp. 223* ff.

60. Until 1567, the prince-bishops of Münster ruled with the assistance of an informal group of advisers and the territorial estates. Under Bishop Johann, the Chamber Court and the Finance Chamber (*Rechenkammer*) were created. An institutionalized Privy Council took on definite form after 1574; it comprised two noblemen, two canons of the cathedral, one chancellor, and two learned councillors. See Reinhard Lüdicke, "Die landesherrlichen Zentralbehörden im Bistum Münster. Ihre Entstehung und Entwicklung bis 1650," *WZ* 59 (1901), pp. 1–169; esp. 113–15.

appeals in the land. Although the magistrates in Münster and in the larger Westphalian towns claimed judicial autonomy, clinging to the traditional common-law courts in their cities, the newly expanded terri- torial judiciary provided both an alternative channel for litigants and employment for ambitious Münster burghers.

Even Münster could not remain isolated from the larger legal reforms which had been shaping the Empire since the beginning of the sixteenth century.[61] Involved in litigation at the Imperial Cameral Court (*Reichskam- mergericht*) and represented in the territorial estates, the Hansa Diets, and the Westphalian Circle Diets, the city needed jurists with academic de- grees to serve as advocates and diplomats.[62] After 1555, five of the twelve Bürgermeisters had university degrees in law; whereas only one magis- trate had a law degree in 1565, seven out of twenty-four magistrates had law degrees in 1618.

Obviously, the increasing importance of jurists in the magistracy re- flected the overall esteem for men with academic training. The trend also reveals the transformation of Münster's ruling elite from a mercantile- burgher class into an academic-jurist class that served in the law courts while maintaining its hold on civic power.[63] A number of magistrates enjoyed dual careers, moving between the bureaucracies and the city council: Bürgermeisters Lic. Albert Mumme, Willbrandt Plönies, Jo- hann v. d. Berswordt, Dr. Hermann Heerde, Dr. Heinrich Vendt, and the councillors Lic. Albert Bockhorst and Lic. Heinrich Frie served vari- ously as privy councillors, and assessors and procurators at the courts.[64]

61. Precocious in the reception of Roman law and in the building of the state bureau- cracy, Bavaria carried out legal reforms between 1500 and 1520. The new class of officials was partially recruited from the ruling elite of the cities who had invested in a legal education for their sons. See Heinz Lieberich, "Die gelehrten Räte. Staat und Juristen in Baiern in der Frühzeit der Rezeption," *ZfBLG* 27 (1964), pp. 120–89. On the growing importance of lawyers in Germany, see Georg Dahm, "Zur Rezeption des Römisch- italienischen Rechtes," *HZ* 167 (1943), pp. 229–58.

62. Between 1549 and 1618, eight Münsteraners matriculated as notaries at the Impe- rial Cameral Court; see Helmut Lahrkamp, "Münsterische Reichskammergerichtsnotare 1549/1651," *QFGSM*, n.f. V (Münster, 1970), pp. 263–70.

63. This point is made by Helmut Lahrkamp; see his "Das Patriziat in Münster," in Rössler, *Deutsches Patriziat,* pp. 202–03. The ambivalence of the burgher elite between civic magisterial office and service in the law courts has been pointed out by Clemens Stein- bicker, who argues that appointments in the territorial bureaucracy remained unattractive to the patriciate and the burgher elite before 1660; see his "Das Beamtentum in den geistli- chen Fürstentümern Norddeutschlands im Zeitraum von 1430–1740," in Günther Franz, ed., *Beamtentum und Pfarrstand 1400–1800* (Limburg, 1972), pp. 138–40. In light of the evidence presented here, it seems that Steinbicker's assertion needs to be modified.

64. Cf. Lüdicke, "Zentralbehörden," pp. 117, 133, 140–41; StdAM, AII, 20, RP, 1589, Aug. 21, fol. 39; StAM, MSS. I, 37, "Bestallungsbücher," fols. 108–09. An interest- ing parallel was the development in Protestant Lippe. The consolidation of the territorial government attracted members of the ruling families in Lutheran Lemgo to state service;

Two examples should suffice to illustrate the transformation of the mercantile burgher elite into an academic-jurist class. When the merchant and magistrate Christoph Höfflinger died in 1599, none of his three sons succeeded him in business: one became canon of the cathedral in Lübeck, another entered the Society of Jesus, and the third served as *Landrentmeister,* the highest financial official of the state.[65] Another example was the Wedemhove family. From the late fifteenth to the end of the sixteenth century, three generations of Wedemhoves were engaged in long-distance trade as clothiers. The men appeared as guild Aldermen and magistrates; the women married Plönies, Oesedens, Vendts, Dettens, and Huges, all magisterial or mercantile families. By the end of the sixteenth century, the new strategy to maintain the social prominence of the family was to shift connubial alliances away from the mercantile to the official-jurist families.[66] Johann Wedemhove, whom we have encountered as the disillusioned merchant, had eight siblings; Johann himself married Elizabeth Erkelenz, daughter of Vitus Erkelenz, protonotary of the Chamber Court, who had previously served as lawyer in the Imperial Cameral Court in Speyer and secretary of the chancery of the Münster Bishopric.[67] Two other sisters also married jurists.[68] The metamorphosis was completed during the next generation, when most Wedemhove men became judges, lawyers, and clergymen. Other families of the burgher elite were also undergoing a similar transformation. By the early seventeenth century, the Heerdes and the Plönies, the two most prominent families in the burgher elite, had abandoned trade and were sending sons exclusively to the Church and to the civic government. Leading guild families who were not represented in the ruling circles also experienced a comparable change in the course of their upward social mobility: the Timmerscheids and the Forckenbecks gained access to the center of civic power in the middle of the seventeenth century by providing legal education for sons of the family.[69]

---

when Count Simon VI converted to Calvinism at the beginning of the seventeenth century, many of these burgher officials became zealous Calvinists and advocated strong measures against their recalcitrant Lutheran home town. See Heinz Schilling, *Konfessionskonflikt und Staatsbildung. Eine Fallstudie über das Verhältnis von religiösem und sozialem Wandel in der Frühneuzeit am Beispiel der Grafschaft Lippe* (Gütersloh, 1981), pp. 266–71.

65. Cf. his will, StdAM, B, Test. I, no. 113; and the settlement between the brothers, papers deposited in StAM, FM, SFG, II. Loc. 6, fols. 95–100.

66. Cf. Richtering, "Chronik Wedemhove," pp. 133f.

67. Ibid., p. 139, n. 54.

68. Clara married Anton Hontemb, assessor at the Ecclesiastical Court and later syndic of the cathedral chapter; Katherina's husband, Gerhard Kronenberg, was respectively assessor at the Ecclesiastical and Chamber Courts; ibid., p. 140, n. 63; p. 141, n. 68.

69. For the Timmerscheids, see Clemens Steinbicker, "Vom Geschlechterkreis der münsterischen Rats- und Bürgermeistersfamilie Timmerscheidt. Ein Beitrag zur Geschichte des münsterischen Honoratiorentums des 17. Jahrhunderts," *WZ* 111 (1961), pp.

Naturally, this avenue of social advancement was not open to all; long years of university education entailed great financial sacrifices for all but a few rich families. But the many positions created by the courts created opportunities for Münsteraners across the social spectrum, provided that they adhered to the correct religion. After 1597, the profession of Catholic faith was required of all candidates before their appointments to the law courts; and in the decades thereafter, the territorial bureaucracy remained loyal to the Roman Church.[70] Below the top ranks in the chancery and courts, many clerks were needed to ensure the smooth functioning of the bureaucratic and judicial machinery. Under the chancellor, judges, and assessors served the procurators and the proto-notaries, who prepared cases, collected legal data, and waited in the wings for promotion. Further down the bureaucratic ladder a host of notaries kept minutes of the court proceedings, transcribed and summarized long legal briefs, drew up business and marriage contracts, and wrote out and certified last testaments. They found employment not only in the state judiciary but also in the municipal government and in independent service.[71] Since a little knowledge of Latin was sufficient for the performance of the notary's normal tasks, the majority of notaries had little or no university education at all. They were recruited from families representing a great diversity of occupations. A considerable number grew up and succeeded their fathers in the scribal occupation. Many originated from the small towns of the bishopric where one generation back their families might have been artisans. The shift from the handicrafts to the judicial-clerical world and the move from the small towns to the capital city of Münster represented for many notaries parallel tracks in the journey of upward mobility.[72]

Needless to say, within the juristic occupations existed a clear-cut pecking order. True, it would be misleading to exaggerate the degree of

---

95–117. The Forckenbecks have not been the subject of definitive genealogical research. They probably came from Deventer and some members of the family were identified as Protestants. The first of the Münster Forckenbecks seemed to have been Aleff, whose two sons, Erasmus and Heinrich, were enrolled in the shopkeepers' guild. Erasmus's son Bert studied in Marburg and Basel, received his doctorate in law, and later became magistrate and Bürgermeister, apparently after having converted to Catholicism. See Ketteler, "Vom Geschlechterkreis," p. 423; Hövel, *BB*, p. 117, no. 1479; p. 192, no. 3133.

70. The episcopal edict stipulating the profession of faith as a condition for appointments in the courts came after the controversy surrounding the burial of Lic. Dietrich Seveker, procurator at the Chamber Court, who refused to communicate in the Catholic rite before his death. See Röchell, *Chronik,* p. 129.

71. Cf. Hövel, *BB*, pp. 52–54; and Franz-Ludwig Knemeyer, "Das Notariat im Fürstbistum Münster," *WZ* 114 (1964), pp. 1–142.

72. The place of origin is given in many cases in the rolls of notarial matriculation; see Kohl, "Notariatsmatrikel"; and Ketteler, "Katalog."

upward social mobility provided by the expansion of the territorial bureaucracy, nor can we speak of a massive desertion of the mercantile and
handicraft trades, but there was a clear and gradual shift of resources
away from the productive sectors of society to the administrative sectors,
and a corresponding adjustment of all social classes, especially among the
burgher elite, was clearly discernible. The unmistakable change in the
social prestige of various occupations went hand in hand with the emphasis of religio-political goals over the pursuit of wealth. In a tract
soliciting funds to turn the Münster Jesuit College into an university,
Matthaeus Timpe contended that such an academy would enable children from poorer families to continue their studies, "otherwise they
would be separated from [their studies] and bound to a sordid, unfree, or
unclean handicraft."[73]

While most of the trades were stagnating, except for the lowly occupation of linen weaving,[74] the proportion of inhabitants in Münster associated with the academic and judicial circles rapidly increased. After the
linenweavers, the notaries ranked second in the number of new citizens
sworn in during the first third of the seventeenth century. There were
over three hundred jurists and notaries in Münster at the beginning of the
seventeenth century; litigation and linen weaving represented the two
fastest growing sectors of the city's economy.[75] To the notaries and
jurists must be added the thousand students at the Jesuit College and the
more than five hundred clergymen, church officials and servants. Together with family dependents, these obviously strong supporters of the
Counter-Reformation comprised roughly one-third of Münster's population around 1600.

The world of academics, the Church, and the law courts was separated
from the world of the markets, the workshops, and the guildhalls by
mutual dislike. Aside from the common disrespect between men who
worked with their heads and those who worked with their hands, the
cultural separation between the two worlds was reinforced by the traditional anti-clericalism of the artisans and the social ideology of the guilds.

73. Matthaeus Timpius, *Erhebliche unnd wichtige Ursachen/warumb weise unnd fürsichtige
Leuth/ auss gottseligem eiffer/bey sich beschlossen haben/von dem so Gott ihnen gnadiglich verliehen/
hülff zu thun/dass man in der wollöblichen Statt Münster/welche die Hauptstatt ist inn Westphalen
oder alten Saxen/ anfange eine hochberühmbte Universitet oder Academiam zu fundieren unnd zu
stifften: unnd warumb billich alle Vaterlands liebende hertzen zu solchem hochpreisslichen Werck
unnd frewdenreichen anfang behülfflich seyn sollen* (Münster: Lambert Raesfeldt, 1612), sig. C1.

74. After many years of petition, in 1613 the city council finally approved the linenweavers' appeal that they be allowed to form a corporation. The linenweavers formed a
fraternity, not a formal guild, and were supervised by overseers appointed by the city
council. The statutes of the corporation, drawn up by the magistrates, stipulated that
illegitimate children could also enter the craft. See Krumbholtz, pp. 298ff.

75. Cf. Hövel, *BB,* pp. 50ff.

Central to the self-image of the guild merchants and artisans was the notion of honor (*Ehrlichkeit*). It informed business transactions wherein fairness outweighted greed and the common good (*Gemein Nutz*) took precedence over individual profit; a sense of honor also governed the social intercourse of the guildsmen. Medieval guilds were much more than mere occupational unions and represented integrated religio-cultural-economic microcosms which regulated relations of guildsmen with the larger urban community. All of the pre-1535 guilds in Münster required members to be of "honorable birth": excluded were children born out of wedlock, clerical offspring, and "dishonorable sorts" such as millers, linenweavers, musicians, actors, gravediggers, executioners, and many others.[76] The stigma of dishonorable birth, passed down from one generation to another, could haunt families who had already attained some measure of social success. Lic. Wilhelm Rick and Bernd Huge the Older, who were elected to the city council in January 1595, were at first barred from taking office because their wives descended from clerical concubinages.[77] Excluded from the practice of a handicraft or trade because of illegitimate birth, offspring of the clergy and the bastards of noble or patrician lineages usually entered the priesthood, served in the territorial administration,[78] or pursued a legal-notarial career,[79] or, in the cases of bastards descended from burghers or peasants, learned trades that were not incorporated or did not bar their entry. Here, the more important distinction was progeny and class, not illegitimacy; officials and jurists did not hesitate to marry bastards of the nobility and the patriciate, either clerical or lay.[80] The notion of guild honor persisted into the eighteenth century even as the social prestige and the political power of the guilds gradually declined in the course of the seventeenth century.[81]

76. For an excellent study of social outcasts in medieval and early modern Germany, see Werner Danckert, *Uneheliche Leute. Die verfemten Berufe* (Bern, 1963); for the discrimination by guildsmen against the "dishonorable peoples" in Münster, see Helmut Lahrkamp, ed., *Die Geburtsbriefe der Stadt Münster 1548–1809* (= *QFGSM*, n.f. IV; Münster, 1968), pp. 16–17 and birth certificates nos. 19, 21, 30–32, 40, 41, 43, 44, 46, 53, 54, 56, 174, 192.

77. Cf. StdAM, AII, 20, RP, Jan. 30, Feb. 3 and 13; vol. 27, fols. 4–4v, 5v–7v, 10–11.

78. Cf. Steinbicker, "Beamtentum," p. 137.

79. Cf. Knemeyer, "Notariat," pp. 122f.

80. Cf. Günther Aders, "Der Domdechant Arnold von Büren (+ 1614) und seine Nachkommen. Zugleich ein Beitrag zur Verfassungsgeschichte der Zünfte in Münster," *Westfalen* 40 (1962), pp. 123–32; see also Steinbicker, "Beamtentum," p. 132.

81. See the Imperial Ordinance concerning the abolition of abuses in the handicraft guilds, promulgated in 1731. One of the abuses was the multiple birth certificates demanded by master artisans to ascertain without doubt the honorable family background of prospective apprentices. The ordinance is published in Michael Stürmer, ed., *Herbst des Alten Handwerks. Zur Sozialgeschichte des 18. Jahrhunderts* (Munich, 1979), pp. 54ff.

There existed, therefore, two alliances in Münster. The mutual dislike
between the legal profession and the guilds was superimposed upon the
obvious opposition between Protestants and militant Catholics. It is important, however, to remember that the two clusters of opposing groups
did not completely overlap, and that the conflicts between the Gesamtgilde and the territorial officialdom were complicated by differences between traditional Catholics, Münsteraners with deep roots in the city
who valued the religion of their fathers, and the militant Catholics, often
recent immigrants, who saw the same faith with rather different eyes. In
spite of intermarriages, the officials and the burgher elite remained distinct social groups, and although they both supported the religious goals
of the Catholic Reformation, they took rather different views of the
political aspects of the Counter-Reformation. We shall deal with the
complicated relations between Protestants, traditional Catholics, and the
militants in another chapter. Let us now look into the ideology of the
Counter-Reformation militants.

THE IDEOLOGY OF THE COUNTER-REFORMATION

In his discourse on ways to revive the glory of the Holy Roman Empire,
Matthaeus Timpe compared the fate of Germany to that of Byzantium:
the latter was conquered by the Turks because it fell away from Rome;
similarly, the Empire, by tolerating Lutherans and Calvinists, incurred
the wrath of God and invited a repetition of Constantinople's tragedy.
Timpe blamed the Lutherans for undermining the war against the Turks
and accused Protestants as instigators of all bloody uprisings.[82] Although
far removed from the war-ravaged Hungarian plains, Münsteraners were
nevertheless deeply conscious of the Turkish menace.

From the late fifteenth century onward, a flood of pamphlets, proph-
ecies, and sermons describing and interpreting the Turkish threat struck
terror in the hearts of most German burghers.[83] Throughout the sixteenth century, Münsteraners witnessed many living proofs of the Turkish scourge as beggars periodically passed through the city, some crippled and disfigured, telling horror tales of former captivity or lamenting
the fate of missing relatives, presumably victims of Turkish cruelty.

---

82. *Ernewerte Welt/das ist: Heylsamer rath das H. Römisch Reich/ja das gantze H. Christen-
thumb/zu vorigen reichthumben/gewalt/zier/unnd wolstandt widerumb zu bringen. Auss H. Biblis-
chen Schrift/hochgelehrten Theologen/unnd dess H. Römischen Reichs Ordnungen/Satzungen unnd
Abschieden/dem alten Christenthumb fürnemblich Teutschen Nation zu ehren/auffnemmen unnd
gedeyen zusammen getragen* (Münster: Lambert Raesfeld, 1610), sig. A2–A5v. Hereafter cited
as *Ernewerte Welt*.

83. See Winfried Schulze, *Reich und Türkengefahr im späten 16. Jahrhundert* (Munich,
1978), pp. 21ff.

It did not matter whether some wandering beggars were telling tall tales to win sympathy and alms, as long as others believed them. The city fathers never refused alms to these wretched creatures, as the entries in the Gruetamt account books well document.[84] Through heightened awareness of the Turkish threat, Münster felt the rekindled sense of solidarity in Christendom. After the Spanish-Venetian fleet crushed the Ottomans at Lepanto (1571), the Münster city fathers ordered seven preachers to give thanks to the Lord, and to "remind the commonfolk that God Almighty had delivered the Turks into the hands of Christians."[85] In 1591, after nearly half a century of quiet, the Turks started a new offensive in central Europe which was to last until the conclusion of an armistice in 1606. The war engendered a new crusading spirit, especially in the Catholic lands of the Empire, and greater support for the Imperial Hapsburgs.[86] Emperor Rudolf's victory in 1593 was celebrated in Münster with the ringing of all church bells and magnificent processions rendering thanks to the Lord.[87] The Turkish threat was also a favorite theme in Jesuit and Baroque sermons; the brothers in the Jesuit sodalium B.M.V. Assumptionis were exhorted to defend the Imperial-Catholic cause against the Ottoman infidels.[88] A few young men actually left Münster for the front, their crusading spirit attested to by wills drawn up prior to their departures.[89]

Not only did the Counter-Reformation inspire support for the Empire, it conjured up a new missionary spirit which helped to expand the terrestial confines of the Catholic Church. While Dutch and English voyages of exploration were undertaken by merchants and adventurers in search of profits and loot, the missionary motive formed a central theme in the overseas expansion of the Iberian Peninsula.[90] The Society of Jesus participated actively in the endeavors of the Spanish and Portuguese crowns; and the patres sailed with officials and conquistadores to

84. Between 1561 and 1600, some eighty former Turkish slaves and prisoners passed through Münster, according to Helmut Lahrkamp's compilations from the entries of the account books of the Gruetamt. See his "Rückwirkungen der Türkenkriege auf Münster 1560–1685," *WZ* 129 (1979), p. 91. See also the older work by Georg Schreiber, "Deutsche Türkennot und Westfalen," *WF* 7 (1953–54), pp. 62–79, which deals more with the financial aspects of the Turkish levies.

85. StdAM, A VIII, 188, GR, vol. 7, fol. 142.

86. See Robert J. W. Evans, *Rudolf II and His World* (Oxford, 1973), pp. 24, 75–76.

87. On January 23, 1594, all church bells rang in Münster to celebrate the Imperial victory. See Röchell, *Chronik,* pp. 121, 123.

88. Cf. StAM, MSS. VII, 1034, "Liber Sodalitatis," fol. 3, 1614, March 9.

89. See the wills of Conrad Tzwyvel, son of the printer Dietrich, and Johann Mennemann; StdAM, B, Test. I, no. 302 (1596) and Test. II, no. 1679 (1624).

90. See Charles R. Boxer, *The Church Militant and Iberian Expansion, 1440–1770* (Baltimore, 1978).

the far shores of the Americas, Africa, and Asia. Through the *Litterae Annuae* and through Jesuit plays and sermons, Catholic Europe followed the activities of Francis Xavier and rejoiced in the conversion of the Japanese. After the canonization of Ignatius and Xavier, the two Jesuits became favorite saints of the militant Catholics and patrons of the further expansion of the Catholic cause in the Empire as well. When the Tokugawa government in Japan expelled foreign missionaries and started to root out native Christians in 1613, after sixteen years of sporadic persecutions, the news even reached remote Münster, and fervent militants in the sodalities prayed for the deliverance of their coreligionists halfway around the world.[91]

One word summarizes the mood of the Catholic world in the opening years of the seventeenth century—triumphant.[92] The Turks were checked, Protestantism was rolled back, new lands were won, and the Catholic princes in Germany had found a common front in the Catholic League. Political centralization, especially in lands under the Wittelsbachs and the Austrian Hapsburgs, facilitated the advance of the Counter-Reformation: the one pushed forward like a plow, breaking new ground, the other followed like a peasant, sowing seeds of the "true faith."

Uniformity, unity, and universality characterized the world view of the Counter-Reformation, which saw human events in terms of universal truths rather than as individual acts influenced by historical circumstances. Carried forward by the political might of Catholic princes and the spiritual rigor of the Society of Jesus, the Counter-Reformation in Germany represented a new and dynamic movement, one which attracted the young, to whom Protestantism was an aberration of their parents' generation. How did Catholic militants understand the social order? Matthaeus Timpe's voluminous writings, which were very influential in Münster, provide us with a picture of the mental world of the Catholic militants.[93] The multifarious themes presented in his works fall

91. Cf. StAM, MSS. VII, 1034, "Liber Sodalitatis," fol. 22v. The entry under April 10, 1616, reads: "Orationis punctum: pro Romano Imperio et Japonia."

92. Cf. Leonhard Intorp, *Westfälische Barockpredigten in volkskundlichen Sicht* (Münster, 1964), p. 30: "Die prunckvoll ausgestattete Fronleichnamsprozession übernahm weitgehend die Rolle der fürstlichen Einzüge der Renaissance, nun das religiöse Triumphgefühl real zu gestatten. Es wertete sich vor allem zu einer machtvollen demonstratio catholica aus, wenn ein neuer Sieg über die Türken errungen war."

93. Timpe was born in Lette, a little town in Münsterland south of Coesfeld, where his father served as pastor. He studied in Münster and at the university in Cologne, after which he taught in various schools, the longest tenure being in Osnabrück at the Gymnasium Carolinum. Called to Münster to head the Collegium Dettensiam, a private foundation attached to the Jesuit College, Timpe continued his polemics against the Protestants. The article by Paul Bahlmann in *ADB* 39, pp. 53–55, is based only on autobiographical

under three headings: the reassertion of sacerdotal authority over the laity, the reordering of the body politic and social, and finally, the confessional interpretation of history.

The first theme in his writings is the restating of clerical authority. Essential to the success of the Catholic Reformation was a morally irreproachable clergy. "If the clergy had integrity," he writes, "the whole Church would flourish; if, however, they were corrupt, the faith of all would wither away."[94] In the same tract, *The Mirror of Clerics,* Timpe lists two hundred signs of the good cleric compiled after diligent reading of the lives of past great churchmen. A good cleric should "flee adultery" (sign 2), "collect a library" (sign 11), "convert infidels" (sign 51), "love eloquence" (sign 70), "be prepared to die for the Catholic Faith" (sign 71), "abhor heretical books and gatherings" (sign 87), and "inveigh harshly against heretics" (sign 90). Chosen by God to be shepherds, the clergy "must preach His Word, punish sins, and exhort his flock to do all sorts of good deeds," writes Timpe in another tract.[95] Perhaps the most distinguished sign of the new Counter-Reformation clergy was sexual abstinence; celibacy and chastity differentiated the clerics from the larger Catholic community, endowing the former with an inherent moral authority. Timpe elevated celibacy to a virtue with mystical qualities and praised virginity in twenty-six sermons which expound on the blessings associated with the virtue.[96] He claimed that chastity was the loftiest merit a Christian could achieve because it inevitably led to the religious life. In a collection of seventy-two funeral orations and Lenten sermons, Timpe associated a theological theme with an occupation or a stage in

---

information in Timpe's numerous writings; the wills of his mother and sister (StAM, FM, SFG, III. Loc. 1) provide new biographical information on this important figure of the Counter-Reformation in Münster. The following folios are especially useful in the three volumes of papers—vol. 1, fols. 1–2 (will of his father); fol. 25 (will of his mother); fols. 5–6v, 12–13, 15–19 (information on his brothers and sister, Johann, Albert, Wennemann, Bernt, and Catherine).

 94. *Speculum Magnum episcoporum, canonicorum, sacerdotum et aliorum Clericorum omnium tam Secularium quam Religiosorum, ex admirandis pontificum, episcoporum, sacerdotum, aliorumque Ecclesiasticorum dictis et factis in gratiam Concionatorum et eloquentiae Studiosorum per locos communes iuxta Alphabeti seriem digestis* (Mainz: Lambert Raesfeld, 1614), p. 1.

 95. *Sehr nothwendigen Reguln dess Lebens/ in welchen ein jeglicher Christ/ wess Standts oder Würden er ist/ als in einem Spiegel erlernen kan/ wie er sich nach Gottes Wort/ in seinem Ampt unnd Beruff unverweisslich verhalten soll* (Münster: Bernhard Raesfeld, 1649), p. 195. The *Amtspiegel* was published together with his collections of New Year sermons.

 96. *Lustgarten der Jungfrauwen/ oder: sechs und zwenzig Paradiessgärtlin und Predigten/ von grossen Wirde/ Schönheit/ und nutzbarkeit der Jungfrauwschaft von vielen mitteln dieses unvergleichliches Perlin unverletzt zubewahren/ und sich wider das unverschambte Laster der unzucht zubewapnen, von den fürnembsten Tugenten mit welchen sich die Jungfrauwen aussbutzen müssen, und endtlich von vielen fürtrefflichen gaben und gnaden dess geistlichen Ordenstands* (Münster: Lambert Raesfeld, 1611).

life. Whereas the death of a poor man brings to mind the misery of life and that of a nobleman occasions a diatribe against false, courtly ways, the passing of a monk, priest, or nun is invariably associated with the reward of heaven.[97]

In the reordering of the social and political orders, the clergy occupied the apex in the Catholic world order. The tripartite division of society into clerics, temporal authorities, and subjects (*Untertanen*), which Timpe spelled out in a sermon entitled "The Mirror of Office," gave precedence to the clerics. The ideal Christian ruler was to be a pious man who exercised his God-ordained authority with wisdom and humility. The rest of society, lumped together as "subjects", were told to obey authorities and not rebel against the divine order.[98] Those who disrupted the harmonious social order, either by serving as mercenaries or by engaging in trade, got no kind words from Timpe. Likewise, he showed hostility and intolerance toward groups which had, according to him, no rightful place in Catholic society—Protestants and Jews. Since the family constituted the basic unit in society, Timpe lavished much attention on the proper ordering of relations within the household. He composed a handbook for parents concerning the proper upbringing of children in the love and fear of God[99] and preached on the duties of the sacraments of marriage. Catholics, he warned, should not marry moneylenders, heathens, or heretics.[100]

Society could not be reordered without the proper performance of ceremonies. The explication and defense of the seven sacraments implied more than a theological exercise; they formed the foundation of the new Counter-Reformation edifice. Timpe described the sacraments in great detail, elucidating the meaning behind every single gesture.[101] Some of the explanations were rather imaginative, such as the ones on confession:

97. *Leich- Trost- und Busspredigten auch Anweisung wie dieselbigen in Auslegung Sonn- und Freyrtag- Evangelien gebraucht werden konnen . . .* (Münster: Lambert Raesfeld, 1613).

98. *Amtspiegel,* pp. 196ff.

99. *Kinderzucht/ oder Kürtzer Bericht von der Eltern sorg unnd fürsichtigkeit in aufferziehung unnd unterrichtung ihrer Kinder* (Münster: Lambert Raesfeld, 1597).

100. *Spiegel der Eheleuth/ oder Kürtzer Bericht/ wie die Prediger nicht allein in ihren Braut- und hochzeitlichen/ sondern auch andern Predigen die Eheleut von ihrem Ampt und schuldiger Pflicht/ oder wie ihr Standt nach Gottes Ordnung/ Willen und Befehl anzufangen/ und in guten Frieden Ruhe/ und Einigkeit/ zuhalten sey/ underweisen sollen* (Münster: Bernhard Raesfeld, 1632), pp. 15–22.

101. *Der Ceremonien warumb/ das ist Lautere unnd klare ursachen unnd ausslegungen der fürnemmsten Ceremonien/ welche auss einsprechung des H. Geists bey dem H. Gottesdienst inn der gantzen H. Christenheit von alters her gleichförmig unnd einhellig gebrauchet werden, sampt etlichen ungereimpten/ widerspennigen Ceremonien unnd Geberden der Sectischen* (Münster: Lambert Raesfeld, 1609).

"Why should one fold one's hands? Answer: To gather one's sins."
"Why does the priest sit during confession? Answer: Because the judge
sits in court."[102] Others, however, conveyed explicitly invective confessional messages, such as his discussion of baptism: "Why do they [the
Protestants] like to give their children Jewish names and forsake the
customary names of the saints? Answer: Because a particular Jewish
Demon is behind this who wants to lead us gradually away from Christendom to Judaism, just as many sectarians have become Jews."[103] In
addition to the sacraments, ceremonies, properly observed, reinforced
the social hierarchy, hence the importance of the pecking order in processions. Processions were "a loud prayer" which turned away wars and
plagues and gave victory to the Catholics over their enemies.[104]

In Timpe's "historiography," the past is turned into a theater of divine
punishments and rewards; historical events serve no purpose other than
as illustrations for moral theology. The Counter-Reformation was fundamentally anti-historicist in that it refused to recognize the chronological progression of human events as worthy of serious study. Timpe's
Theatrum historicum is organized thematically and arranged alphabetically
according to the two main headings of "sins" and "virtues." After every
sin or virtue, he tells a story from late antiquity, the Middle Ages, or
from his own age which conveys the basic message that God punishes
sins and rewards good Christians. Under the heading "sins against the
Eucharist," for example, he cites the "sad and lamentable death" of a
certain Calvinist burgher of Wesel, who died of the plague after he had
blasphemed against the Eucharist.[105] To illustrate the "punishments and
unhappy deaths of heretics," he juxtaposes ancient and modern examples, comparing the Anabaptist Kingdom to the Donatists of the early
Christian centuries.[106]

To the city fathers, however, the lesson of the Anabaptist Kingdom
was that religious fanaticism could tear asunder the carefully woven
fabric of society. Timpe's crude, confessional view of history contrasted

102. Ibid., pp. 105ff.

103. Ibid., p. 265.

104. *Processionpredigten/ oder: Deutliche Anweisung/ wie die Seelsorger zur Zeit der H. Bett-
fahrten/ Creutzgäng und Processionen/ bevor ab an S. Marcus Tag/ in der H. Car und Creutzwo-
chen/ und am Hohen Fest des H. Fronleichnams Christi/ das Gemeine Volck lehren und underweisen
sollen/ wie die abwendung der Thewrung/ des Krieges/ der weit umb sich fressenden Kranckheiten/
und aller andern Trübseligkeiten von Gott zu erhalten sey* (Münster: Bernard Raesfeld, 1632),
pp. 6, 40–41.

105. *Theatrum Historicum, continens Vindictas Divinas, et Praemia Christianarum Virtutum*
(Münster: Michael Dalius, 1625), pp. 87–90.

106. Ibid., p. 112.

strongly with the proud republican tradition cherished by the burghers of Münster. As far as the ruling elite was concerned, loyalty to the Roman Church did not mean subservience to the clergy; the traditions of civic independence must be defended against all religious fanatics, Anabaptist rebels as well as Catholic militants.

CHAPTER FIVE

In Defense of Civic Liberties

As early as 1580, John of Nassau, the brother of William of Orange, cautioned Münster that the United Provinces could not tolerate the election of Ernst of Bavaria to the Münster episcopal see,[1] warning of Dutch intervention should the Catholic Wittelsbach candidature be successful. In 1583, when warfare broke out over the deposition of Gebhard Truchsess, the archbishop of Cologne turned Calvinist, both Dutch and Spanish troops poured into the Rhineland and Westphalia to support their respective candidates. Ernst of Bavaria, chosen by the Catholic canons of Cologne to be their next archbishop, triumphed over Truchsess, thanks to Spanish military support.[2] His election to the Münster See two years later realized the worst fears of the Münsteraners: the bishopric rapidly turned into another battlefield of the Dutch War for Independence as bands of marauding mercenaries pillaged the countryside and terrorized the populace. In the last two decades of the sixteenth century Westphalia offered a taste of the horrors which were to come in the Thirty Years' War.

The general instability in the region and the fear of warfare on the part of the burghers determined the pattern of conflict between city and prince-bishop. Weary of religious fanaticism and a possible division of the body politic, the city fathers of Münster were resolved to defend every bit of tradition and privilege, especially the right of the city republic to attend to its own religious affairs. When Archbishop Ernst forbade the burial of non-Catholics in the city's parish churches and instructed the Münsteraners to elect only Catholics to serve on the city council, to the majority of the magistrates it appeared all the more critical to separate religion from politics. Meanwhile, Protestants and militant Catholics formed factions on the city council, and open confessional antagonism poisoned relations between citizens. From the perspective of the prince-bishop and his officials, however, the towns and their archaic, particularist privileges, often invoked to protect Protestants, became the major

---

1. Cf. Keller, I, doc. 487, 488, pp. 497ff.
2. See Ritter, I, pp. 607, 618–20 and Franz Petri, "Im Zeitalter der Glaubenskämpfe," in F. Petri et al., eds., *Rheinische Geschichte*, vol. 2 (Düsseldorf, 1976), pp. 83ff.

obstacles to the Counter-Reformation. Thus, the reduction of autonomous civic rights constituted the first task of the Catholic territorial state.

PRINCE-BISHOP AND CITY-REPUBLIC

Not all disagreements between Archbishop Ernst and Münster stemmed exclusively from the implementation of Counter-Reformation policies. Long-standing issues of contention between princely and republican authority took on a new poignancy when they had implications for the exercise of religion. Disputes over jurisdictional competence were the most important of these long-standing differences.

An episcopal edict of March 6, 1590, proclaimed the establishment of Catholic schools, the dismissal of all clerics with Protestant sympathies, and a general ban on evangelical worship in the diocese.[3] The bailiffs (*Amtmann, Drosten*) and other territorial officials were instructed to denounce Protestants, cite suspicious clerics, and expel Anabaptists. The towns, especially Münster, proved to be recalcitrant. To undermine the power of the proud city, Archbishop Ernst disputed Münster's traditional right to exercise lower jurisdiction (*Gogericht*) over the neighboring village of Senden. He also tried to increase episcopal authority by appointing episcopal city judges from the ranks of the officialdom and not from the city's leading families. Most medieval German town councils had evolved from colleges of jurors (*scabini, Schöffen*) who assisted episcopal or royal city judges, originally the highest authority in the cities. During the twelfth and thirteenth centuries, the office of city judge declined in proportion to the rising importance of the civic magistracy and was often absorbed by the emerging town councils.[4] Although the office of city judge survived in Münster, it was commonly filled by men recommended by the city council, whose acceptance by the bishops was taken for granted. The city judge swore burgher oath, sat with two councillors in the city's court, and acted as a mediator between the city council and the prince-bishop. Between 1535 and 1574, the office was in the hands of the Wesselinck family, who shared bonds of friendship and marriage with the families represented on the city council.[5]

In 1589, Archbishop Ernst broke with tradition and explicitly instructed the city judge, Goddert Leistinck, that he owed allegiance solely to the territorial lord and not to the city republic. The magistrates tried in

---

3. Keller, II, doc. 281, pp. 325ff.

4. Cf. Planitz, pp. 295ff., esp. 298, 302.

5. They were Lic. Johann Wesselinck, who served as city judge from 1536 to 1549. He was succeeded by Dr. med. Johann Wesselinck, personal physician to Bishop Franz von Waldeck, who exercised the office between 1550 and 1566. The first judge's son, also a Johann, served from 1567 to 1574. In 1575 Goddert Leistinck succeeded to the office.

vain to persuade Leistinck and the judges on the Chamber Court in Münster to swear burgher oath and promise respect for the city's customs. Thereafter, relations changed for the worse, and civil cases were heard by magistrates without the presence of the city judge.[6]

More serious was the challenge to customary civic jurisprudence posed by the Chamber Court. Although an agreement in 1573 between the episcopal government and Münster recognized the judicial autonomy of the city's own court, the Chamber Court provided an alternative channel of litigation for those burghers who did not find a favorable hearing before the city court. Moreover, when disputes arose between Münsteraners and outsiders, the latter tended to present their cases before the Chamber Court. The first lawsuit which called to question the conflict in jurisdiction between the two courts was brought by Heinrich Herding, Bürgermeister of Bocholt, against his brother Hermann, who was a city councillor in Münster. Their late father, Johann Herding (+1573), had been Bürgermeister of Münster and the two brothers quarreled over the division of the immense paternal inheritance. When the case had dragged on for some years in Münster, Heinrich filed suit at the Chamber Court to enforce a speedier decision. Hermann refused to obey the summons of the Chamber Court, a decision supported by his colleagues on the city council.[7] In subsequent years—in 1593, 1595, 1597, and into the seventeenth century—the city council repeatedly protested and ignored the summoning of burghers by the Chamber Court.[8]

The dispute between Münster and the Chamber Court was an example of a larger pattern of conflict between the towns and the territorial government. Between 1583 and 1600, numerous disputes over jurisdictional competence embittered the towns of the bishopric when episcopal bailiffs arbitrarily arrested their citizens and repeatedly summoned the townsfolk to appear before the Chamber Court. Warendorf, Bocholt, Rheine, Haltern, Beckum, Ahlen, Telgte, Werne—the smaller towns of the bishopric—kept turning to Münster for leadership and support in their conflicts with territorial officials.[9]

6. On the conflict between the magistrates and the city judge, see StdAM, AII, 20, RP, 1589, March 3–4, August 21, vol. 21, fols. 8–16v, 39; and RP, 1593, Jan. 19, vol. 24, fol. 144.

7. Cf. StdAM, AII, 20, RP, 1584, Feb. 17–18, March 2, vol. 16, fols. 5–8v, 11–13v.

8. See StdAM, AII, 20, RP, 1593, June 18, vol. 25, fol. 51; 1595, Feb. 27 and March 14, vol. 27, fols. 15–16, 19v–20, 21–21v; 1597, Feb. 28, vol. 29, fol. 11; 1601, Dec. 6, vol. 33, fol. 311; 1604, May 21, vol. 36, fol. 47v; 1615, April 27, vol. 47, fol. 150.

9. For the appeals of the other town councils, see StdAM, AII, 20, RP, entries under the following dates: Feb. 1, 1583 (vol. 15, fols. 2v–3); Nov. 19, 1584 (vol. 16, fol. 43v); March 22, 1585 (vol. 17, fol. 12v); April 21 & Dec. 19, 1589 (vol. 21, fols. 23, 49–49v); Sept. 10, 1593 (vol. 25, fols. 73v–74); July 21, 1594 (vol. 26, fol. 52); April 30, 1599 (vol. 31, fols. 39–40); Sept. 13, 1600 (vol. 32, fols. 61v–63).

To further aggravate the conflict, Archbishop Ernst tried to raise money to strengthen the bishopric's defenses against the undisciplined bands of Dutch and Spanish troops by imposing direct taxation on the smaller towns, contrary to traditional rights, whereby only the estates could constitutionally grant the lord extra subsidies.[10] As a skillful ruler, Archbishop Ernst exploited the differences between the estates to isolate the towns; he took advantage of the conflict between Münster and the cathedral chapter over the minting of copper coins and the punishment of delinquent clergy to forge an anti-urban alliance between the territorial administration and the most powerful member of the territorial estates.[11] In June 1599, an alliance of cathedral canons and noblemen at the *Landtag* voted to place the burden of defense taxes entirely upon the burghers by agreeing to an excise tax on corn milling in the towns.[12] Representing the other towns, Münster protested and disputed the constitutionality of such a move at the Imperial Cameral Court.[13] The magistrates were especially incensed because the towns had repeatedly consented to raising generous monetary subsidies and providing troops for the defense of the bishopric. In the case of Münster, the efforts entailed great sacrifices on the part of the citizens and additional voluntary contributions from the city fathers themselves.[14] On July 15, 1600, twelve towns joined Münster in a *Städtebund,* swore allegiance to one another, and promised help in the event that their rights or liberties were infringed upon.[15]

The hostility of Archbishop Ernst and the territorial officialdom to the

10. Cf. StdAM, AII, 20, 1589, Dec. 19, vol. 21, fols. 49–49v.

11. The anti-urban sentiments of the cathedral chapter were manifest in an incident which took place in Münster on September 20, 1599. In a tavern, the syndic of the chapter proclaimed loudly in the presence of two magistrates that the chapter would teach the Münsteraners to dance to its tunes. StdAM, AII, 20, RP, vol. 31, fol. 90: "Und haben daneben referirt, dass Capitale Syndicus, Lic. Sickman in anwesen Herman Herdinck und Thomas Egbers sich offentlich im weingelage horen lassen, dass man der Stadt Münster bürgere nache dess Capituli Pfeiffen zu dantzen leren sollte."

12. See StdAM, AII, 20, RP, 1599, June 4, vol. 31, fol. 57.

13. See StdAM, AII, 20, RP, 1600, Dec. 15., vol. 32, fol. 90v. The first years of the seventeenth century saw a vastly increased volume of litigation between cities and lords at the *Reichskammergericht* in Speyer and at the *Reichshofrat* in Prague. The cities were not without success in defending their traditional rights against the encroachments of the territorial states; the dispute between the Lutheran city of Lemgo and its Calvinist lord, the count of Lippe, was adjudicated to the burghers' advantage, both at the Cameral and the Aulic Courts. See Schilling, *Konfessionskonflikt,* pp. 294–319.

14. Cf. StdAM, AII, 20, RP, 1590, May 14 (vol. 22, fol. 13v); 1594, Oct. 7 (vol. 26, fol. 70); 1598, Nov. 28, Dec. 5 and 18 (vol. 30, fols. 49v, 50v–51, 52v), and many other entries in the council minutes and financial records of the city during the 1590s.

15. The towns were, besides Münster, Coesfeld, Warendorf, Bocholt, Borken, Beckum, Ahlen, Rheine, Dülmen, Haltern, Vreden, Werne, and Telgte. See StdAM, AII, 20, RP, 1600, July 13–14, vol. 32, fols. 49–50v. For the articles of federation, see Keller, II, doc. 320, pp. 356–58.

towns was doubtless inherent in their absolutist and hierarchical views of the state, in which there was no place for autonomous city republics; the feeling was further reinforced by the fact that the towns harbored the strongest Protestant sentiments in the bishopric, and that within the city walls were to be found not only "heretics," but also potential rebels. Already the 1571 diocesan visitation reported that "the majority of clerics outside of Münster live[d] in degenerate concubinage" and that most of the towns in the bishopric had adopted Lutheran worship.[16] The town of Warendorf, third largest in the bishopric, had replaced Catholic liturgy by Lutheran rites as early as the 1530s without the formal adoption of a new Protestant church ordinance.[17] In towns close to the Dutch border, such as in Ahaus, Bocholt, and Vreden, many Anabaptists (the pacifist Mennonites) were enriching the communities by their hard work and skills. Episcopal edicts of expulsion in the 1590s failed simply because the town magistrates quietly disobeyed orders of the episcopal government to exile model citizens. The Reformation influenced many Westphalian towns not by formal adoption but rather through gradual infiltration of ideas of reform. By the last decades of the sixteenth century, clerical marriages, communion in both kinds by the laity, and the singing of German hymns had become part of the customs of many townsfolk. Thus, to enforce Catholic orthodoxy, it was imperative for the prince-bishop first to reduce the customary rights of the towns and to impose central administrative authority. The suppression of a second Protestant movement in the episcopal cities of Würzburg, Bamberg, and Eichstätt in the second half of the sixteenth century was the result of direct political force exercised by the prince-bishops as territorial lords who exiled Protestants, filled city councils with reliable Catholics, and appointed officials to supervise civic affairs.[18] Persuasion alone did not suffice to bring about a Catholic revival; and the conflict between towns and lord in the Bishopric of Münster echoed similar conflicts in Germany, engendered by the Counter-Reformation and leading to the Thirty Years' War.[19]

Nobody felt the threats of religious violence more than the townsfolk of the sixteenth century. Münsteraners watched anxiously as the war in the Netherlands slowly engulfed their land. In his journal, the guild Alderman and shopkeeper Arnold von Guelich noted the ominous beginning of troubles in the Netherlands, recording the 1566 iconoclastic riots in Flanders, Brabant, Holland, and Friesland. For the next forty

16. Keller, I, doc. 292, p. 384.
17. Keller, I, doc. 289, pp. 382–83.
18. Hans-Christoph Rublack, *Die Gescheiterte Reformation* (Stuttgart, 1980), pp. 124ff.
19. The most prominent and bloody example of such a conflict was that between Bishop Dietrich von Fürstenberg and the city of Paderborn between 1597 and 1604; see below, pp. 132–33 and n. 44.

years, entries of family and civic matters became more and more interspersed with references to warfare in the neighboring Netherlands. In the 1570s, Guelich noted the sack of Antwerp by the Spanish army, the campaign of Don Juan of Austria, and the massacre of Maastricht by the Spaniards; in the early 1580s, he recorded the assassination of William of Orange and the War of Cologne; by 1589, the journal started to take note of the many attacks by Dutch and Spanish troops in Münsterland itself.[20]

Perhaps most alarming to the burghers was the seeming insensitivity of the zealous Catholic clergy to the horrors of war. The sentiments of Hermann von Weinsberg, magistrate in Cologne and author of a well-known family chronicle, best exemplified the feelings of many townsmen. After the 1572 Saint Bartholomew Day's Massacre in France, he commented:[21]

> At this time, the Pope ordered the minting of a coin, on which a slaughtering angel with the words "Vindicta Dei" are engraved. However one may take it, the matter is really beyond my understanding to pass judgment on people in such high places. But Catholics as well as Protestants in many lands are uttering all sorts of things about it.

The capture and sack of Neuss by the Spanish army in 1586 brought forth another contrast in attitude between burgher and clergy: whereas Arnold von Guelich noted the sack of Neuss by the troops of the Duke of Parma in his journal, undoubtedly with horror, the same occasion inspired Everwin von Droste, dean of Saint Martin, to compose a poem praising the "orthodox, apostolic, Roman Catholic Church."[22] Melchior Röchell's contemporary chronicle reflected the growing fear of the Münsteraners as Dutch and Spanish incursions became more frequent, and as the details of atrocities committed became more vivid before burgher eyes. Between 1584 and 1600, the magistrates of Münster received scores of letters from other town councils in the bishopric in which were reported troop movements, attacks, and sieges, and which begged for help.[23] While Dutch and Spanish incursions were about

---

20. The journal (354 folios) was bound together with a copy of the police ordinance. Entries from 1554 to 1609 were kept in Arnold von Guelich's own hand; additional entries in another hand carried the chronicle up to 1660. Records of interest payments on annuities owned by Guelich are entered on fols. 59–95. This document is also very valuable in the genealogical reconstitutions of other families of the ruling elite. See StAM, AVM, MS. 172.

21. See *Das Buch Weinsberg. Aus dem Leben eines Kölner Ratsherrn,* ed., Johann J. Hässlin (Munich, 1964), p. 397.

22. See Guelich, Chronicle, fols. 39, 41. Droste's poem is published in Huyskens, *Everwin von Droste,* pp. 47ff.

23. A huge bundle of letters is still extant and is now deposited in StdAM, AXIV, "Spanisch-Holländischer Krieg."

equally frequent between 1585 and 1590, thereafter, the uncontrollable Spanish army became the major threat to peace and order in the bishopric. Both the United Provinces and Münster wanted to maintain neutrality,[24] but the Spaniards spoliated the bishopric for provisions and used Westphalia as a strategic front to outflank the Dutch. During the 1590s, Münsteraners came to identify the Spaniards as the threat to peace and taxes raised by the *Landtag* for defense were directed against the Spanish army. The Münsteraners' hatred of the Spaniards inevitably blackened the image of the Counter-Reformation; high-handed measures by the archbishop to revive Catholicism were perceived by citizens as constituting an inquisition and not a Catholic reform. When Spanish troops spent the winter of 1598–99 in the bishopric, they occupied several towns and forced Catholic worship on the inhabitants. Welcomed by Archbishop Ernst and the militant Catholic officials as help in restoring orthodoxy in the bishopric, Spanish arms symbolized instead tyranny in the eyes of the burghers. To them, what mattered was not religious conformity, but peace and tradition; essential to the preservation of peace and tradition were the rights of the city republic to bury its own dead and to elect its own leaders.

CONFLICT OVER BURIALS AND ELECTIONS

The first conflict between secular and ecclesiastical authorities over the burial of Protestants in Münster arose in 1587. In November of that year, Master Bernt Capellaen, teacher at the cathedral school, was critically ill and yet he refused communion and confession at the hands of the clergy. After his death, Dean Everwin von Droste of Saint Martin's asked the magistrates to forbid his burial in the parish church. The city fathers refused the dean's request, defended the schoolmaster as "neither Anabaptist, schismatic, nor Calvinist," and permitted his burial in the church cemetery.[25] Three months later, Dean Droste again denied permission to bury another burgher who had refused to receive communion in one kind before his death. To avoid confrontation, the parish provisors

---

24. In 1591, Münster sent two ambassadors to Prince William of Maurice to declare the city's neutrality; they were, however, robbed ("durchaus spoliert und ihre Kleider beraubt") near Nijmegen and never made it to The Hague (StdAM, AII, 20, RP, 1591, June 11, vol. 23, fols. 55–55v). Two years later, Maurice sent two letters to Münster asking the bishopric and city to remain neutral (RP, 1593, May 7, vol. 25, fols. 34–34v). The magistrates also strictly prohibited burghers from service in the mercenary bands and barred recruitment in the city; see RP, 1586, March 3, vol. 18, fol. 7; 1600, March 13, vol. 32, fol. 18v; 1602, March 22, April 17, May 3, vol. 34, fols. 67–68, 100, 124–25.

25. StdAM, AII, 20, RP, 1587, Nov. 16, vol. 19, fol. 94.

buried the dead man, Werner Docht, in the cemetery of the Franciscan cloister instead.[26]

For the next nine years, similar cases did not arise, but beginning with 1597 secular and ecclesiastical authorities were engaged in a number of controversies over the burial of Protestant burghers. When the procurator at the Chamber Court, Lic. Dietrich Seveker, died, having refused to communicate in the Catholic rite, the clergy at Überwasser forbade his burial and the ringing of church bells. At this time, the guild leaders, already engaged in a campaign to force the Jesuits to pay wine excise, took up Seveker's case to counter what appeared to them as the meddling by clergy in civic affairs.[27] The incident turned into a contest of rights, with the magistrates claiming authority over all religious matters when citizens were involved, while the cathedral chapter based its claims on medieval archdeaconic ecclesiastical jurisdiction over the city.[28] In any case, alarmed at the strength of Protestants and the audacity of the magistrates, Archbishop Ernst ordered all pastors to start keeping parish registers and to report on suspicious parishioners.[29] Anxious to show that their action had not violated the laws of the Empire, the magistrates in Münster expelled several Anabaptist families while they defended the rights of Lutheran burghers whose freedom of conscience was legally guaranteed by the 1555 Religious Peace of Augsburg, while the Anabaptists remained outlaws after the 1529 Imperial Diet at Speyer.[30] The problem was compounded by the deaths of visiting merchants and journeymen from Protestant cities in Münster. The epidemics of the 1590s and 1600s proved to be a double health hazard to the citizens because zealous Catholic pastors refused burial to sojourning Protestant artisans who had fallen victim to the plague. In 1599, on the occasion of one such controversy, the magistrates admonished the pastors to report on the religiously suspect while they were alive and not to deny them the basic right of burial after their death.[31]

26. StdAM, AII, 20, RP, 1588, Feb. 19, vol. 20, fol. 7.

27. For the Seveker case, see StdAM, AII, 20, RP, 1597, Jan. 24, Feb. 3, vol. 29, fols. 3v and 4v. See also Röchell, *Chronik,* pp. 128f.

28. Cf. StdAM, AII, 20, 1597, March 10, vol. 29, fols. 13–13v.

29. Cf. Keller, II, doc. 300, p. 338. In Calvinist Lippe the territorial Church also functioned as a moral police to enforce the religious and social policies of the territorial state. See Schilling, *Konfessionskonflikt,* pp. 190–200.

30. One man was denounced as Anabaptist when he refused guard duty while others were discovered because they refused to baptize infants and held clandestine conventicles. For investigations and sentences of exile passed by the magistates, see StdAM, AII, 20, RP, 1597, Feb. 3, 7, March 10, 14, 17, 27, and April 9, 14; vol. 29, fols. 5, 6–7, 13–14v, 16v–18. Unlike the Anabaptists of 1534–35, the Mennonites of the later sixteenth century were pacifists and the wave of executions in the first half of the sixteenth century was replaced by the milder sentences of exile.

31. StdAM, AII, 20, RP, 1599, June 14, vol. 31, fol. 59v.

The cause célèbre occurred in 1604. On March 25, Wilhelm Niehuis (Neuhaus), a prominent merchant who had also served as elector, died without confession or communion.[32] Nicolaus Arresdorff, pastor of Saint Lambert's, prevented Niehuis's burial, whereupon the man's sons and some citizens, including the Protestant magistrates Andreas Wilckinghoff and Johann Block, forced entry into Saint Lambert's and buried Niehuis. Episcopal officials charged the action as a violation of ecclesiastical sanctity, while the guild leaders and Protestants defended their action by claiming that the church buildings and grounds belonged to the parishioners and not to the clergy. Although displeased with the rash actions of the burghers, the magistrates did not punish the participants.[33] The Ecclesiastical Court, however, summoned the magistrate Andreas Wilckinghoff to face charges,[34] an order which was ignored by the councillors. In September, an episcopal edict arrived in Münster and explicitly forbade the burial of non-Catholics in the churchyards.[35]

The magistrates were divided on how to respond. Led by Bürgermeister Heinrich Vendt and the syndic Heinrich Wittfeld, the clerical faction on the city council argued against drawing up a protest note, saying that Münster had already acquired a reputation for defiance; they feared that an angered prince-bishop would rescind the city's charters (which bound Münster to Catholicism) and suggested that the clergy should be allowed a free hand in denouncing heretics.[36] The guild leaders, several of whom also sat on the city council, feared that the clergy wanted to eliminate lay control over the parish churches and recommended drawing up a protest note to reject the episcopal edict. Andreas Wilckinghoff gave the most persuasive speech:[37]

> I worry that hidden behind this [edict] is the Spanish Inquisition. Until this time, both Catholics and Lutherans are allowed to practice their religion in

32. Niehuis was Kurgenosse of Ludgeri in 1590 and 1594; see Schulte, "Kurgenossen," p. 189.

33. The details of the incident are recorded in minutes of the city council; for a description and subsequent investigation, see StdAM, AII, 20, RP, 1604, March 26, 27 and April 9, vol. 36, fols. 22v–25, 29v–34. See also the reports by ecclesiastical officals in Keller, II, docs. 335, 336, and 337, pp. 368–69.

34. See the summons issued by the episcopal offical Hermann Bisping to Wilckinghoff, StdAM, AXIII, no. 28.

35. Cf. StdAM, AII, 20, RP, 1604, Sept. 6, vol. 36, fol. 82.

36. The core members of the clercial faction were Bürgermeister Vendt, syndic Wittfeld, councillors Bernt van Detten, Lic. Heinrich Frie, and Konrad Grüter; they were supported by Bernt Meyer, Jakob Stöve, and Johann Boland, who voted with them on this motion but also sided with the "political faction" of Catholic magistrates on other issues. For the council's deliberations and the positions of the different magistrates, see StdAM, AII, 20, RP, 1604, Sept. 6 and 7, vol. 36, fols. 82–85v.

37. StdAM, AII, 20, RP, 1604, vol. 36, fol. 83v.

the Empire and in all cities. If matters should now stand otherwise, let us beware of a bloodbath!

In the subsequent voting, the combined numbers of Protestants and politiques[38] prevailed over the clerical faction and a note was drawn up to repudiate the episcopal edict.[39]

Meanwhile, a second assault on civic privileges had been launched in 1601 with another episcopal edict which prohibited the election of non-Catholics to serve on town councils in the bishopric.[40] The smaller towns rejected the edict without exception.[41] After having ignored the edict for three years, the magistrates in Münster replied to episcopal officials in 1604 that the edict could not concern the city and that the citizens cared little anyway about the religious affiliation of prospective magistrates.[42] The next two years saw a number of heated exchanges between episcopal officials and magistrates, the latter often acting under pressure from the guild leaders. Every time the judge admonished the magistrates to heed the edict, the city fathers told the citizens to ignore it during elections; every time the clergy forbade the burial of Protestants, the magistrates and the guild leaders interceded and declared the city's right to bury its own dead. To intensify the conflict there was also the ongoing dispute over granting the Jesuits exemption from wine excise. To complicate matters further, many burghers interpreted Archbishop Ernst's motives in light of recent attempts to suppress civic liberties and revive Catholicism in neighboring Dortmund and Paderborn. A handful of Catholics

38. The term "politiques" was used by contemporaries to characterize those Catholics who supported Henry of Navarre and royal authority over the ultramontane, militant Catholic supporters of the House of Guise in the French Wars of Religion. It came to mean all Catholics and Protestants who put pragmatic political considerations over the ideology of the Counter-Reformation, and suggested occasional opposition to the goals of the zealous clergy. In the Hapsburg court at Vienna, the supporters of the Jesuits were known as the *clerici*, while their opponents were called the *politici*. See Bireley, *Lamormaini,* p. 23.

39. The Protestant councillors were Andreas Wilckinghoff, Bernhard Burmann, Heinrich Meinertz, and Johann Beifang; they were supported by Johann Wernike, Johann Schonebeck, Bernhard Smithues (alias Ickinck), and two patricians, Bürgermeister Warendorp and Travelmann. The protest note, signed by all the councillors and the guild leaders, was dated August 27; it protested the episcopal interdict as an infringement of the ancient customs and rights of the republic; it asked Archbishop Ernst to rescind the edict; and it argued the council's position based on customary magisterial jurisdiction over both temporal and spiritual affairs. The note, 23 folios long, is now deposited in BDAM, PfA Lamberti, Akten, Kart. 60, C7.

40. Cf. Keller, II, doc. 328, pp. 364–65.

41. Cf. Keller, II, docs. 329, 331–33, pp. 365–67.

42. The edict was first related to the Münster city council in 1602 by the bailiff of Wolbeck and the city judge Leistinck; see Keller, II, docs. 330, 343, pp. 365–66, 373. For the formal rejection by the city fathers, see StdAM, AII, 20, RP, 1604, Jan. 12, vol. 35, fol. 188.

in Dortmund agitated for the full restoration of church properties in that Protestant Imperial city by allying themselves with the clergy and by appealing to Emperor Rudolf II.[43] In Münster itself, the Jesuits toyed with the idea of settling in Dortmund to strengthen the Catholic cause. While these attempts largely ended in failure, events in Paderborn thoroughly alarmed the Münsteraners. Elected in 1585, Bishop Dietrich von Fürstenberg, a firm supporter of the Jesuits and the Counter-Reformation, undertook steps to gradually undermine the independence of the largely Protestant metropolitan city. After an unsuccessful armed conflict, in 1604 Bishop Dietrich von Fürstenberg took the city by deceit, tortured Bürgermeister Dietrich Wickard to death, abolished the traditional rights of the city, and imposed Catholic worship on all.[44] The guild leaders in Münster mentioned the two cities by name when they warned the magistrates in January 1606 that the edict forbidding the burial of Protestants could become the spark to ignite the fire of warfare between bishop and city.[45]

Tempers were running short. In November 1605, when Nicolaus Arresdorff forbade the burial of an artisan from Nuremberg who had died of the plague, the guild leaders threatened to place the corpse in the pastor's house or on the high altar in Saint Lambert's until the stench would force a change of mind.[46] During the next year, a number of Protestant burghers died, each time provoking a fresh confrontation between civic and ecclesiastical authorities. On the one hand Archbishop Ernst renewed the edict regarding burial[47] and the clergy wrote and preached against the burial of Protestants.[48] On the other hand the parishioners organized to defend the rights of the laity and the city council appealed to the Imperial Cameral Court.[49] The most serious incident in 1606 surrounded the denial of burial to the Protestant magistrate Mel-

43. For confessional conflicts in Dortmund at the end of the sixteenth and the beginning of the seventeenth centuries, see the contemporary chronicle by the merchant Detmar Mühlherr, published in *Beiträge zur Geschichte Dortmunds und der Grafschaft Mark* 68 (1973), esp. pp. 50–55, 59–75; see also Luise von Winterfeld, *Geschichte der Freien Reichs- und Hansestadt Dortmund* (Dortmund, 1934), pp. 139ff.

44. For the Reformation, attempts at Catholic revival, and the struggle between bishop and city in Paderborn, see Karl Hengst, *Kirchliche Reform im Fürstbistum Paderborn unter Dietrich von Fürstenberg (1585–1618)* (Paderborn, 1974), pp. 98–100; Keller, *Gegenreformation* II, pp. 433–53; and Klemens Honselmann, "Der Kampf um Paderborn 1604 und die Geschichtsschreibung," *WZ* 118 (1968), pp. 229–338.

45. StdAM, AII, 20, 1606, Jan. 20 and 23, vol. 37, fols. 123–24.

46. Cf. StdAM, AII, 20, RP, 1605, Nov. 24 and 25, vol. 37, fols. 154v, 156–57.

47. Cf. Keller, II, doc. 348, pp. 376–77.

48. Cf. StdAM, AII, 20, RP, 1606, March 31, April 3, vol. 38, fols. 43v–45v, 48v; see also Keller, II, doc. 347, pp. 375–76.

49. Cf. StdAM, AII, 20, RP, 1606, April 17, vol. 38, fol. 73.

chior Steinhoff. When the canons of Saint Martin's locked up the church, the magistrates and citizens cut a new key, opened the church, and buried Steinhoff.[50] Meanwhile, the city council was still divided between the clerical faction and the politique-Protestant majority. The clericals reiterated the religious provisions of the 1554 Edict of Restitution; they did not want the council to undertake any actions, and even advised burghers who could not tolerate the clergy to leave town.[51] The position of Dr. Heinrich Vendt, leader of the clericals, was of considerable interest. In the meeting of June 30, he "warned of Stutenbernt's [Bernhard Rothmann's] example, who was initially Lutheran but later turned radical and Anabaptist so that all may take heed; further, those who could not thus defend their religion must yield because the terms of the restitution must be observed."[52] The guild leaders advanced the argument that intolerant confessional orthodoxy would keep apprentices away and ruin the city's economy,[53] and the Protestant magistrates urged the city council to acknowledge publicly its duty to protect Lutheran citizens against clerical tyranny.[54]

Already, Archbishop Ernst had complained to Emperor Rudolf II about the disobedience of Münster. In August 1607, a letter arrived from Prague which reminded the magistrates that Münster was only a territorial city under both the temporal and spiritual jurisdiction of the prince-bishop. Rudolf II further admonished the city fathers to obey the episcopal edicts concerning the burial interdict and the election of Catholics to the city council; once again, the disobedience was compared to the tumultuous events leading up to the Anabaptist Kingdom of 1533–34.[55] Upon receipt of the Imperial letter, the magistrates and guild leaders convoked an assembly of the entire citizenry, an extraordinary political move undertaken only when the city fathers needed to mobilize broad civic support and to assure consensus in the face of external pressure.[56] Having reached a consensus among the citizens, the city council persisted in ignoring the episcopal edicts[57] and drew up a polite, but firm, reply to explain why the Imperial injunction could not be obeyed. A delegation was also sent to Prague to plead Münster's case before Emperor Rudolf

50. On the Steinhoff case, see Keller, II, docs. 351–54, pp. 377–80; see also StdAM, AII, 20, RP, Dec. 7, vol. 38, fol. 255v.

51. Cf. StdAM, AII, 20, RP, June 9, vol. 38, fol. 94v.

52. StdAM, AII, 20, RP, vol. 38, fol. 119.

53. StdAM, AII, 20, RP, March 31, vol. 38, fol. 45v.

54. StdAM, AII, 20, RP, June 9, vol. 38, fol. 94v.

55. The letter, dated May 3, 1607, is published; see Keller, II, doc. 359, pp. 384–88.

56. StdAM, AII, 20, RP, 1607, protocol extraordinarium, Aug. 23 and 25, vol. 39, fols. 124–29.

57. See StdAM, AII, 20, RP, 1608, Jan. 19 and 21, vol. 40, fols. 14–14v, 16.

himself.[58] In addition, the city council also approached Lübeck to intercede on Münster's behalf with the prestige of the Hansa.[59]

The letter to the emperor can be summarized by fourteen points:[60] (1) Münster was a prestigious Hansa city for centuries. (2) All past bishops had promised to respect the city's liberties, justice, and customs, including Archbishop Ernst. (3) Münster had served Archbishop Ernst well through generous contributions. (4) The archbishop, however, did not reside in the bishopric and the councillors who ruled in his place were drawn exclusively from the cathedral chapter and the nobility, contrary to the past practice of including magistrates from Münster. (5) The city of Münster had the right to grant passage and punish clerical delinquents; hence, she was not absolutely subject to the bishop; moreover, after 1555, Lutherans had lived, died, and were buried in Münster without anyone's objections. (6) The magistrates obeyed Imperial laws and did not tolerate Anabaptists. (7) The present troubles had been stirred up by restless foreign clerics. (8) The episcopal edicts would frighten off journeymen and ruin the city's economy. (9) Münster was not an enclosed world and she had Protestant neighbors: in these times, no one could be forced to confess what he did not believe in. (10) The churchyards and churchbells were at the disposal of the laity and not the clergy. (11) The magistrates would continue to follow the 1554 Edict of Restitution and would allow only Catholic church services. (12) Free councillor elections were a custom from time immemorial. (13) The episcopal city judge had exceeded his rights in interfering with civic affairs. (14) The city had been slandered: one simply could not compare the situation to the unrest in 1533; the only question was whether Lutherans were to be treated as men beyond the pale of law, like the Anabaptists.

The conflict had reached a stalemate. For the next decade the magistrates would consistently intercede on behalf of Protestants who were denied burial by the clergy.[61] Regarding the episcopal injunction to elect only Catholics to the city council, the episcopal officials and the magistrates would continue to exchange admonitions and protests into the first years of the 1620s; the disagreement came to a resolution only in 1661,

58. StdAM, AII, 20, RP, 1608, July 14, vol. 40, fol. 120.

59. StdAM, AII, 20, RP, 1608, April 28, fol. 94v.

60. See StdAM, AII, 5, draft of letter dated Jan. 10, 1608, written in the hand of secretary Heinrich Holland. For other copies, see StAM, AVM, MSS. 86 and 221.

61. For examples, see the decisions of the magistrates in the following controversies over the denial of burial: StdAM, AII, 20, RP, 1609, Dec. 3 and 4, vol. 41, fols. 274v, 276v; 1611, Sept. 10 and 12, vol. 43, fols. 173, 174v, 176; 1612, Nov. 21/22 (the burial of magistrate Andreas Wilckinghoff), vol. 44, fols. 403–06; 1613, Feb. 5 and Nov. 12, vol. 45, fols. 63, 456. Imperial pressure did not cease: in 1622, Emperor Ferdinand II wrote from Vienna to order the magistrates to obey the episcopal edicts; see letter dated March 30, 1622, StdAM, AII, 5c.

when the prince-bishop crushed civic liberties by military might. In the years in which the city republic stubbornly resisted the centralizing political measures associated with the Counter-Reformation, the balance of forces on the city council gradually tipped in favor of the clerical faction. While the growing influence of the clericals partly resulted from the increasing animosity between guild leaders and magistrates, the shifting balance of power reflected the more fundamental fact that a new generation of burgher elite that had been educated by the Jesuits was coming into power.

MAGISTRATES, GUILDSMEN, AND CITIZENS

The antagonism between city council and Gesamtgilde, manifest in the former's opposition to the restoration of guilds in the years between 1552 and 1554, surfaced again in 1587, when the breakdown of order in the bishopric urgently forced the city republic to bolster her defenses. The mobilization of all able-bodied male citizens gave rise to strong disagreements between the magistrates and the guild leaders; at stake were the command and organization of the civic militia. The magistrates planned to replace the 1584 militia model and integrate the artisans into an enlarged militia, which was to comprise twelve companies based on the six city districts (*Leischaften*). At first, the guild Aldermen and masters insisted on maintaining the old structure in which each guild would supply a separate contingent under the command of its own masters. Two years later, in 1589, they agreed to recruitment based on the district but took over forty of the fifty-five commanding positions in the new civic guard.[62]

62. On the disagreements between city council and guilds over the organization of the civic militia and the subsequent compromise, see StdAM, AII, 20, RP, 1587, many entries, especially those under Feb. 27, March 17, April 6 and 29, vol. 19, fols. 10v–11, 18, 32–34, 40v–41v; see also Röchell, *Chronik*, p. 102. For the names of the company commanders, see Röchell, *Chronik*, p. 133; and RP, 1591, July 1 and 5, vol. 23, fols. 64, 65v–66v. The 1598 militia commanders included many Protestants who were leading guild leaders. The militia was a pivotal element in city politics, and city councils stood or fell depending upon the support of the civic guard. The organization of the civic militia reflected the division of power in the cities: where guild influence predominated, the burgher guard was usually organized along craft lines; where the magistracy had the upper hand, the district or quarter would be the basic organizational unit; where towns had lost their liberties and were ruled directly by territorial officials, civic militias were prohibited and contingents of mercenaries held the towns against external attacks as well as against possible rebellions. On the civic militia in Münster, see Henrich Marré, *Die Wehrverfassung der Stadt Münster von den Wiedertäuferunruhen bis zur Regierungszeit Christoph Bernhards von Galen 1536–1650* (Münster, 1913). For a broad and comprehensive study of civic militias in early modern Germany, see Jürgen Kraus, *Das Militärwesen der Reichsstadt Augsburg 1548–1806. Vergleichende Untersuchungen über städtische Militäreinrichtungen in Deutschland 16.–18. Jahrhundert* (Augsburg, 1980).

In the 1590s, constant friction between guild leaders and magistrates over the treatment of the Jesuits eventually hardened the city council's attitude toward the guilds. Conversely, emboldened by the knowledge that external threats made Münster more dependent on the artisans who constituted the major part of the civic militia, guild leaders arrogated the position of spokesmen for the entire community and began to rival the authority of the city council. The magistrates viewed the growing boldness of the Gesamtgilde with misgivings. In attempting to reduce the power of the guilds, the magistrates acted out of two sets of motivations. The politiques were primarily concerned with freeing the city council from internal pressures in order to give themselves greater flexibility in dealing with the emperor and the archbishop. To these men, politics and religion were separate, distinct spheres of activity, and the implacable anti-clericalism of the guilds threatened to enmesh the city republic in a confessional struggle with the prince-bishop. A second group of magistrates, who were in the minority, identified the stubborn guild leaders as the major opponents of the Counter-Reformation. Together with the archbishops and the Jesuits, they shared the vision of a Catholic renewal in Münster, a goal whose attainment entailed modifying the traditional view of the city republic as an autonomous polity and adopting one in which the community formed but a link in the much greater Roman Catholic world.

The changing social structure in Münster also helped to widen the gap between city council and Gesamtgilde. In the first decade of the seventeenth century, the mercantile and craft guilds no longer dominated the economic and social life of the city; in addition to the quick expansion of the legal and scribal professions, Münster was becoming an academic and consumption center, and several occupational groups began to assume a new numerical and social prominence, chief among which were the beer-brewers, innkeepers, physicians, and apothecaries.[63] The rising number and wealth of occupations not organized in the Gesamtgilde, both in absolute terms and in comparison with the guilds, supplied the social dimension in the conflict between magistrates and guild leaders.

In 1606, the *Gemeinheit,* the Münsteraners not organized in the guilds, protested the haughty arrogation of power by the guild leaders. Furious, the guild Aldermen and masters pressured the magistrates to punish "the

---

63. On beer brewing in Münster, see Josef Grewe, *Das Braugewerbe der Stadt Münster* (Leipzig, 1907), which deals only with the economic and technical aspects of the industry. The more interesting question of the social status of the beerbrewers is hardly touched on. For Münster's brewers, see Krumbholtz, pp. 483–502. For the growth of the industry in Münster, the income from the brewing tax is revealing: in 1567, the city received 5,414 marks from beer brewing (StdAM, AVIII, 188, GR, vol. 6, fols. 233–233v); half a century later, in 1618, tax on beer brewing totaled 14,389 marks (GR, vol. 13, fols. 138v–140).

slanderers," and, when the magistrates refused to take action, hinted at unfavorable guild reaction at the next election.[64]

There was a simple reason why the magistrates refused to punish the representatives of the Gemeinheit in 1606: it was most probable that several councillors were involved, either as direct instigators or as relatives of instigators. Although the names of those who presented grievances against the guild leaders in 1606 are not known, those who composed a similar list of grievances in 1614 were named in the council minutes.[65] The twenty-two representatives of the Gemeinheit included five present or future magistrates;[66] in terms of occupations, they included twelve lawyers and notaries, three merchants, and two patricians. More important, at least six men were members of the Jesuit sodality B.M.V. Assumptionis.[67] The real motive behind the criticism of the guilds was religion. The very first article of grievances blamed the guild leaders for calling up the civic militia during the 1603 Papal Jubilee celebrations in Münster, a move, the article argued, aimed at intimidating the clergy as well as preventing the citizens from participation in the processions.[68] The other articles attacked the guildsmen for occupying the majority of commanding positions on the militia, for favoring their own in disputes between artisans and other citizens, and for presuming that they alone represented the entire civic community in the political process of the republic. Moreover, by meddling in affairs which did not

64. See StdAM, AII, 20, RP, 1606, many entries, see especially those under Feb. 23, Dec. 7, 14, and 19, vol. 38, fols. 24–26v, 258–59, 264–265v, 271–271v; see also fols. 33, 44, 75, 78–79, 175.

65. See StdAM, AII, 20, RP, 1614, June 13, vol. 46, fol. 240. The names have not yet been published and analyzed; the twenty-two representatives were Dr. Johann Heerde, Dr. Johann Droste, Dr. Johann Loges, Lic. Dietrich zum Sande, Lic. Reinert Ketterich, Wilhelm Bockhorst, Lic. Hermann Voss, Lic. Johann Alers, Johann Averhagen, Bernhard Buck, Christian Lordenbeck, Johann zur Lippe, Hermann Frie, Johann Grüter, Edo Elertz, Christopher zu Schloet, Dietrich Schoettler, Gert Hase, Heinrich Nunning, Bernt Uphaus, Johann Joddevelt, and Heinrich Sterneman. I have identified all but three of the twenty-two men from membership rolls of the Jesuit sodalities, published matriculation rolls of lawyers and notaries, the *Bürgerbuch* published by Eduard Schulte, membership list of the Saint Anne Confraternity of clothiers, and my prosopographical file on city councillors. Of the three men I have not been able to identify, two—Bernhard Buck and Johann Grüter—were patricians.

66. They were Dr. Johann Heerde, Lic. Dietrich zum Sande, Wilhelm Bockhorst, Lic. Johann Alers, and Johann Averhagen.

67. They were Johann Heerde, Johann Droste, Dietrich zum Sande, Reinert Ketterich, Wilhelm Bockhorst, and Johann Alers.

68. The gravamina of the Gemeinheit has been published; see Krumbholtz, pp. 129ff. In the city council's reply to Emperor Rudolf II, the magistrates explained the mobilization of the militia as a precaution to protect the procession against possible attacks from the Dutch. It seems to me that this explanation was offered merely as an excuse and that the real motive of the guild leaders corresponded to the charge in the grievances.

concern them (no doubt, references to the guilds' positions regarding the Jesuits and the burial and election edicts), the guild leaders had brought a bad name to the city and disadvantages to all her citizens. In conclusion, the *gravamina* stated that being more numerous and wealthy than the artisans, the citizens in the Gemeinheit would no longer tolerate the presumption of power by the Gesamtgilde, and would henceforth recognize only the city council as the sole legitimate political authority in the city.

It seemed that the Society of Jesus played a coordinating role behind these political maneuvers. The patres followed elections to the city council with great interest and rejoiced whenever their opponents lost out.[69] Moreover, Jesuit sodalities served as an informal politico-confessional party; and strategies to remove Protestant magistrates were discussed during meetings.[70] The Jesuits and their supporters were alarmed because Protestant strength on the city council grew in the first years of the seventeenth century. In 1605 and 1606, the peak years, nine out of twenty-four magistrates each year were Protestants.[71] Thereafter, especially beginning with 1610, the strength of the Protestants declined while that of the clerical faction on the council rose. Biological attrition played a role here. Many Protestant magistrates died within a few years of one another: Melchior Steinhoff died in 1606, Johann Block in 1611, Andreas Wilckinghoff in 1612, Hans Laeke also in the 1610s, Johann Beifang in 1620, and Bernhard Burmann in 1621. Conversely, a new generation of burgher elite from Catholic families who had been educated by the Jesuits started to reinforce the ranks of the clerical faction in the 1610s: Wilhelm Bockhorst was elected in 1609, his brother Heinrich attained magisterial office in 1611, together with Hermann Heerde, Nicolaus von Berswordt (son of Bürgermeister Johann von Berswordt), and Wilhelm Lageman were elected in 1612, Heinrich Frie-Vendt in 1614, Johann Alers and Johann Averhagen in 1615, and Dr. Johann Heerde in 1616. The change in the relative strength of the Protestants and the militant Catholics on the city council is presented in table 5.1. While the other magistrates cannot be identified as strong supporters of the Jesuits, most belonged, nevertheless, to prominent families whose ties to the Catholic

69. Cf. StAM, FM, SFG, "Comp. Hist. Coll.," fols. 48v, 59v, 71v, 78v.

70. StAM, MSS. VII, 1034, "Liber Sodalitatis," Jan. 20, 1615, fol. 14: "In festo S.S. Fabiani et Sebastiani electii novis senatii, tres eiecti, tres subrogati, certatum de insigni calvinista eii irende ab hora 2 ad qua vespertina inter paria vota contraria, nec haeretici alea fortuna conmittere auso, tandem peraicerent, nec eiectii Calvinista. Interim catholici in aliis personis magis catholicas obtinverent, quod optabant. Marre in templo uno hora 7 cantatum horam missa. Intimista et mediani in aula audiverunt famam non impeditis lectionibus, etsi esset dies Martis: na die Electionis non solet dari venia, ne in foro fuit studiosi insolentes, turba populari immixti."

71. Analysis based on council lists for relevant years; see StdAM, AII, 01, vol. 3 (B).

Table 5.1   Protestants and Clericals on the City Council of
Münster, 1600–18

Protestants		Clericals	Protestants		Clericals
1600	2	6	1610	5	5
1601	3	6	1611	3	5
1602	5	5	1612	5	7
1603	5	5	1613	2	7
1604	6	5	1614	4	6
1605	9	4	1615	3	8
1606	9	4	1616	5	7
1607	8	4	1617	4	7
1608	8	4	1618	4	8
1609	6	5			

Source: StdAM, AII, 01, vol. 3 (B); and appendix 1.

Church in Münster remained unquestioned. Hence, the increasing strength of the clerical faction on the city council specifically reflected the growing support for the Counter-Reformation among the ruling families of Münster.

Like the city council, the larger community also came to be increasingly polarized in the years immediately before the Thirty Years' War. Almost all clashes in Münster occurred between supporters and opponents of the Jesuits. None of these resulted in fatal casualties, but a tavern brawl of 1615 sounded a distinctly ominous note. On January 15, two burghers almost came to blows in the city's Überwasser beer cellar. Intoxicated, Johann Lemgo boasted that "the sodalities in this city are already four companies strong, and the fifth is right there because the students would come if they were to attack the new fortifications at the *Georgskommende* and the *Fraterhaus*." A neighbor, Caspar Meinertz, retorted, and the heated exchange would have ended up in bloodshed had the two not been hauled off to the town hall.[72] Behind the frequent fights between hotheaded students at the Jesuit College and impetuous journeymen lurked the hostility between two parties in the citizenry; only the self-restraint exercised on both sides prevented a major outbreak of civil violence in those years.

72. See StdAM, AII, 20, RP, 1615, Jan. 16, vol. 46, fos. 518–20. The Jesuits were also very concerned that the incident would incite a riot directed against the Society and tried to cool tempers among their own supporters. See StAM, MSS. VII, 1034, "Liber Sodalitatis," Jan. 27, 1615, fol. 14v: "Die martis fuit consultatio usque ad hora 11 in aula et actum de Lemgoro et Casparo Meiners, conclususque, rem non negligendus se predendus, diffamatores predictos et Aldemenner que rem detulerant ad senatu. Das Rottereien verhindern würden."

A NEW BREED OF CLERGY

Among those who resisted the Counter-Reformation in Münster were not only Catholic magistrates and citizens but also some members of the clergy. After 1585, an increasing proportion of clerics in Münster was made up of men and women born and trained outside of Westphalia. Their presence aroused resentment among the native clergy, especially when the newcomers brought with them ideas and rules for moral reform. The Society of Jesus was the most obvious example: patres from many parts of the Empire staffed the college at Münster, and the expansion of the Society treaded on many entrenched clerical privileges and excited much jealousy. The early seventeenth century also represented a historical landmark of the spread of religious orders in German cities, a period comparable to the thirteenth century. In the years just before the Thirty Years' War, the Sisters of Poor Clare and the Capuchins established congregations in Münster; the Dominicans came later, in 1621.

Even the secular and parochial clergy included more and more men alien to the traditions of the city of Saint Ludger; they usually occupied the highest administrative positions in the diocesan hierarchy and represented the ecclesiastical counterparts to the territorial officials appointed by archbishops Ernst and Ferdinand to help consolidate the Catholic clerical-territorial state. Nicolaus Arresdorff, a native of Luxembourg and guardian of the Cologne Province of the Franciscans from 1584 to 1587, was appointed pastor of Saint Lambert's in Münster.[73] Arnold von Bocholtz, a native of Roermond (then part of the Spanish Netherlands), was a canon at Münster, Hildesheim, and Liège and holder of a number of other benefices; he served as the leading diplomat under the Wittelsbach archbishops of Cologne.[74] A third important figure was Johann Hartmann, vicar of Archbishop Ferdinand and plenipotentiary of ecclesiastical affairs in the Bishopric of Münster. A native of Bonn, he, like Bocholtz, was educated at the Collegium Germanicum in Rome and became one of Archbishop Ferdinand's most trusted advisers.[75] Characteristic of this new breed of clerical bureaucrats was their extensive legal training, both in canon and Roman law, reflecting the judicial emphasis placed on the Counter-Reformation by the Roman Curia itself.

Arresdorff and Bocholtz, together with Dean Everwin von Droste and four other Münster clerics, comprised the commissioners of the Clerical Council, an organ created by Archbishop Ernst in 1601 to supervise and

---

73. For a brief biographical note, see Adolph Tibus, *Geschichtliche Nachrichten über die Weihbischöfe von Münster* (Münster, 1862), pp. 136–67.

74. Cf. Herbert Immenkötter, *Die Protokolle des Geistlichen Rates in Münster 1601–1612* (Münster, 1972), pp. 29ff.

75. For Hartmann's biography, see chap. 4, n. 30.

discipline the clergy in the bishopric.[76] The commissioners were empowered to suspend clerics suspected of heresy or moral depravity.[77] The move to tighten clerical discipline frightened many who had been eschewing the rigors of the religious life. In the early years of the seventeenth century, monks and nuns ran away from cloisters and a few converted to Protestantism to flee the measures of the Counter-Reformation.[78]

The most bitter clerical opposition to the Counter-Reformation surrounded the confrontation between the Ringe beguines in Münster and the Observants from Cologne. The friars, who served as confessors to the beguines, sponsored the introduction of the Poor Clares to Münster by taking over the beguinage and integrating the sisters into the new religious order. This confrontation aligned Archbishop Ferdinand, the cathedral canons, the Observants, and the Poor Clares on one side, the magistrates, the guild leaders, the Münster Franciscans, and the Ringe beguines on the other; it provides us with a most instructive example of the resistance offered by local, urban, and traditional Catholicism to the innovations of the Counter-Reformation.

Ringe beguinage in the parish of Saint Ludger was traditionally associated with the leading guild and mercantile families of Münster.[79] In the fifteenth century, the beguines adopted the Third Rule of Saint Francis and the beguinage was visited by the Observant Franciscans from Hamm. In March 1613, two Observants approached the magistrates in Münster, informing the city fathers of the order's plans to reform the beguinage and introduce the Poor Clares into the reformed house. The magistrates, however, refused to support them.[80] On their own, the Observants informed the beguines of the impending reform.

In April, the mother superior of Ringe beguinage appealed for help at the city council, pleading that the beguinage was founded by citizens for daughters of the city, and that it should never be taken over by strangers.[81] A second letter from the beguines in May warned the magistrates of the pressures they were under: the Observants strongly disapproved of the ambiguous clerical character of the house and wanted to

76. For the names of the other commissioners on the Clerical Council, see Immenkötter, pp. 24–36.

77. Cf. Immenkötter, pp. 36ff.

78. In 1602, Lucas Reddeker, a runaway monk from Marienfeld cloister, was expelled from Münster by the magistrates; see StdAM, AII, 20, RP, 1602, Feb. 15, vol. 34, fol. 29. A year earlier, the council minutes also recorded that two nuns, Stine N [N = unknown name] and Maria Wolterinck, ran away from Aegidii cloister; see RP, 1601, Dec. 17, vol. 33, fol. 323.

79. See chap. 2, pp. 40–41.

80. StdAM, AII, 20, RP, 1613, March 15, vol. 45, fols. 147–48.

81. Cf. letter of beguines to the city council dated April 26, 1613; StdAM, AXIII, 426.

put the beguines under cloistered rules. When the beguines resisted, Archbishop Ferdinand, a benefactor of the Poor Clares and the Obser- vants, threatened the beguines with excommunication. He sent Johann Hartmann and Nicolaus Vigerius, provincial of the Lower Rhine Prov- ince of the Observants, to visit and warn the beguines of the conse- quences of their obstinance. The beguines regarded the policy as an infringement of their liberties as well as an attack on civic rights. They implored the magistrates to defend their cause as they had no one else to turn to.[82] A few days earlier, the guild Aldermen Heinrich Dickmann and Ludolf Buermeister had already interceded on their behalf before the city council. The guild elders emphasized that the beguinage was intended for "honorable burgher children" and that the interest of the civic commu- nity as a whole was at stake.[83] The city council wrote to Archbishop Ferdinand defending the traditional practice of the beguines of attending church services in Saint Ludger's and mixing freely with their fellow citizens; a cloistered religious life had never been part of the heritage of the Ringe beguinage.[84] In his reply to the magistrates, Archbishop Ferdi- nand blamed the beguines for leading a too-worldly life and wanted to impose a stricter religious rule on them.[85] In July, two Observants visited the beguines to put further pressure on the women. While the beguines added a new supplication in their daily prayer—"Deliver us, o Lord, from the snares of the evil monks!"[86] —the guild leaders urged the magis- trates to intervene openly. Although the city council refused to act di- rectly in what appeared to be an internal ecclesiastical matter, it agreed to appeal to the archbishop and to Rome.[87]

Meanwhile, the Poor Clares had slipped into Münster without prior magisterial approval and were lodging in a house on Lobachsstegge owned by the former city councillor Bernd van Detten the Younger.[88] The city council summoned Detten to face hearings because civic laws barred clerical habitation of burgher houses and the residence of strangers without magisterial residence permit. In an early September meeting, both the magistrates and the guild leaders concurred that there were

82. Letter, dated May 20, 1613, is in StdAM, AXIII, 426.

83. Their letter is dated May 14, 1613; StdAM, AXIII, 426.

84. Cf. letter of the city council of Münster to Archbishop Ferdinand dated May 20, 1613; StdAM, AXIII, 426.

85. Cf. letter of Archbishop Ferdinand to the city council of Münster dated June 28, 1613; StdAM, AXIII, 426.

86. Cf. StdAM, MS. 4, Franciscan Chronicle, fol. 69.

87. Cf. StdAM, AII, 20, RP, 1613, July 26, vol. 45, fol. 307.

88. See StdAM, AII, 20, RP, 1613, Aug. 23, vol. 45, fols. 351–52. Bernd was son of Bernd van Detten the Older, also a city councillor; he and his siblings were co-founders of the Collegium Dettensiam and were all strong supporters of the Counter-Reformation; see appendix 1, no. 36.

already too many clerics in Münster, and that two more religious orders—and begging orders at that—were certainly not welcomed. They asked the episcopal officials to reconsider allowing the Observants and Poor Clares to settle in the city.[89] By the time Bernd van Detten and his son Heinrich appeared before the city council in late September, more Poor Clares had arrived in Münster.[90] The Dettens said that the sisters wanted to stay for only one year, but the magistrates and guild leaders instructed them, under penalty of a heavy fine, to evict the nuns.[91] The Poor Clares, nevertheless, stayed on, and were negotiating for the purchase of a house on Bispinghof. The magistrates complained to the episcopal officials, citing that the Jesuits had already been allowed to establish a congregation; moreover, the difference between the fathers and the Poor Clares was one between a teaching and a mendicant order, and the latter would only be a nuisance to the citizens.[92] To the delight of the guild leaders, the magistrates again denied the Poor Clares permission to reside.[93] Negotiations continued into December until the magistrates were convinced of the determination of Archbishop Ferdinand and the cathedral canons to support the Poor Clares; they began to consider the possibility of allowing the nuns to stay but without granting them tax exemption. The guild leaders, however, urged the magistrates not to yield.[94]

By February 1614, under mounting pressure from the archbishop, the magistrates finally agreed to grant a residence permit to the Poor Clares, a decision hotly contested by the guild Aldermen and masters, who pointed out that there were too many beggars, poor people, and clerics in Münster. The only concession the guild leaders would make was to allow the Poor Clares to live in an already established ecclesiastical house, with the stipulation that they not buy burgher property.[95] The magistrates reported the continued opposition of the community to the episcopal officials.[96] At the end of May, Archbishop Ferdinand wrote directly to the magistrates, informing them that he himself had just purchased the disputed house on Bispinghof for the Poor Clares, and asked that the city fathers humor him and not raise more objections to the sisters' settlement in Münster.[97] The magistrates persuaded the guild

89. StdAM, AII, 20, RP, 1613, Sept. 3, vol. 45, fol. 371.
90. StdAM, AII, 20, RP, 1613, Sept. 13 and 14, vol. 45, fols. 374, 378–79.
91. StdAM, AII, 20, RP, 1613, Sept. 20, vol. 45, fols. 385–87.
92. StdAM, AII, 20, RP, 1613, Sept. 11, vol. 45, fols. 416–17.
93. Ibid., fol. 418.
94. StdAM, AII, 20, RP, 1613, Dec. 13 and 16, vol. 45, fols. 515–16, 522–23, 528–29.
95. StdAM, AII, 20, RP, 1614, Feb. 14, 18, and 21, vol. 46, fols. 65, 76, 79–80.
96. StdAM, AII, 20, RP, 1614, March 7 and 17, vol. 46, fols. 103, 112.
97. StdAM, AII, 20, RP, 1614, May 23, vol. 46, fol. 203.

leaders to consent, fearing that Ferdinand might otherwise be offended and punish the city.[98] The guild leaders, obdurate as ever, provoked a violent disagreement with the magistrates; the acrimonious debates threatened to degenerate into civic confrontations. Both the city council and the Gesamtgilde appealed to the citizenry. The former exclaimed that the condescension and contumacy on the part of the guild leaders could simply no longer be tolerated; the latter claimed to represent the voice of the burghers. It was during this confrontation that an extraordinary delegation was called from the Gemeinheit which then proceeded to present a list of grievances against the guilds.[99] Eventually, the guild leaders agreed to let the Poor Clares stay, but only on condition that they promise not to buy burgher houses, failing which they should be expelled and Bernd van Detten deprived of his citizenship. The magistrates reasoned that the nuns were already in Münster and expelling them would only intensify ill feelings on both sides; if a consensus could not be reached, they would act without the guilds. Only when the magistrates had produced the gravamina of the Gemeinheit did the guild leaders soften their stand.[100] The councillors further accused the guild leaders of stirring up the burghers, forming a faction in secret, and planning an uprising. Faced with these charges, the guild Aldermen and masters excused their behavior and agreed to allow a specific number of Poor Clares and Observants to settle in Münster.[101] After the agreement, minor irritations kept straining relations into the summer.[102] The hostilities engendered by the dispute were evident on the Feast of the Assumption of the Blessed Virgin (August 18), when boys climbed trees to get into the courtyard of the Poor Clares' cloister and taunted the nuns, who were listening to a sermon.[103]

Scarcely had tempers cooled over the dispute when another mendicant order, the Capuchins, asked permission to establish a congregation in Münster.[104] The guild leaders again objected, arguing that too many

98. StdAM, AII, 20, RP, 1614, May 30, vol. 46, fols. 214–16.

99. StdAM, AII, 20, RP, 1614, June 2, 6, 7, 13, vol. 46, fols. 221–22, 228–29, 230–31, 240–41.

100. StdAM, AII, 20, RP, 1614, June 16, vol. 46, fols. 246–49.

101. Eight to ten nuns, four to five lay sisters, and two monks were allowed; see StdAM, AII, 20, RP, 1614, June 16 and July 4, vol. 46, fols. 260–61.

102. The Poor Clares did not wait for the council's permission before they moved from Detten's house into the house on Bispinghof; guild leaders saw this as an insult to civic authority and talked anew of expulsion. The magistrates refused to consider extreme measures. See StdAM, AII, 20, RP, 1614, Aug. 1, 11, 22, 25, vol. 46, fols. 301–04, 319–20, 327–28, 331–32.

103. The city council said it would investigate and punish the culprits, probably suspecting someone had put the boys up to the act; see StdAM, AII, 20, RP, 1614, Aug. 18, vol. 46, fol. 323.

104. StdAM, AII, 20, RP, 1614, Dec. 12, vol. 46, fol. 489.

properties had already passed into clerical hands and been removed from taxation.[105] When the Capuchins agreed not to purchase civic properties or beg, the magistrates readily granted permission to reside; the guild leaders were now simply opposed to seeing any more clerics in the city.[106] Throughout 1615, the Capuchins did not succeed in finding a house in Münster due to the opposition of the guildsmen.[107] The key issue in the 1616 negotiations was whether the Capuchins would add a further burden to the already overtaxed burghers. When the friars offered to give Münster 1,000 dalers to help the poor citizens bear their share of taxes in exchange for the right to buy a burgher house, the magistrates raised no more obstacles.[108] The guild leaders fought and lost every inch of the way, first objecting to granting permission at all,[109] then wanting to keep the friars outside of the city,[110] and finally, trying to shove the new religious order aside to an undesirable lot at the edge of the city walls.[111]

Concurrent with the disputes over the admissions of the Poor Clares and the Capuchins, renewed pressure was exerted on the Ringe beguines to submit.[112] Upon the appeal to civic liberties by the beguines and the guild leaders,[113] the magistrates wrote to the provincial of the Observants in Cologne.[114] The local Franciscans also supported the beguines. Angered by the resistance, Archbishop Ferdinand instructed the provincial of the Franciscans in Cologne, Brother Johann Pelking, to warn the Münster friars to withdraw their support of the beguines. Winand Alstorff, guardian of the Münster Franciscans, ignored repeated warnings not to oppose the Observants, whereupon he was suspended and later excommunicated.[115] Alstorff then begged the magistrates as the secular

105. StdAM, AII, 20, RP, 1615, Jan. 15, vol. 46, fol. 515.

106. StdAM, AII, 20, RP, 1615, Feb. 13, vol. 47, fols. 43–44.

107. StdAM, AII, 20, RP, 1615, Sept. 4, Dec. 11 and 18, vol. 47, fols. 324, 512–13, 522–23.

108. StdAM, AII, 20, RP, 1616, June 3, vol. 48, fols. 184–86.

109. StdAM, AII, 20, RP, 1616, May 27, vol. 48, fol. 178.

110. Ibid., July 8, Oct. 3, 7, 14, and 24, vol. 48, fols. 236–38, 396–97, 401–02, 416–19, 425–27.

111. Ibid., Dec. 2, 19, and 20, vol. 48, fols. 498–99, 536–38, 541–43.

112. Cf. letter of beguines to the city council dated Oct. 23, 1615, complaining of renewed pressure and beseeching the magistrates to defend a three-hundred-year-old civic religious institution; StdAM, AXIII, 426. See also StdAM, C (Stiftungsarchiv), Kloster Ringe, 46–48, documents covering the period from 1613 to 1619.

113. StdAM, AII, 20, RP, 1615, Dec. 7, vol. 47, fol. 505.

114. Cf. letter dated Dec. 16, 1615, StdAM, AXIII, 426.

115. Cf. StdAM, MS. 4, Franciscan chronicle, fol. 69: "Unde irritatus serenissimus Ferdinandus Episcopos acerrimas tam ipsi Provinciali quam Ordini minas scripsit P. Joanni Pelkingio Provinciali, nisi P. Guardianum Monasteriensem Windarum Alstorff a sua moniales istas contra Observantes defendendi sententia revocaret. . . ."

arm to protect him against impending prosecution.[116] Simultaneous pressure was brought on the beguines: the Observants forced the habit and the cloistered rules on the sisters, and forbade them to appeal the actions.[117] When the magistrates interceded on behalf of Alstorff and the beguines to the superiors of the mendicant orders in Cologne, the friars replied that clerical obedience was at stake; supported by Archbishop Ferdinand, the orders must hold on to their positions.[118] With civic liberties and religious traditions thus challenged, the city fathers appealed to the College of Cardinals and to the pope on behalf of the beguinage.[119] The slow machinery of papal government eventually referred the dispute back to Cardinal Marone, papal nuncio in Cologne.[120] A final compromise was not reached until 1621: The beguines were to wear the habit and follow cloister rules, but they were allowed to retain certain traditional practices; the Observants were told not to bother the sisters any longer.[121]

More significant than the irritations caused by these confrontations was the general pattern of change apparent in the mendicant orders and in their relations with the Münsteraners. Plans to reform the Franciscan cloister in Münster had been hatched already in the 1580s, when Duke Johann Wilhelm wanted to turn the cloister over to the Jesuits.[122] Although the friars enjoyed widespread support among the burghers at the end of the sixteenth century, the cloister stood in sad need of reform.

The guardian friar Anton Boeker misappropriated the funds of the cloister to enrich his relatives and was only deposed in 1600, four years after he was elected superior of the Münster Franciscans.[123] Even though lay support for the friars grew in the 1600s (the first decade of the century saw the foundation of a new confraternity of Saint Francis), the Münster Franciscans were criticized by the Observants in Cologne for cor-

116. Cf. StdAM, AII, 20, RP, 1615, Dec. 18, vol. 47, fol. 525; see also his letter to the city council dated Jan. 4, 1616, StdAM, AXIII, 326.

117. Cf. letter of beguines to the city council dated Jan. 7, 1616, StdAM, AXIII, 426.

118. Cf. letter by the Observants and the Franciscans to the city council dated Feb. 1, 1616, StdAM, AXIII, 426.

119. Cf. copy of letter from the city council to the College of Cardinals dated Feb. 21, 1616, and letter by the same to the pope dated Jan. 3, 1618, both in StdAM, AXIII, 426.

120. Cf. letter of papal chancery to the city council dated Dec. 16, 1619, StdAM, AXIII, 426.

121. Cf. letter from Dean Johann Weiden of Saint Sevesin in Cologne to the city council of Münster dated Dec. 15, 1621; Weiden had been appointed arbitrator by the Apostolic Chamber in Rome and by the papal nuncio in Cologne, StdAM, AXIII, 426. Still the dispute dragged on until 1628 because the beguines kept complaining of harassment by the Observants; see StdAM, C, 51.

122. See chap. 3, pp. 60ff.

123. StdAM, MS. 4, Franciscan chronicle, fols. 42, 56–57.

ruption.[124] Jealousy certainly fueled the quarrel between the Franciscans and the Observants over the beguines. The Münster friars also resented the Rhinelanders, who relied on central ecclesiastical authority to intimidate the local friars. The Observants and the Jesuits, on the other hand, viewed the Franciscans as the decayed remains of an older, delapidated Church; they coveted the properties of the friars and wanted to use these to further the work of the Counter-Reformation and their own orders as well.[125] After Winand Alstorff had been excommunicated, he and two other ex-friars, Caspar Martin of the Capuchins and Nicolaus Fuchs of the Observants, waged a war of polemics against the high-handed policies of their Cologne superiors. Alstroff himself eventually became a Protestant.[126]

Under pressure from the Counter-Reformation, the Münster Franciscans also distanced themselves from the burghers, with whom they had enjoyed centuries of rapport. In 1610, they refused burial to a child of David Wöstmann. He had already given one daler to the friars and obtained permission to bury his child, but when the funeral procession reached the cloister, another friar (probably Nicolaus Arresdorff) accused him of failure to go to confession and communion, and the friar refused to bury the dead child.[127] The friars also forbade burghers to hold meetings in their cloister. When questioned by the magistrates and guild leaders in 1613 as to why they had refused permission for the smiths' guild to gather in the cloister, they replied that they were acting under orders from the provincial in Cologne. From now on, the provincial ordered, the Franciscans must lead a secluded life, avoid contact with the laity, and exclude worldly affairs from the cloister. The displeased magistrates threatened to cut off support for the friars.[128]

The social composition of the mendicant orders in Münster was changing, too. Whereas most of the friars between 1535 and 1610 came from the little towns and villages of Münsterland, the new mendicant

124. StdAM, MS. 4, Franciscan chronicle, fol. 62.

125. In 1615, for example, the Observants and Jesuits clashed with the Franciscans over the cloister at Noresien, near Cologne, because the inmates wanted to transfer their allegiance from the Franciscan to the Observant order. See StdAM, MS. 4, Franciscan chronicle, fols. 73–74.

126. The tract they wrote was: *Ausgang auss Babel/ Sodama/ Egypten und eingang in die Stadt des lebendigen Gottes/ ins himlische Jerusalem/ in das hauss Gottes, da Christus allein das fundament und Eckstein ist, dreyer Vornehmer Geistlicher Ordens leuth der dreyerlei unterschiedener Franciscaner Mönche orden eines Obersten der Capuciner zu Uranien/ prasidenten der Observanten zum Hamm/ Obersten der Gaudenten zu Münster in Westfalen* (Johann Horenburg, 1616). Alstorff became a strong proponent of clerical marriage. See StdAM, MS. 4, Franciscan chronicle, fols. 70–71.

127. StdAM, AII, 20, RP, 1610, May 7, vol. 42, fols. 83–83v.

128. StdAM, AII, 20, RP, 1613, Aug. 5, Sept. 2 and 9, vol. 45, fols. 328, 362, 365–66.

orders included many Rhinelanders. The Franciscans were mainly recruited from humble burgher ranks and from the villages; the new mendicant orders, in contrast, enjoyed the support of the nobility, the patriciate, and the civic elite. A noblewoman, Dorothea Smisinck, headed the first Poor Clares in Münster; among the other eight sisters was another noblewoman as well as daughters from rich burgher families.[129] Neither poor nor humble, the new mendicant orders symbolized the new dignity and self-confidence of the Counter-Reformation clergy; they were ready once more to win salvation for all.[130] After almost a century of declining reputation and sagging membership, brought about in large part by the Reformation, the fortunes of the mendicant orders had gone full cycle; once again, they attracted noblemen, patricians, and the leading families of Münster, and regained their status as elite sacerdotal and social institutions.

These conflicts point to the strong differences between two types of Catholicism. One was the Counter-Reformation militancy of the prince-bishop, the territorial officials, the Jesuits, and new religious orders; the other embodied traditional, civic piety, and was supported by magistrates, local clergy, and citizens. Between the religious reforms and political centralization called for by the Counter-Reformation and the traditions of civic piety and autonomy, the Münsteraners faced a most difficult dilemma.

129. The other noblewoman was Mechtchild von Plettenberg; a nun was named Margaretha Alers, probably a sister of magistrate Lic. Johann Alers; another, Magdelena Kock, probably belonged to the rich baker family of the same name. See StdAM, MS. 4, Franciscan chronicle, fol. 77.

130. Nicolaus Arresdorff, for example, bequeathed 2,234 dalers to the clergy and the poor; for his will (Feb. 11, 1616), see StdAM, MS. 4, Franciscan chronicle, fols. 88–90.

CHAPTER SIX

Changes in Civic Culture

It was not primarily through political pressure that the Counter-Reformation gained influence in Münster, but rather through the introduction of a new culture, through linguistic and educational innovations, through the printing press, and through assaults on traditional popular culture. The three-quarters of a century between the suppression of the Anabaptist revolt and the beginning of the Thirty Years' War, especially the forty years after the advent of the Jesuits in Münster, saw drastic and fundamental changes in the culture of Westphalia.

At the beginning of the sixteenth century, Münster was bound by trade, marriage, population movements, language, and customs to the Hanseatic cities of the Baltic coast and to her Dutch neighbors.[1] The prominent role played by Netherlanders in the Anabaptist Kingdom attested to the close relations between the two regions.[2] By the end of the

1. For relations between Münster and the Hanseatic cities of the Baltic, see J. Rondorf, *Die westfälischen Städte in ihrem Verhältnis zur Hanse bis zum Beginn des 16. Jahrhunderts* (Münster, 1905); J. Berres, *Münster und seine handelspolitischen Beziehungen zur deutschen Hanse* (Münster, 1919); and Luise von Winterfeld, "Das westfälische Hansequartier," *Der Raum Westfalen* II:1 (Münster, 1955), pp. 257–354. The area between the IJssel and the Weser formed a linguistic, cultural, familial, and commercial unity in the late Middle Ages and the early sixteenth century. Westphalian Low German was more closely related to East Middle Dutch than to the Rhinish-Hessian dialects to the south or to the other Low German dialects of the Baltic port cities. Between Deventer and Münster an open border existed until the late sixteenth century; Overijssel and western Münsterland are rather similar in landscape, and the cities of Deventer and Münster enjoyed very close commercial and cultural ties. The Dutch-German border today is the result of historical forces which pulled eastern Netherlands toward Amsterdam and Westphalia toward Cologne. See Franz Petri, "Vom Verhältnis Westfalens zu den östlichen Niederlanden," *Westfalen* 34 (1956), pp. 161–68; F. Petri and W. Jappe Alberts, *Gemeinsame Probleme Deutsch-Niederländischer Landes- und Volksforschung* (Groningen, 1962); W. Jappe Alberts, "Die Beziehungen zwischen Geldern und Münster im 14. und 15. Jahrhundert" *WF* 9 (1956), pp. 83–95; and Robert S. Platt, *A Geographical Study of the Dutch-German Border* (Münster, 1958). For familial ties and migration patterns between Westphalia, the Hanseatic Baltic, and east Netherlands, see Ketteler, "Geschlechterkreis," and W. Moorrees, *Het Münstersche Geslacht van der Wyck* (The Hague, 1911).

2. The links between the Dutch and Münster Anabaptists have been thoroughly investigated by Albert F. Mellink; see his *Amsterdam en de Wederdopers in de zestiende Eeuw* (Nijmegen, 1978), esp. pp. 40–66; "Das niederländisch-westfälische Täufertum im 16.

century, however, Münster's ties with the Netherlands had weakened because of the war between Spain and the new republic; the Westphalian metropole also felt the stronger pull of the Rhineland, of Central and South Germany, thanks to the ascendancy of the Counter-Reformation. While some of the factors at work were clearly political, the long-term currents of cultural change need to be more closely examined.

THE DECLINE OF LOW GERMAN

Whereas pre-Tridentine, late medieval popular piety in Münster was closely related to the *Devotio Moderna* of the Low Countries and expressed itself in the tongue of the burghers, Middle Low German, the Counter-Reformation looked to Munich, Vienna, and Rome, and spoke in refined, foreign tongues—Latin and High German.

The process of the displacement of Low German as a written language in the North German chanceries began in the late thirteenth century, a time when High German reigned supreme through the *Minnesänger* and through the political ascendancy of South Germany during the dynasties of the Hohenstauffen and the Hapsburg.[3] The glacial invasion of the Low German realm by High German in the Middle Ages turned into an avalanche with Luther's translation of the Bible into Saxon, a Middle German dialect more closely related to High German than to Low.[4] A second assault on Low German in Westphalia came through Bavaria: under the Wittelsbach archbishops Ernst and Ferdinand, Bavarian High German radiated from Cologne to transform slowly the official written language of the extensive territories of the archiepiscopal principality.[5] After the establishment of the Society of Jesus in Germany around the middle of the sixteenth century, patres from South Germany streamed to the North in search of lost souls, while sons of the Catholic urban elite in the North went south to Cologne, Mainz, Freiburg, Dillingen, and Munich to study and assimilate more of the ascendant High German language. After 1570, High German had replaced Low in the official records

---

Jahrhundert," in Hans-Jürgen Görtz, ed., *Umstrittenes Täufertum 1525–1975* (Göttingen, 1975), pp. 206–22; and his ground-breaking study, *De Wederdopers in de Noordelijke Nederlanden 1531–1544* (Groningen, 1953).

3. Cf. Hans Eggers, *Deutsche Sprachgeschichte III. Das Frühneuhochdeutsche* (Hamburg, 1969), pp. 21–38; and Kurt Böttcher, *Das Vordringen der hochdeutschen Sprache in den Urkunden des niederdeutschen Gebietes vom 13. bis 16. Jahrhundert* (Berlin, 1916), pp. 71ff.

4. Luther's role in the shaping of modern German is discussed by Eggers, pp. 161–79; see also Hugo Moser, *Deutsche Sprachgeschichte* (Stuttgart, 1950), pp. 122ff.

5. Eggers, p. 189.

of Münster.[6] By the end of the sixteenth century, notarial instruments appeared without exception in High German, as did increasing numbers of private letters and account books.[7]

The displacement of Low German by High was not an even process; linguistic stratification followed social and political distinctions as well. The city council, documented by the language of the protocols and the official correspondence, was in the forefront of the linguistic innovations.[8] Account books of the parishes kept by lay overseers persisted in Low German until the early seventeenth century.[9] Along juristic lines, the Chamber Court used High German, the Ecclesiastical Court Latin, and the city court, which followed customs, Low German. Linguistic division also partially reflected class stratification: the ruling elite was more likely to adopt High German than the craftsmen or the barely literate day laborers. But within the civic elite, families associated with the academic-juristic milieu favored High German, while leading guild and mercantile families often held on to Low.[10] Women of the civic elite, too, used Low German well into the seventeenth century.[11] Certain occupational groups spearheaded the adoption of High German—the notaries, the lawyers, copyists, academicians, and officials of the consolidating territorial state. Others, notably the guildsmen, were repositories of tradition.[12] Different ecclesiastical bodies responded differently to the

6. Council minutes of Münster are extant beginning with the year 1564; they were still kept in Low German. In November 1571, Johann Pagenstecker, a native of neighboring Warendorf, was appointed secretary of the city council; thereafter the protocols were kept in High German.

7. This generalization is based on linguistic analysis of wills deposited in the StdAM, B, Test. I, 19 volumes. Perhaps the most telling indicator of change is the way numbers and names were written. The "ing" ending in names, for example, had replaced the traditional "inck" orthography. Another important indicator was the general adoption of the dative article which differentiates the usage of "de" in Low German.

8. In the territories the princes were generally the innovators, leading the cities and the ecclesiastical institutions in adopting High German. Within the cities, the city council usually took the lead. See Böttcher, pp. 75f. See also his discussion of the reception of High German in Lübeck, "Das Vordringen der Hochdeutschen Sprache in den Urkunden des niederdeutschen Gebietes vom 13. bis 16. Jahrhundert," *Zeitschrift für Deutsche Mundarten* (1921), pp. 62–67.

9. Cf. StdAM, C, Stiftungsarchiv, account books of the parish poorfunds; also, BDAM, PfA Ludgeri, B, Kart. 48; PfA, A103–08.

10. The will of the merchant and magistrate Rotger Ossenbrügge, drawn up in 1611 by a notary, is in High German; the codicil, however, which was written in Ossenbrügge's own hand, is in Low German. See StdAM, B, Test. II, no. 1712, vol. 63, fols. 157–58.

11. Cf. the will of Klara Heerde, sister of Bürgermeister Dr. Hermann Heerde, written in her own hand; StdAM, B, Test. II, no. 437.

12. The minutes of the Schoehaus (Gesamtgilde) were kept in Low German until as late as 1614. Cf. StdAM, AXI, 76, vol. 3.

influence of High German. Parish clergy recruited locally tended to persist in the use of Low German in preaching, while Latin and High German were preferred by the Jesuits and the clerical bureaucrats, who were often ignorant of the local dialect. The difference was also one of generation. Michael Rupert and Matthaeus Timpe, the former a preacher at the time of the initial Catholic revival in the seventies and eighties, the latter a zealot of the Counter-Reformation around the turn of the century, were natives of Westphalia. Rupert wrote in Low German for the common folk, while Timpe composed in Latin and High German for the clergy and the educated elite. One can say that Low German remained the language of traditional Catholic piety in Münster and High German and Latin became the languages of the Counter-Reformation. Clerical institutions which resisted the Counter-Reformation tended to hold on to the language of tradition. As late as the mid-seventeenth century, some cathedral canons from venerable Westphalian noble families still resented the High-German-speaking, clean-shaven, "Italianized" younger canons, who were educated in Rome and South Germany and were strong partisans of the Jesuits.[13]

These resentments represented, however, isolated rearguard actions rather than whole-hearted resistance. It took the Jesuits just one generation to establish the supremacy of High German over Low German as the language of devotion in Münster. When the first Jesuit Father, Peter Michael (Brillmacher), preached in 1588, no one understood his accent.[14] In 1622 a memorandum written by a Jesuit in Cologne painted a completely different picture:[15]

> In all of Rhineland, including Neuss and Düsseldorf, one prefers to listen to preachers in the Mainzer or Speier dialects rather than the Lower Rhine tongue; this is also the case in Aachen and has been true for some time in Münster and Paderborn, because the chief preachers were from South Germany. Earlier, the South Germans were less well understood, but now the inhabitants of North Germany have smoothed out their tongues and in general people try to make the High German dialect their own. This is due

13. In 1650, the dean of the cathedral, Bernhard von Mallinckrodt, characterized his younger colleagues in the chapter who had been educated by the Jesuits and in the Collegium Germanicum as "bartlose, italienische Komödianten." He scorned their foreign ways and their "sanfte, zierliche und schmeidige wörter und dictiones." Dean Mallinckrodt also happened to be supported by the burghers against his rival in the episcopal election, Bernhard von Galen; the latter enjoyed the support of the Jesuits. Quoted by Wilhelm Kohl, in "Die Durchsetzung der tridentinischen Reformation im Domkapitel zu Münster," *Reformatio Ecclesiae. Festgabe Erwin Iserloh,* ed., Remigius Bäumer (Paderborn, 1980), p. 745.

14. Cf. BDAM, MS. 180 "Spicilegum Ecclesiasticum," vol. 19, fols. 19–28; and Röchell, *Chronik,* pp. 98f.

15. Quoted in Duhr, II:2, pp. 5f.

to [the work] of our Fathers, to schools, sermons, and vernacular devotional tracts. Nowadays almost no book is published in the Cologne or Westphalian dialects, but only in the pure German dialect; and so the people are getting used to the better German language, and it pleases them so much that even in the Westphalian and Cologne regions those who speak High German are more highly regarded.

The supremacy of High German also meant a greater distance between city and country in the cultural and linguistic landscape of Westphalia. The distinction between High-German-speaking burghers in Münster and the *Plattdütske* rural dwellers endured until the early decades of the present century.

Parallel to the gradual supplantation of Low German by High was the advance of Latin at the expense of the vernacular. This process could not be separated from the educational revolution introduced by the Jesuits in Catholic Europe. The rules of Jesuit colleges required the speaking of Latin by students at all times and contributed to the latinization of the educated lay elite.[16] The growing importance of the knowledge of Roman law as prerequisite for service in the various imperial, territorial, and civic bureaucracies also hastened the laicization of Latin.[17] Lawyers began to dominate most city councils, Catholic or Protestant.[18] Latin formulae appeared more and more often in notarial instruments and council minutes, and Latin expressions became commonplace in the writings and speeches of the learned. Purged of its medieval corruptions, Latin in its neo-classical purity was no longer the obsession of the philologists and humanists; it had become a bourgeois mark of distinction.

In late medieval Germany the laity and the clergy were divided by Latin. The spread of humanistic and legal education in the sixteenth century, however, redrew the line of demarcation in the Empire. Latin was no longer the dividing line between clergy and laity, but between the elite and commoners, cutting across the former distinctions. The knowledge of Latin served as an instrument of social advancement for the civic elite. From the leading families of the German cities came the learned councillors, the lawyers, and the judges

16. Cf. Bernhard Duhr, *Die Studienordnung der Gesellschaft Jesu* (Freiburg, 1896), pp. 236f.

17. Cf. Fritz Hartung, *Deutsche Verfassungsgeschichte vom 15. Jahrhundert bis zur Gegenwart* (9th ed., Stuttgart, 1969), pp. 60f.

18. In Protestant Hamburg, two of the twenty council seats in 1575 were occupied by lawyers; the number of jurists rose to seven in 1620; and in 1650 more than half of all councillors were jurists. Similarly, whereas only one of the four Bürgermeisters in 1600 was a lawyer, in 1643, all four possessed law degrees; see Martin Reissman, *Die Hamburgische Kaufmannschaft des 17. Jahrhunderts im sozialgeschichtlichen Sicht* (Hamburg, 1975), p. 344.

of the consolidating territorial states,[19] as well as the clerical bureaucrats of the Counter-Reformation.[20]

Knowledge of Latin also created divisions within the ranks of the clergy and the laity. The lower secular clergy and the female religious houses in general, as well as many inmates of male religious houses, notably the Franciscans in Münster,[21] were blissfully ignorant of Latin. Fluency in the language was a badge of distinction worn by the Jesuits and the clerical officials in the episcopal territorial administration. A similar division was discernible among the Catholic laity in Münster. Traditional confraternities embodied organizations of mutual help among the laity in search of sanctity and salvation; membership was usually open to all social classes; the brothers and sisters prayed to their local saints in their local tongue. In contrast, the Marian sodalities sponsored by the Jesuits aimed at recruiting the best students at their colleges and the socially most prominent members of the civic community. These coteries of elite Christians were closely supervised by the Fathers and often the members spoke Latin, not German, in their gatherings.[22]

The inroads made by High German and Latin in Münster differentiated the written from the spoken language, accelerated the growing divergence between the ruling elite and the common burghers, and served the cultural pretensions of a reinvigorated corporate society (*Ständestaat*). The ruling elite and the commune were divided not only by the exercise of political office, but also by the cultural trappings of newly

19. The "correct" confessional allegiance became one of the prerequisites to civil service in the German territorial states of the late sixteenth century. Two tendencies were at work, discernible in both Protestant and Catholic states: first, officials of burgher origin, usually holders of law degrees, became numerically the most important group within the administration while the nobility and especially the clergy lost influence. Second, although noblemen usually still held the highest ranks of office, as a group their confessional loyalties were divided and they often tried to oppose the confessional policies and centralism of the state in the estates. The burgher officials, in contrast, adhered strongly to the religion of their rulers and pushed through measures enforcing confessional orthodoxy and political obedience. Calvinist Palatinate and Catholic Bavaria are cases in point. See Volker Press, "Stadt und territoriale Konfessionsbildung," in Franz Petri, ed., *Kirche und gesellschaftlicher Wandel in deutschen und niederländischen Städten der werdenden Neuzeit* (Cologne, 1980), pp. 251–96, esp. pp. 295f; and his *Calvinismus und Territorialstaat. Regierung und Zentralbehörde der Kurpfalz* (Stuttgart, 1980). For Bavaria, see Maximilian Lanzinner, *Fürst, Räte und Landstände: Die Entstehung der Zentralbehörden in Bayern 1511–1598* (Göttingen, 1980), pp. 150ff., 224ff.

20. A prosopographical study of the leading clerical officials of the Counter-Reformation in Germany remains a *desideratum* in historical research. The best study of the social recruitment of Protestant clergy is the work by Bernard Vogler, op. cit., esp. pp. 18–23.

21. Cf. StdAM, MS. 4, Franciscan chronicle, fol. 38, where the chronist laments that most of the novices, rustics from around Münster, knew not a word of Latin.

22. The minutes of the meetings of the sodality B.M.V. Assumptionis were kept in Latin; certain entries were made in a code-alphabet. Cf. StAM, MSS. VII, 1034.

consolidated power and the consciousness of aristocracy which it entailed. The Catholic renewal of the late sixteenth century reinforced the social hierarchy. The Counter-Reformation depended upon the ruling elites in the cities and in the territories for its propagation; it, in turn, sanctioned the ideology of a God-ordained, sacred society and provided the language for the articulation of a new aristocratic consciousness on the part of the civic elite.

PRINTING AND PAINTING

The new synthesis of cultural and religious changes was perhaps most visible in the battle over the control of the printing press and artistic expression in Münster. Movable type first came to Münster in 1485 and the earliest books were produced for the clerical and humanistic markets.[23] Breviaries, missals, the Psalms and other books of the Vulgate, Latin grammars, works by authors of Latin antiquity (Virgil, Ovid, Pliny, and Terence), a few works of the Italian Renaissance, and compositions of the Münster humanists themselves comprised the corpus of the earliest printed works in the Westphalian metropole.[24] No German work was printed until 1532 when Dietrich Tzwyvel the Older published Bernhard Rothmann's Confession of Faith.[25]

Dietrich Tzwyvel came to Münster in 1513 from Jülich. He took over the printing press of Lorenz Bornemann, who had worked in Münster for only three years (1509–11), and became the first permanent printer of the city.[26] When the Reformation came, printing was pressed into the

23. For discussions of the advent of printing and its impact on Europe, see Lucien Febvre and Henri-Jean Martin, *The Coming of the Book: The Impact of Printing, 1450–1800,* trans. David Gerard (London, 1976); Elizabeth Eisenstein, *The Printing Press as an Agent of Change: Communications and Cultural Transformations in Early Modern Europe,* 2 vols. (Cambridge, 1979). For printing in Münster, see Josef Benzing, *Die Buchdrucker des 16. und 17. Jahrhunderts im deutschen Sprachgebiet* (Wiesbaden, 1963); Joseph Niesert, *Beiträge zur Buckdruckergeschichte Münsters oder Verzeichnis der vom Jahr 1486–1700 zu Münster gedruckten Bücher* (Coesfeld, 1828) and supplementary volume published in 1834; J. B. Nordhoff, *Denkwürdigkeiten aus dem Münsterischen Humanismus. Mit einer Anlage über das frühere Press- und Bücherwesen Westfalens* (Münster, 1874); Clemens Baumer, "Neue Beiträge zur Bibliographie des münsterischen Humanisten Murmellius und zur münsterischen Druckergeschichte," *WZ* 40 (1882), pp. 164–72; Alois Bömer, "Der münsterische Buckdruck in dem ersten Viertel des 16. Jahrhunderts," *Westfalen* 10 (1919), pp. 1–48, and his "Der münsterische Buckdruck vom zweiten Viertel bis zum Ende des 16. Jahrhunderts," *Westfalen* 12 (1924), pp. 25–76; Otto Zaretzky, "Unbeschriebene münsterischen Drucke aus dem ersten Viertel des 16. Jahrhunderts," *Westfalen* 14 (1928), pp. 62–66.

24. Cf. Bömer and Zaretzky.

25. Cf. Bömer, "Zweiter Viertel," p. 64; see also Robert Stupperich, ed., *Die Schriften Bernhard Rothmanns* (Münster, 1970), pp. 64–68.

26. Cf. R. Pick, "Dietrich Zwivel der Ältere," *Annalen des Historischen Vereins für den Niederrhein,* 26–27 (1874), pp. 399–401; A. Bömer, "Dietrich Tzwyvel," in *Westfälische Lebensbilder,* Hauptreihe II:1 (1931), pp. 15–29.

service of the movement. Both Dietrich Tzwyvel and the painter Ludger tom Ring the Older, with whom Dietrich was later to collaborate in designing and building the astronomical clock in the cathedral, supported the reform movement before things took on a radical, Anabaptist twist. Rothmann's pre-Anabaptist tracts were printed by Tzwyvel, but when the reformer turned to Anabaptism in the summer of 1533, the printer and painter immediately disassociated themselves from him.[27] In fact, both Tzwyvel and tom Ring were active in the Lutheran opposition to the Anabaptists. They printed a Low German translation of Bucer's open letter to the city of Münster which attacked Melchior Hoffmann's teachings.[28] Both men apparently fled Münster before the Anabaptists took power in February 1534 and returned only after the downfall of the Anabaptist Kingdom.[29]

Tzwyvel's fonts served as instruments of propaganda for the millenarian regime after Rothmann had taken over the printing shop; hundreds of tracts proclaiming the end of the world and defending the cause of the saints rolled out from under Rothmann's pen and the press. After the destruction of the Anabaptist Kingdom no book was printed in Münster for ten years, a reflection of the destitution of the besieged, conquered, and pillaged city. Dietrich Tzwyvel died after 1542, but his son, Gottfried Tzwyvel, resumed business in 1545. It is worth noting that both Gottfried Tzwyvel and Hermann tom Ring, Ludger's son, were fervent Catholics, in stark contrast to their fathers' sympathies for the Reformation. Ludger himself returned to Münster, shaken by the iconoclastic fury of the Anabaptists and the destruction wrought upon his beloved city. He rejoined the Catholic Church, and received commissions in the rebuilding of churches.[30] After the brief alliance with the Reformation and the debacle of Anabaptism, printing and painting in Münster returned to the fold and patronage of the Catholic Church and the Catholic ruling elite. One of Gottfried Tzwyvel's first works was a tract commissioned by the cathedral chapter celebrating the decennial of the liberation of Münster from the Anabaptists, in which the Catholics who fled Münster were compared to the Israelites who had been oppressed by the Pharisees.[31] The image of Israel in exile also appeared in one of Hermann

27. Cf. Kerssenbroch, p. 738.

28. Cf. Bömer, "Zweiter Viertel," p. 65; Carl A. Cornelius, *Geschichte des münsterischen Aufruhrs. II. Die Wiedertaufe* (Leipzig, 1860), doc. 24, pp. 356–57. Bucer's original text is to be found in Robert Stupperich, ed., *Strassburg und Münster im Kampf um den rechten Glauben* (= *Martini Buceri Opera Omnia Series I: Deutsche Schriften V,* Gütersloh, 1978), pp. 109–258.

29. Cf. Kirchhoff, "Bürgerliste 1535," p. 82.

30. Cf. Max Geisberg, "Die tom Rings," in *Westfälische Lebensbilder* II:1 (1931), pp. 30–37.

31. *Festum Liberationis nostrae, ab impiissimo Cathabaptistarum impetu et tumultu, de mirabili uictoria, et anniuersario festo. Contra furiosos Anabaptistas postridie natalis Ioannis Baptiste solenniter obseruando* (Münster, 1545), sig. A3v.

tom Ring's first paintings. A votive picture dated 1548 depicted Ludger, his father, and the whole family: in the background Moses receives the Ten Commandments while the Israelites worship the Golden Calf; two tablets stand in the center of the picture—the Ten Commandments on one side, verses from Exodus 20 and Deuteronomy 5 on the other.[32] The iconography is explicit. The idolatry of the Israelites symbolizes the godlessness of the new Israelites—the Anabaptists—and the reference to Exodus points to the tom Ring family in exile, steadfast to the true Church.

In the eleven years he was active as printer in Münster (1545–56) Gottfried Tzwyvel produced eleven works, all except three in Latin.[33] The Latin books were in demand from the clerical and pedagogic markets; the German works included two devotional tracts printed in Low German and the police ordinance of the bishopric. After his death in 1562, Gottfried's shop passed into the hands of his son, Dietrich Tzwyvel the Younger; meanwhile, Johann Ossenbrügge came to Münster from Cologne and opened up a rival press.[34] The Tzwyvel Press, the larger of the two, printed twenty-five works between 1562 and 1580; the eighteen Latin books put out by the press included thirteen school texts and two editions of the small Catholic catechism. The German-language works were all orders from the territorial government and included the *Carolina,* episcopal edicts, and mint, Chamber Court, and other governmental ordinances.[35] The two presses struggled to survive; the school and ecclesiastical markets were simply too small to provide enough profits. Almost everywhere in Germany the Reformation and the expansion of printing went hand in hand; Luther's numerous tracts served both the spread of the message of reform and the business of the printers.[36] Even in staunchly Catholic Cologne, several printers could not resist the financial temptation or the urges of conscience to print Lutheran tracts clandestinely.[37] Prospects were gloomy for the Catholic presses in Germany in the middle decades of the century.

The painters, however, did a good business. Reconstruction in Münster was still going on half a century after the siege of the city in 1534–

32. Cf. *Ausstellung des Landesmuseums des Provinz Westfalen. Juli/Sept. 1924 (Katalog): Die Werke der Münsterschen Malerfamilie tom Ring* (Münster, 1924), catalogue no. 10. The picture is now kept in the Church of Überwasser.

33. Cf. Bömer, "Zweiter Viertel," pp. 66–67.

34. Ibid., pp. 38–39.

35. Ibid., pp. 68–71.

36. Cf. S. H. Steinberg, *Five Hundred Years of Printing* (rev. ed., Bristol, 1961), p. 194; Eisenstein, p. 407; Febvre and Martin, pp. 291–95.

37. Cf. Robert Scribner, "Why Was There No Reformation in Cologne?" *Bulletin of the Institute of Historical Research* 49 (1976), pp. 234–35.

35.[38] Hermann tom Ring, now master painter and important guild leader, dominated the guild of painters, glassmakers, and sattlers, and left his imprint on the artistic recovery of the city. Second guild master in 1556, he was elected first guild master in 1559 and remained in that position until his death in 1597.[39] His brother, Ludger tom Ring the Younger, a painter with Protestant leanings, left Münster for Brunswick in 1556 or 1557. Whether Hermann was involved in his brother's decision to leave is a question that cannot be answered from the sources.[40]

Hermann tom Ring was a fervent Catholic, a friend of the Franciscans, and the artistic champion of the Catholic restoration.[41] Between 1544 and his death, he left behind no less than eighteen major paintings, most of them commissioned by prominent Catholic clients, including the count of Hatzfeld, dean of the cathedral chapter Gottfried von Raesfeld, patron of the Jesuits, and two Bischopinck brothers, patricians and canons at the collegiate Church of Saint Mauritz.[42] One of his most famous paintings, *The Last Judgment,* was commissioned by Bishop Bernd von Raesfeld in 1558 for the Chapel of Saint Michael in the cathedral. Hermann's style stands in sharp contrast to those of his father and brother: whereas the two Ludgers excelled in portraits and a certain naturalism may suggest a lack of deep interest in religious themes, Hermann's paintings are intensely and almost exclusively religious, expressing both his own intense piety and his theological convictions.[43] *The Annunciation,* painted in the seventies or the eighties, was the major artistic creation of Marian devotion in post-Anabaptist Münster.[44] He also worked closely with Gottfried and Dietrich Tzwyvel, supplying the woodcuts that illustrated the various governmental ordinances. Although his paintings are less well known than those of the Cranachs, the Holbeins, and Dürer, Hermann tom Ring was one of the best artists of North Germany in the sixteenth century and was perhaps the only artist of stature who remained steadfast

38. In 1581, the spire of Saint Aegidius, which was never properly repaired after 1535, collapsed and severely damaged the choir, necessitating further, expensive repairs; cf. StdAM, AXIII, 43.

39. Cf. Krumbholtz, pp. 346ff.

40. Cf. Geisberg, "tom Rings."

41. Cf. StdAM, MS. 4, Franciscan chronicle, fol. 35: "Anno 1579: Renovatus est chorus . . . eodem die M. Herman Maler by uns was cum uxore et filius, wante dat malen im choro volendiget was und de lefte thosamen drüncken."

42. Cf. *Ausstellung Katalog tom Ring* and discussion of a picture not included in the 1924 exhibition by Paul Pieper; see his "Hermann tom Ring als Bildnismaler," *Westfalen* 34 (1956), pp. 72–101.

43. Cf. Karl Hölker, "Die Malerfamilie tom Ring," *Beiträge zur Westfälischen Kunstgeschichte,* Heft 8 (Münster, 1927), esp., pp. 56–60; Theodor Riewerts, "Deutsches und Niederländisches bei Hermann tom Ring," *Westfalen* 23 (1938), pp. 276–87.

44. Cf. *Ausstellung Katalog,* no. 36; the painting is now kept in the Church of Überwasser.

to the Catholic Church. He was a transitional figure: a man deeply attached to traditional Catholicism, he did not yet fully experience the spiritual grandeur of the Counter-Reformation which was to inspire many masters of the Baroque.[45]

After the death of Dietrich Tzwyvel the Younger in 1580 the press continued operations under the management of his widow, Christina Kock. When their son Konrad Tzwyvel came of age in 1596, the twenty-two-year-old left Münster "to go out of the country to Hungary to fight the arch-enemies of the Christian faith."[46] The Tzwyvel Press itself had closed down in 1589 when Lambert Raesfeld, a printer from Cologne, purchased the typefonts from Christina Kock.

A man who combined militant confessionalism and good business sense, Lambert Raesfeld was a Counter-Reformation printer par excellence.[47] He cooperated with the Jesuits from the very beginning and set up his presses in the basement of the Jesuit College in 1591.[48] Close to half of his early titles represented works by the rector of the Jesuit College in Münster, Father Peter Michael, alias Brillmacher.[49] Of the 127 works published by the Raesfeld Press between 1589 and 1618 (Lambert himself died in 1617 and his widow continued the business) twenty-eight came from the pens of the patres.[50]

Compared to the Tzwyvel Press, the Lambert Press enjoyed robust financial health.[51] Whereas Dietrich Tzwyvel the Younger brought out on the average no more than two books each year, the Raesfeld Press turned out four or more titles annually. Several factors accounted for the

45. Hermann's younger brother, Herbert, and his son Nicolaus both continued to paint works commissioned by the clergy. Herbert became master of the painters' guild in 1560 and Nicolaus served as guild master between 1607 and 1612. Their works, however, were artistically inferior to those of Hermann. See Geisberg, "tom Rings."

46. Cf. StdAM, B, Test. I, no. 302.

47. The milieu of printing in the second half of the sixteenth century is described very well by Febvre and Martin, p. 153: "From the end of the 16th century the attitudes of printers and booksellers changed, as did relations between authors and publishers. . . . After a hundred years of exceptional prosperity printing was in crisis: the innumerable editions of books had glutted the market, capital to finance publishers was not forthcoming because of the general economic crisis, and unrest and strikes broke out among the workers. . . . [B]ooksellers and printers had by now formed into guilds and corporations. . . . The leading firms were those on the side of the Counter-Reformation—important merchants but humble servants of Jesuit policy, supporters of the ultramontane faction."

48. Cf. Krumbholtz, pp. 503ff.

49. Cf. Bömer, "Zweiter Viertel," pp. 71ff.

50. Ibid.; see also Niesert, "Verzeichnis," for catalogue of books printed between 1600 and 1618.

51. Cf. B. Lucas, *Der Buckdrucker Lambert Raesfeldt. Ein Beitrag zur Buchdruckereigeschichte Münsters im 16. und 17. Jahrhundert* (Münster, 1929). For the financial success of Catholic printers in general, see Eisenstein, p. 354.

boom of the printing industry in Münster after 1590. First, there were the Jesuits. The patres created a steady supply of pedagogic, polemical, and theological tracts, and their teaching and literary battles with neighboring Protestants kept their works in demand.[52] Moreover, book production in Münster was then integrated into an international market for the first time. Previously, presses in Münster produced essentially for Westphalia; the distribution network centered on Münster, and none of the works reached supra-regional circulation. Lambert Raesfeld, on the other hand, had established good professional contacts in Cologne before coming to Münster. He had close business contact with the firms of Johann Gymnich and Peter Henning in Cologne and with Matthaeus Pontanus (Brückner) in Paderborn. The Gymnich and Raesfeld presses arranged to publish one another's works, thereby sharing the financial risks while extending simultaneously the network of distribution. Through the Henning Press, two books accepted by the Raesfeld Press also came out in Mainz. Thanks to his business associates, Lambert Raesfeld could exhibit his titles at the Frankfurt Bookfair when he could not attend in person.[53] The last reason for the financial success of the press was the monopoly exercised by Lambert Raesfeld. His collaboration with the Jesuits paid off handsomely when Archbishop Ernst, a pupil of the Jesuits himself when he was growing up in his father's Munich court, granted Lambert the sole right to print in the Bishopric of Münster, banning once and for all any potential competition, economic or confessional.[54] In 1612 Archbishop Ferdinand appointed him official censor of the bishopric; Lambert Raesfeld had the power to confiscate all books suspected of heresy solely on his own authority and to dispose of them as he saw fit.[55]

The alliance between confessional polemics and printing success in Münster is clearly demonstrated by the character of the output of the Raesfeld Press. About one-third of all titles (seventeen Latin and twenty-two German works) which came out of the press in Münster during those years were books of polemical character, several of which were diatribes written by Münster Jesuits directed against theologians of the nearby Calvinist Academy of Burgsteinfurt. Increasingly, the boundaries between works of devotion, theology, and polemics disappeared; toward

---

52. On the subject of the Society of Jesus and the revival of Catholic printing, see Febvre and Martin, pp. 193–95.

53. Cf. Bertram Haller, "Köln und die Anfänge des Buchdrucks in Westfalen," *Köln Westfalen 1180–1980. Landesgeschichte zwischen Rhein und Weser* (Catalogue of the exhibition in the Landesmuseum Münster, Oct. 26, 1980, to Jan. 18, 1981), ed., Landschaftsverband Westfalen-Lippe, vol. 1 (Beiträge), (Lengerich, 1980), pp. 441–44.

54. Cf. Krumbholtz, p. 505.

55. Cf. Krumbholtz, p. 507.

the end of the sixteenth century, devotional tracts usually contained negative examples of the perversion of true faith by Protestants, while the defense of Catholic sacramental theology was often coupled with occasional vituperations thrown across the confessional lines. In fact, devotional tracts, handbooks for the clergy, and polemical works constituted by far the most important portion of the titles of the Raesfeld Press: thirty-one of the fifty-five Latin works and sixty of the seventy-two German works came under these three genres. Titles from classical antiquity and school texts which were prominent in the agenda of the Tzwyvel Press occupied a very modest place in the stock of the Counter-Reformation Raesfeld Press.[56]

The shift away from Low German to High German is also clearly manifest when we look at the inventory of the Raesfeld Press. Only four of the seventy-two books in the vernacular were in Low German: three of these were writings of Michael Rupert and one was a compilation of prayers from the Latin Fathers and from medieval devotional tracts—the *Oldtvedder Boick* (1593), edited by Johann van Detten, son of the councillor Bernd van Detten the Older and canon of the Old Cathedral.[57] Significantly, when Detten's *Oldtvedder Boick* was reprinted in 1609 it appeared in High German as the *Altväter Buch*.[58] Everywhere in Catholic North Germany, Low German disappeared as a printed language, although Lutheran Lübeck and Hamburg still retained a strong sense of linguistic identity. The two Hanseatic cities continued to print books in Low German throughout the seventeenth century.[59] The tenacity of Low German in Protestant North Germany was no doubt reinforced by the exultation of lay piety, by preaching in the vernacular, and by the more democratic, popular nature of the Reformation.[60]

56. Analysis is based on the printed catalogues in Bömer, "Zweiter Viertel," and Niesert, "Verzeichnis."

57. Cf. Bömer, "Zweiter Viertel," p. 73, no. 9. For the Detten family see appendix 1, nos. 35 and 36.

58. Cf. Niesert, "Verzeichnis," pp. 80f., no. 37.

59. Hamburg and Lübeck were the most prominent cities which printed books in Low German; between 1601 and 1650, the Protestant presses of the Hanseatic North turned out on the average 13.9 titles annually in Low German (in addition to High German works). The calculations are based on volume 2 of Konrad Borchling and Bruno Claussen, eds., *Niederdeutsche Bibliographie. Gesamtverzeichnis der niederdeutschen Drucke bis zum Jahre 1800*, 3 vols. (Neumünster, 1941–57).

60. In Hamburg, the Reformation precipitated a change in government and the adoption of a more democratic constitution; in Lübeck, the populist Wullenwever regime rose to power on the back of demands for church reform as well. See Bernhard Studt and Hans Olsen, *Hamburg. Die Geschichte einer Stadt* (Hamburg, 1951), pp. 77ff. See also Heinrich Reincke, *Hamburg am Vorabend der Reformation*, ed., Erich von Lehe (Hamburg, 1966). For Lübeck, see the standard work by Georg Waitz, *Lübeck unter Jürgen Wullenwever und die Europäische Politik*, 3 vols. (Berlin, 1855–56).

The printed word was a double-edged sword. The control of the book trade in Münster by the Counter-Reformation did not go unchallenged. During the night of December 22, 1583, copies of a vehemently anti-Catholic pamphlet, entitled *Mönstersche Inquisitio,* were thrown into the homes of sleeping burghers. The pamphlet attacked the 1571 diocesan visitation ordered by Bishop Johann von Hoya and labeled fifty-four Tridentine articles designed for carrying out diocesan reform "guidelines for the Inquisition." The anonymous author, a partisan of the deposed Calvinist archbishop of Cologne, Gebhard Truchsess, exhorted the burghers of Münster to join the Calvinist camp.[61]

A more direct challenge presented itself in 1603, the year of the Jubilee proclaimed by Pope Clement VIII.[62] Tracts composed by Calvinist theologians in Burgsteinfurt attacked the dispensation of papal indulgences; to the chagrin of the Catholics, these tracts were openly peddled on the market in Münster while the clergy was staging a magnificent procession in honor of the occasion.[63]

In light of these and similar events, Archbishop Ernst published an edict of censorship in 1609.[64] His successor (and nephew) Ferdinand rewarded the cooperation of Lambert Raesfeld, who acted as official censor, by granting him protection against pirate editions,[65] a protection also guaranteed by the city council in 1616.[66] The firm alliance between the book trade and Catholicism in Münster was evident in the statutes of the Fraternity of Bookbinders, incorporated in 1608, which forbade members to bind Lutheran, Calvinist, and other heretical books.[67]

ASSAULT ON POPULAR CULTURE

Recent studies argue that the Reformation and the Counter-Reformation successfully mobilized forces to suppress traditional popular festivities; underlying the attack on popular culture was the emergence of a new breed of clerics and their understanding of the proper relationship between the sacred and the profane realms.[68] Still another view sees the

61. Cf. Paul Bahlmann, "Mönstersche Inquisitio," *WZ* 47 (1889), pp. 98–120.

62. The Jubilee was proclaimed by Pope Clement VIII in 1600 but was not celebrated in the archdiocese of Cologne until 1603. Cf. Ludwig von Pastor, *The History of the Popes,* vol. 24 (London, 1933), pp. 269–80.

63. Cf. StdAM, AII, 20, RP, 1603, May 16 and July 24, vol. 35, fols. 53v and 87.

64. The censorship edict is printed in Krumbholtz, p. 507.

65. Cf. Krumbholtz, pp. 507–08.

66. Cf. StdAM, AII, 20, RP, 1615, Dec. 18, vol. 47, fol. 524; Krumbholtz, pp. 509–10.

67. Cf. Krumbholtz, p. 189.

68. Cf. Keith Thomas, *Religion and the Decline of Magic* (New York, 1971), esp. pp. 51–77, 151–73; Peter Burke, *Popular Culture in Early Modern Europe* (New York, 1978), esp. pp. 207–34, 259–81.

consolidation of the state as the major enemy of popular culture: the centralization of power, the enoblement of the urban elite, and the growing distrust of the lower orders widened the gap between high and low cultures.[69] At these high levels of generalization the contexts in which the changes discussed took place have tended to be ignored. In the following discussion I will attempt to view this cultural transformation within the context of the city and identify the social groups which were attacking or defending popular culture.[70] But first, let us look at the major festivals of the Münsteraners.

A summer festival common to Westphalian towns and villages, *Gude Maendag* was celebrated the Monday after Trinity Sunday. The festival represented a celebration of the vitality of summer with overtones of a pagan-agrarian fertility rite. Journeymen of the guilds selected their *Meigraven* and *Meigräfin*. They sang, danced, rode, and paraded about in the open countryside. The activities of the festival lasted anywhere between two and ten days.[71]

As early as 1565, possibly even earlier, Gude Maendag was suppressed by episcopal orders as part of the campaign against popular festivals. The bishops declared the general ban again in 1592 and in 1617, suggesting the ineffectiveness of coercive ordinances.[72] The magistrates succeeded only in controlling the "excesses" (*Üppigkeiten*) which disturbed the peace: loud music-playing, horse-riding in the narrow streets, and fights between drunken and agitated journeymen of different guilds were repeatedly censured. In spite of magisterial suspicions and hostilities toward popular spontaneity, the celebrations of Guden Maendag endured and remained part of the civic calendar of Münster.[73]

Fear of social disorder, the disapproval of magistrates and guild elders, and the general violence which accompanied traditional festivities were general themes that characterized urban festivals in Münster. The carnival best exemplified the confluence of these themes.

A chronicle composed at the turn of the sixteenth century describes the

69. See the excellent study by Robert Muchembled, *Culture Populaire et Culture des Élites dans la France Moderne (XVe–XVIIIe Siècles)* (Paris, 1978).

70. Muchembled's discussion of urban popular culture is based on studies of the cities of the French-Flemish border region, in particular the city of Arras. Since both the political and the social structures of the North French-Flemish cities differed from those of Münster, his conclusions need to be modified here.

71. On Guden Maendag, see R. Brockpähler, "Der 'Gute Montag' der Bäckergilde Münster, Sage und historische Wirklichkeit," *RWZfVK* 16 (1969), pp. 123–63; Klaus Gimpel, "Patriotische Einflüsse im münsterischen Gute-Montags-Brauch des 19. Jahrhunderts," *WF* 28 (1976–77), pp. 197–99; see also Röchell, *Chronik,* p. 45.

72. Cf. Brockphäler, p. 156; Krumbholtz, p. 98; Röchell, *Chronik,* p. 43.

73. Cf. Viktor Huyskens, "Der Gute Montag," *WZ* 61 (1903), pp. 217–19.

celebrations in vivid detail.[74] At carnival mummered and masked servants went around to the houses of rich burghers, where they were entertained with food and drink; some women went about in men's clothing and men disguised themselves in feminine attire; still others dressed up as Turks, Poles, heathens, or even as the Devil or other evil spirits. Journeymen and apprentices chose among themselves the handsomest, who formed various troops; they marched in pairs behind their guild banners to the houses of their masters and asked for money, sausages, and beer. Having assembled the food and drink, they then invited the daughters and maids of their masters to a dance the next day. The occasion also permitted the journeymen to criticize and make fun of their masters and the magistrates with impunity.

Carnival, however, was not the preserve of the lower classes alone; all social strata in Münster participated. It is more accurate to say that in carnivals, the social classes expressed their separate identities through segregated activities. The most prestigious carnival society was the Saint Anne Fraternity, called the Great Company. Sons of the richest burghers, mostly young merchants engaged in the Münster-Lübeck trade, comprised the membership. Governed by strict statutes, the brothers pledged to observe the carnival according to prescribed sets of ceremonial and vestimentary guidelines.[75] "They were the ones," wrote our chronist, "who turned day into night and night into day."[76] Young merchants from Lübeck, Hamburg, and Bremen came together to celebrate together at the invitation of the Great Company.

On Maundy Thursday brothers of the Great Company rode out to Kinderhaus carrying a strawman in a cart. There they named him "Doctor," honored and invited him to preside over the carnival season in Münster. They rode back into town and paraded the carnival lord through all quarters of the city before taking him to the main market. The carnival lord, the Fool, the *Geck*,[77] lodged with the brothers at the house of the fraternity during the days of revelry that followed. On Shrove Tuesday the brothers paraded around the streets in their outlandish costumes and ended the merrymaking with a dance, to which

---

74. Cf. Röchell, *Chronik*, pp. 32ff.

75. An account book of the Great Company pertaining to the years 1607–08 is extant; it is MS. 403 of the Altertumsverein Münster, deposited in StAM. I have not examined the manuscript and rely here on the summary of the contents rendered by Offenberg, *Bilder und Skizzen*, II, pp. 89–91. There is, however, a protocol of the Company for the years between 1556 and 1607 which Offenberg was not aware of; it is MS. 139 of the StdAM.

76. Röchell, *Chronik*, p. 37.

77. For the possible etymologies and meanings of the name "Geck," see Karl-Heinz Kirchhoff, "Kleine Beiträge zu münsterländischen Volkskunde um 1535," *RWZfVK* 8 (1961), pp. 92–105.

daughters of prominent families and many civic dignitaries were invited. The day after Ash Wednesday was the day of reckoning for the carnival fool. When the brothers were all exhausted and nauseated from their debauchery, they realized "that they had been misled and betrayed by the lord [of the carnival]. . . . they became angry at him, blamed him for all their ills, hit him mercilessly . . . scolded him, calling him a rogue, traitor, murderer, and thief; he had betrayed them all and should and must die without mercy."[78]

A platform at the market served as the place of execution; the event was attended by many cheery spectators. Dressed as a priest, a brother heard confession from the condemned; three other brothers mimicked a judge and two assessors, accusing the now-dethroned carnival lord, the strawman, the Fool, of being a corrupter of youth, a whoremonger, an inventor of all tomfooleries, a destroyer of peace and unity, a murderer, rapist, and breaker of all divine laws. Thereafter, tied to the stake, the strawman was set aflame; the ashes hovering over the city symbolized the collective purgation of sin.[79]

Unlike the journeymen, the apprentices, the servants, and the maids, the brothers of the Saint Anne Fraternity ruled their corporation with two annually elected Aldermen.[80] Well-endowed and strictly governed, the fraternity had little in common with the relatively impromptu and dependent carnival groups of the lower classes. The latter depended on their masters and employers for money, food, and drink, for approval and supervision; the young merchants were self-governing and financially independent. The spontaneous outbursts of joy by the lower classes represented a counterpoint to the well-defined ceremonies of the Great Company.

Primarily a display of social hierarchy, of the pomp, opulence, and power of the elite, carnival was a civic event which marked off the limits of lawlessness and a chaos well controlled by ceremonies.[81] The sporadic carnivalesque violence was by no means limited to the lower classes: when the artisans challenged the social order in the 1580 carnival at

78. Röchell, *Chronik*, pp. 39–40.

79. Röchell, *Chronik*, pp. 40–41.

80. Cf. Röchell, *Chronik*, pp. 42; Offenberg, II, pp. 89ff.

81. For carnival as social control, see Burke, pp. 199–201. It is essential to strike a balance between the political and the festive aspects of carnival in our interpretation. Although many folklorists do not venture beyond mere descriptions of popular festivals, it is equally misleading to emphasize unduly the political character of the festival per se. An example of this extreme position is Peter Weidkuhn's article "Fastnacht-Revolte-Revolution," *Zeitschrift für Religions- und Geistesgeschichte*, 21:4 (1969), wherein he writes: "Ich behaupte nun, dass die Fastnacht eine archaische Form dieses politischen Klassenkampfes darstellt, dass sie eine kulturelle Institution ist, die den permanenten gesellschaftlichen Konflikt regelt oder ritualisiert" (pp. 297–98).

Romans, the ruling elite did not hesitate to turn the feast into a massacre.[82] The attack on carnival in the sixteenth century cannot be viewed primarily as an assault by the elite on popular culture, because they themselves were participants. Rather, it reflected a metamorphosis within civic culture itself which differentiated the sacred from the profane, the elite from the common folk. The main agents forcing this differentiation were the religious and cultural values introduced by the Counter-Reformation and the Jesuits.

Anxiety over the cohesion of the body social, especially in times of religious strife and warfare, was reinforced by the perennial magisterial concern over the spiritual well-being of the city.[83] The sinfulness of the burghers brought on plagues, natural calamities, rising prices, and general disorder under heaven.[84] In 1565 the city council published an ordinance which governed the proper observance of public and private festivities; the magistrates lamented the gluttony, the drunkenness, and the general moral depravity of private and public behavior. They specified the number of guests permissible at baptisms, weddings, and other gatherings, and set limits to the amount of food and drink that could be consumed. A similar ordinance was promulgated for the bishopric in 1571.[85] The carnival was to be done away with altogether.[86] These prohibitions met strong resistance, and in 1571 the council gave permission to celebrate carnival but urged moderation. The same year, a fine was imposed on those who worked on Sundays and other feastdays.[87]

For ten years the council refrained from intervention.[88] But in the 1580s the Cologne War and the campaigns in the Netherlands spilled over into Westphalia. External threats reminded the council of potential internal disorder and the sinfulness of the burghers which angered God; in 1585 the magistrates forbade mummery and arms-bearing at carnival,

---

82. Cf. Emmanuel Le Roy Ladurie, *Carnival in Romans,* trans. Mary Feeney (New York, 1979).

83. Cf. Huyskens, *Zeiten der Pest, II,* pp. 8ff. See also Keller, I, p. 346.

84. This idea was central to the consciousness of the burghers in the Middle Ages, as the brilliant study of medieval German city chronicles by Heinrich Schmidt shows; see his *Die deutschen Städtechroniken als Spiegel bürgerlichen Selbstverständnisses im Spätmittelalter* (Göttingen, 1958), pp. 87–93, 119–23.

85. Cf. StAM, AVM, MS. 24, "Extract auss der Münsterischen Gemeindenordnung am letzten Octobris anno 1571 auffgerichtet/ von Brautwirtschafften/ Vogelschiessen/ der Haussleute Kleidung und dergleichen." The ordinance is bound together with a work by Matthaeus Timpe.

86. Cf. Röchell, *Chronik,* p. 43.

87. Cf. StdAM, AII, 20, RP, 1571, Feb. 6 and Dec. 3, vol. 7, fols. 9v and 31v.

88. The only magisterial injunction in the decade was in 1582 when the city council asked the Company brothers not to place the Geck on the main market. See StdAM, AII, 20, RP, Feb. 23, vol. 14, fol. 5v.

and outlawed Maigang.[89] All celebrations were banned the next three years "on account of these dangerous times."[90] Although carnival celebrations resumed in 1589, the council attempted to outlaw certain excesses; mummery and the eating of meat, which were contrary to canon law, bearing arms, and the playing of drums and trumpets, with their ominous martial tidings, were banned.[91] In 1591 the council prohibited the festival of Guden Maendag for good.[92] Four years before, the Jesuits had already forbidden their students to take part in the vulgar feast.[93] The magistrates took more stringent steps to enforce their authority in the face of general indifference. They fined the Company brothers 5 marks each in 1594 because the latter welcomed the carnival lord in spite of explicit magisterial injunction.[94] The Ipsen brothers, another carnival society, were each fined 3 marks two years later for eating meat during Lent.[95] The following years saw alternations of complete prohibitions and reluctantly granted permissions, depending on the magisterial perception of the state of the city's security and sanctity.

The spirit of the Catholic Reformation left strong marks on the magistracy. A greater concern with moral propriety on the part of the councillors was revealed in 1601 when the Company brothers petitioned the city council, asking to be exempted from the general carnival prohibitions. Bürgermeister Dr. Heinrich Vendt agreed that the brothers were all "decent people" (*anständige Leute*) and that the young merchants had had a long corporative and festive tradition, but added that exempting the Company brothers would set a bad precedent in dealing with the other carnival societies. Bürgermeister Dr. Lambert Buck rejected the petition on the ground that mummery was an ancient heathen custom; the syndic, Lic. Heinrich Wittfeld, said that "mummery was not only forbidden by canon law but also in the Old Testament."[96] Heinrich Vendt and Heinrich Wittfeld were both strong supporters of the Society of Jesus, and the Fathers certainly encouraged the magistrates to root out the ancient, pagan customs. Prohibitions against mummery, the playing of drums and trumpets, riding horses, and bearing arms were repeated every single year thereafter,[97] obviously to no avail, because the city

89. StdAM, AII, 20, RP, 1585, Feb. 25, vol. 17, fol. 7v.

90. StdAM, AII, 20, RP, 1586, Feb. 10, vol. 18, fol. 4v; 1587, Jan. 30, vol. 19, fol. 3v; 1588, Feb. 19, vol. 20, fol. 7v.

91. StdAM, AII, 20, RP, 1589, Feb. 6, vol. 21, fol. 4.

92. StdAM, AII, 20, RP, June 7, vol. 23, fol. 53.

93. StdAM, AII, 20, RP, 1587, May 8, vol. 19, fol. 34v.

94. StdAM, AII, 20, RP, Feb. 18, vol. 26, fol. 12v.

95. StdAM, AII, 20, RP, 1596, April 22 and 26, vol. 28, fols. 18v–19.

96. Cf. StdAM, AII, 20, RP, Feb. 26, vol. 33, fols. 46–48.

97. Cf. StdAM, AII, 20, RP, vol. 34, fols. 20–21; vol. 35, fols. 4v–5; vol. 36, fol. 10v; vol. 37, fols. 24v, 28–29; vol. 39, fols. 35–36v.

secretary Heinrich Holland wrote in 1608 that carnival was still celebrated with mummery and great disorder.[98] Determined once and for all to eradicate these excesses, the council imposed the enormous fine of 20 dalers for infringement of the ordinances.[99]

Not only did these stern legislations go unheeded; violence, in fact, kept mounting.[100] Hostilities, however, were not directed against the civic authorities but rather against the Jesuits, who had openly preached against the festivals.

Latent anti-clericalism burst out into the open during the 1608 carnival.[101] The Ipsen brothers, joined by some students of the gymnasium, ridiculed the Jesuits while the latter held the forty-hour prayer vigil for the first time in Münster. The brothers made an enormous strawman, put a Jesuit cap on his head, glasses on his nose, and let a foxtail run down his neck. Hidden inside the strawman, a brother moved the limbs and lips of the puppet, mimicking the speech and gestures of the local *patres* and giving out benedictions, to the great amusement of the spectators. The city council did not punish the perpetrators probably because, true to the charges of the Jesuits, the leading Protestant magistrates and guild leaders had organized the mockery.[102] Carnival had clearly counterattacked in the war declared by Lent.[103]

98. StdAM, AII, 20, RP, 1608, Feb. 29, vol. 40, fol. 48.

99. Ibid.

100. It has been argued that popular festivals became more and more politicized in the course of the sixteenth and seventeenth centuries. Fearful of revolts in the guise of festivals, civic authorities attempted to suppress popular feasts, which in turn provoked greater hostilities on the part of the lower classes. See Burke, pp. 259–70; Yves-Marie Bercé, *Fête et Révolte* (Paris, 1976).

101. The incident is described in a manuscript, StAM, AVM, MS. 261c. An article by Ludwig Remling arrived too late to be incorporated into the discussion here. Dr. Remling has transcribed and published all Jesuit sources relating to the attempts at the suppression of carnival in Münster. See his "Fastnacht und Gegenreformation in Münster: Diarien, Chroniken und Litterae annuae der Jesuiten als Quellen," *Jahrbuch für Volkskunde* (1982), pp. 51–77.

102. On February 29, the magistrates questioned Heinrich Deitermann and Johann Korman, Aldermen of the Ipsen Company, as to whether they had approved of the recent carnival mockery of the Jesuits. The two denied foreknowledge; see StdAM, AII, 20, RP, vol. 40, fol. 47v. The Jesuits, however, told quite a different story. They named Andreas Wilckinghoff, Christopher Hesse, Hans Balcke, [Johann?] Greving, and Wermelinck as the ringleaders, accusing them of taking revenge because the fathers opposed the burials of their heretical friends. See StAM, FM, SFG, "Comp. Hist. Comp.," 1608, Feb. 19, fol. 40v.

103. Unlike France, where popular resentments at festivals were often directed against the symbols of state power, carnival in Germany loved to mock the clergy, both Catholic and Protestant. Cf. Gerald Strauss, *Nuremberg in the Sixteenth Century* (Bloomington, 1976), p. 215; Robert Scribner, "Reformation, Carnival and the World Turned Upside-down," *Social History* 3 (1978), pp. 303–29.

Tensions continued to rise. Four carnivals later the copyists ran amok, damaging two houses owned by the Jesuits and completely destroying the door of the building of the procurators and notaries. The council saw no alternative but to fine each culprit 20 marks, warning them of more severe punishments if similar actions were repeated.[104] The incident revealed the anti-Jesuit sentiment built up over class and group differences. The copyists stood outside or occupied the lowest rung on the ladder of the judicial apparatus, whereas the procurators and notaries were among the higher- and middle-ranking officials and were some of the most fervent supporters of the Jesuits. Conflict between clerical and anti-clerical groups broke out again in 1613 and in 1618, when students of the Jesuit College and journeymen of the tailors' and goldsmiths' guilds threw stones at one another on Guden Maendag and were on the verge of armed clashes.[105] The hard times after the outbreak of the Thirty Years' War aided the magistrates in the suppression of carnival and other popular festivities, but the customs survived repeated prohibitions and were never completely rooted out.[106]

The celebrations of carnival, Gude Maendag, and other popular and neighborhood feasts were integral parts of the civic experience in Münster; they expressed the sense of group and communal solidarity inherent in traditional, pre-Tridentine Catholicism.[107] Carnival's successful resistance against the onslaughts of the Counter-Reformation depended upon the support of a part of the elite in Münster. In 1608 the twenty-four brothers of the Great Company included at least four future city councillors or close relatives of magistrates.[108] Among the guests they invited to their carnival ball were the cathedral canon Lucas Nagel, the city judge Dr. Johann Römer, the councillor Bernd Meyer, and girls from patrician, notable, and the leading mercantile and guild families. A general ban on merrymaking was intended primarily for the journeymen and the lower sorts; the magistrates conceded in 1618 that the ban on drinking during carnival evenings did not apply to solid property-owning burghers.[109]

While complete eradication of traditional forms of popular culture

104. StdAM, AII, 20, RP, 1612, Jan. 26, vol. 44, fols. 28v–29.

105. Cf. StdAM, AII, 20, RP, 1613, June 8 and 10, vol. 45, fols. 229, 231–32; 1618, June 15, vol. 50, fols. 244–46.

106. Cf. Norbert Humburg, *Städtisches Fastnachtsbrachtum in West- und Ostfalen* (Münster, 1976), pp. 127ff.

107. Cf. Muchembled, p. 328; Irmgard Simon, "Fastnachtsbräuche in Westfalen," *RWZfVK* 6 (1959), pp. 56–69; Siegfried Sieber, "Nachbarschaften, Gilden, Zünfte und ihre Feste," *Archiv für Kulturgeschichte* 11 (1914), pp. 455–82, and 12 (1914), pp. 56–78.

108. Offenberg, pp. 89f. The four were Wilhelm Bockhorst, Johann Huge, Johann Stöve, and Heinrich van Detten. See also appendix 1, no. 20, and under nos. 36, 71, 131.

109. Cf. StdAM, AII, 20, RP, March 17, vol. 50, fols. 123–24.

proved impossible, the Counter-Reformation succeeded in slowly transforming the nature of some of the festivities and substituting alternative
forms of culture. We have seen that Gude Maendag was originally a
celebration of summer and vitality by journeymen; by the early seventeenth century it had become an occasion for pilgrimage undertaken by
the students to the nearby Marian shrine at Telgte.[110] Sponsored by the
Jesuit Marian sodalities, Gude Maendag pilgrimages took on an aca-
demic-religious character in opposition to the artisanal-anthropological
nature of the original feast.

The repression of traditional popular festivals went hand in hand with
the promotion of religious processions, in which the clergy now took the
leading role.[111] What was new in Counter-Reformation processions was
the renewed definition of the proper relationship between clergy and
laity; the former was the head, the latter the body, of the *corpus christianum* of the revitalized Catholic world.[112] In the second half of the sixteenth century, and especially at the beginning of the seventeenth, religious processions in Münster assumed a new character. Superimposed
on the consciousness of the civic community was the clerical view of
ecclesiastical and civic history. The annual Saint John the Baptist procession in commemoration of the deliverance of Münster from the Anabaptists was an example of this new definition of civic historical consciousness by the clergy. The first procession took place on June 24,
1545, the decennial of the downfall of the Anabaptist Kingdom.[113] This
originally clerical ceremony eventually became a civic event; in 1635 the
city councillors also marched in the procession celebrating the centennial
of the deliverance of the *civitas christiana et catholica* from the hands of the
ungodly heretics.[114]

THE WORLD AS THEATER

An alternative Counter-Reformation civic culture was most visible on
stage. The sixteenth and seventeenth centuries loved the theater. In an

110. Cf. Wilhelm Schmülling, "325 Jahre Marienwallfahrt Telgte," *RWZfVK* 25
(1979–80), pp. 283–87.

111. Promoting Corpus Christi and other religious processions on the one hand, the
Counter-Reformation clergy attacked "rival" popular processions on the other. Agrarian
processions praying for good harvests—the field perambulations (*Flurumzüge*)—were condemned by the clergy for their sexual manifestations. Cf. H. L. Cox, "Prozessionsbrauchtum des späten Mittelalters und der frühen Neuzeit im Spiegel obrigkeitlicher Verordnungen in Kurköln und den vereinigten Herzogtümern," *RWZfVK* 22 (1976), pp. 51–85.

112. Cf. Muchembled, p. 212.

113. For details of the ceremonies, see *Festum liberationis nostrae* (1545).

114. A document recording the cost of candles for the magistrates and the guild leaders
in their procession through the city is extant. See StdAM, AXIV, 45a.

age before cinema and television, theater provided the most ready form of mass entertainment. Mystery plays, biblical drama, and carnival farces constituted a central element in the synthesis of holiness and profane entertainment in pre-Reformation civic culture. In the initial years of the Reformation, the theater served as a powerful weapon in the hands of the Protestants.[115] In Switzerland, Pamphilius Gengenbach and Niklaus Manuel incorporated virulent anti-papist polemics into traditional carnival plays.[116] The Bavarian Thomas Naogeorg combined humanist drama and Reformation propaganda in his enormously popular work *Pammachius* (1537).[117] Elsewhere in Germany carnival plays often ridiculed the Catholic Church and satirized the ignorance and corruption of the clergy. German drama, a close ally of the new religious message, gained much success through works such as Sizt Birk's *Judith* or Paul Rebhun's *Susanna* (1535).[118] The Münster Anabaptists also lashed out dramatically at the Catholic Church; they put on farces which mimicked Catholic mass and performed *Rich Man and Poor Lazarus* during the siege of the city to encourage the defenders and to express the egalitarian and radical strains of the millenarian revolution.[119] The Anabaptist Kingdom itself was a *theatrum historicum*, with a cast of thousands under the direction of a former Leiden actor, Jan Beukelszoon, enthralling the whole of Europe.[120]

After the downfall of the Anabaptist Kingdom, dramatic activities centered around the rhetorical education of the students at the cathedral school. Between 1551 and 1574, primarily under the rectorship of Hermann von Kerssenbroch, the students performed various plays with biblical themes, among them *Judith* (1551), *Susanna* (1553), *Joseph* (1558), *Tobia* and *Johannis Baptistae* (1563), *Saint Lawrence* (1572), and *Hestar* (1573).[121] These plays followed the civic festive calendar and were mostly carnival plays.[122] Bourgeois in their content and appeal, many were adaptations of Protestant school and humanist drama.

115. Cf. Hans Rupprich, *Die Deutsche Literatur vom späten Mittelalter bis zum Barock. II Teil. Das Zeitalter der Reformation 1520–1570* (Munich, 1973), pp. 318ff.

116. Ibid., pp. 333ff.; Steven Ozment, *The Reformation in the Cities* (New Haven, 1975), pp. 108–16.

117. Cf. Rupprich, pp. 360–65.

118. Ibid., pp. 372ff.

119. Cf. Kerssenbroch, p. 518.

120. Many broadsheets and newsletters kept Germany informed of the details of the siege of Münster; see Günther Vogler, "Das Täuferreich zu Münster im Spiegel der Flugschriften," in Hans-Joachim Köhler, ed., *Flugschriften als Massenmedium der Reformationszeit. Beiträge zum Tübinger Symposion 1980* (Stuttgart, 1981), pp. 309–51. I wish to thank Dr. Köhler for providing me with a copy of the article.

121. Cf. Albert Wormstall, "Das Schauspiel zu Münster im 16. und 17. Jahrhundert," *WZ* 56 (1898), pp. 75–85.

122. Cf. Humburg, pp. 63ff.

The Jesuits continued the humanist dramatic tradition when they took over the cathedral school in 1588. Jesuit drama readily found a sympathetic audience and satisfied to a large extent the theater-going urges of the burghers. The element of continuity, however, was deceptive; Jesuit theater represented an instrument for the missionary and ultramontane goals of the Society and introduced a new religious message in familiar cultural form into the city.

The first rector of the Jesuit College in Münster, Peter Michael *alias* Brillmacher, enjoyed some fame as a playwright. Born in 1542 in Cologne, he entered the Society in 1558 and served with distinction as preacher in Trier, Mainz, Speyer, and Düsseldorf.[123] It was as confessor to Duke Johann Wilhelm of Jülich-Cleve that he was called to Münster. All his plays were composed before 1588: some of them had biblical themes—*Daniel* was performed in Mainz (1565) and in Cologne (1579), *Absalon* in Speyer (1571), and *Magdelena* in Cologne—and others were of a didactic-polemical character.[124] His earliest play, *Vita Hominis militia*, stresses the central Ignatian concept of *electio* and urges men to undertake an active role in the service of God and the Catholic Church.[125] The play *Magdelena* shows the conversion of the sinner, the gathering together of committed Christians and later martyrdom. The plot called for the mobilization of moral forces among coteries of "elite Christians," who would then actively serve the true cause of Christ.[126]

It seems most likely that the first repertoire of the Jesuit theater in Münster consisted of the works of Brillmacher. The first play was performed in 1589 to the great delight of the magistrates and the better citizens; the council rewarded the players with money and many praises.[127] Performances were given every school year, usually at the beginning and end of terms. Some of the productions are known to us: the play *Saint Peter* was put on in 1598, *de Aulico Impoenitente* (on the life of Bede) in 1611, and *Tobias* in 1613.[128]

Technically, Jesuit theater was superior to earlier humanist and carni-

123. Cf. Johannes Müller, *Das Jesuitendrama in den Ländern Deutscher Zunge vom Anfang (1555) bis zum Hochbarock (1665)*, 2 vols. (Augsburg, 1930), vol. 2, pp. 7ff.

124. The list of works by Brillmacher given by Müller is incomplete; for the complete works of Brillmacher, see Müller, pp. 7ff. and Jean-Marie Valentin, *La Théatre des Jésuites dan les Pays de Langue allemande 1554–1680*, 3 vols. (Bern, 1978), vol. 1, pp. 408–10. See also Duhr, I, pp. 335–36.

125. Cf. Valentin, I, p. 408.

126. Ibid., pp. 409–10.

127. Cf. Sökeland, p. 66.

128. Cf. Müller, p. 53; *Litt. Ann.*, 1611, p. 551; and StAM, FM, SFG, "Comp. Hist. Coll.," fol. 63v.

val drama: the stage design was more sophisticated.[129] Casts were usually quite large, involving at times up to one hundred students.[130] Backed by the literary skills of the patres and the financial support provided by the city council and noble patrons, Jesuit drama offered spectacular visual entertainment. Jesuit theater represented different things to different people: for the students, it provided rhetorical practice and exercise in Latin memorization; for the parents, it showed tangible results of the pedagogic achievements of the patres; for the councillors, patricians, noblemen, and the educated elite, it honored them as the most esteemed members of society, who alone could understand the exclusive inner message; for the common crowd, it offered a spectacle of sounds and sights, of histrionic extravaganzas and heroic actions; for the Jesuits themselves, it served as an instrument for the propagation of faith.[131] Behind the histrionics and pageantry the Jesuits conveyed an explicit confessional message. In contrast to the earlier humanist school drama, with its bourgeois-biblical themes, Jesuit plays depicted scenes and actions far from the daily experiences of the civic community. Church history and the lives of saints formed the stuff of most of the plays performed in Münster.[132] Of the 323 Jesuit plays known to have been written in Germany between 1555 and 1665, 149 depicted episodes from church history or from the lives of saints; another 122 showed the blessed careers of kings, queens, and princes when they conformed to the will of God and, conversely, their tragic ends if they dared to oppose the one true Church.[133]

This new weapon of the Jesuits aroused the ire of their enemies. The great Protestant playwright of the sixteenth century, Johann Fischart,

129. Cf. Willi Flemming, *Geschichte des Jesuiten-Theaters in den Ländern Deutscher Zunge* (Berlin, 1923), pp. xv–xvi, 270ff.

130. Cf. L. van den Boogerd, *Het Jezuietendrama in de Nederlanden* (Groningen, 1961), pp. 69–72; Elida Maria Szarota, *Das Jesuitendrama im deutschen Sprachgebiet,* 2 vols. (Munich, 1979–80), vol. 1, pt. 1, p. 7.

131. On the appeal of Jesuit theater to the social elite, see Flemming, pp. 1–2; Valentin, II, pp. 959–60. Compared to Jesuit theater in Munich and Vienna, North German Jesuit drama was more didactic, polemical, and confessional in character. In the face of non-Catholic spectators the Jesuits in North Germany emphasized the function of drama as sermons and catechism; in Catholic Bavaria and Austria, the artistic elements were given full chance to develop. Cf. Fritz Rediger, *Zur dramatischen Literatur der Paderborner Jesuiten* (Emdsdetten, 1935), pp. 34f.

132. The texts of the earliest Jesuit plays in Münster have not survived. Plots of Jesuit drama performed in Münster between 1632 and 1648 are summarized by Paul Bahlmann in his *Jesuiten-Dramen der Niederrheinischen Ordensprovinz* (= *Beihefte zum Centralblatt für Bibliothekswesen* 15, Leipzig, 1896), pp. 99–108. I base my observations here on the repertoire of Brillmacher and the isolated references to performances in the *Litterae Annuae* and the history of the college.

133. Cf. Müller, pp. 91–96.

also wrote a piece entitled *Jesuitenhütlein* and other polemical works to deride the Society. As catechism and as a means of conversion, Jesuit theater appealed to the intellect and to faith through emotions and senses. In 1611 the Jesuits proudly reported a conversion: the play *de Aulico Impoenitente* moved a heretic to return to the bosom of the Mother Church.[134]

Jesuit drama embodied the essential principle of late medieval popular piety. It was a form of "salvific display" which conferred grace upon its beholders, a means of salvation directed at the eyes of the devout.[135] Thus, it represented a continuation of the Catholic emphasis on the visual aspects of piety, in contrast to the often-observed intensely aural aspects of Protestant devotion. The former depended on spectacles, images, and gestures; the latter praised sermons, the reading aloud of Scripture, and the singing of hymns. In the early Reformation, the explosion of production in woodcuts attacking the Catholic clergy and propagating Luther's cause made use of this intensely visual popular piety. However, as the Reformation gained acceptance, the Protestant clergy abandoned many of these early cultural weapons, attacking them as vestiges of a sinful and heathen past: carnivals were banned, scurrilous woodcuts and broadsheets censored, and the rowdy and scatological *Fastnachtspiele* of a Hans Rosenplüt or a Hans Folz became the long-winded and didactic plays of Hans Sachs. The splendor of Jesuit drama appealed to the religious and aesthetic feelings of the burghers who had created in the first place the cultural world of the Passion plays and the paintings, woodcuts, figurines, and statues of Pre-Reformation Germany.

The success of Jesuit theater can be understood in two ways. The students, the future elite, emulated the saints, the godly rulers, and the martyrs, and practiced the roles they were being trained to play as prelates, priests, councillors, lawyers, professors, princes, and rulers; they acted out historical roles in preparation for their own active role in shaping the course of history. The spectators, the masses, remained passive. They were on the receiving end of the Counter-Reformation idea of a sacred *ordo rerum*. Although they, too, belonged to the hierarchical order of things, they were the inferior parts who were to obey and marvel at the new order of the universe. The model of the heroic, godly individual was not directed at them; Jesuit drama was a theater of power, of moral and spiritual strength, and of actual political might. It was a theater of power for the powerful and was thus in harmony with the new con-

---

134. *Litt. Ann.*, 1611, p. 551.
135. For the importance of visual forms of devotion in pre-Reformation and early Reformation Germany, see Robert Scribner, *For the Sake of Simple Folk: Popular Propaganda for the German Reformation* (Cambridge, 1981).

sciousness of the civic elite.[136] Weakened in their ties to the urban community through service in the territorial state, disdainful of traditions by
their legal and humanistic education, and more aware of the dignity of
political office and the gulf between *Obrigkeit* and commune, the greater
part of the elite in Münster came to identify their destiny less with the
confined urban space of the craftsmen and more with the dynamic, ex-
pansive world of the Counter-Reformation. By dramatically presenting
the struggle between heaven and hell, by depicting the struggle between
the Empire and the Turks, and by re-enacting the martyrdom of Christians in faraway Japan,[137] Jesuit theater vastly expanded the spiritual horizons of the ruling elite. The salvation of the civic community was no
longer something between God and the particular city alone, but constituted a chapter in the universal war between God and Satan, and shared
the fortunes of Empire and Papacy.

136. For the social influences of Jesuit drama, see Valentin, II, pp. 959f., and Flemming,
pp. 299ff.

137. After 1603, news of the persecutions of Christians in Japan prompted the performance of many Jesuit plays depicting Christian martyrdom both in contemporary Japan
and in the early Christian centuries; see Szarota, I:1, pp. 58–59.

CHAPTER SEVEN

A Profile of Popular Piety

To understand the impact of the Reformation and the Counter-Reformation on popular religious attitudes in the sixteenth century, we now turn to perhaps the most solemn moment in life and to records which capture, however fleetingly, the concerns and moods of that moment: death and last testament. The more than twelve hundred wills of burghers in Münster which have come down to us from the period under consideration are repositories of the wealth, kinship, love, fear, and piety of men and women caught up in a time of rapid historical change. Through these wills, we come to know our Münsteraners as individuals, often intimately; we get acquainted with their family, relatives, and friends and catch a glimpse, sometimes even a good view, of their material and spiritual being. Again, through the wills, we can observe changes in the collective impulses of the age; we touch central historical forces which compelled individuals to partake in common destinies as members of distinct social and religious groups.

Historians of ancien régime France have led the way in analyzing wills over "long durations" in order to reconstruct changes in religious mentalities. The work of Michel Vovelle stands here as the model for such investigations.[1] In Germany, jurists, linguists, and economic historians have studied medieval urban wills; these sources provide the fullest evidence for investigations into the rights of inheritance, synchronic and diachronic characteristics of the German dialects, and urban economic life. The publication of the wills of medieval Lübeck by Ahasver von Brandt represents the most important undertaking in this direction of

---

1. Michel Vovelle, *Pieté Baroque et Déchristianisation en Provence au XVIIIe Siècle. Les Attitudes devant la Mort d'après les Clauses des Testaments* (Paris, 1973). For other works, see Claude Aboucaya, *Le Testament lyonnais de la Fin du XVe au Milieu du XVIIIe Siècle* (Paris, 1961); Pierre Chaunu, *La Mort à Paris: XVIe, XVIIe, XVIIIe Siècles* (Paris 1978); and Wilma J. Pugh, "Catholics, Protestants, and Testamentary Charity in Seventeenth-Century Lyon and Nimes," *French Historical Studies* 11:4 (1980), pp. 479–504. Aboucaya's study deals more with the technical aspects of wills—their legal status, typology, and contents. Vovelle's study concentrates primarily on the wills as documents for religious history.

Table 7.1   Wills of Münster Burghers, 1510–1618

| | No. of wills made by | | |
	single testator*	joint testator	Total
before 1530	2	—	2
1530–39	18	1	19
1540–49	44	7	51
1550–59	71	24	95
1560–69	50	37	87
1570–79	121	55	176
1580–89	121	51	172
1590–99	103	88	191
1600–09	150	107	257
1610–18	120	65	185
Total	800	435	1,235

*Under this category are included widows, widowers, and husbands and wives making separate wills.

research.[2] For Reformation and Counter-Reformation Germany, there is as yet no systematic study of wills as documents of religious sentiments and practices. While Münster burgher testaments have served as the basis for several genealogical reconstructions, they are analyzed here for the first time in respect to clauses of pious legacies, religious invocations, relations between laity and clergy, and popular attitudes toward death.

Our sources are 1,235 extant wills dictated and executed in the years between 1510 and 1618.[3] They were made by 719 men and 910 women, including couples dictating joint testaments. The male/female ratio of testators is 1:1.266, reflecting closely the ratio of the sexes in Münster, where the presence of many clergymen and the higher death rate among men resulted in a sex ratio of 1:1.349 in favor of females.[4] Table 7.1 shows the distribution of wills according to decades.

From the estimated death rate for the late sixteenth and early seven-

2. See Ahasver von Brandt, ed., Regesten der Lübecker Bürgertestamente des Mittelalters. I: 1278–1350 (Lübeck, 1964) and II: 1351–1363 (Lübeck, 1973). See also his Mittelalterliche Bürgertestamente. Neuerschlossene Quellen zur Geschichte der materiellen und geistigen Kultur (Heidelberg, 1973); a bibliographic appendix lists published wills and related studies for other medieval German cities (pp. 30f.).

3. StdAM, B (Gerichtsarchiv), Testamente I (sixteenth century), 19 vols.; Testamente II (seventeenth century), 51 vols., plus unbound pergaments. For a detailed discussion of the legal aspects and the procedure of drawing up a will, as well as a description of the formats and styles, see R. Po-chia Hsia, "Civic Wills as Sources for the Study of Piety in Münster, 1530–1618," SCJ 14 (1983).

4. The sex ratio is calculated from the 1591 population figure given by Lethmate; see his Bevölkerung, pp. 46f.

teenth centuries, I have reckoned that the 1,629 testators of 1,235 wills represented probably one-third of all potential testators, the upper and middle strata of the citizenry being better represented than the lower classes.[5] Moreover, a sample check of wills prepared by a number of notaries shows that the notarial formulations which give the wills a certain uniformity do not distort the religious sentiments of the testators. Even in wills drawn up by the clergy, there is no consistent pattern of invocation or commendation; the religious vocabulary reflects the sentiments of the testators and not those of the notaries.

HOW CATHOLIC WAS MÜNSTER?

There are two ways to measure support for the Catholic Church in the wills—by noting formulae of invocation and commendation and by identifying legacies to the clergy.

A distinct traditional, pre-Reformation Catholic style of will can be identified through references to the Virgin Mary, saints, and guardian angels when the testator commended his soul to God. This style is manifest in both of the pre-1530 wills and appears with decreasing frequency in wills after 1535. A typical commendation was that of Maria thon Eule, widow of the baker Hermann Werninck. Her 1554 will states that after her soul separates from its mortal body and leaves this vale of tears, she would commend it to "God of Heaven, Mary his lovely mother, my holy angels, my apostles . . . [and] all the heavenly hosts *[Godde vann hemelryck, Marien syner leven moder, mynen hilligen Engell, mynen apostell . . . allen hemmelsschen heer]*.[6] Figure 7.1 shows the frequency of occurrence of this traditional Catholic pattern of commendation. Use of this formula declined continuously until it almost disappeared around the turn of the century. Even in the early decades of the seventeenth century, when the Catholic revival was underway, it turned up in only a tiny fraction of all wills (0.78 percent and 1.6 percent for 1600–09 and 1610–18, respectively). The change points to a definite decline of traditional forms of piety after 1535, even though Münster remained a Catholic city. In particular, the decline indicates a precipitous drop in devotion to the Virgin Mary among burghers throughout the sixteenth century, in

5. The crude death rate is calculated from the changes in population for the period between 1591 and 1603, when complete sets of demographic data are available. Taking into consideration the net gain in population through immigration, I arrived at the crude death rate of 7.7 per thousand, which corresponds to the adult death rate of many early modern European cities. For the methodology and sources, see Hsia, "Civic Wills," *SCJ* 14 (1983). See also Roger Mols, *Introduction à la Démographie Historique des Villes d'Europe du XVIe au XVIIIe Siècle,* vol. 3 (Louvain, 1956), pp. 213–14, table 8.

6. StdAM, B, Test. I, no. 226, vol. 6, fol. 121v.

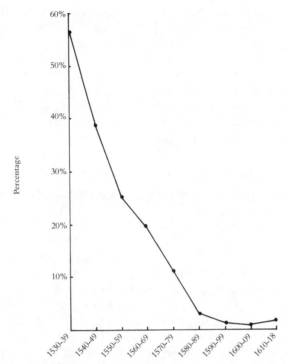

Figure 7.1 Frequency of Catholic Commendation Formula

strong contrast to the decades before the Reformation.[7] Residual devotion to the Virgin Mary was equally weak among men and women: 56 men (7.79 percent of all testators) and 71 women (7.8 percent of all testatrices) specifically commended their souls to the Virgin Mary.

After the Reformation years, the commendation formulae show a decidedly more Christocentric piety, reflecting, perhaps, the lingering influence of Reformation beliefs and the quiet infiltration of Protestant ideas in post-Anabaptist Münster. The new emphasis on Christocentrism, however, was also a direct result of the Catholic response to the Reformation in Münster. Dean Michael Rupert of Liebfrauen Church (1551-98), the best-loved popular preacher in Münster during the second half of the sixteenth century, focused on Christ's passion in his sermons and writings.[8] His popular book of catechism, written in the local dialect,

7. Marian devotion was central to the heightened popular piety in Germany before the Reformation; see Willy Andreas, *Deutschland vor der Reformation. Eine Zeitenwende* (7th ed., Berlin, 1972), pp. 153f.

8. Michael Rupert also founded the confraternity of Saint Peter in Liebfrauen parish and served as one of the commissioners in the 1571 diocesan visitation; for a brief biography see Rudolf Schulze, *Liebfrauen-Überwasser*, pp. 193-206.

went through two printings; in it he tried to show "how mankind was doomed because of Adam's pitiful fall and redeemed by Jesus Christ the Son of God and Mary."[9] Representative of this new Christocentrism was the will of Gertrud Niehuis (1581), in which she commended her soul into the hands of "Our Lord Jesus Christ my only mediator and sanctifier *[unsers Hern Jesu Christi meines einigen midlers und salichmachers]*."[10] The intense fear of death and the great uncertainty over eternal salvation which characterized popular piety in Germany on the eve of the Reformation seemed to have been mitigated by a trustful hope in the merits of Christ's sufferings and God's boundless mercy among both the Lutherans and the Catholics.[11] This would explain the decline in the popularity of the traditional Catholic style of commendation; for Catholics, imploring one omnipotent, merciful redeemer and sanctifier proved more comforting than invoking the dubious efficacy of a heavenly paraphernalia of angels and saints.

If the virtual disappearence of the traditional Catholic commendation formula points to a change in style and to new religious sensibilities among the Catholics of post-Anabaptist Münster, legacies to the clergy irrefutably indicate the level of support for the institutional Church. Figure 7.2 shows the change in lay support for the clergy as indicated by the percentage of wills containing legacies to ecclesiastics.

The trend of development is clearly manifest. The middle of the century represented a turning point. The generations reared in traditional Catholicism who remained faithful to the Roman Church had died out; the generation who matured in the years of the Reformation and left behind their wills in the 1560s was a generation whose ties to Catholicism were most tenuous. Until 1570 the Roman Church in Münster took hardly any effective measures to retain the laity in its fold. Beginning with 1568 a new determination of Catholic renewal was embodied in the person of Bishop Johann von Hoya and the work of a few outstanding

9. *Catechismus und Betböklin mit heylsamen Betrachtunge und Gebetlin vermehret und gebettert . . . dorch Michaelem Rupertum Werlensem Decken unser lieven frauwen Kercken tho Oeverwater binnen Münster. Gedruckt tho Münster in Westphalen by Lambert Raesfeldt/ in verlegung Matthae Pontani genandt Brückner. 1596*, sig. A4: "wie dat menschlige Geschlechte dorch den erbermligen Fall Adams verloren und dorch Jesum Christum den Sohn Gots und Marie wederum verlöst ist." He mentions also that the first edition has been sold out for a long time and that upon many requests he is now authorizing a new printing. The entire second part of the catechism is on the life and passion of Christ: "Dat Leven unsers Herren und Erlösers Jesu Christi ader Passionalböcklin welchs ethwan van den Gottsaligen Voralderen und adlen Catholischen Christen/ Dat Paradyss ader Der Seelen Lustgarde/ ist genant worden."

10. StdAM, B, Test. I, no. 656, vol. 17, fol. 57v.

11. For the intense fear of death in pre-Reformation Germany, see Andreas, pp. 184–88.

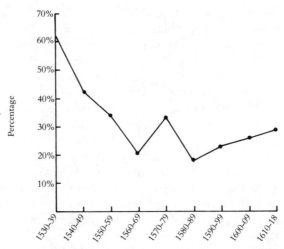

Figure 7.2 Legacies to the Clergy as a Percentage of Wills

pastors.[12] In 1571 the Tridentine Decrees were published for the first time in the Bishopric of Münster, and Bishop Johann appointed a commission to carry out the first diocesan visitation. The contrast with the previous decade is immediate. The slight drop in support during the 1580s probably resulted from civic fears of Münster's entanglement in the Cologne War; the downturn reflected burgher suspicions of an over-zealous clergy. It was also the decade when strong forces for Protestantism among the cathedral canons touched off the struggle for power between Catholics and Protestants in the cathedral chapter. After 1588, with the arrival of the Jesuits, the forces of the Counter-Reformation slowly but steadily gathered strength; the upswing in the last decade of the sixteenth century was the beginning of a long process of recatholicization in Münster.

The general trend of development discussed above is corroborated by an analysis of pious legacies: these included money for the repair of church buildings, candles for the eucharist and altars, the endowment of preacherships, and gifts to confraternities, often willed by the same testators who gave money to the clergy. The secular trend shown in figure 7.3 closely resembles the pattern in figure 7.2.

Having plotted the general line of development regarding support for the Catholic Church, we need to examine more closely the donations to the clergy. Altogether 335 wills (27.1 percent of all wills) contain 483 clauses of bequests to the clergy; these wills represented the testaments of

---

12. For a biography of the humanist-reformer Bishop Johann von Hoya see Wilhelm Kohl, "Johann von Hoya (1529–1574)," *Westfälische Lebensbilder* 10 (1970), pp. 1–18.

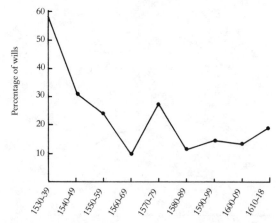

Figure 7.3 Pious Legacies as a Percentage of Wills

253 women and 148 men (27.8 percent and 20.58 percent of all testatrices and testators). More than one-third of them were giving to relatives: from the texts of the wills it can be ascertained that at least 138 of the 335 wills in question were dictated by men and women who had siblings, children, or cousins as clerics. If the exact relationships between all testators and clerical beneficiaries can be established, the proportion of bequests to clerical relatives would undoubtedly be even higher.

Among the different groups of clerics, the seculars received the greatest number of bequests, the majority of which went to the pastors and vicars of the parish churches; of the 483 legacies to the clergy, 228 (47.2 percent) named them as beneficiaries. Legacies to male religious orders and houses comprised 16.8 percent (81 clauses) of the 483 bequests. Support rose sharply after 1590, an increase due to the establishment of two new congregations in Münster: the Jesuits in 1588 and the Capuchins in 1615. Donations to the convents declined steadily after the 1560s, a sign of the diminished attraction of the cloistered life for women; the situation only changed for the better after the arrival of the Jesuits, when the Patres encouraged a new religious movement among women.[13] The decline may also reflect decreasing burgher support for the convents, which continued, nonetheless, to receive daughters of the nobility. Still, legacies in this category comprise 24 percent of all clauses. The last 12 percent of the 483 legacies went to the beguines. Donations fluctuated little between 1540 and the end of the century; after that they declined steadily. Figure 7.4 shows legacies to different ecclesiastical groups as percentages of all clauses of donations to the clergy.

13. See chap. 3, pp. 81–84.

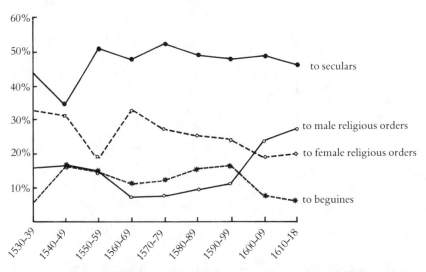

Figure 7.4 Legacies to Different Clerical Groups as Percentages of All Donations to the Clergy

Several characteristics of legacies to the clergy deserve our attention. First, the strong burgher support for the parish clergy expressed a sense of civic solidarity. As we have seen, the city council exercised extensive presentation rights over the parish vicarages.[14] These benefices were endowed by burghers for native sons who prayed and worked for the salvation of their fellow citizens. The close rapport between the citizenry and the lower clergy was often based on actual kinship ties; before the appointment of foreign priests to implement the Counter-Reformation in the parish churches, the closeness between burghers and the civic clergy was a constant theme in the vacillating relationship between Church and society in Münster.

The wills also reflect the differing prestige of the religious orders by the amount of donations to each. Whenever both Jesuits and Franciscans appear as beneficiaries in the wills, the Fathers always received more donations than the friars. On the other hand, many wills contain legacies to the Franciscans but none to the Jesuits. In fact, several wills drawn up by members of the burgher elite mention donations to every religious order but the Jesuits,[15] an unmistakable indication of the existence of anti-Jesuit sentiment among pious Catholics.

14. See chap. 2, pp. 36–38.
15. In 1637 the brothers Heinrich and Johann Herding gave 200 dalers to the Sisters of Poor Clare, the Capuchins, the Observants, and the Franciscans, but nothing to the Jesuits (StdAM, B, Test. II, no. 1999); a similar pattern with legacies to the mendicant orders and the parish clergy but nothing to the Jesuits is also found in the wills of Johann Borchorst and Katherina Nünning, and of Bürgermeister Johann Herding (see Test. II, nos. 569 & 682).

The last point to be noted is that at the beginning of the seventeenth century, a smaller percentage of testators was giving much larger sums to the clergy. In other words, lay support for the clergy in the earlier decades of the sixteenth century was more diffused among the citizenry, whereas in the first two decades of the seventeenth century, donations to the clergy stemmed from a much smaller, but more powerful and wealthy, segment of urban society. The most extreme example is that of Lic. Dietrich zum Sande, procurator at the Ecclesiastical Court and magistrate in 1632, who gave his entire fortune of over 30,000 dalers to the Roman Catholic Church.[16]

Can we make some general statements about the strength of Catholicism in Münster? The difficulty is that the majority of wills contain no clues concerning the confessional loyalty of the testators. Many were made by burghers of modest means who bequeathed their meager possessions only to relatives and friends. Most wills have religious formulae which are ambiguous to interpret: they invoke the Holy Trinity and Christ but make no mention of the Virgin and the saints, although in many cases the testators specifically characterize themselves as Catholics. The absence of positive indicators of Catholicism does not necessarily mean the testators were Protestants, but it can be assumed that only a small portion of the citizenry were active supporters of the clergy. The confessional loyalty of the leading burgher families comes out clearly through their legacies to the clergy, who were often their kinsmen. But the silent majority—the lower classes—are just as reticent in the wills. Except for domestic servants of magisterial families who shared the household and confessional allegiances of their masters and mistresses,[17] the laconic statements of the lower classes probably reflect a sense of religious, or at least, confessional indifference.

Since no organized Protestant community existed in post-Anabaptist Münster, it is much more difficult to gauge sentiments for the Lutheran and Calvinist confessions. However, the wills of known Protestant leaders suggest a few characteristics which may be indicative of the religious sentiments of other testators.[18] The most obvious characteristics are, of course, the absence of references to saints, angels, or the Virgin Mary, or of donations to the clergy. Coupled with the absence of the above, generous almsgiving is a strong suggestion of Protestant senti-

---

16. His will, account books, and the inventories of his possessions fill 207 folios and an entire bound volume in the city archive; see StdAM, B, Test. II, no. 10, vol. 20, fols. 1–95 (his will and codicils); fols. 97–207 (inventory of his library and other material possessions). The bulk of his fortunes were in 35 annuities worth 24,500 dalers.

17. See StdAM, B, Test. I, no. 219; Test. II, no. 1306.

18. See the wills of Bernhard Burman (Test. II, no. 752), Christine Stummel (the widow of Melchior Steinhoff) (Test. II, no. 980), Lic. Dietrich Seveker (Test. I, no. 334), and Peter Varwick (Test. I, no. 355).

ments. A number of wills stand out in this respect. They were made by merchants of considerable wealth who gave large sums to the poor but nothing to the clergy. Heinrich Scholbrock, a wine merchant with over 10,000 dalers, gave the poor 370 dalers but nothing to the clergy.[19] Or take the example of the merchant Johann zum Klei: he gave one-quarter of his possessions to the poor but not a single penny to the clergy.[20] This testamental pattern stands out in sharp contrast to the wills of the Catholic burghers in the same social class who bequeathed large sums to many ecclesiastical institutions, and suggests the existence of strong anti-clerical, if not actual Protestant, sentiments.

VAGABONDS AND GOD'S POOR

Catholic piety in Münster before the Counter-Reformation was strongly influenced by the practical burgher piety of the *Devotio Moderna*. In his catechism, Dean Michael Rupert urges his parishioners to give alms by arguing the merits of practical acts of charity. He wrote, "Man is justi-fied by good works and not by faith alone, and whoever does justice, he is just."[21] Figure 7.5 examines the effectiveness of the appeal of the Cath-olic message in reference to poor relief. Altogether 691 out of 1,235, or 56 percent of all wills, contain clauses of almsgiving. For the entire period, the wills of the 1550s and 1560s have the lowest percentages of charitable bequests (34.7 percent and 25.2 percent respectively). There are several factors which may explain this ebb in the mid-sixteenth cen-tury. The wills of the year 1530 to 1549 were dictated by the same generations which we have seen retained their Catholic faith in the stormy years of the Reformation; these wills also show the highest fre-quency of occurrence of the traditional Catholic formula of commenda-tion. It is characteristic that many wills of these decades which gave alms to the poor also stipulated reverse services from the benefited. The poor were asked to follow the funeral processions of the benefactors, to attend vigils and memorial masses, to pray for the souls of the departed—to participate, in short, in the reciprocal economy of collective salvation. Thus for those who died between 1530 and 1550, the willingness to give to the poor expressed adherence to the Catholic doctrine of salvation through good works.

The men and women who died between 1550 and 1570 were less likely to give alms because many of them came to Münster as immigrants in the immediate post-Anabaptist years; they were, on the whole, humble

19. StdAM, B, Test. I, no. 181. His son, however, was a supporter of the Jesuits. See appendix 1, no. 120.

20. StdAM, B, Test. I, no. 484.

21. *Catechismus und Betböklin, sig. C 12v: "Uth guden wercken/ und nicht alleine uth dem Geloven/ wert de Mensche gerechtferdiget/ unde wer da doet de gerechtigheit/ de ist gerecht."*

charitable legacies as percentage of all wills

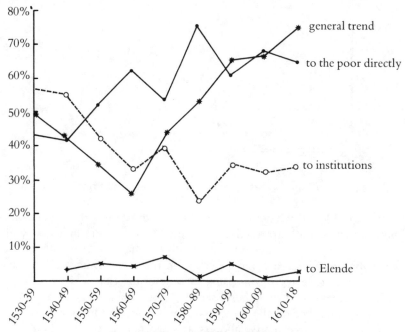

Figure 7.5 Poor Relief in Münster

folks—artisans and day laborers—who had little money to spare. These two decades also represented a low point in lay support for the clergy; the low level of poor relief could also suggest widespread indifference among less wealthy citizens, who were more concerned with their livelihood than with helping the clergy or the poor.

The decisive upturn began in the 1570s, when the fruits of the Catholic renewal and economic recovery began to show. Whereas the seventies were comparable to the forties in terms of the intensity of poor relief, the years after 1580 represented new heights in public charity. These advances show unmistakable signs of a local Catholic renewal, brought about before the coming of the Jesuits mainly by the filtering down of the Catholic reform to the parish level through the workings of a few outstanding pastors. It is no accident that testators at the end of the sixteenth century often bequeathed small sums to their confessors "out of friendship."

Aside from a renewed Catholic piety, the rise in charitable donations also resulted from two sets of factors. First of all, there was a greater willingness to give and more money around. By the 1570s, Münster had recovered from the economic setbacks caused by the Anabaptist rebel-

Index 1537 = 100

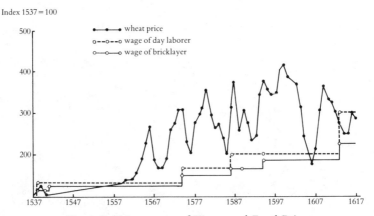

Figure 7.6 Movement of Wages and Food Prices

lion; in the last three decades of the sixteenth century the expansion of
beer-brewing, the introduction of a new linen-weaving industry, and a
flourishing trade in wine, cattle, and other agricultural products (which
partially compensated for the decline in the long-distance cloth trade)
were clearly reflected in the rising income of the city.[22]

This brings us to the second set of factors: the increasing number of
persons who relied on charity to make ends meet. In Münster, poor relief
certainly kept alive many laborers and workers in the building trades
whose wages were strictly regulated by the city council. Figure 7.6 com-
pares the rate of wage increase and the much faster rise in the price of
wheat between 1535 and 1618. To put it in words, the price of basic
foodstuffs rose twice as fast as wage increases. The deteriorating standard
of living for working men and women in fifteenth- and sixteenth-century German cities has been well documented by Ulf Dirlmeier.[23]

Unlike the Flemish and Brabantine cities, Münster was not a major
center of weaving with a large urban proletariat; the swollen ranks of the
poor toward the end of the sixteenth century comprised more refugees
than poor laborers. When the Bishopric of Münster became another
battleground between the Spaniards and the Dutch in the 1580s, peasants
from around Münster sought protection behind the city walls from marauding bands of mercenaries.[24]

22. Revenues from the cloth-tax, and tolls on cattle and agricultural products passing
through Münster rose from 504 marks in 1567 to 1,594 marks in twenty years' time. These
figures are from StdAM, AVIII, GR, vols. 6 & 9.

23. See Ulf Dirlmeier, *Untersuchungen zu Einkommensverhältnissen und Lebenshaltungskosten in oberdeutschen Städten des Spätmittelalters (Mitte 14. bis Anfang 16. Jahrhunderts)*
(Heidelberg, 1978), pp. 171–75, 213–19, 533f.

24. The council minutes of 1599 report daily increases in the number of refugees
fleeing war; see StdAM, AII, 20, RP, May 14, vol. 31, fol. 51v.

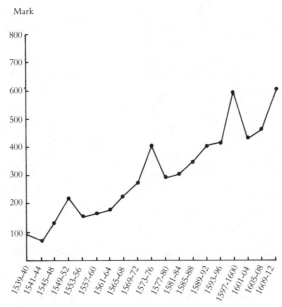

Figure 7.7 Aegidii Almissenkorff Income: Four-Year Averages
Source: BDAM, PfA Aegidii, Akten, A103-108

Magistrates and citizens undertook massive efforts to raise funds for
the poor. The sharp increase in charitable donations after 1590 is manifest
not only in testamentary bequests but also in the income of poorfunds
partly or wholly dependent on money from the city council. Figures 7.7
and 7.8 chart the rising income of the alms-box of Aegidii parish and the
"bacon fund" of Saint Lambert's; the former was administered by parish
provisors who were often magistrates and the latter was managed by two
city councillors.

Even with public and private initiatives, there was simply not enough
money to go around. Concomitant with providing food, clothing, and
alms, the magistrates also sought to restrict the number of refuges and
control the poor. The problem of dealing with the massive influx of
refugees accelerated magisterial measures to differentiate the poor from
the vagabonds. Many cities had already published ordinances against
wandering beggars in the late fifteenth century; the distinction between
poverty and mendicancy became more sharply defined in the course of
the late Middle Ages.[25] In Münster, the first documented prohibition
against foreign beggars is a councillor ordinance of 1564.[26] In 1585, an

25. Cf. Michel Mollat, *Les Pauvres au Moyen Âge* (Paris, 1978), pp. 281ff. See also
Études sur l'histoire de la Pauvreté, 2 vols. (Paris, 1974), ed. Michel Mollat.
26. Cf. StdAM, AII, 20, RP, 1564, March 8, vol. 1, fols. 11–11v. If earlier council
minutes were extant, similar ordinances could most likely be found.

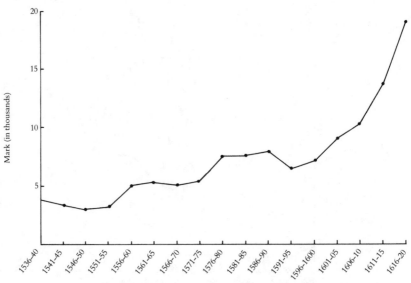

Figure 7.8 Lamberti Speckpfründen Income: Five-Year Averages
Source: StdAM, C, Speckpfründen Lamberti

ordinance for the poor was drawn up by the magistrates to cope with the influx of refugees.[27] City officials organized beggars into work-gangs to repair streets and buildings in exchange for alms.[28] The magistrates also regulated the number of refugees who could lodge in garden sheds to prevent exploitation by greedy landlords; no more than one couple could stay in a garden shed.[29] Parish provisors were charged to register the poor who received alms from the various parish poorfunds; those living on charity had to wear badges (*Armenzeichen*), an administrative measure which brought humiliation on the poor and an opportunity for fraud.[30] Local beggars also came under strict supervision. Not only were the able-bodied forced to work, but women, children, and the handicapped were permitted to beg in the streets only in the early morning and late evening hours.[31]

Who were the poor in Münster? Here, we have to distinguish between

27. Cf. StdAM, AII, 20, RP, May 31, vol. 17, fol. 24.

28. StdAM, AII, 20, RP, 1592, Sept. 15, vol. 24, fol. 90.

29. StdAM, AII, 20, RP, 1598, May 7, vol. 30, fols. 19–20 and RP, 1602, Feb. 25, vol. 34, fol. 41.

30. The ordinance requiring the poor to wear badges in Münster was first publicized in 1599; see StdAM, AII, 20, RP, 1599, July 1, vol. 31, fols. 64–64v. Half a year later, some citizens sold the badges of their dead relatives; the magistrates were prompted to deal severely with the fraudulent use of public charities; see RP, 1600, Jan. 31, vol. 32, fol. 6v.

31. In 1609 the city council forbade begging between eight in the morning and six in the evening; see StdAM, AII, 20, RP, 1609, July 3, vol. 41, fol. 115.

contemporary perceptions and the actual groups of impoverished Münsteraners. The actual composition of the poor can be reconstructed from extant account books of the poorfunds. The register of the poor-box of Saint Ludger's parish lists a corps of poor parishioners, the majority of them poor widows, whose names were entered in the book when they received periodic alms. A few poor artisans and disabled men also appear in the account book.[32] In the wills, these are usually described as the *"Gottesarmen," "kentliche Huisarmen," "heimliche Huisarmen,"* or the "genuine poor." Implied is the notion that they truly deserved Christian charity and help from their fellow citizens. The term *heimliche Huissarmen* refers to those who lived in their own homes and not in poorhouses, and were too ashamed to beg openly in the streets;[33] these included poor artisans, day laborers, and impoverished widows who hung on to the margins of respectability while making ends meet. Another group were the beggars, the vagabonds. As outsiders and parasites, they represented a threat to the already overburdened good will and charity of the burghers. In the second half of the sixteenth century, discretion to help these outside wretches rested with the magistrates, who could turn them away, give alms, even grant them permission to reside in Münster.[34] Paradoxically, while magistrates and burghers made sharper distinctions between undeserving vagabonds and the genuine local poor, the social status of the latter also approached the former group. From a Christian virtue with the promise of compensation in eternal life, poverty became more of a shame to society by the end of the sixteenth century.[35] The best illustration of the new, negative attitude toward Christian mendicancy was the fate of the Guest House in Münster: while it provided lodging for pilgrims in the Middle Ages, the place became an asylum, a prison for the insane, in the seventeenth and eighteenth centuries.[36]

A third group of poor people consisted of the inmates of the hospitals, the poorhouses, the orphanage, and the house for lepers. The orphanage was founded in 1599 by the magistrate Johann Verendorp and his wife, a

32. See BDAM, PfA Ludgeri, B (Akten), Kart. 48, "Reygyster unde Recken-schup . . . almyssenn korviss . . . Ludgerij bynnen Monster ffan de anno 1572."

33. In their will, Johann zum Klei and Anna Hülsow gave one-quarter of their possessions to help "der haussitzenden armen und burgher disser stadt Münster, welche sich des haussbettelens schamen." StdAM, Test. I, no. 484, vol. 13, fol. 20v.

34. In 1562, for example, the magistrates gave alms to "a pious man" who had lost everything in a shipwreck so that he could lodge at a local poorhouse and not go around begging; see StdAM, AVIII, 188, GR, vol. 6, fol. 80v. The account books of the Gruetamt also record many instances where outside beggars were permitted to beg for a day or two in Münster or were given small sums by the magistrates and expelled from the city.

35. Cf. Mollat, *Les Pauvres,* pp. 303ff.

36. See Klaus Gimpel, "Das Gast- und Irrenhaus in Münster," *Historia Hospitalium. Zeitschrift der deutschen Gesellschaft für Krankenhausgeschichte* 14 (1981). I would like to thank Herrn Gimpel for providing me with a copy of his article before publication.

childless couple; the house attracted donations from other childless couples in Münster, a touching aspect of a practical act of charity linking the benefactor to the beneficiary.[37] The refuge for lepers in Kinderhaus near Münster was established in the Middle Ages to house unfortunate burghers. The Saint Magdelane's Hospital within the city walls, the Saint Anthony's Hospital outside the city walls, and the poorhouses had livings which supported citizens in their old age. The livings were generally purchased by burghers who had saved up enough money from long years of hard work, or by relatives of the inmates on their behalf. These sixteenth-century retirement homes catered primarily to burghers of modest means who could not find enough security in their household or did not have fellow guildsmen to support them in their old age. Those too poor to purchase a living worked as servants in these institutions to earn room and board. Compared to those who depended on public and private charities, the inmates had the security of food and lodging for the rest of their life; the tendency of poorhouses to become retirement homes for burghers of the lower strata reflected the widespread pauperization among broad segments of urban society.

The *Elende* represented still another type of poor relief institution. These were parish plague-houses intended for domestic servants, apprentices, students, and outsiders who succumbed to sickness or destitution while working or sojourning in Münster. Table 7.2 shows the distribution of alms to the individual poor and to the various institutions of poor relief.

The pattern of distribution demonstrates two salient facts. First, poor relief in Münster was primarily a civic act of charity, instituted by more fortunate burghers to help their fellow citizens and neighbors. Good neighborliness and civic consciousness were thus two underlying factors in the initial Catholic renewal in Münster. Second, there was a significant difference between men and women regarding donations to institutions of poor relief. Whereas women and men were just as likely to give to the poor directly (41.4 percent of all testatrices and 41.3 percent of all testators), many more women gave to the poorhouses (23.3 percent of all testatrices and 18.7 percent of all testators), the reason apparently being that widows and old women constituted the largest group among the inmates. Of the twenty poorhouses in existence at the end of the sixteenth century (including the guesthouse for pilgrims), eleven housed only women, six housed both sexes, and only two were exclusively male institutions.[38] The Elende, which were intended primarily for outsiders,

---

37. For the endowment of the orphanage, see the will of Johann Verendorp and Margarete Plate, StdAM, B, Test. I, no. 41; for other donations, see Test. I, nos. 198 and 366.

38. Cf. Lethmate, *Bevölkerung*, pp. 24–26.

Table 7.2   Distribution of Charitable Legacies

	To institutions			To poor directly			To Elende			Total
	C	M	F	C	M	F	C	M	F	
pre-1530	—	1	1	—	—	1	—	—	—	3
1530–39	—	5	3	1	3	2	—	—	—	14
1540–49	1	6	9	2	3	7	—	—	1	29
1550–59	2	2	13	4	7	10	1	—	1	40
1560–69	2	—	6	7	3	5	1	—	—	24
1570–79	7	8	19	12	12	22	2	—	4	86
1580–89	4	7	13	24	22	31	1	—	—	102
1590–99	19	9	22	42	19	26	—	4	3	144
1600–09	25	11	25	50	30	49	—	—	1	191
1610–18	15	11	26	37	19	45	—	—	4	157
Total	272 (34.4%)			495 (62.6%)			23 (3%)			790

Key:
C = Legacies willed by couples
M = Legacies willed by men
F = Legacies willed by women
Note: The numbers refer to clauses of poor relief donations; multiple clauses of donations in a single will are quite common.

beggars, also suffered from the stigma associated with the civic disdain for mendicancy and received few bequests. The very uneven distribution of legacies to the poor bears out the tendency of the age to differentiate between types of poor people because larger multitudes of destitute men and women competed for limited good will. Under the Counter-Reformation, confessional allegiance became another criterion for receiving alms; Lic. Gerhard Kleinsorgen, episcopal official at Werl, specified in his will that alms were to be given only to the Catholic poor.[39]

Initiatives to organize poor relief in sixteenth-century Münster passed almost completely from ecclesiastical to lay hands. Short of establishing a central bureau of poor relief, similar to the Aumône-Generale of Lyon or to the Common Chest in Strasbourg,[40] the magistrates exercised tight control over the dispensation of alms to the poor. Two systems of public relief, in fact, existed in Münster. The need to make efficient use of limited funds in order to benefit the genuine poor necessitated a system of rational magisterial control. The poor ordinances, the prohibitions

39. Cf. StAM, FM, SFG, III Loc. 1, no. 22, fols. 19–20.
40. See the excellent study of poor relief in Lyon by Natalie Z. Davis, "Poor Relief, Humanism, and Heresy," in her *Society and Culture in Early Modern France* (Stanford, 1975), pp. 17–64. For Strasbourg, see Miriam Chrisman, "Urban Poor in the Sixteenth Century: The Case of Strasbourg," in Miriam Chrisman and Otto Gruendler, eds. , *Social Groups and Religious Ideas in the Sixteenth Century* (Kalamazoo, 1978), pp. 59–67.

against foreign beggars, and the registration of welfare recipients were expressions of this system of charity. Parallel to the official system of welfare was private charity; giving alms to the poor continued to be a way to earn salvation in Catholic Münster. Most wills with charitable legacies spell out the expectations of the testators: they hoped to benefit from the prayers of the poor and win eternal life. Protestants, too, gave to the poor as an expression of their evangelical beliefs. Sustaining the official, magisterial system of poor relief was the wealth and class consciousness of the ruling elite. At the end of the sixteenth century, three major charitable institutions were founded by magistrates.[41] For the Catholic elite who identified the fortunes of their families with the fate of their city, generous help for their fellow citizens expressed their responsibility of governance and represented a public display of their wealth and piety.[42] For the larger multitude of Münsteraners, almsgiving represented an investment for salvation affordable by all and a safe deposit for the final reckoning.

THE VALE OF TEARS

Anyone who looks at the paintings of Hieronymus Bosch is immediately struck by late fifteenth-century imaginations of the terror of hell. Woodcuts, paintings, carnival plays, and dances of the age portrayed the imminence of Death with vivid horror. The skeleton with sickle and hourglass was the great leveler, striking indiscriminately at rich and poor, at the mighty and the humble.[43] This feverish fear of death sounded the prelude to the Reformation, a revolution which liberated men from obsession with hell, and the laity from dependence upon the clergy. The wills of Münsteraners show three successive views of death in the course of the sixteenth and the early seventeenth centuries; these different attitudes helped to determine the changing relationship between laity and clergy from the Reformation years to the beginnings of the Counter-Reformation in Westphalia.

The intense fear of death in pre-Reformation Germany expressed itself in horrible imaginations of the devil; human suffering in this life and the next reflected the equivocal outcome in the eternal battle between God

41. Elende Aegidii was founded by Bürgermeister Dr. Heinrich Vendt; see BDAM, PfA Aegidii, Urk. 107. Johann Verendorp and his wife endowed the first orphanage in Münster. StdAM, Test. I, no. 41. And the Bürgermeister Boldewin Warendorp founded another poorhouse.

42. See also Brian Bullan's study of poor relief as statecraft and class ideology of the Venetian ruling elite, *Rich and Poor in Renaissance Venice: The Social Institutions of a Catholic State* (Cambridge, Mass., 1971).

43. See Johann Huizinga, *The Waning of the Middle Ages* (New York, 1954), chap. 11.

and Satan.[44] Mortal men and women thus banded together in confraternities, bought indulgences, venerated a host of saints and angels, and gave money for requiem masses and vigils, erecting elaborate measures of collective defense against the malignant forces of death. Wealthy Münsteraners enrolled in various confraternities in order to benefit from the prayers of a larger collectivity; they handed out alms to all the poor in the city, bidding them to follow the funeral processions and ward off the evil spirits with massive demonstration of Christian solidarity.[45]

Luther's doctrine of justification was simultaneously an assertion of the omnipotent power of God over evil and a theology of hope. It liberated the believer from the clutches of hellish imaginations and directed his glances to the boundless mercy of Christ. In our wills, all except two dating after the Reformation years, the devil was mentioned merely six times as the *"boser Viende"* or as the *"hellerscher Hunde,"* he appeared only once after 1569. It seems that the appeal of Luther's theology of hope was not limited to territories which went over to the Augsburg Confession; liberation from the fear of death must have struck a sympathetic chord in most men. The Christocentrism of commendation formulae in our wills points to the triumph of hope over despair, and life over death.

A sign of reduced fear of death was the decline in legacies for requiem masses. Out of the 1,235 wills only 34 contain clauses for endowing or paying for requiem masses; these wills were made out by 26 women and 10 men, a tiny fraction of all testators.[46] For all wills of the sixteenth century only two men gave money for requiem masses. The numerical distribution of the 33 wills are shown in table 7.3. The two generalizations we can make from the slight variation from decade to decade are that proportionally testators between 1560 and 1600 were least likely to request requiem masses, and that this type of pious bequest became slightly more popular again after the turn of the century.

Besides the less intense fear of death there was a material reason why memorial masses were not commonly requested in wills: they were too expensive. While a single service cost only one gulden or daler, an endowed perpetual requiem mass required 500 guldens or dalers in invest-

44. The earliest printed books in Germany included many *Teufelbücher* and *Sterbebüchlein*. The invention of printing might have, in fact, helped to communicate anxieties of death and evil. For inventories of printed literature of the two genres and their popularity see Max Osborn, *Die Teufelliteratur des 16. Jahrhunderts* (Berlin, 1893) and Franz Falk, *Die deutschen Sterbebüchlein von der ältesten Zeit des Buchdruckes bis zum Jahre 1520* (Cologne, 1890; reprinted Amsterdam, 1969).

45. Cf. StdAM, B, Test. I, nos. 379, 515, and 568.

46. The wills are: StdAM, B, Test. I, nos. 221, 288, 341, 393, 415, 421, 468, 479, 520, 528, 550, 554, 559, 600, 635, 649, 679, 691, and Test. II, nos. 279, 676, 683, 853, 885, 1033, 1079, 1200, 1301, 1359, 1419, 1605, 1615, 1616, 1895, 1927.

Table 7.3   Legacies for Requiem Masses

	Wills dictated by			
	couples	men	women	Total
pre–1530	—	—	1	1
1530–39	1	—	—	1
1540–49	—	—	2	2
1550–59	—	—	5	5
1560–69	—	—	1	1
1570–79	—	—	3	3
1580–89	—	1	3	4
1590–99	—	—	1	1
1600–09	—	5	3	8
1610–18	1	2	5	8
Total	2	8	24	34

ment, a figure out of reach for over 90 percent of the faithful.[47] The sum represented the entire possession of an average family in the medium tax brackets and a significant cut in the wealth of many families in the upper strata. Only the very richest families could afford this spiritual luxury. In fact, only one of the 34 wills specified perpetual requiem service; the others merely bequeathed much smaller sums for one to several memorial masses.

Not only were requiem masses of doubtful efficacy for the salvation of the laity, the moral integrity and the sanctity of the practitioners of that service also came under suspicion. Facing an inadequately educated and poorly motivated clergy, the Catholic laity in Münster saw a more efficacious supplicant in the swollen ranks of the poor; placed out of reach of endowing masses and vicaries, they turned to prayers. Almsgiving and praying offered a chance of winning merits and salvation to all social classes; they represented less capital-intensive, more available instruments of spiritual investment. After 1550 the testators were less likely to ask the poor to attend their funerals and more ready to ask for prayers. Legacies to the clergy too were accompanied by requests for prayers. Dean Michael Rupert places prayers first among the good works listed in his catechism,[48] explicates the meaning of the Lord's Prayer, and teaches the prayers of Bede, Saint Gregory, and Saint Bernard. He also offers

47. In 1517 Elsa Smithues endowed a perpetual memorial mass and two antiphons at the cost of 500 guldens (see BDAM, PfA Lamberti, notata Bursae Lambertinae (sig. XIXc 1a), fols. 78v–79, copy of the Urkunde of May 14, 1517. In 1560 and 1575, two endowments by Mechtild Hesselinck and Margaretha Herding also cost 500 guldens/dalers each (see BDAM, PfA Lamberti, Urk. 35, 1560 IV 25; Urk. 44, 1575). For Hesselinck's will see StdAM, B, Test. I, no. 554.

48. Michael Ruperti, Catechismus und Betböklin, sig. C 12v.

prayers compiled for different times of the day, for various feasts, for deliverance from the Turks, for times of trouble or sickness, and for the hour of death.[49]

This second period of peaceful death was threatened by more rapid outbreaks of epidemics toward the end of the sixteenth century.[50] In 1605, the Jesuits attributed part of their success to "the scourge of God." They wrote:

> This paternal scourge of God benefits not only the health of the sick but also of the strong. Many have been brought over from lax and sinful lives to lives of Christian severity; many who have hitherto stubbornly closed their ears to truth eagerly frequent Catholic services.[51]

At the same time, confidence in the clergy was restored among the laity with the arrival of Counter-Reformation ecclesiastical orders. The general quality of the parish clergy, too, improved after 1572. These two reasons may well explain the revival of requesting requiem masses in wills. Another indication of change was the tendency to favor the clergy and students over the poor; seven wills of the early seventeenth century contain legacies to ecclesiastics but give no alms to the poor.[52] Signs of greater class consciousness are discernible in the devotional practices of the Counter-Reformation: the ruling urban elite was won back to endowing perpetual memorial masses.[53]

The stronger presence of death, however, did not bring back the old horror of hell and intense fear of the devil; instead, it became "untimely death" which reminded Christians of the shortness and transience of life. Earthly existence was "a vale of sorrows" (*Jammertal*), a sojourn before

---

49. Ibid., sig. C9–10v, D5v, E6v, F4v–8v, G10v–11, H2–8v.

50. For sixteenth-century Westphalia, there seemed to have been two major periods of epidemic outbreaks. In the late 1520s and early 1530s, Münster was hit by an outbreak of fever, the "English sweat." The chronicle of Melchior Röchell gives us a rough idea of the intensity of epidemics. While various outbreaks of the plague affected Münster throughout the sixteenth century, the epidemics of the 1590s and the early seventeenth century were especially deadly. See Erich Püschel, "Untersuchungen über die Verbreitung einer epidemischen Krankheit in Westfalen. Der Englische Schweiss des Jahres 1529," *WF* 10 (1957), pp. 57–63; Röchell, *Chronik*, pp. 24 & 145; and Huyskens, *Zeiten der Pesten*.

51. *Litt. Ann.*, 1605, p. 723: "Nec aegrotis solum, sed valentibus etiam ad salutem profuit paternum hoc Dei flagellum. Multi a laxiore vita deliciisque ad Christianam severitatem traducti sunt; multi qui veritati pertinacius hactenus aures occluserant, ad conciones Catholicas ventitare caeperunt."

52. Cf. StdAM, B, Test. II, nos. 609, 610, 797, 799, 1302, 1359, 1820.

53. Wills of patrician and burgher magistrates in the 1620s and 1630s again show frequent endowments of requiem masses; see the testaments of the patricians Konrad and Johann Grüter zu Ulenkötten, father and son, the wills of Hermann Heerde and Anna Holthaus, Bürgermeister Johann Herding and Klara Volbert, and the brothers Heinrich and Johann Herding; StdAM, B, Test. II, nos. 609, 610, 679, 682, 1999.

the faithful found final repose in eternal life. Action, rather than fear, was the Counter-Reformation's answer to the fragility of human existence. The Church militant expressed a vigor and purpose which anchored the existence of the faithful to this-worldly pursuits and prevented its drift to despair over ultimate fate in the next world.[54]

Whereas death was the great leveler in pre-Reformation Germany, social divisions intruded into the deaths of the Counter-Reformation. The new genre of funeral orations best demonstrated the greater inequality in this ultimate human experience. In his funeral sermons, Matthaeus Timpe expounds on individual meanings of deaths. His book of funeral sermons (seventy-two chapters) is organized for particular social orders: there are orations for kings, princes, prelates, officers, scholars, noblemen, Bürgermeisters, magistrates, judges, merchants, soldiers, watchmen, organists, physicians, widows, virgins, husbands, wives, for the poor, the rich, the blind, the deaf, for those who died of the plague, at sea, and by accidents.[55] Within the guilds and the confraternities, collective solidarity in the face of death also gradually disappeared. Masters no longer attended the funerals of journeymen at the end of the sixteenth century, and the rich in confraternities hired others to take their places in the funeral processions.[56] These changes indicated a dissolution of communal obligations and collective religious solidarities, and their replacement by religious practices and attitudes which accentuated divisions in urban society, between the ruling elite and the common burghers, and between a spiritual elite and the larger multitude of the faithful.

54. In his admirable and stimulating study of western attitudes toward death, Philip Ariès treats the High Middle Ages and the early modern centuries as a continuum, characterized by "death of the Self." He does not, however, take into consideration the discontinuities represented by the Reformation and the Counter-Reformation. Ariès's study of the popularity of requiem masses is based mostly on seventeenth-century French wills; the result of the analysis of Münster wills seems to suggest major differences. See Philip Ariès, *The Hour of Our Death,* trans. Helen Weaver (New York, 1981), pp. 173, 602ff.

55. Matthaeus Timpe, *Leich- Trost- und Busspredigen auch Anweisung wie dieselbigen in Auslegung Sonn- und Freyrtag- Evangelien gebraucht werden konnen . . .* (Münster: Lambert Raesfeld, 1613).

56. Cf. Peter Löffler, *Studien zum Totenbrauchtum in den Gilden, Bruderschaften und Nachbarschaften Westfalens vom Ende des 15. bis zum Ende des 19. Jahrhunderts* (Münster, 1975), pp. 293ff.

CONCLUSION

Of the complexity of changes between 1535 and 1618 there were but two essential developments: first, the conflict between city and territorial state and, closely associated with it, the tensions between different forms of religiosity; second, the gradual, but successful, implementation of the Counter-Reformation and its impact on the lives of the people.

The half century after the defeat of the Anabaptists saw a successful accommodation between Catholics and Protestants in Münster. After 1555, Lutherans could reside (though not worship) in Münster, and even the once-feared Anabaptists (now pacifist Mennonites) were no longer hunted down. An atmosphere of religious toleration existed, although Jews, Anabaptists, and Calvinists were still considered to be groups outside of acceptable, respectable urban society. Münster approached the model of a bi-confessional city; its example shows that in Westphalia a strong confessional identity was uncharacteristic of urban religious life until the end of the sixteenth century, in contrast, for example, to the early, emphatically Lutheran, identity of Strasbourg.[1] Trade, manufacture, intermarriages, and the simple fact of co-habitation within the narrow confines of the city walls fostered a degree of mutual acceptance among burghers. Above all, the religious fanaticism of the Anabaptists which had earlier brought disaster to the city became a part of civic consciousness both in support of the Catholic Church and in opposition to religious intolerance.

In the cities, the Lutheran Reformation meant homegrown piety; clerics who were native sons; local, lay control over ecclesiastical affairs; and liberation from a universal Church with its overextended, international preoccupations. The reform movement also meant a simplified, more understandable, accessible, and "democratic" form of piety, one which was close to the hearts of the burghers. The existence of many of these elements in Münster sustained Catholicism after 1535. The Devotio Mo-

---

1. Strasbourg developed a strong Lutheran identity very early as was manifest in the fierce civic opposition to the Interim and to the toleration of Catholic mass. See Erdmann Weyrauch, *Konfessionelle Krise und soziale Stabilität. Das Interim in Strassburg 1548–1552* (Stuttgart, 1978).

derna with its traditions of popular and practical lay piety was responsible for the continuing allegiance of a large Catholic minority in Calvinist-dominated Netherlands.[2] Similarly, in Westphalia, where the Devotio Moderna exerted a strong influence, traditional Catholicism was able to persist in spite of the challenges of the Lutheran and radical Reformation movements. The Fraterherren, the beguinages, and lay control of parish affairs imparted to Münster the most distinctive qualities of the city's Catholicism. Compared to the Franconian episcopal cities, in Münster the magistrates also exercised a far greater degree of control over the lower clergy. In terms of the composition of the parish clergy and the religious orders, Münsteraners and natives of Westphalia predominated until the coming of the Society of Jesus. In other words, common to both traditional, urban Catholicism and the Reformation movement in the cities was the fact that religion reinforced the sense of communal solidarities. Unlike South German Imperial cities where the Reformation reasserted communal civic consciousness which had been weakened by the process of greater wealth differentiation and class formation in the late fifteenth century, in Münster the Reformation went too far, and the civic movement for religious renewal turned into a millenarian revolution which threatened to destroy the city. Thus, after the suppression of the Anabaptists, traditional Catholicism provided the only institutional means of rebuilding the fabric of socio-religious solidarities.

After 1585 the aims of the Catholic city and the Catholic territorial state began to diverge. With the extension of Wittelsbach power to the Rhineland and Westphalia, the model of the Bavarian Counter-Reformation also began to threaten the distribution of power between lord and estates in the northwest German bishoprics. The success of the Catholic Reformation in Bavaria was based, above all, on the identification of interests between the central, ducal government and the goals of the Counter-Reformation. Thus, the absolutist power of the Bavarian dukes followed upon the defeat of the estates, among which, especially among the nobility, Protestantism had found strong support. The new officialdom in Bavaria, drawn from the nobility but heavily from the civic elite, was loyal to the dukes and dedicated to the Catholic cause; these burgher officials were the ones who helped to consolidate the Catholic territorial state in Bavaria.

In Westphalia, however, traditional political forces strongly resisted the absolutist tendencies of the prince-bishops. In the case of Paderborn, the conflict between city and prince-bishop broke out in open warfare,

2. In Deventer, as in many Dutch cities, the Calvinists comprised only a minority of the populace. See A. C. F. Koch, "The Reformation at Deventer in 1579–1580: Size and Social Structure of the Catholic Section of the Population during the Religious Peace," *Acta Historica Neerlandica* 6 (1973), pp. 27–66.

inflamed by the passions of religious antagonism. While confessional differences added bitterness to the struggle between lord and city, not all such conflicts were between absolutist Catholic prince-bishops and "democratic" Protestant burghers. Many patterns of religio-political conflict were possible in the second half of the sixteenth century in Germany: the Calvinist city of Emden, backed by the United Provinces, won independence from its Lutheran lord, the count of Friesland; the Lutheran city of Lemgo successfully defended its liberties against the count of Lippe, who went over to the Calvinist confession. Confrontations between cities and lords who were both on the same side of the confessional front also existed: the Lutheran city of Brunswick lost its autonomy to a Lutheran prince, whereas in Münster, a predominantly Catholic ruling elite vigorously defended civic rights against the Wittelsbach prince-bishops.

In most of these conflicts, the towns in question were small enough that communal solidarity overrode potential or actual divisions within the civic community in order to present a common front against the territorial lord. Where an internal split did occur, as when in 1609 the Lemgo burghers refused to obey their Calvinist lord in matters religious, only a small part of the magistracy sided with the count against the community.[3] In Münster, a city of considerable size, the Counter-Reformation obfuscated the conflict between lord and city and created an internal confessional antagonism which could weaken civic resistance to the prince-bishop. It was in the 1580s, when the Spanish-Dutch warfare spilled over to Westphalia and when the Counter-Reformation made itself felt in Münster, that a greater tension between the guilds and the city council also became noticeable. Except for a minority of militant Catholic magistrates who supported the Society of Jesus without reserve, the majority of councillors and guild leaders were united in upholding civic autonomy against the prince-bishop; they differed only in respect to the methods to be employed. The magistrates, more keenly aware of the implications that internal policies had for the city's foreign relations in the Empire, were careful to avoid open confrontation and stressed, instead, legal channels of settlement through the Imperial Cameral Court. The guild leaders, many of them Protestant in belief, were under pressure from the rank and file of the crafts, and were much more combative in tone. Moreover, even the Catholic guild elders felt threatened by the Counter-Reformation because they were the ones who were most closely associated with those civic ecclesiastical institutions, such as the beguinages and the Franciscan cloister, which came under the direct criticism of the Counter-Reformation clergy.

3. Schilling, *Konfessionskonflikt*, pp. 262ff.

Traditional Catholicism in Münster, shaped by the city's social and pietistic particularities, thus served as a civic ideology in the struggle between the burghers and the officials of the territorial state; concretely, it meant burghers defending the right of local control over local church affairs and honoring the religion of their fathers against the arrogant presumptions of outsiders. While the presence of a Protestant minority among the citizenry complicated the conflict between city and lord before 1618, after 1623 confession was no longer an issue of contention between prince and city.

In 1623, when the troops of the Catholic League (of which Archbishop Ferdinand was a member) demanded quarters in Westphalia, Münster came to a separate understanding with the prince-bishop. In exchange for the right to furnish its own garrison, Münster abandoned the smaller towns of the bishopric to the mercy of the prince-bishop and the army of the Catholic League. The magistrates promised as well not to tolerate Protestant burghers within the city walls. While the city council succeeded in upholding traditional Catholicism and civic liberties in 1623, the conflict between the city and the prince-bishop was not over. The outcome of the contest between prince-bishop and city ended only in 1661 when Christoph Bernhard von Galen forced the burghers to surrender after a siege.[4]

In many ways Münster remained a "medieval city" in the sixteenth and early seventeenth centuries. The city struggled to win complete freedom from the prince-bishops and to attain the status of an Imperial city.[5] The numerous and persistent conflicts between laity and clergy, too, echoed medieval precedents. Münster, however, was trapped between the Counter-Reformation and her traditional loyalty to Catholicism. If clear-cut confessional differences had existed, they might have strengthened the forces of civic liberties against a territorial lord of a different religious persuasion. The consolidation of the Counter-Reformation, especially the work of the Society of Jesus, gradually but unmistakably undermined the strength of civic unity by transforming the way Münsteraners thought of their city and their religion.

The Counter-Reformation affected the lives of Münsteraners in two fundamentally different, yet complementary ways: it strengthened the parochial organization from above and reasserted sacerdotal control over the

4. For the struggles between Münster and the prince-bishop after the Thirty Years' War, see Wilhelm Kohl, *Christoph Bernhard von Galen* (Münster, 1964).

5. The city fathers' desire to gain the status of an Imperial city for Münster can be documented as early as 1576. In September of that year, the city council wanted to send a representative to the Imperial Diet at Regensburg, but desisted on account of the expenditures involved. See StdAM, AII, 20, RP, 1576, Sept. 10, vol. 10, fol. 62.

daily lives of the laity in the first place; it also liberated the individual Catholic from the confines of his parish and enlisted his talents for the work of the universal papacy through the Society of Jesus. The first development brought about effective Church control over the masses of the faithful for the first time, binding them to their ecclesiastical locality by the use of parish registers and pastoral supervision. The second development elevated a spiritual elite above the geographical and pietistic confines of the parish, and redirected their energies to the service of the Church militant in the world. These two developments expressed the twin, essential impulses of the Counter-Reformation: to restore the authority of the Roman Church by keeping the faithful in check, and to reinvigorate Catholicism by inspiring and tapping the energies of a spiritual elite for the propagation of Roman faith and the reconquest of lost souls.

The Council of Trent provided for the establishment of seminaries in every parish and the strengthening of episcopal authority over particularistic clerical institutions as indispensable prerequisites for the re-establishment of sacerdotal, Roman control over the laity. In Münster, although a priestly seminary was not yet founded in our period, episcopal authority increased significantly through the 1571 diocesan visitation, through the increase in authority of the central episcopal staff, and through the establishment in 1601 of the clerical council to supervise the behavior of the clergy. Concomitant with the strengthening of central episcopal authority was the elevation of the secular clergy over the laity. This was accomplished by means of the Tridentine definition of the sacraments and the re-confirmation of the role of the parochial clergy as sole curators of sacramental rituals. Thus, in Münster, the first steps in the re-establishment of sacerdotal authority over the laity took the form of clerical censure and interdict over burials of Protestant suspects and the refusal of the clergy to continue administering communion in both kinds, as was the custom after 1535. The laity was required to confess and receive communion at least once a year; those who failed to do so were marked as suspects in religion. Moreover, to better establish clerical control over the laity, parish registers recording the baptism, marriage, and burial of all parishioners were kept for the first time, beginning with the early years of the seventeenth century. These novel administrative measures enabled the clergy and the secular authorities to keep record of the external religious practices of the laity and were of paramount importance in enforcing religious conformity in Münster after 1623.

The second development, the elevation of a spiritual (often social) elite above the masses of the Catholic faithful, was enshrined in the preeminence of a supra-regional organization, the Society of Jesus, over the geographically based and restricted parochial system. While membership in this elite was based on the individual, parochial membership was compulsory and automatic for all residents. The contrasting elements of volition and compulsion, enthusiasm and conformity, elite and masses, reflected the social hierarchy in Catholic Germany and represented a fundamentally different socio-religious principle from the Lutheran emphasis on the community of all believers. This spiritual elite also transcended the division between clergy and laity which governed the life of the parishes; instead, the Counter-Reformation elite, represented on the clerical side by the Jesuits, also included many laymen who held important positions in society: organized in Jesuit sodalities, princes, noblemen, councillors, officials, magistrates, professors, and lawyers were found in their midst. The alliance between the Jesuits and their supporters in high political and social positions—the two sides often connected by family ties—constituted the major driving force behind the Counter-Reformation in Germany.

The two motivating forces of the Counter-Reformation, one based on individual initiative, the other based on the central administrative control of the laity by the Church, ran contrary to the spirit and social basis of traditional Catholicism in Münster. The latter was inseparable from the family and from kinship ties, natural or artificial, be it the extended family or the craft guild. Traditional Catholicism in Münster, by virtue of having survived the Reformation, proved much more resistant to the impact of the Counter-Reformation. Hence, alongside Jesuit sodalities, traditional confraternities continued to flourish. The resistance of the beguinages and Franciscan cloister to measures of the Counter-Reformation showed that traditional Catholicism existed in Münster, parallel to institutions bearing the distinctive mark of the Counter-Reformation, and that the introduction of religious reforms from outside was strongly opposed by the Münster clergy and laity.

The importance of family ties in the social expression of traditional Catholicism in Münster was manifest in the ambivalent attitude of the ruling magisterial families toward the Counter-Reformation. The strongest support the Jesuits enjoyed in the immediate years after they settled in Münster did not come from those ruling families who had enjoyed generations of preeminence in the city; instead, magisterial backing for the Society of Jesus came from families who served on the city council for the first time. These families had either moved to Münster recently, as was the case with Bürgermeister Johann von der Berswordt, who came from Dortmund, and the councilman Christoph Höfflinger, who originated from Austria, or had only recently risen to civic political prominence, as was the case with Bürgermeister Heinrich Vendt and councilman Heinrich Frie. Families of the traditional patrician and burgher ruling elite, who remained steadfastly

Catholic during the Reformation movement, were at best reserved in their support for the Jesuits in the beginning. In short, the magisterial supporters for the Counter-Reformation were all *homines novi* who had weaker ties with the civic tradition and who had served, as was the case with Heinrich Vendt, in the territorial government as well. Likewise, the lesser supporters of the Jesuits were also homines novi—the officials, lawyers, and notaries, many of whom settled in Münster because of their careers and owed their promotion to the consolidation of the Counter-Reformation clerical territorial state. Substantial patrician and burgher elite support for the Jesuits came much later, only in the middle of the seventeenth century, when the Society had already established itself in Westphalia for over sixty years and when the traditional civic elite was less committed to political service and the preservation of the republican traditions of their city.

Crucial to the successful implementation of the Counter-Reformation was the elimination of particularist civic privileges. Not only did traditional urban liberties stand in the way of centralized state and ecclesiastical reforms, fierce loyalty to urban liberties also expressed the civic consciousness which believed that the city was the fundamental unit for attaining sanctification and salvation in the world.[6] The medieval idea of a *corpus christianum* wherein all citizens were linked by a common fate in their striving for salvation still exercised a very powerful force in the sixteenth century.[7] Without this consciousness, the transformation of the urban Reformation movement in Münster into a millenarian city of the saints cannot be understood. The underlying idea in this medieval sacral-political civic ideology was self-sufficiency, both in material terms, as in the safety from attacks and the freedom from famine, and in the spiritual fusion of the body politic and the body sacred.

The Counter-Reformation, however, undermined the civic ideology of self-sufficiency by its uncompromising confessionalism. Polluted by heretical doctrines and rituals, the civic community was no longer seen by the Jesuits as the pristine corpus christianum. The presence of Protestants in the midst of Münster invalidated the claim of the city as the entity capable of helping all citizens to win salvation. What inspired the Jesuits and their supporters was not the grandeur of the church spires or

---

6. Medieval burghers saw in the order and laws of their city the realization of the will of God and salvation itself: "In dem vortrefflichen Zustand der Natur spiegelt sich geradezu die hohe Rechtsstellung der Stadt. Wie Gottes Heil im Recht der Stadt ist, so auch in ihren Äckern und Geländen." The quotation is from Heinrich Schmidt, *Die Deutschen Städtechroniken als Spiegel des bürgerlichen Selbstverständnisses im Spätmittelalter*, p. 80. Schmidt's book is a most sensitive and imaginative analysis of medieval civic consciousness; see also pp. 87–99, 112–26, 141–42.

7. Cf. Moeller, *Imperial Cities*.

the sacral traditions of the city of Saint Ludger, but the fate of the one, true, universal Church, fighting her enemies in Europe and winning new souls in faraway lands. The stakes were much higher than the spiritual well-being of the community within the walled confines of Münster or any other city; the Counter-Reformation weakened local traditions of the civic community in the war between God and Satan and subsumed the lives of the Münsteraners under the fortunes of the Empire and the Papacy.

APPENDIX ONE

A Prosopography of Magistrates in Münster, 1536–1618

The prosopographical material in this appendix has been compiled from a great diversity of sources, both published and archival. The primary reference is the two-volume "Ratsliste" in the Stadtarchiv (no signature), compiled by the former and present archivists, Eduard Schulte and Helmut Lahrkamp. The Ratsliste represents a work "in progress." Biographical entries vary greatly in details; they are generally reliable for the late sixteenth and seventeenth centuries. Several magistrates who served in the mid-sixteenth century, however, have not been included in the list. I have added many more biographical details for the magistrates of the sixteenth century. These additional references are indicated in the prosopographical entries; citations follow the table of abbreviations and the shortened titles listed in appendix 2. Since council minutes before 1564 are not extant it is impossible to determine precisely the tenures of office between 1536 and 1564. Where possible, I have extracted fragmentary references from account books of the Gruetamt, Kämmerei, and from judicial and testamentary records. For years after 1564, the positions of the magistrates within the city council are given; these different magisterial offices reflected the hierarchy within the ruling regime and indicated the prestige and power of different city councillors. The offices are ranked in the following order: Bürgermeister, Richtherren, Weinherren, Kämmerer, Gruetherren, Stuhlherren, Hospitalherren, Sterbherren, Bierherren, Kapellenherren, Kinderhausherren, and Ziegelherren. The responsibilities of most of these offices are self-explanatory. The Hospitalherren supervised the city hospital of Saint Magdelene; the Kapellenherren had the charge of the Saint Antony Hospital and Chapel; the Kinderhausherren administered the house of lepers at Kinderhaus; and the Ziegelherren managed the brick-making workshop of the city. The first five offices (Bürgermeister, Richtherren, Weinherren, Kämmerer, and Gruetherren) were positions occupied by the ten senior magistrates on the city council; the most powerful families of the civic elite were usually represented. Magistrates from the guilds or patricians who accepted civic office unwillingly generally took over the lower offices.

KEY: I/ Biographical and familial data
   a. date of birth and death
   b. parents
   c. marriage(s)
   d. children
   e. godchildren
   f. siblings

II/ Wealth and occupation
   a. occupation
   b. district of residence
   c. ownership of land and houses
   d. annuities
III/ Political activities
   a. city council
   b. Kurgenosse (elector)
   c. Gesamtgilde
   d. parish administration
   e. territorial government
IV/ Religion
   a. confession
   b. membership in confraternity
   c. endowments
V/ Education
   a. university
   b. academic degree
VI/ Other information

1)   ALERS (Ahlers, Alertz), Johann
I   a. +1639
      b. Heinrich A. and Gertrud van Detten
      c. 1610 with Anna Meyer (+1633), daughter of Lic.
         Lubbert Meyer and Dorothea Vendt
         (Hövel, *BB,* no. 2089)
      d. 1/ Lic. Johannn A., canon of Saint Martin's
         2/ Heinrich, canon in Essen
         3/ Lubert 4/ Bernt 5/ Klara 6/ Anna
III   a. 1615, 1618–19, Ziegelherr, 1620–39
         (1636–38, Richtherr)
IV   a. Catholic
      b. Jesuit sodality B.M.V. Assumptionis
         (StAM, MSS. VII, 1034)
V   b. Licentiat of Law

2)   AVERHAGEN (Overhagen), Gerhard
I   c. 1545 Anna Ocken
      d. 1/ Johann (see no. 3)
         2/ Gertrud = Hermann Holtappel (no. 68)
         3/ Klara = Johann Stöve (cf. no. 129)
         4/ Bernt, emigrated to Lübeck (Test. I, no. 151, fol. 130v)
         5/ Maria (+1596), beguine ?
II   a. merchant
      b. Lamberti, Prinzipalmarkt
      c. the estate Hegentorp in Rinckerode parish
III   a. 1536–41, 1542 Stuhlherr, 1545–48?

      c. 1524 ML, 1529 OL (Krumbholtz, 40)

      d. 1545, 48 provisor Speckproven Lamberti

IV   a. Catholic, he lent Bishop Franz 500 guldens to suppress the Anabaptists (*QFGSM* VIII, 23)

3)   AVERHAGEN, Johann

I   a. 1514–Nov. 28, 1582 (*QFGSM* II, 74)

      b. Gerhard A. and Anna Ocken

      c. Christine (Test. I, no. 151, fols. 124v–125v)

      d. 1/ Anna = Dietrich Körler (no. 81)

         2/ Johann (no. 4)

         3/ Christine = Bernt Meyer II (no. 94)

         4/ Hermann, master of the clothiers' guild, died of the plague in 1582 as a young man (Guelich, chronicle, fol. 32)

II   a. clothier

      b. Jodefeld

      c. assessed 6 guldens in 1548, richest man in Jodefeld district (StdAM, AVIII, 259, 1548 SR Jodefeld, vol. 1, fol. 7v); assessed 4 dalers in 1568 for houses in Lamberti (*QFGSM* IX, 53)

III   a. 1554, 55, 1561 Hospitalherr, 1565–69, 71, 74, 76, 79–82 Kämmerer

      d. 1554–55 provisor of Speckproven Lamberti

IV   a. Catholic

4)   AVERHAGEN, Johann

I   a. 1576–?

      b. Johann A. and Christine

      c. Margaretha ? (+before 1607) (*QFGSM* II, 190) Gertrud Bockhorst, daughter of Albert B. (no. 18) and Gertrud von Werden

      d. Anna

II   a. clothier?

      b. Lamberti, Salzstrasse

III   a. 1615–19 Ziegelherr, 1620–21 Kapellenherr, 1622 Stuhlherr, 1623 Kinderhausherr, 1626 Stuhlherr, 1627 Bierherr

IV   a. Catholic

5)   BEIFANG, Johann

I   a. 1562–June 11, 1620

      b. Johann B., Freigraf in Burgsteinfurt

      c. Gertrud von Oeseden, widow of Johann Loerenick, daughter of clothier Wilhelm v. O. and Margaretha Wedemhove

      d. none

II   b. Martini, Fischmarkt

III   a. 1595 Kapellenherr, 1597–98 Hospitalherr, 1599–1604 Richtherr, 1605–20 Weinherr

IV   a. Calvinist (see appendix 4, no. 1)

V   b. Licentiat of Law

6)   BERNING, Peter

I   a. 1558–1626 (Test. II, no. 821)

      b. Heinrich B. (KG Ludgeri 1575, 82, 85, 88, 91, 93, 95, 99) and Alheit Hundestegge

      c. Richtmot Potken, daughter of guild Alderman Johann P. and Margaretha Boikman

      d. 1/ Heinrich, magistrate 1654, 55

          2/ Johann, magistrate 1637–38, 40–42, 44

          3/ Christoph 4/ Peter 5/ Maria 6/ Gertrud

II   b. Ludgeri, Königsstr., am Kirchhoff

      c. another house on Hundestegge; 2 estates, 3 fields, and 2 cottages in Münsterland

III   a. 1605–09 Ziegelherr, 1610–12, 14, 16–17 Kapellenherr, 1618–19 Bierherr, 1620–26 Sterbherr

IV   a. Lutheran (See appendix 4, no. 2)

7)   BERSWORDT, Johann von der, zu Dieckburg

I   a. 1540(?)–1591

      b. Nicolaus (+1567), Bürgermeister of Dortmund and Catherine Schwarte (+1572)

      c. Margaretha Mumme (+Sept. 10, 1584) (Guelich, chronicle, fol. 38)

      d. 1/ Johann v. d. B. zu Hüsten (cf. *ADB* II, 509)

          2/ Nicolaus v. d. B. zu Dieckburg (no. 8)

          3/ Elizabeth, (+1643) nun in Überwasser cloister (see appendix 3, no. 1; Test. II, no. 612)

          4/ Maria, (1574–1631), nun in Marienfeld (see appendix 3, no. 2; Test. II, no. 913)

      f. brother Hildebrand (+1606), Bürgermeister in Dortmund (see G. Krippenberg)

II   a. Dortmunder patrician family; merchant, rentier

      b. House Dieckburg in Münsterland

      c. 200 guldens in city bonds (StdAM, GR)

III   a. 1567 Ziegelherr, 1568 Kapellenherr, 1569, 71, 74 Stuhlherr, 1576 Richtherr, 1579–83 Bürgermeister, 1584–89 Weinherr; represented Münster at 1580 Hansa Drittelstag in Cologne

      e. Landrat under Bishop Ketteler (StAM, MSS. I, 37)

IV   a. Catholic

      b. strong supporter of the Jesuits

8)   BERSWORDT, Nicolaus von der, zu Dieckburg

I   b. Johann v. d. B. and Margaretha Mumme

      c. 1609 with Catherine von Hellerscheidt

III   a. 1612 Kinderhausherr, 1613 Kapellenherr, 1614 refused magisterial office

IV   a. Catholic

9)   BISCHOPINCK (Bisping), Everhard, zu Bispinck   patrician

I   b. Everhard B. and Anna von Langen, founders of the poorhouse Bispinck

II   c. assessed 4 dalers for houses in Lamberti in 1568 (*QFGSM* IX, 53)

III   a. 1568–69 Ziegelherr

10) BISCHOPINCK, Johann, zu Hacklenborg   patrician

I   b. Bertold B. zu Rumphorst and Anna Aspelkamp zu Telgte

      c. 1549 with Anna Warendorp (+1571), daughter of Heinrich (no. 147) (Test. I, no. 723)

      d. 1/ Johann (no. 11)

         2/ Elsa = Johann Renkerinck

      f. Bertold B. zu Telgte (elector of KG in 1555) Christine = Albert Clevorn (no. 30) (Fahne, p. 104)

II   b. Lamberti, Prinzipalmarkt

III   a. 1496 Hospitalherr? 1529–31, 1536–48 Kämmerer, 1553–54 Bürgermeister

      e. City Judge, 1521, 24–25 (Aders, *WZ* 110, 73) paid 100 guldens in 1534 to fight Anabaptists (*GQBM* VIII, 11)

11) BISCHOPINCK, Johann, zu Hacklenborg, II   patrician

I   a. ca. 1535–86

      b. Joh. z. B. and Anna Aspelkamp

      d. Johann ? (no. 12)

II   b. Lamberti, am alten Steinweg

      c. assessed 1.5 dalers for houses in Lamberti (*QFGSM* IX, 52)

III   a. 1565 Stuhlherr, 1566–69 Hospitalherr, 1571, 79–83 Weinherr, 1574, 76, 83–86 Bürgermeister

      b. elector of KG in 1555

12) BISCHOPINCK, Johann, zu Hacklenborg, III   patrician

I   b. Johann z. B. ? (no. 11)

III   a. 1589 Ziegelherr, 1590–91, 93–95 Kinderhausherr; did not want to serve (RP, 1589 III/10, vol. 21, fol. 18)

13) BISPINCK, Heinrich, zum Geist   patrician

I   a. +1562

      b. Heinrich B. (magistrate 1503–07, 1511, 14, 29–30) and Elsa Brockman

      c. Elsa Heerde, daughter of magistrate Hermann Heerde I and Ursula Lowerman (see no. 58 below)

      d. 1/ Hermann (no. 11)

         2/ Heinrich 3/ Bernt 4/ Ursula

II   a. rentier

      b. Lamberti, Prinzipalmarkt

      c. assessed 5 guldens in 1539 Aegidii district tax (SR Aegidii, 1539, fol. 1); fief in Altenberg parish (StAM, AVM, MS. 51, fol. 40v)

      d. 400 guldens in city bonds (StdAM, GR)

III   a. 1546–48 Kämmerer, 1551, 54 Richtherr

      d. provisor of Saint Lambert's 1545 (PfA Lamberti, no. 16)

      e. paid taxes and provided feudal levy to the episcopal army in 1534 (*GQBM* VIII, 11 & 101)

IV   a. Catholic

14) BISPINCK, Hermann
I   a. born in 1539
       b. Heinrich B. (no. 10) and Elsa Heerde
       c. Maria
II   a. rentier, merchant (member of Great "Saint Anne" Company)
       b. Aegidii, Rothenburg
       c. assessed 2 dalers in 1539 Aegidii tax; fief "Udinck" in Handorf parish
          (StAM, AVM, MS. 51, fol. 39v)
III   a. 1593 Bierherr, 1596 Kapellenherr, 1597–1600 Sterbherr,
       b. KG Aegidii 1578, 80, 84, 86, 90
       c. Mesterlude 1591

15) BISPINCK, Johann, zu Kückelinck   patrician
I   b. Heinrich B. ?
       c. Margaretha Boland, daughter of Johann B. (no. 23) and Elizabeth
          Brechte (Test. I, no. 437)
II   b. Lamberti, Prinzipalmarkt
III   a. 1569, 76 Kapellenherr, 1571 Ziegelherr, 1574, 79–81 Bierherr, 1586
          Hospitalherr, 1582–84, 91 Richtherr, 1585, 88–90 Kämmerer
       b. KG Lamberti 1565

16) BISPINCK, Jürgen   patrician
I   a. +1577
       b. Sweder B. and Jutta; Sweder was elector of KG in 1555 and vassal of
          Bishop Franz (StAM, AVM, MS. 51, fols. 13v & 87)
       c. 1551 with Gertrud von Heiden, daughter of Gograf Lütze v. H. and
          Matta
       d. 1/ Sweder
          2/ Heinrich
          3/ Elsa = Jacob Stöve (Test. I, no. 421)
          4/ Anna = Johann Grotegese
          5/ Jürgen (bastard)
       f. Sweder junior, vassal of bishop
          (StAM, AVM, MS. 51, fol. 87)
          Elsa = 1. Wilbrand Ploenies II (no. 112)
               = 2. Johann Wesselinck (Test. I, no. 421)
II   b. Ludgeri, Ludgeri Str.
       c. Südmuehle in Werne village (Dopelmann, 91)
III   a. 1554, 1557, 74 Kinderhausherr, 1565, 76 Hospitalherr, 1566 Bierherr,
          1571 Kapellenherr

17) BLOCK (Bloccius), Johann
I   a. 1562–161?
       b. Johann B.
       c. 1596 with Elske Hesseling from Warendorf
       d. 1/ Johann

2/ Anna Margaretha
3/ Georg
II   b. Ludgeri, Hundestegge, Ludgeristrasse
III   a. 1605 Kinderhausherr, 1606–10 Stuhlherr
     b. KG Ludgeri 1600, 04; Martini 1602
IV   a. Calvinist (see appendix 4, no. 4)
V   a. Marburg, 1578 (B.A.?); 1592–93 Basel (*UM Basel*, 409)
     b. Licentiate of Law

18)   BOCKHORST (Boichorst), Albert
I   c. Gertrud von Werden
     d. 1/ Heinrich (no. 19)
       2/ Gertrud = Johann Averhagen
       3/ Wilhelm (no. 20)
       4/ Johann, canon of Old Cathedral, 1593–1616
       5/ Anna = Lambert Holthaus (no. 70)
       6/ two bastard daughters (StdAM, causae discussionum 38)
II   a. merchant
     b. Martini, Vossgasse
     c. assessed 5 dalers for houses in Lamberti in 1568, "Unter den Boggen" (*QFGSM* IX, 53)
III   a. 1566–67 Weinherr, 1568–69, 71 Bürgermeister
IV   a. Catholic

19)   BOCKHORST, Heinrich
I   a. +1627
     b. Albert B. and Gertrud von Werden
     c. 1598 with Katherina Helskamp from Rees
     d. 1/Albert, Dr. of Law, syndic of Münster Cathedral Chapter = Maria Witton
       2/Heinrich, Dr. of Law, assessor at Chamber Court = 1. Elizabeth Heerde 2. Klara Otterstedde
       3/Johann, canon in Wesel (+1665)
       4/Rotger, canon in Old Cathedral
       5/Wilhelm, canon of Saint Martin's
       6/Hermann, canon of Saint Ludger's
       7/Johann Wilhelm, Dr., councillor in Osnabrück
       8/Anna = Hilbrand Hermann Plönies
       9/Klara, nun in cloister at Bocholt
       10/Jacob, canon in Xanten
II   a. lawyer
     b. Lamberti, Alter Steinweg
III   a. 1599 Sterbherr, 1600 Hospitalherr, 1601 Stuhlherr, 1601 in Rees, 1611–18 Richtherr, 1619–27 Bürgermeister
IV   a. Catholic
     b. supporter of Jesuits
V   b. Doctorate of Law

20)   BOCKHORST, Wilhelm
I   b. Albert B. and Gertrud von Werden
       c. Anna Frie (+1618), daughter of Heinrich Frie (no. 49) and Anna Vendt
          (Test. II, no. 1200)
       d. none
II   a. clothier, alderman of Great (Saint Anne) Company (Offenberg II, 89)
       b. Aegidii, Aegidiistr.
       c. his wife had 4,000 dalers in land and annuities
III   a. 1609 Kinderhausherr, 1610 Bierherr
       b. KG Lamberti 1608, Aegidii 1613, 17
IV   a. Catholic

21)   BOLAND, Goddert (Gottfried)
I   a. +1616
       b. Johann B. (no. 22) and Alheid
       c. Margaretha Herding (+1613), daughter of Johann H. (no. 64) and
          Christine Wesselinck
       d. Christine = Bernd Meyer junior (son of no. 94)
II   b. Aegidii, Aegidii Strasse
III   a. 1586, 88 Ziegelherr, 1594–95 Bierherr, 1603–04 Sterbherr, 1605–08
          Gruetherr, 1610–12 Hospitalherr, 1614 Stuhlherr, 1616 Bierherr
       b. KG Aegidii 1599
       d. Roggenherr (StdAM, AVIII, 277, KR, vol. 5, fol. 166v)
IV   a. Lutheran (see appendix 4, no. 6)

22)   BOLAND, Johann
I   a. +1568?
       b. Johann B., magistrate 1513–26, including 1514 and 1523 as Bürger-
          meister
       c. Alheid
       d. 1/ Albert (+1605) = Gertrud Holtappel (+1634)
          2/ Heinrich (+1612)
          3/ Elizabeth (+1606) = Johann Wylertz
          4/ Goddert (no. 21)
          5/ Schmallink
          6/ Hermann (+in Lisbon)
          7/ Gertrud (+1612) = Werner Kock, judge in Billerbeck
       f. 1/ Heinrich, in Cologne
          2/ Konrad
          3/ Anna = Johann Grüter (no. 54)
          4/ Klara, in cloister Rengering
II   a. merchant
       b. Lamberti, Roggenmarkt
       c. assessed 4 dalers for houses in Lamberti in 1568 (QFGSM IX, 51)
       d. 140 guldens in city bonds (StdAM, GR)
III   a. 1554–55, 57–66 Kämmerer, 1567–68 Stuhlherr, represented Münster at
          1556 Hansa Drittelstag in Cologne
       d. 1550–55, provisor of Saint Lambert's parish

23) BOLAND, Johann
I   a. +1558 (*QFGSM* II, 38; Test. I, no. 456)
     b. Konrad (Cord), judge in 1528 and 1530 (*QFGSM* III, 116; Aders, *WZ* 110) and N Heerde
     c. Elsa Brechte (+1583)
     d. 1/ Johann
        2/ Margaretha = Johann Bispinck zu Kükelinck
        3/ Elizabeth = Bernhard Frie zu Backhaus
        4/ Anna = Jobst Frie zu Böddinck
II   b. Lamberti, Alter Steinweg
     c. estate "Böddinck" in Altenberge parish; gardens and summer house outside Mauritz Gate and another garden inside Münster
     d. 260 guldens in city bonds (StdAM, GR)
III   a. 1549–57 Gruetherr
IV   a. Catholic

24) BUCK, Hermann, zu Heimsburg   patrician
I   a. +1626
II   c. 1. Benedicta von der Tinnen, daughter of Jobst
        2. Anna von der Tinnen
     d. Lambert, from 2nd marriage
III   a. 1610–11 Kinderhausherr, 1613–21 Hospitalherr, 1622–26 Weinherr

25) BUCK, Lambert, zu Heimsburg   patrician
I   a. +1559
     b. Lambert B., magistrate in 1469
     c. Anna Travelmann, daughter of Heinrich (no. 139) (BDAM, PfA Aegidii, Urkunden Inventar, no. 222, p. 72)
     f. Evert, elector of KG in 1555
II   b. Servatii
     c. estate "Kampman" in Dreinsteinfurt parish
III   a. 1536–45 magistrate, 1546–55 Gruetherr, 1556 Kämmerer
     b. elector of KG in 1555
     e. paid taxes and provided feudal levy for the episcopal army in 1534 (*GQBM* VIII, 11 and 101)
IV   a. Catholic

26) BUCK, Lambert, zu Sentmaring and Grevinghoff   patrician
I   a. +1604
     b. Bernhard B. and Johanna von der Rühr
     c. Maria Bischopinck, daughter of Johann B. and widow of Johann Steveninck zu Broite
     d. 1/ Hans-Eberhard
        2/ Lambert
        3/ Maria
        4/ Richtmot
II   b. Ludgeri
     c. assessed 3 dalers for houses in Lamberti in 1568 (*QFGSM* IX, 52)

III   a. 1591 Kapellenherr, 1593–96 Hospitalherr, 1597 Kämmerer, 1598–1604
          Bürgermeister

27)   BUERMEISTER, Ludolf
I   a. ca. 1574–163?
       b. Georg B. (KG Martini 1566, 74–75, 77, 80, 82, 86) and Anna Halver
       c. 1. Maria von Detten (+1617), daughter of Bernd (no. 35) and widow
             of Hermann Dreihaus (Test. II, no. 1156)
          2. Anna Langermann, daughter of Werner and Agnes Wedemhove,
             widow of Bernd Hobbeling
       d. from 2nd marriage: Anna = Balthasar Hofsherr zu Bergeickel
II   a. clothier
       b. Martini, Hörsterstrasse
       c. estate "Bergeickel" near Ahlen
III   a. 1614 Ziegelherr, 1615 Kapellenherr, 1616 Sterbherr, 1617–21 Bierherr,
          1623–24 Kapellenherr, 1625 Bierherr
       b. KG Martini 1603, 11, 28, 31, 33
       c. Alderman
       d. provisor of Saint Aegidius 1604 (*QFGSM* IX, 30)
IV   a. Protestant (see appendix 4, no. 7)

28)   BURMANN, Bernhard
I   a. +1621 (Test. II, no. 752)
       c. Agnes Glandorp (+1621), daughter of shopkeeper Johann G. and Matta
          Westhove
       d. 1/ Johann (+in Gotha)
          2/ Hermann, in Lübeck
          3/ Bernhard (+1642) = Agnes Huge, daughter of Bernhard (no. 71)
II   a. shopkeeper, guild master 1599–1601
       b. Lamberti, am Fischmarkt
       c. house worth 800 dalers; 2 gardens outside Mauritz Gate with summer
          house and pond, worth 400 dalers altogether
III   a. 1602 Ziegelherr, 1603–04 Kapellenherr, 1605–09 Bierherr
       b. KG Lamberti 1598, 1601
       c. Meisterlude
IV   a. Protestant (see appendix 4, no. 8)

29)   BUTHMANN, Johann
III   a. magistrate 1536–?
       b. KG Aegidii 1523, 30
IV   a. Catholic

30)   CLEVORN, Albert   patrician
I   c. Christine Bischopinck
       d. 1/ Albert (no. 31)
          2/ Johann, canon at Saint Ludger's
III   a. 1503–07, 09, 11, 15–24, 26–27 Richtherr, 1536–41? probably withdrew
          from city council in 1541 (Kerssenbroch, 903ff.)

      e. paid taxes and raised feudal levy for the episcopal army in 1534 (*GQBM* VIII, 11 & 101)

IV   a. Catholic

31) CLEVORN, Albert, zu Darvelt
I   a. ca. 1531–96
      b. Albert C. and Christine Bischopinck
      c. 1. Stephenea
         2. Gertrud von der Tinnen, daughter of Jacob and Anna von der Rühr
      d. from 1st. marriage: Egbert (no. 33)
II   b. Lamberti, Alter Steinweg
      c. House Darvelt in Saint Mauritz parish
III   a. 1571 Kapellenherr, 1574, 76 Stuhlherr, 1583, 84, 93 Kämmerer, Weinherr 1585–92, 94–96

32) CLEVORN, Egbert   patrician
III   a. 1536–?
      e. paid taxes and raised feudal levy for episcopal army in 1534 (*GQBM* VIII, 11 & 102)
IV   a. Catholic

33) CLEVORN, Egbert, zu Darvelt   patrician
I   b. Albert C. and Stephenea
      c. Elizabeth Travelmann
      d. Jacob = Gudula Elizabeth Travelmann
II   b. Lamberti, Alter Steinweg
III   a. 1614–15 Kinderhausherr, 1617–20 Kapellenherr, 1621 Kinderhausherr, 1628–31, 39, 47 Stuhlherr

34) CLUTE (Cloeth), Christoph
I   b. Dietrich (?) Rentmeister at Horstmar; purchased Anabaptist houses (Kirchhoff, Täufer, p. 8, also nos. 201, 224, 472, 671)
      c. Klara Groll, daughter of Dietrich and Anna Stöve
      d. 1/ Dr. Christoph Clute, learned episcopal councillor (StAM, MSS. I, 38, fol. 125)
         2/ Anna (= 1610) = Hermann Herding (no. 62)
II   b. Lamberti, Prinzipalmarkt
      c. assessed 2 dalers in 1560 for house in Aegidii with 1 servant and 3 maids (StdAM, AVIII, 259, Aegidii SR 1560, vol. 1, fol. 66v)
III   a. 1566–67 Ziegelherr, 1568 Bierherr, 1569, 71 Richtherr, 1574 Kämmerer
      b. KG Aegidii 1565
IV   a. Catholic

35) DETTEN, Bernhard van, the Older
I   a. +1583 (*QFGSM* II, 74)
      b. Johann and Geseka
      c. Matta Hassing

    d. 1/ Heinrich, student at Cologne Univ., vicar at Münster cathedral (*UM Köln*, 1568)

        2/ Gese, in Hofringe beguinage

        3/ Johann, (+1617) canon in Old Cathedral, composer of the "Atlvater Buch" and leading supporter of the Jesuits

        4/ Bernhard (no. 36)

        5/ Katherina = Johann Joddeveld, (son of no. 73)

        6/ Rotger = Elizabeth Schottelen

        7/ Maria = 1. Hermann Dreihaus 2. Ludolf Buermeister (no. 27)

        8/ Gertrud = Heinrich Alers, (father of no. 1)

        9/ Hermann

II   a. tanner and oxen merchant

      b. Lamberti, am Roggenmarkt

III   a. 1568–69 Ziegelherr, 1571, 76 Kinderhausherr, 1574, 79–83 Sterbherr

      b. KG Überwasser 1555, 57, 60, 62, 64, 66

      c. Meisterlude 1560; Alderman 1564–67 (Krumbholtz, 35, 41f.)

IV   a. Catholic

36) DETTEN, Bernhard van, the Younger

I   b. Bernd and Matta Hassing

      c. 1. NN 2. Anna Wedemhove, daughter of Johann (no. 150) and Katherina Pael

      d. 1/ Heinrich, magistrate 1635–52

        2/ Johann, canon of Old Cathedral

        3/ Anna = Johann Lageman

        4/ Klara = Bernd Pauck, shopkeeper

        5/ Bernd, canon of Old Cathedral

        6/ Gertrud = Dietrich Langenhorst in Werne

        7/ Katherina, in cloister Niesing

II   a. tanner

      b. Lamberti, Roggenmarkt

III   a. 1591 Ziegelherr, 1593, 96 Bierherr, 1597–98 Hospitalherr, 1599 Gruetherr, 1600–04 Kämmerer

      b. KG Ludgeri 1583, 90

      c. Mesterlude, 1581, 86–90 (Krumbholtz, 44)

IV   a. Catholic

      c. co-founder (with his siblings) of the Collegium Dettensiam attached to the Jesuit College; he also housed the first Sisters of Poor Clare in Münster in 1613

37) DICKMANN, Heinrich

I   a. 1564–1630?

      c. 1. 1586 with Elsa Forckenbeck

        2. Anna Wilckinghoff

        3. 1608 with Katherina Hesseling from Warendorf

II   a. shopkeeper, guildmaster

      b. Martini, Roggenmarkt, bei Münze

III   a. 1616 Ziegelherr
        c. Alderman, 1607

IV   a. Calvinist (see appendix 4, no. 11)

38) DROLSHAGEN, Arnold von   patrician
I   a. +1545 (Test. I, no. 91)
      b. Bernd (magistrate in 1527) and Richtmot Kerckerinck
      d. Jürgen (father of no. 39), elector of KG in 1555
II   c. held fiefs from the bishops
III   a. 1536–45
      e. paid taxes and raised feudal levy for episcopal army in 1534 (*GQBM* VIII, 11 & 101)
IV   a. Catholic

39) DROLSHAGEN, Bernhard, zu Lütkenbeck   patrician
I   a. +1622
      b. Jürgen (son of no. 38) and Anna Thomas v. d. Rühr; father was elector of Kurgenosse in 1555 and vassal of the prince-bishop (StAM, AVM, MS. 145d)
      c. 1. Anna von der Tinnen, daughter of Jacob and Anna v. d. Rühr
           2. Mechtild von Vörst, daughter of Reinert and Agnes Maria von Mulert
      d. from 1st. marriage:
          1/ Heinrich
          2/ Jacob zu Rorup
          3/ Everwin
          4/ Anna Thomas
          from 2nd. marriage:
          1/ Johann
          2/ Bernd
          3/ Mechtild
          4/ Adolf
          5/ Bernd
III   a. 1576 Kapellenherr

40) DROSTE, Alard   patrician
I   b. Everwin, (no. 43)
      c. Anna Kerckerinck, daughter of Heinrich
III   a. 1538–54, not reelected in 1554 (Kerssenbroch, 949)
      b. elector of KG in 1555
      e. paid taxes and feudal levy, and served in the episcopal army (*GQBM* VIII, 92 & 108)
IV   a. Catholic

41) DROSTE, Alard, zu Mühlenbeck   patrician
III   a. 1609 Kapellenherr, refused magisterial office
      b. armigerous vassal of the bishop (StAM, AVM, MS. 145d)

42) DROSTE, Bernhard, zu Hülshof patrician
I a. 1546–?
   c. Richtmot Travelman
   d. Heinrich zu Hülshof ? magistrate in 1626, 28
II b. Lamberti, Salzstrasse
III a. 1576 Kinderhausherr, 1579–80 Stuhlherr, 1582–86, 88–91 Hospital-
     herr, 1592–1604, 1619–21 Weinherr, 1605–18 Bürgermeister

43) DROSTE, Everwin patrician
I d. 1/ Alard (no. 40)
     2/ Everwin, dean of Saint Martin
     3/ Johann, canon of Saint Martin (Huyskens, *Everwin v. Droste*, 26, n.
        3)
II c. fief "Spellbrinck" in Handorp parish (StAM, AVM, MS. 51, fol. 13)
III a. 1492, 98, 99, magistrate, 1503–09 Kämmerer, 1510–15, 22–31
     Bürgermeister, left Münster in 1532 when Lutherans dominated the
     city council, magistrate 1536–? represented Münster in 1506, 07 Hansa-
     tag in Lübeck and 1512 Drittelstag in Cologne
   e. paid taxes for episcopal army in 1534 (*GQBM* VIII, 11)
IV a. Catholic

44) DROSTE, Everwin, zu Ulhenbrock patrician
III a. 1589, 93 Kapellenherr, 1607 Kinderhausherr, did not want to serve
     (RP, 1593 III/23, vol. 25, fol. 23v)

45) DROSTE, Heinrich, zu Hülshof patrician
II b. Liebfrauen, Honekamp
   c. 7 fiefs in Everswinckel, Altenberg, Roxel, Telgte, and Saint Mauritz
     parishes (StAM, AVM, MS. 51, fol. 42v)
III a. 1536–53 (1538 Kinderhausherr, 1543–53 Hospitalherr) represented
     Münster in 1549 Hansatag in Lübeck
   b. elector of KG in 1555
   e. paid taxes and raised feudal levy for episcopal army in 1534 (*GQBM*
     VIII, 92)
IV a. Catholic

46) DROSTE, Johann patrician
III a. 1550–63 ?
   e. paid taxes for episcopal army in 1534 (*GQBM* VIII, 92)
IV a. Catholic

47) EGBERTS, Heinrich
I a. 1525–1602 (Test. II, no. 1106)
   c. 1. Elsa Wilckes
     2. Margaretha Grüter (+1607), no children
   d. 1/ Thomas (no. 48)
     2/ Heinrich, glassmaker, = Judith Blising (Krumbholtz, 350)
     3/ Matta
     4/ Klara
     5/ Anna

II a. glassmaker, guild master
   b. Martini, Hörsterstrasse
   c. another house on Ludgeristr., house on Hörsterstr. worth 800 dalers, total wealth over 1,200 dalers
III a. 1596 Ziegelherr, 1597–1600 Kapellenherr
   b. KG Lamberti 1575, 81, 83, 85, 87, 90, 98
   c. Mesterlude 1570, 74, 77; Alderman 1578–85, 88, 95 (Krumbholtz, 43f; *QFGSM* III, 178f., Test. I, no. 127; Röchell, 128)
   d. 1575 provisor of Saint Martin's

48) EGBERTS, Thomas
I a. +1611
  b. Heinrich and Elsa Wilckes
  d. 1/ Gertrud
     2/ Heinrich, glassmaker (Krumbholtz, 348)
II a. glassmaker, guild master in 1596
III a. 1607–11 Ziegelherr
   b. KG Aegidii 1594, 1606
   c. Alderman 1602–06 (Krumbholtz, 350)

49) FRIE, Heinrich
I a. +1612
  b. Bernd ?
  c. 1. Anna Vendt (+1590), daughter of Heinrich (no. 142) and Klara Wedemhove
     2. Klara Grüter (+1610), childless marriage; she committed suicide "ex melancolia" or "defecta sensuum" (RP, 1610 VIII 16, vol. 42, fols. 165–165v)
  d. 1/ Klara, unmarried
     2/ Anna (+1618) = Wilhelm Bockhorst (no. 20)
     3/ Heinrich Frie-Vendt (no. 50)
     4/ Hermann = Christine Meyer
     5/ Johann (+1613)
     6/ Agnes = Johann Heerde (no. 61)
II b. Lamberti, Salzstrasse
III a. 1585–86 Kinderhausherr, 1588–91, 1602 Hospitalherr, 1593–1601 Stuhlherr, 1609–10 Gruetherr
   e. learned episcopal councillor (StAM, MSS. I, 37, fol. 108)
IV a. Catholic
   c. contributed toward the endowment of the Aegidii poorhouse in honor of his 1st wife
V b. Licentiat of Law

50) FRIE-VENDT, Heinrich
I b. Heinrich Frie (no. 49) and Anna Vendt
  c. 1/ Klara = Dr. Heinrich Römer (BM after 1618)
     2/ Agnes = Dr. Bernd Schöpping (BM after 1618)
     3/ Anna = Lic. Johann Timmerscheidt (BM after 1618)

II   b. Aegidii, Aegidiistrasse
III   a. 1614–16 Kapellenherr, 1617–18 Sterbherr, 1619–26 Richtherr, 1627
            Weinherr, 1628–34 Bürgermeister
IV   a. Catholic
        b. Jesuit sodality B.M.V. Assumptionis (StAM, MSS. VII, 1034)
V   a. Cologne (*UM Köln* 1600)
        b. Doctorate of Law

51)   GRAL, Heinrich   patrician
I   a. +1578 (Guelich, Chronicle, fol. 18)
        c. Elsa Bischopinck, daughter of Bertold
        d. 1/ Hilla = Heinrich Bischopinck zu Telgte
            2/ Elizabeth
II   b. House at Nünninck
III   a. 1565–66 Kapellenherr, 1567–69 Kinderhausherr, 1571 Hospitalherr,
            1572–74, 76 Weinherr

52)   GROLLE, Bernhard
I   a. +1539
        b. N. Grolle and Anna Kerckerinck (+1520), daughter of Bürgermeister
            Johann K. (Aders, *WZ* 110, p. 72)
        c. 1525 with Margaretha Herding (+1580), daughter of Johann (no. 63)
            (Test. I, no. 691)
        d. 1/ Johann
            2/ Katherina ? = judge Johann Wesselinck
II   a. clothier
        c. His widow had a house on Rothenburg, assessed 4 g. in 1539 (SR
            Aegidii, vol. 1, fol. 4v), worth 1,800 dalers in 1580; another house on
            Ludgeristr. taxed 4 dalers in 1560 (SR Aegidii, vol. 1, fol. 76); a third
            house on Spieckerhof, worth 1,000 dalers; a fourth house on Salzstr., 19
            fields and 10 gardens near Münster; 3 estates in Sendenhorst, and a
            house in Bremen: her total wealth was ca. 15,000 dalers
        e. 260 guldens in city bonds (StdAM, GR)
III   a. 1524, 1536–39
IV   a. Catholic

53)   GRÜTER, Bernhard, zu Ulenkötten   patrician
I   c. Klara Grolle, daughter of Dietrich, judge 1517–19
        d. 1/ Elseke = Hermann Holtappel (no. 68)
            2/ Dietrich
            3/ Johann ? (no. 54)
II   d. 260 guldens in city bonds (StdAM, GR)
III   a. 1526–27 Hospitalherr, 1529–31 Gruetherr, 1536–?
        b. KG Lamberti 1526, 29
IV   a. Catholic

54)   GRÜTER, Johann, zu Ulenkötten   patrician
I   a. +1572

	b. Bernhard ?
	c. Anna Boland, daughter of Johann (no. 22)
	d. 1/ Konrad (no. 55)
	2/ Heinrich
II	c. assessed 4 dalers in 1568 Lamberti tax (*QFGSM* IX, 51)
III	a. 1549–54, 1565–69, 71 Stuhlherr, represented Münster at 1554 Hansa Drittelstag in Wesel

55) GRÜTER, Konrad, zu Ulenkötten   patrician

I	a. +1631 (Test. II, no. 609)
	b. Johann and Anna Boland
	c. Katherina Herding, daughter of Johann (no. 64) and Christine Wesselinck
	d. 1/ Johann (+1625) (Test. II, no. 610)
	= 1. Katherina Frie
	2. Elseka Hardtland
	2/ Anna, nun (+1667)
	e. Johann Herding
II	c. 9 estates in Nienberge, Greven, Neuenkirchen, Rheine, Altenberge, Everswinckel, and Roxel parishes and 4 other fields
III	a. 1583–85 Ziegelherr, 1586 Kapellenherr, 1588–89 Kinderhausherr, 1590–91, 1602 Stuhlherr, 1593–95 Hospitalherr, 1596–1615, 17, 19–26 Gruetherr, 1628–29 Weinherr
IV	a. Catholic
	c. family vicarage of Saint Catherine in Nienberge parish church

56) GUELICH, Arnold van

I	a. 1529–1602, born in Jülich
	c. 1. Klara Elverfeld
	2. Anna Beckhaus
	d. from 1st. marriage:
	1/ Albert, procurator = Elsa Stael, daughter of Johann
	2/ Anna = Johann Wernike (no. 152)
	3/ Klara (+young)
	4/ Rembert, Fraterherr, entered religious life in 1577, worked in Coesfeld
	5/ Johann, baker apprentice (+1579 of the plague)
	6/ Klara = 1. Bertold Poetken
	2. Matthaeus Ossenbrügge (son of no. 107)
II	a. shopkeeper, entered guild in 1554, guild master (Krumbholtz, 43f.)
	b. Martini, Hörsterstrasse
	c. assessed 1.5 dalers for house in Lamberti in 1568 (*QFGSM* IX, 50); house in Aegidii assessed at 32 schillings in 1591 (SR Aegidii, vol. 2, fol. 7) purchased house on Hörsterstr. in 1575 from the goldsmith Johann Beckenfeld for 700 dalers
	d. 1573, 1,020 guldens in principal in 3 annuities to 3 noblemen; 1593, 1,800–1,900 dalers principal to 4 noble and 2 patrician debtors

III   a. 1599–1601 Kinderhausherr, 1602 Sterbherr
       b. KG Aegidii 1577, 79, 81, 83, 85, 88, 91, 99
       c. Mesterlude, 1573, 75, 77, 80–81 Aldermen, 1582–86, 90–92, 96–97 (Krumbholtz, 43f.)
       d. provisor of Poorhouse Saint Elizabeth (Guelich, Chronicle, fol. 5)
IV   a. Catholic
       b. Franciscan confraternity (StAM, MSS. I, 273)
VI   a. composer of family chronicle (StAM, AVM, MS. 172)

57)   HEERDE, Borchard
I   a. +1539 (Test. I, no. 106)
       b. Walter and Elsa Liderman
       c. Kunne Beckers from Beveren
       d. 1/ Elsa
          2/ Anna, both in Saint Anne's Convent in Coesfeld
          3/ Johann, clothier, = 1. Anna Huge
                                 2. Anna Wesselinck
          4/ Borchard (+1578), clothier, KG Martini 1558, 65, 67, 70
             = 1. Klara von Oeseden
             = 2. Klara Rodde (Test. I, no. 435)
       e. 1/ son of Wilbrand Plönies (no. 112)
          2/ son of Bernd Grolle (no. 52)
          3/ son of Dietrich Grolle
          4/ son of Schramen
          5/ son of Johann Schenckel
          6/ daughter of judge Johann Wesselinck
          7/ daughter of Hermann Heerde (no. 58)
          8/ daughter of Wolter Plönies
       f. Heinrich, a clergyman (Test. I, no. 106) sister = Johann Boland
II   a. clothier
       b. Lamberti, Roggenmarkt
       c. over 10,000 guldens in wealth (cf. Test. I, no. 435)
III   a. 1536–39
IV   a. Catholic
       c. endowed 6 cells for the Carthusian monastery Marienburg near Dülmen

58)   HEERDE, Hermann, II
I   a. 1502–71
       b. Hermann I, (+1529), magistrate 1510–23, and Ursula Lowerman
       c. 1. Gertrud Boland
          2. Maria Ossenbrügge (+1546)
          3. Katherina Brechte, daughter of Bürgermeister Werner Brechte in Hamm, widow of Hermann Buttel
       d. from 1st. marriage:
          Ursula (+1553) = Johann Herding (no. 64)
          from 2nd. marriage:

1/ Hermann (no. 59)

2/ Katherina = Bürgermeister Gerhard Schürkman of Hamm

3/ Ursula = Hermann von Oeseden (no. 104)

4/ Anna = Johann Plönies (no. 111)

5/ Klara, nun (+1602) (Test. II, no. 437)

e. Bernhard, son of Bernhard Frie (see RP, 1568 IV/8, vol. 5, fols. 16–17)

f. 1/ Johann, KG Martini 1522, 55, Lamberti 1560–61, = Anna Ossenbrügge

2/ Borchard, Bürgermeister in Reval

3/ Elsa = Heinrich Bispinck (no. 13)

II a. clothier, rentier

b. Martini, Vossgasse

c. assessed 4 dalers for house in Lamberti in 1568 (*QFGSM* IX, 51); house in Wolbeck (*GQBM* VIII, 115), total wealth ca. 30,000 dalers

d. 580 guldens in city bonds

III a. 1532 Kämmerer (*QFGSM* II, 155), magistrate 1536–44, 1545–71 Bürgermeister, represented Münster in 1549 Hansatag in Lübeck and 1554 Drittelstag in Cologne

b. KG Martini 1522

d. provisor of Saint Lambert's in 1537 (BDAM, PfA Lamberti, Kart. 16, A5)

IV a. Catholic, left Münster in protest in 1532 when Lutherans dominated the city council (Kerssenbroch, 271)

59) HEERDE, Hermann, III

I a. +1601

b. Hermann, II, and Katherina Brechte (no. 58)

c. Elizabeth Herding (+1589), (Test. I, no. 626), daughter of Johann Herding (no. 64) and Christine Wesselinck

d. 1/ Hermann (no. 60)

2/ Johann (no. 61)

3/ bastard, Jobst

II a. lawyer

b. Martini, Vossgasse

III a. 1584 Kinderhausherr, 1585–86, 88 Stuhlherr, 1589 Weinherr, 1590–91, 93–97 Bürgermeister; he did not want to serve at first in 1584 (RP, 1584 VI/15, XII/17, vol. 16, fols. 30v, 49–49v)

e. assessor at the Chamber Court, 1578 (StAM, MSS. I, 37, fol. 109)

IV a. Catholic

V b. Doctorate of Law

60) HEERDE, Hermann, IV

I a. +1638 (Test. II, no. 679)

b. Hermann, III and Elizabeth Herding

c. Anna Holthaus (+1634), daughter of Lambert (no. 70)

II a. clothier?

b. Martini, Vossgasse

III   a. 1611 Kapellenherr, 1612–15 Sterbherr, 1637–38 Bierherr
      b. KG Martini 1617, 20, 22, 27
IV   a. Catholic
      b. Jesuit sodality B.M.V. Assumptionis (StAM, MSS. VII, 1034)
V   a. Cologne (*UM Köln*, 1585)

61)   HEERDE, Johann
I   a. +1636
      b. Hermann III and Elizabeth Herding
      c. Agnes Frie (+1654), daughter of Heinrich (no. 49) and Anna Vendt
      d. 1/ Johann Heinrich = Johanna Klara Katherina Plönies, doctor of law
           and secretary of cathedral chapter, learned councillor and magistrate
           in Münster after 1656
         2/ Hermann, studied at the Collegium Germanicum in Rome, later
           provost of Saint Aegidii
         3/ Heinrich
         4/ Klara = Dr. Everwin Droste
         5/ Elizabeth = Dr. Heinrich Bockhorst, son of no. 19
         6/ Agnes = Lic. Johann Kaspar Bispinck
III   a. 1616–20 Kinderhausherr, 1621–23 Gruetherr, 1624 Richtherr, 1625–31
         Gruetherr, 1632–34 Weinherr, 1635–36 Bürgermeister
      b. KG Martini 1613, Überwasser 1615
IV   a. Catholic
V   a. Cologne (*UM Köln*, 1612)
      b. Doctorate of Law

62)   HERDING, Hermann
I   a. (+before 1610)
      b. Johann (no. 64) and Ursula Heerde
      c. Anna Clute (+1610), daughter of Christoph (no. 34) (Test. II, no. 1277)
      d. 1/ Margaretha = Kaspar Schlettbrügge
         2/ Elizabeth, nun at Marienfeld (+1666)
         3/ Johann, holder of the family vicarage and canon in Vreden
         4/ Anna = Werner Bischopinck zu Kückeling
         5/ Christoph = Sara Steinhardt
II   a. clothier
III   a. 1579–81 Kapellenherr, 1583, 92 Kinderhausherr, 1584–90 Bierherr,
         1593–98 Kämmerer, left for Livonia in 1599
VI   For the Herdings, see Joseph Ketteler's study

63)   HERDING (Herdinck), Johann, I
I   d. 1/ Heinrich, father of no. 64
         2/ Gerhard (+1554)
         3/ Margaretha (+1580) = Bernd Grolle (no. 52)
II   a. clothier, Alderman of guild in 1528 (Krumbholtz, 40)
III   a. 1518–25 Gruetherr, 1536–?
      b. KG Martini 1521, 24
      e. paid 100 g. in taxes to fight Anabaptists (*GQBM* VIII, 12–13)
IV   a. Catholic

64) HERDING, Johann, II
I   a. 1527–73
    b. Heinrich (+1537), son of no. 63, and Mechthild Buschof (+1546)
    c. 1. Ursula Heerde (+1553), daughter of Hermann (no. 58) and Gertrud
       Boland
      2. Christine Wesselinck, daughter of judge Johann and Katherina
       Grolle
    d. from 1st. marriage:
      1/ Hermann (no. 62)
      2/ Heinrich, Bürgermeister in Bocholt = Margaretha zum Bortert
      from 2nd. marriage:
      1/ Elizabeth (+1589) = Dr. Hermann Heerde (no. 59)
      2/ Mechthild = 1. Johann Mumme
                 2. Engelbert von Scheick in Rees
      3/ Ursula = Gerhard v. d. Steine in Emmerich
      4/ Katherina = Konrad Grüter (no. 55)
      5/ Johann (no. 65)
      6/ Gerhard, Lic. jur. in Cologne
      7/ Maria, unmarried
II   a. rentier
    b. Liebfrauen, Frauenstrasse; Aegidii, Rothenburg
    c. assessed 5 dalers for 3 houses in Lamberti in 1568 (*QFGSM* IX, 54);
      house in Liebfrauen and Aegidii parishes; total wealth over 40,000
      dalers
III a. 1556–70 Gruetherr, 1571–72 Bürgermeister, represented Münster in
      1567 Hansa Drittelstag in Emmerich 1567
IV a. Catholic
VI fought in Charles V's army at Mühlberg as Rittmeister; for his account
    book see StdAM, MS. 120

65) HERDING, Johann, III
I   a. +1634 (Test. II, no. 682)
    b. Johann (no. 64) and Christine Wesselinck
    c. Klara Volbert (+1636)
    d. 1/ Heinrich ? Jesuit in Austria
      2/ Johann
      3/ Christine = Ernst Höfflinger, grandson of no. 66
      4/ Klara = Johann Heinr. Willbrandt Plönies
      5/ Gottfried, priest
II   a. rentier
    b. Lamberti, Salzstr.
    c. 3 houses in Münster (2 on Prinzipalmarkt, 1 on Salzstr.), 10 estates in
      Münsterland, 8 pieces of land and gardens, 2 cottages, total wealth over
      45,000 dalers
III a. 1599 Kinderhausherr, 1600–04 Gruetherr, 1605–15, 17, 19–27,
      Bürgermeister
IV a. Catholic

      b. Jesuit sodality B.M.V. Assumptionis (StAM, MSS. VII, 1034)

      c. family vicarage in Saint Lambert's

V   a. Cologne, 1583 (*UM Köln*, 1583); Siena 1592 (*UM Siena*, 2173)

66) HÖFFLINGER, Christoph

I   a. +1599 (Test. I, no. 113)

      c. 1. Ursula Joddeveld (+ca. 1580), daughter of Kaspar and Ursula Bute-
          seige

         2. Agatha Langermann

      d. from 1st. marriage:

         1/ Christoph, cathedral canon in Lübeck

         2/ Balthasar, Jesuit (see appendix 2)

         3/ Kaspar (1560–1608), Landrentmeister, = Margaretha Bisping, a
           son, Ernst, was magistrate 1625–36, Bürgermeister 1637–55,
           1661ff.

         4/ Ursula (+1633) = Hermann Mennemann (no. 92)

         5/ Anna = Hermann Wedemhove

II   a. clothier, partner with Borchard Heerde junior (son of no. 57)

      b. Liebfrauen, Frauenstrasse

      c. an inventory of his credits and debits is in StAM, FM, SFG, II Loc. 6,
         no. 37, fols. 101–103v

III   a. 1574, 76, 79–81 Sterbherr, 1582–89 Gruetherr

      b. KG Überwasser 1591

IV   a. Catholic

67) HOLTAPPEL, Bernhard

I   a. +1555

      b. Wilhelm, Kinderhausherr 1498–1514, Kämmerer 1515–16, Gruetherr
         1520, and Kunneke (Aders, 71ff.)

      c. Gertrud

      d. 1/ Gerhard

         2/ Johann

         3/ Wilhelm

         4/ Gertrud (Test. I, no. 391)

II   a. clothier

      b. Martini, Hörsterstrasse

      d. 80 guldens in city bonds

III   a. 1542–47 Kinderhausherr, 1548–50 Richtherr, 1551–54, not reelected in
         1554

      b. KG Martini 1555

IV   a. Catholic

68) HOLTAPPEL, Hermann

I   b. Wilhelm and Kunneke

      c. Gertrud Averhagen, daughter of Gerhard (no. 2)

      d. 1/ Gertrud = Albrecht Boland

         2/ Dr. jur. Franz = Anna Wulffers

II   a. clothier

c. estates "Salinck" and "Moddehof" in Laerbeck and "Hoppe" in Sendenhorst

d. 240 guldens in city bonds

III   a. 1554–60, including 1558–60 Gruetherr

d. provisor of Saint Lambert's, 1550–55 (BDAM, PfA Lamberti, Akten 17, fol. 1)

IV   a. Catholic

69) HOLTEBUER, Johann

I   c. Elsa Huge

II   a. shopkeeper, guild master (Krumbholtz, 41f., RP, 1565 XI/16, vol. 2, fol. 53v)

c. assessed 4.5 dalers in 1568 Lamberti tax (*QFGSM* IX, 52)

III   a. 1574 Kapellenherr

b. KG Lamberti 1554–55, 63, 65, 68

c. Alderman 1555–56, 68, 70 (Krumbholtz, 41f.)

70) HOLTHAUS, Lambert

I   a. +1610

b. Jobst and Margaretha Vendt, daughter of Hermann Vendt and sister of Heinrich (no. 142)

c. 1. Anna Plönies (+1588), daughter of Wilbrand (no. 113) and Maria Wedemhove (Test. I, no. 433)

2. 1589 with Anna Bockhorst, daughter of Albert (no. 18) and Gertrud von Werden

d. 1/ Albrecht, Lic. = Gertrud Kronenberg, daughter of Lic. Gerhard K., assessor at Chamber and Ecclesiastical Courts

2/ Johann, canon of Old Cathedral

3/ Heinrich, Dr. of Law = Elizabeth Plönies, daughter of no. 110

4/ Anna = Hermann Heerde IV (no. 60)

f. Elizabeth = Heinrich Jonas, son of Hermann (no. 74); Heinrich ? KG Aegidii 1564, 81, 83, 87, 89

II   b. Lamberti, Roggenmarkt

III   a. 1583–84 Kapellenherr, 1585–90, 93–98 Richtherr

IV   a. Catholic

V   a. Cologne (*UM Köln*, 1567)

b. Licentiat of Law

71) HUGE, Bernhard

I   a. 1529–1601

b. Bernd ? A Bernd Huge was in the service of the episcopal army in 1534–35 (*GQBM* VIII, 29, 32, 60)

c. 1. Anna Kock, daughter of Hermann Kock, Rentmeister in Meppen

2. Judith Rupe

d. from 1st. marriage:

1/ Anna = Heinrich Stael

2/ Katherina = Johann v. Oeseden (son of no. 103)

3/ Elsa = Christian Wedemhove (son of no. 149)

4/ Bernd (+1624), Gograf at Sandveld, = 1. Agnes Wedemhove; their son Bernd was magistrate 1639–61 = 2. Gertrud Jonas (Test. II, no. 427)

from 2nd. marriage:

1/ Johann (+1623), magistrate 1621–23 = Margaretha Alers, daughter of Heinrich A. and Gertrud v. Detten and sister of no. 1 (Test. II, nos. 201, 887)

2/ Klara Agnes = Bernd Burman (son of no. 28)

II   a. shopkeeper (Krumbholtz, 255)
      c. assessed 1.5 dalers in 1568 Lamberti tax (*QFGSM* IX, 50)
III   a. 1579–81 Ziegelherr, 1582, 85–86 Kapellenherr, 1583–84 Kinderhausherr, 1587–91 Bierherr, 1595 Kapellenherr, 1596–98 Bierherr, 1599 Hospitalherr, 1600 Sterbherr
      b. KG Martini 1564, 76

72) ICKINCK, alias SMITHUES, Bernhard
I   a. +1621 (Test. II, no. 1793)
      c. Elsa Körler (+1638), daughter of Heinrich (no. 82) and Katherina Wesselinck
      d. none
II   a. clothier, guild master (RP, 1598 VIII/28, vol. 30, fol. 35)
      b. Lamberti, Salzstrasse
      c. fields and garden, total wealth over 2,000 dalers
III   a. 1599–1600 Ziegelherr, 1601–04 Bierherr, 1605–12 Hospitalherr, 1613–15, 17, 19, 20 Gruetherr
      b. KG Lamberti 1597
      d. Roggenherr 1588–99 representing the Gemeinheit (RP, 1588 II/1, vol. 20, fol. 5)

73) JODDEVELT (Jodefeld), Johann
I   a. +1604 (Test. II, no. 261)
      b. Jaspar, Lutheran and Bürgermeister in 1533, and Klara Holtappel
      c. Kunne Kock, daughter of Johann K., Gograf in Billerbeck
      d. 1/ Johann (+1638), magistrate, = Katherina v. Detten
         2/ Ursula = Arnold Pünning
         3/ Elseke = Dr. jur. Goddert Grotegese
II   a. clothier
      c. Liebfrauen, Frauenstrasse
III   a. 1565–69 Kinderhausherr, 1571–74 Bierherr, 1576, 88–91, 93, 96–98 Sterbherr, 1579–84, 1599–1604 Richtherr
IV   a. Catholic

74) JONAS, Hermann, the Older
I   a. +1565
      c. Gertrud Blumen (Blomen) from Greven
      d. 1/ Heinrich (+1603), oxen-merchant and butcher, KG Überwasser 1574–79, = 1. Elizabeth Holthaus = 2. Margaretha v. Senden (Test. I, no. 247)

2/ Gertrud = Christian Wedemhove (no. 149)

II   a. butcher and oxen merchant
      b. Überwasser

III   a. 1531 Kinderhausherr, 1536–57
      b. KG Überwasser 1529
      c. Mesterlude, many years (Krumbholtz, 41f.)

IV   a. Catholic

75) KERCKERINCK, Bertold, zu Gieseking and Stapel   patrician
I   b. Matthias and Margaretha Travelmann, daughter of Bertold (no. 135) (Test. 1, no. 446, fol. 26v)

III   a. 1594 Kapellenherr, did not want to serve (RP, 1594 II/17, vol. 26, fols. 11v-12)

76) KERCKERINCK, Dietrich, zu Amelsbüren   patrician
III   a. 1584 Stuhlherr, he joined a princely army and was crossed off the civic roll (RP, 1584 III/2, 1585 I/18, vol. 16, fols. 10v, 54v-55)

77) KERCKERINCK, Hermann, zu Borg   patrician
I   b. Johann ? A Johann K. zu Borg paid 100 g. in 1534 tax to fight Anabaptists (*GQBM* VIII, 11), was elector of KG in 1555, and Freigraf and Gograf of Senden

III   a. 1606 Kinderhausherr, 1613–16 Stuhlherr, 1617–18 Weinherr, 1619–20 Stuhlherr, 1621–25 Weinherr

78) KERCKERINCK, Johann, zu Angelmodde   patrician
I   a. +1624
III   a. 1611 Kinderhausherr, 1612, 15, 17, 19–21 Stuhlherr, 1613–14, 22 Hospitalherr, 1623–24 Stuhlherr

79) KERCKERINCK, Johann, zu Rinckerode   patrician

I   There were four Johann Kerckerincks in Münster around the middle of the sixteenth century; for the best available genealogical study of the many branches of this patrician clan, see the two works by Anton Fahne in the bibliography
III   a. 1550–56?
      e. paid taxes and raised feudal levy for episcopal army in 1534 (*QFGSM* VIII, 11 & 101)

80) KERCKHOFF, Dietrich
I   a. +1642
      c. Anna Stael, daughter of Johann S., widow of Heinrich Berning
II   a. jurist
      b. Jodefeld, Bergstrasse
III   a. 1610 Kinderhausherr, 1611 Sterbherr, 1613 Kapellenherr, 1614–21, 23, 25–31, 35–39, 41 Richtherr, 1642 Weinherr
IV   a. Catholic

81)   KÖRLER, Dietrich
I   a. +1634
       b. Heinrich (no. 82) and Katherina Wesselinck
       c. 1603 with Anna Averhagen (+1644)
       d. 1/ Heinrich, clothier, magistrate 1647–49, 55
           2/ Anna = Hermann Soens
           3/ Katherina = Heinrich Soens
           4/ Maria = Johann Schmidt, Rentmeister in Ahaus
       f. Johann (no. 83)
II   a. clothier
       b. Aegidii, Rothenburg, vor St. Michael
III   a. 1612 Ziegelherr, 1613–15 Bierherr, 1616–24 Hospitalherr, 1625–27
           Stuhlherr, 1628–29, 1632–34 Gruetherr
       b. KG Ludgeri 1603, Aegidii 1606, 11
       d. provisor of Saint Lambert's 1608 (BDAM, PfA Lamberti, Urk. 58)
IV   a. Catholic
       b. Jesuit sodality B.M.V. Assumptionis (StAM, MSS. VII, 1034)

82)   KÖRLER, Heinrich
I   a. 1532–99
       b. Peter K., wine-merchant and master of the cellar in Bishop Franz von
           Waldeck's court; awarded a house in Münster after 1535 (Kirchhoff,
           Täufer, 19, no. 443) and N. Schuirman
       c. Katherina Wesselinck, daughter of judge Johann and Katherina Grolle
       d. 1/ Elseke (+1638) = Bernd Ickinck (no. 72)
           2/ Peter, Dr., clergy
           3/ Dietrich (no. 81)
           4/ Katherina = Bernd Scholbrock (no. 120)
           5/ Heinrich
           6/ Maria = Lic. Johann Kramer
           7/ Johann (no. 83)
           8/ Anna
       f. sister (+1599) = Veit Ercklentz, secretary of the chancery and protono-
           tary of the Chamber Court (Wedemhove, Chronik)
II   a. wine merchant; imported 109 ohm of wine in 1592, assessed 103 dalers
           4 schillings in excise, second largest wine merchant after Johann tor
           Mollen (StdAM, AVIII, 153)
       b. Aegidii, Rothenburg, vor St. Michael
       c. assessed 3 dalers in 1560 for house (SR Aegidii, vol. 1, fol. 65)
III   a. 1559–64 magistrate, 1565–69 Sterbherr, 1571–75, 90 Gruetherr, 1576,
           79–89, 91–92, 96 Kämmerer
       d. 1559, 63–65 provisor of Speckproven at Lamberti; 1574 Verordneter
           der Kirchenscheffer (QFGSM IX, 47)
       e. served in 1575 as city judge for his late in-law Johann Wesselinck (RP,
           1575 I/14, vol. 19, fol. 106v)

83)   KÖRLER, Johann
I   a. +1609

b. Heinrich (no. 82) and Katherina Wesselinck

c. Klara Holter, daughter of Franz, notary at Ecclesiastical Court, and Elsa Leistinck

d. 1/ Goddert (=Gottfried), Jesuit (see appendix 2)
   2/ Johann

II a. shopkeeper, wine merchant

III a. 1597–98 Ziegelherr, 1599–1601 Bierherr

84) LAEKE, Hans
I   a. 1550–161?

d. 1/ Katherina = Heinrich Stöve (son of no. 131)
   2/ Maria = Heinrich Kros
   3/ Gertrud = Gerhard Groeninger, master of sculptors' guild

II a. sculptor guild master

b. Martini, Hörsterstrasse

III a. 1599–1600, 04 Ziegelherr, 1601–02, 05–08 Kapellenherr, 1609–10 Sterbherr

b. KG Lamberti 1590, 98

c. Alderman 1595 (Röchell, *Chronik*, 128)

IV a. Calvinist (see appendix 4, no. 20)

85) LAGEMAN, Wilhelm
I   b. Nicolaus and Fanna in Ibbenbüren

c. Katherina Meyer, daughter of Bernd Meyer II (no. 94) and Christine Averhagen, widow of Dr. Franz Leistinck; through marriage he acquired citizenship in 1610 (*BB*, no. 2082)

d. 1/ Franz Wilhelm, Dr. of Law, Gograf at
      Meest = 1. Maria Bockhorst
             = 2. Christine Margaretha Grüter
   2/ Anna = 1. Dr. Gert Honthen
           = 2. Anton Christoph Bole
   3/ son, canon at Frenswegen, father in Niesing Convent

II a. lawyer

b. Jodefeld, Bergstrasse

III a. 1612–13 Ziegelherr, 1614–15 Bierherr, 1617, 23 Stuhlherr, 1619 Sterbherr, 1622, 24 Richtherr

e. lawyer at the Chamber Court

IV a. Catholic

b. Jesuit sodality B.M.V. Assumptionis
   (StAM, MSS. VII, 1034)
   Franciscan confraternity
   (StAM, MSS. I, 273)

V   b. Licentiat of Law

86) LANGERMANN, Johann, junior
I   a. 1509–84

b. Johann senior, magistrate 1531–33, one of the strongest supporters of the Lutheran Reformation in Münster (+1551 in Hamburg)

c. 1. Elsa Stöve, daughter of Jakob Stöve I (no. 129) and Greta
2. Elsa Heerde, widow of Heinrich Bispinck (no. 13)
d. from 1st. marriage:
1/ Wenner = Agnes Wedemhove
2/ Anna
3/ Albrecht
4/ Bernd
5/ Hermann (+in London), Hansakontor 1578–91
6/ Agatha = Christoph Höfflinger (no. 66)
7/ Jakob, in Hamburg

II a. merchant
b. Lamberti, Prinzipalmarkt
c. assessed 5 dalers for several houses in 1568 Lamberti tax (*QFGSM* IX, 53)

III a. 1554–64? 1565–69, 74, 76, 82–84 Weinherr, 1571 Kämmerer, 1578–81 Gruetherr, represented Münster in 1554 Hansa Drittelstag in Wesel and 1572 Hansatag in Lübeck
d. provisor of Saint Lambert's 1546 (BDAM, PfA Lamberti, Kart. 16, no. 15, fol. 9)

IV a. initially Lutheran but returned to the Catholic Church after 1535 ?

87) LEISTINCK, Gerhard
I a. +1578 (Test. I, no. 2)
c. Anna Schenckinck, daughter of Johann and Kunne Kock (Test. I, no. 241)
d. 1/ Elsa = Franz Holter, notary at the Chamber Court
2/ Anna = Goddert Alerding
3/ Matta
4/ Christine in Rosenthal beguinage

II a. notary; in 1539 he employed 2 copyists (SR Aegidii, vol. 1, fol. 5v)
b. Aegidii, Aegidiistrasse
c. assessed 3 dalers in 1560 (he had 5 servants and 2 maids) (SR Aegidii, vol. 1, f. 67); his house was worth 530 dalers in 1578, a field worth 600 dalers, and a garden outside Aegidii Gate, total wealth ca. 1,500 dalers

III a. 1571 Ziegelherr, 1574 Kapellenherr, 1576 Stuhlherr
b. KG Aegidii 1566
d. provisor of poorfund Aegidii 1559

88) LENNEP, Johann
I a. 1553–1626
b. Christian, Gograf at Bakenfeld and Telgte and Apollonia von Hatzfeld
c. Katherina Heideman (1551–1636)
d. 1/ Johann, Dr of Law, canon of Old Cathedral, studied at Freiburg (*UM Freiburg*, 798)
2/ Katherina = Wilbrand Stael, wine merchant
3/ Melchior = Katherina Witton

4/ Christian, Jesuit (see appendix 2)
5/ Elseka = Dr. Christoph Clute (see no. 34)

II   a. clothier, guild master

III   a. 1603, 20 Ziegelherr, 1621–24 Bierherr, 1625–26 Sterbherr

      b. KG Martini 1610, 12, 15, 17, 19

      c. Alderman

89) LOBACH, Johann

I   b. Johann ? (+ca. 1568) (*QFGSM* IX, 49)

II   a. wine merchant

      b. Lamberti, Prinzipalmarkt

      c. assessed 3 dalers in 1568 Lamberti tax (*QFGSM* IX, 53)

      d. 700 g. annuity to nobleman Hermann v. d. Recke (*RKG*, no. 151)

III   a. 1617, 23 Ziegelherr, 1618–19 Sterbherr

      b. KG Ludgeri 1612

90) MEINERTZ (Meiners), Heinrich

I   b. Johann (+1577), ML 1558, 63, 72, Alderman of Gesamtgilde 1576–77 (Krumbholtz, 41ff.) and KG Ludgeri 1563, 67, 69, 77

      c. Anna Degen, widow of Hermann Hartmann

      d. Johann, Lic. of Law, magistrate 1645–49

II   a. fuller, guild master, 1595–1601 (StdAM, RP)

      b. Ludgeri, Loerstrasse

III   a. 1602–08 Kinderhausherr, 1609 Bierherr, 1612 Kapellenherr

      b. KG Ludgeri 1594, 1601

      c. Alderman 1601

      d. provisor of Saint Servatii 1604 (*QFGSM* IX, 30)

IV   a. Protestant (see appendix 4, no. 21)

91) MENNEMANN, Hermann

I   a. +ca. 1569

      c. Anna Rotgers, daughter of Heinrich, magistrate 1527, 31, 32, and Alderman in 1524

      d. 1/ Heinrich

         2/ Maria

         3/ Agnes

         4/ Hermann

         5/ Gertrud

         6/ Jürgen

         7/ Johann

II   a. clothier?

III   a. 1555–56

92) MENNEMANN, Hermann, zu Welpendorp

I   b. Johann (1493–1578), Alderman of Gesamtgilde, and Gertrud Schmitjohan (Test. I, no. 405)

      c. Ursula Höfflinger

      d. 1/ Ursula

    2/ Gertrud
    3/ Hermann
    4/ Johann, student at Vienna 1615 (*UM Wien*, II S9), +in Bohemia, (*RKG*, H 1341)
  f. 1/ Anna
    2/ Johann
    3/ Hermann
    4/ Gertrud
    5/ Katherina
    6/ Christine, in convent

III   a. 1616

93) MEYER, Bernhard, I
I   a. +1587
    c. Anna Holtebuer
    d. Bernd, II (no. 94) ?
II   b. Martini, Hörsterstrasse
III   a. 1574, 76 Ziegelherr, 1579–81 Kapellenherr, 1582 Sterbherr, 1583–86 Bierherr
    b. KG Martini 1563
    c. Mesterlude, 1562, 66, 71–74 (Krumbholtz, 42f.)

94) MEYER, Bernhard, II
I   a. 1560–1630
    b. Bernd, I ?
    c. 1. Christine Averhagen, daughter of Johann (no. 3) 2. NN
    d. 1/ Bernd, III, magistrate 1631–46, 56–57, KG Aegidii 1621, 23
      2/ Katherine = 1. Dr. Franz Leistinck
             = 2. Lic. Wilhelm Lageman (no. 85)
      3/ Christine = Hermann Frie
    f. Gerhard, goldsmith = Gertrud Isfording
II   a. clothier
    b. Martini, Hörsterstrasse; Lamberti, Roggenmarkt
III   a. 1593–96 Ziegelherr, 1597–1600 Bierherr, 1601 Sterbherr, 1602 Stuhlherr, 1603 Hospitalherr, 1604–15, 17, 19–26, 28–30 Kämmerer
    b. KG Martini 1591

95) MODERSOHN, alias BALCKE, Heinrich
I   c. Maria Hövel, sister of Dietrich H., Amtmann of Saint Magdelene Hospital (Test. I, no. 233, fol. 151v)
II   a. butcher (StdAM, AII, 20, RP, 1564, vol. 1, fol. 42v)
    b. Ludgeri, Ludgeristrasse
III   a. 1565–67 Bierherr

96) MODERSOHN, Heinrich, the Older
I   a. +1593 (Test. I, no. 366)
    b. Johann
    c. Fama (Sophia) Bittinck
    d. none

      f. Heinrich and Michael (Test. I, no. 366)

II   a. butcher
      b. Aegidii
      c. total wealth ca. 1,200 dalers + house

III   a. 1565–69, 71 Hospitalherr
      b. KG Aegidii 1557
      d. provisor of Saint Ludger's 1565–66

IV   a. Catholic

97)   MODERSOHN, Jobst
I   a. +1576
      c. Greta
      d. 1/ Werner
          2/ Bertolt
          3/ Wilhelm
          4/ Helma

II   a. butcher
      b. Ludgeri, Ludgeristrasse

III   a. 1569 Bierherr, 1571, 74 Kinderhausherr
      c. 1555–60, 65, 67–68 Mesterlude, 1565 Alderman (Krumbholtz, 41f.)
      d. provisor of Saint Ludger's 1572

IV   a. Catholic

98)   MÜNSTERMANN, Bertold
I   b. Philip M. zu Velthaus and Katherina Plönies
      d. 1/ Johann, castellan in Wolbeck
          2/ Katherina
          3/ Philip, student at Cologne in 1592 and at Freiburg in 1604 (*UM Freiburg*, 722)
          4/ Richtmot = Gerhard Schreick, judge in Bocholt

II   a. rentier
      b. Lamberti, am Kirchhof
      c. House Velthaus, he moved his residence out of Münster in 1595 (*QFGSM* II, 87)

III   a. 1589, 93–94 Ziegelherr

99)   MÜNSTERMANN, Dietrich, I
I   a. 1507–51
      b. Johann (1459–93) and Gertrud Howers
      c. 1. 1507 with Gertrud (+1514)
          2. 1520 with Richtmot Dreihaus (+1537)
          3. 1539 with Gertrud Dreihaus (+1560)
      d. from 1st. marriage:
          1/ Johann (+ca. 1550), canon at Saint Martin's
          2/ Elizabeth (+1577), in Niesing Convent
          from 2nd. marriage:
          1/ Johann (+1551)
          2/ NN, in Rengering Convent

        3/ Philip (zu Veldhaus) (+1557), canon at Saint Martin's = Katherina
        Plönies; elector of KG in 1555
        4/ Klara = Hermann Hansow, founder
        5/ Heinrich (+1567) = Klara Coesfeld, daughter of Franz (Test. I, no.
        46)
        6/ Dietrich (no. 100)
        7/ Bertold (+1607), canon at Saint Martin's
   f. 1/ Heinrich (+1535), Abbot of Marienfeld
        2/ Johann 3/ Konrad
        4/ Anna, in Reine beguinage

II   a. merchant
III   a. 1524–25 Kämmerer, 1526–33 Bürgermeister, 1536–40 Kämmerer, rep-
       resented Münster in Hansa Drittelstag, 1522 in Duisburg, 1529 in Co-
       logne
    b. KG Aegidii 1520
IV   a. Catholic
VI   See the genealogical reconstruction by Joseph Prinz

100) MÜNSTERMANN, Dietrich, II
I   a. 1536–92
    b. Dietrich (no. 99) and Richtmot Dreihaus
    c. 1566 with Anna Stöve, daughter of Johann (son of no. 129) and Klara
       Averhagen (Test. I, no. 151)
    d. 1/ Klara = Johann Boland, Bürgermeister in Coesfeld
       2/ Dietrich, +1601 in Livonia (Test. II, no. 1703)
       3/ Johann (+1599), murdered (Röchell, *Chronik*, 142)
       4/ Heinrich
       5/ Anna = Wilbrand Baeken
II   a. merchant
III   a. 1579–81 Kinderhausherr, 1582 Bierherr, 1583 Stuhlherr, 1584 Sterb-
       herr, 1585–92 Richtherr
    d. provisor of Saint Aegidii and poorfund

101) MUMME, Albert
I   c. Elizabeth Rodde, daughter of Hermann, magistrate 1492, 1509–15,
       widow of Jobst Smithues (no. 122)
    f. Heinrich, Bürgermeister, and Jaspar, judge in Bocholt; the Mumme
       belonged to an official-patrician family
III   a. 154?–58/59, including 1550–52 Weinherr, 1555–58/59 Bürgermeister
    e. episcopal ambassador to Reichstag at Regensburg in 1541; learned
       councillor in Münster episcopal government
IV   a. Catholic
V   b. Licentiat of Law

102) OESEDEN (Hoeseden), Bernhard van, the Older
I   d. Bernd the Younger (no. 103)
II   a. clothier
    c. assessed 4 dalers for house in Lamberti in 1568 (*QFGSM* IX, 52)

III   a. 1543–72, including 1565, 67–69, 71–72 Richtherr, 1566 Stuhlherr

      c. Mesterlude 1574

      d. 1540, 44 provisor of Saint Lambert's (BDAM, PfA Lamberti, Kart. 16, no. 11, fol. 1 and Urk. 29)

IV   a. Catholic

103) OESEDEN, Bernhard, the Younger

I   a. +1597 (Test. I, no. 668)

      b. Bernd the Older (no. 102)

      c. 1. Gertrud Wedemhove (+1588), daughter of Christian (no. 149) and Gertrud Jonas

         2. Gertrud Rodde, daughter of clothier Johann

      d. Johann = Katherina Huge

II   a. clothier

      b. Lamberti, opposite the church

III   a. 1588–90 Ziegelherr, 1591 Bierherr, 1593 Richtherr, 1594–96 Sterbherr

      b. KG Lamberti 1586

104) OESEDEN, Hermann van

I   a. +1595

      b. Wilhelm, clothier, and Margaretha Wedemhove

      c. Ursula Heerde, daughter of Hermann (no. 58) and Katherina Brechte

      d. 1/ Wilhelm, clothier and magistrate 1627–34

         2/ Klara = Alheit Thiason

         3/ Ursula = Procurator Heinrich Schlade

II   a. clothier

      b. Lamberti, Prinzipalmarkt

III   a. 1590–91 Ziegelherr, 1593–95 Sterbherr

105) OSSENBRÜGGE, Hermann

II   a. clothier

III   a. 1553 (Kerssenbroch, 885)

      d. provisor of Saint Lambert's, 1540, 44 (BDAM, PfA Lamberti, Kart. 16, no. 11, fol. 1 and Urk. 29)

106) OSSENBRÜGGE, Johann

I   a. +1577 (Guelich, Chronicle, fol. 12)

      b. Matthaeus

      c. Engela Buthman, daughter of Heinrich and Anna Tünneken

II   a. clothier

III   a. 1565–66 Kinderhausherr, 1567–69 Bierherr, 1571 Sterbherr, 1574, 76 Richtherr

      b. KG Ludgeri 1577

107) OSSENBRÜGGE, Rotger

I   a. +1612 (Test. II, no. 1712)

      c. Klara Joddeveld

      d. 1/ Kaspar, pastor at Saint Magedelene's Hospital

         2/ Matthaeus = Klara van Guelich

3/ Johann = Gertrud zur Floet
II   a. clothier
     b. Liebfrauen, am Überwasserkirchhof
     c. garden outside Kreuz Gate and camp at Grevenweg, total wealth over 3,000 dalers
     d. annuities with 650 dalers principal
III a. 1579–81 Ziegelherr, 1582 Kapellenherr, 1583–85 Sterbherr, 1586–87, 90–92, 99, 1601–03 Kämmerer, 1594–98, 1604–12 Richtherr

108) PAEL, Jaspar
II   c. assessed 3 dalers in 1568 Lamberti tax (*QFGSM* IX, 50)
III a. 1565 Ziegelherr, 1571 Bierherr
     b. KG Ludgeri 1560–61, 68
     c. Mesterlude, 1561, 63, 66, 68–70 (Krumbholtz, 42)

109) PLÖNIES, Hillbrand
I   a. 1524–98
     b. Wolter (+1532), magistrate and judge, and Elizabeth Buschof (+1586) (Test. I, no. 351)
     c. 1. Margaretha Brechte, daughter of Werner B., Bürgermeister of Hamm
       2. Engela Buthman, widow of Johann Ossenbrügge (no. 106)
     d. from 1st. marriage:
       1/ Willbrand, canon of Old Cathedral
       2/ Werner = Christine Kleinsorge of Geismar; merchant, went to Reval in 1577; their son Dr. Hillbrand P. was magistrate in Münster from 1639–51, including Bürgermeister from 1640–46, 51. (*RKG*, 4404/ P839/ 2626)
       3/ Mechtild = Dr. Georg Kumpsthorst
       4/ Hermann, cathedral canon in Lübeck (StdAM, A281a, VIII, 1599 IX 22)
       5/ Heinrich (1566–1634), studied in Rome and dean of Old Cathedral
       6/ Hillbrand (no. 110)
       from 2nd. marriage:
       1/ Wolter = Anna Frie
     f. 1/ Johann, clergy
       2/ Wolter
       3/ Katherina
       4/ Anna
II   a. merchant
III a. 1557–58 Kinderhausherr, 1565–66 Richtherr, 1567–69 Kämmerer, 1571, 79–81, 90–91, 93–98 Weinherr, 1574–76, 82–86, 88–89 Bürgermeister, represented Münster in Lübeck Hansatage, 1562, 64, 72 and in Drittelstage in Cologne, 1561, 66, 67 and in Wesel, 1564, 79 (*QFGSM* IV, 335, n. 14)
IV a. Catholic

110) PLÖNIES, Hillbrand, zu Ossenbeck
I a. 1558–1623
   b. Hillbrand (no. 109) and Margaretha Brechte
   c. Richtmot Clevorn
   d. 1/ Johann Friedrich, canon of Saint Mauritz
      2/ Hillbrand Hermann = Anna Bockhorst
      3/ Margaretha = Albert Sasse in Lübeck
      4/ Elizabeth = Dr. Heinrich Holthaus (son of no. 70)
      5/ Hermann
      6/ Richtmot, in Ringe beguinage (1628)
II a. rentier
   b. Saint Servatius, am Servatiitor
   c. house Ossenbeck
III a. 1613–14 Ziegelherr, 1615 Kapellenherr, 1616–17, 20 Bierherr
   b. KG Ludgeri 1606
   d. provisor of Saint Servatius 1604 (*QFGSM* III, 190)
IV a. Catholic

111) PLÖNIES, Johann
I a. +1584 as a young man (Guelich, Chronicle, fol. 36v; Test. I, no. 413)
   b. Willbrand, III (no. 113) and Maria Wedemhove
   c. Anna Heerde, daughter of Hermann (no. 58) and Katherina Brechte
   d. none
II c. assessed 4 dalers in 1568 Lamberti tax (*QFGSM* IX, 52)
III a. 1582 Ziegelherr, 1583–84 Kapellenherr
   b. KG Lamberti 1570, 82
IV a. Catholic

112) PLÖNIES, Willbrand, II
I b. Willbrand, I, clothier and Bürgermeister 1503–13, and Matta Liderman
   c. 1. Anna Buschof
      2. Elsa Bispinck
   d. from 1st. marriage:
      1/ Willbrand (no. 113)
      2/ Johann (+1589), elector of KG in 1555 = Halam von Hausen (Test. I, no. 437)
      3/ two bastard daughters, Metta and Anna (Test. I, no. 421)
   f. 1/ Hermann, Bürgermeister in Lübeck, knighted in 1532 by Charles V
      2/ Wolter (father of no. 109)
II a. merchant
   b. assessed 6 g. in 1550 Lamberti district tax (SR Lamberti, vol. 1, fol. 6v); 4th richest man in the district
   d. 260 guldens in city bonds (StdAM, GR)
III a. 1521–22, 25, 27–28 Gruetherr, 1532, 1536–45 Bürgermeister, left Münster in 1532 when Lutherans dominated city council; represented Münster in 1521 Hansa Drittelstag in Wesel
   e. paid 100 g. in taxes for episcopal army in 1534 (*GQBM* VIII, 12) and

procured ammunition for the besieging army (*GQBM* VIII, 61 & 117);
Landrat under Bishop Ketteler (StAM, MSS. I, 37)

IV   a. Catholic

113) PLÖNIES, Willbrand, III
I   a. +before 1571 (Test. I, no. 421)
     b. Willbrand, II (no. 112) and Anna Buschof
     c. Maria Wedemhove, daughter of Hermann (father of nos. 149, 150) and
       Agnes Ossenbrügge
     d. 1/ Anna (+1588) = Lic. Lambert Holthaus (no. 70)
       2/ Willbrand (no. 114)
       3/ Johann (no. 111)
       4/ Hermann = Elizabeth Hansen
II   b. Lamberti, Salzstrasse
     c. house "Ossenbeck" near Dreisteinfurt assessed 5 dalers for houses in
       Lamberti in 1568 (*QFGSM* IX, 52)
III   a. 1565–67 Kapellenherr
     d. provisor of Saint Lambert's 1554–55 (PfA Lamberti, Kart. 16, no. 21,
       fol. 9v)
IV   a. Catholic

114) PLÖNIES, Willbrand, IV, zu Ossenbeck
I   a. +1625
     b. Willbrand, III (no. 113) and Maria Wedemhove
     c. Klara von Hansen, daughter of Johann
II   c. he inherited the title and properties of his childless uncle, Johann
       Plönies zu Ossenbeck (Test. I, no. 437)
III   a. 1593–94, 96 Kapellenherr, 1597–98 Kinderhausherr, 1599, 1600, 1611–
       14, 22–24 Stuhlherr, 1620–21 Sterbherr
IV   a. Catholic
     b. Franciscan confraternity StAM, MSS. I, 273)

115) RICK (Reich), Wilhelm
I   a. +1599
     b. Adam R., Rentmeister at Horstmar, and Anna Ossenbrügge
     c. Gertrud Ralle, widow of Konrad van Delft in Coesfeld
II   a. lawyer
     b. Martini, Neubrückenstrasse
III   a. 1595 Ziegelherr, 1596–97 Kinderhausherr, 1598 Gruetherr
     e. 1591 protonotary of the Chamber Court (StdAM, AXIII, 39, fol. 11)

116) RODDE, Goddert
I   b. Hermann(?) magistrate 1492, 1509–15
     c. Gertrud Schmitjohan
     d. 1/ Johann ?
       2/ Hermann ?
       3/ Bernd ?
       4/ Anna = Johann Volbert (no. 144)

II d. 300 guldens in city bonds (StdAM, GR)
III a. 1542–47

117) RODDE, Johann
I   a. 1529–?
    b. Johann (no. 116) ?
    c. 1. Elizabeth Gerkens
       2. Maria v. Upen
    d. 1/ Gerhard (1565–1644), in Lübeck
       2/ Anna = Johann Pagenstecker, secretary of the city council in
          Münster
       3/ Adolf (1567–1617), magistrate in Lübeck
       4/ Johann, in Colmar
       5/ Gertrud = Bernd v. Oeseden (no. 103)
       6/ Bernd, in Lübeck
       7/ Elizabeth = Bernd Kolns
       8/ Klara = Johann Stöve (son of no. 131)
       9/ Maria = Heinrich Kestering in Ahlen
II a. clothier? The family left for Lübeck after 1589
III a. 1574 Ziegelherr, 1585 Sterbherr
    b. KG Martini 1589

118) SCHENCKINCK, Hermann   patrician
I   a. +1554 (Test. I, no. 577)
    b. Johann and Mechtild Wyck
    c. Mechtild Buck, daughter of Lambert (father of no. 25) and Richtmot
       Bischopinck
    d. 1/ Hermann (no. 119)
       2/ Johann, canon at Saint Mauritz and later cathedral canon in Augs-
          burg
       3/ Otto, bishop in Livonia
       4/ Katherina, in Niesing convent
       5/ Heinrich, in Livonia
       6/ Bernhard, dean of Saint Mauritz
       7/ Christine = N. Nagel
       8/ Everhard = Ida Droste
       9/ Matta = Lubbert Travelmann (no. 140)
II a. rentier and merchant
    b. Lamberti, Alter Steinweg
    c. House "zur Wyck" and 3 fields
III a. 1525 Hospitalherr, 1527 judge, 1536–53, including 1541, 50 as Wein-
       herr, 1553 Kämmerer, represented Münster in Hansa Drittelstag in
       Cologne, 1549
    b. elector of KG in 1555
    e. paid taxes and raised feudal levy for episcopal army in 1534 (*GQBM*
       VIII, 11 & 92)
IV a. Catholic

119) SCHENCKINCK, Hermann, zu Wyck and Vöegedinck   patrician
I   b. Hermann (no. 118) and Mechtild Buck
     c. Alheid Bischopinck, daughter of Bertold
     d. 1/ Bertold = Anna v. d. Porten
        2/ Anna Richtmot = Johann v. Hetterscheidt
        3/ Hermann
II   c. sold his house on Alten Steinweg to the widow of Jacob v. d. Tinnen in 1565
III   a. 1596 Kinderhausherr, 1599–1604 Hospitalherr, 1605, 10–11 Stuhlherr, 1608–09 Kinderhausherr, 1612–15 Weinherr

120) SCHOLBROCK, Bernhard
I   a. 1560–?
     b. Heinrich (+1595) and Anna Averhagen; his father was a very wealthy wine merchant (Test. I, no. 181)
     c. 1592 with Katherina Körler, daughter of Heinrich (no. 82) and Katherina Wesselinck
     d. 1/ Heinrich, canon of Saint Ludger's
        2/ Anna = Heinrich Stael
        3/ Maria = Albert Wulffert
        4/ Elizabeth = Johann Otterstedde
        5/ Bernhard
     f. 1/ Gertrud
        2/ Heinrich
        3/ Elizabeth
II   a. wine merchant and shopkeeper
     b. Aegidii; Lamberti, Fischmarkt, Roggenmarkt
     c. assessed 3 dalers in 1590 Aegidii district tax; his father was assessed 5 dalers (SR Aegidii, vol. 2, fol. 1v); his house on Prinzipalmarkt was worth 1,800 dalers in 1595 (cf. Test. I, no. 181, vol. 5, fol. 83); total wealth over 4,000 dalers
III   a. 1601 Kapellenherr, 1602–08 Bierherr, 1609–13 Sterbherr
     d. Roggenherr 1599– (RP, 1599 III/16, vol. 31, fol. 20v)

121) SCHONEBECK, Johann
I   a. 1554–1612
     b. Hermann (+1576), furrier and Alderman of Gesamtgilde (Test. I, no. 284)
     c. Maria Potken, daughter of Alderman Johann P. and Margaretha Bockman
     d. 1/ Hermann, notary
        2/ Anna = Hermann Bennemann
        3/ Elizabeth = Dietrich Goekeman
II   a. furrier, guild master?
     b. Liebfrauen, am Frauentor
III   a. 1597–98 Ziegelherr, 1599–1600 Kapellenherr, 1601–04 Kinderhausherr, 1605–08 Sterbherr, 1609–12 Bierherr

b. KG Überwasser 1584, 90, 94

c. Mesterlude 1583–95, Alderman 1596 (Krumbholtz, 44; Röchell, *Chronik*, 128)

V a. Cologne 1574

122) SMITHUES, Jobst

I c. Elizabeth Rodde, daughter of Hermann and Katherina

  d. Katherina (Test. I, no. 633)

II c. held episcopal fiefs in Wolbeck, Nordwalde, Amelsbüren, and Alvenskirchen (StAM, AVM, MS. 51, fol. 58v)

  d. 200 guldens in city bonds (StdAM, GR)

III a. 1536–40?

IV a. Catholic

123) SNELLE, Johann

I c. Anna van Vreden

  d. 1/ Elizabeth

   2/ Eva

II c. assessed 2 dalers in 1568 Lamberti tax (*QFGSM* IX, 53)

III a. 1562–66 Gruetherr

124) STEINHOFF, Melchior

I a. +1606

  b. Gerhard, guild master of tailors, and Margaretha Stadeling, alias Boeker

  c. Christine Stummel,(+1611) (Test. II, no. 980)

  d. none

II a. painter, joined guild in 1587 (Krumbholtz, 349f.)

III a. 1605–06 Ziegelherr

  b. KG Überwasser 1596, 98

IV a. Calvinist (see appendix 4, no. 27)

125) STEVENINCK, Everwin, zu Brock patrician

I b. Heinrich (no. 127) and Margaretha v. d. Tinnen

  c. Sibilla von Wendt, daughter of Lubbert and Anna von Altenbecken

  d. 1/ Anna Margaretha = Melchior von Harde

   2/ Johann = Maria Bischopinck, widow of Lambert Buck (no. 26)

   3/ Agnes, abbess of Aegidii cloister

III a. 1576 Bierherr, 1574 Stuhlherr, 1579–81 Hospitalherr; he did not want to serve (RP, 1574, vol. 9, fols. 4v, 70v, 99v–100; 1581 VII/6; 1582 I/8)

126) STEVENINCK, Everwin, zu Wilkinghegge patrician

I b. Johann and Katherina Buck

  c. Margaretha von Ledebur (see appendix 4, no. 28)

  d. Wilhelm Johann (+1652), magistrate 1621–52

III a. 1590–91 Kapellenherr, 1593, 95 Kinderhausherr; did not want to serve (RP, 1594 XII/20, vol. 26, fol. 91)

127) STEVENINCK, Heinrich, zu Brock   patrician
I   b. Everwin, magistrate 1507–25 (Bürgermeister 1516–17, 20–21) and
       Anna Kleihorst
     c. Margaretha von der Tinnen, daughter of Bernd and Nesa von Berns-
       feld
     d. 1/ Everwin (no. 125)
       2/ Agnes = Evert Bischopinck
     f. 1/ Konrad, canon of Saint Mauritz
       2/ Johann (no. 128) = Katherina Buck
II   c. held 6 fiefs from the bishop in Altenberg, Bosendal, Albersloh,
       Amelsbüren, and Billerbeck (StAM, AVM, MS. 51, fol. 39v)
III   a. 1536–50?
     b. elector of KG in 1555
     e. paid taxes and raised feudal levy for episcopal army in 1534 (*GQBM*
       VIII, 11 & 92)
IV   a. Catholic

128) STEVENINCK, Johann   patrician
I   b. see no. 127
     c. = Katherina Buck
III   a. 1554 (Kerssenbroch, 949)
     b. elector of KG in 1555

129) STÖVE, Jakob, I
I   b. Evert, fuller in Warendorf
     c. 1. Greta N.
       2. Anna Rodde, daughter of Johann
     d. from 1st. marriage:
       1/ Greta 2/ Jakob, II (no. 130)
       3/ Elsa = Johann Langermann (no. 86)
       from 2nd. marriage:
       1/ Evert (+1537) in Warendorf = Greta Swolle (+1549)
       2/ Engel (+1515) = Johann Körding of Warendorf
       3/ Johann = Klara Averhagen (+1576) (Test. I, no. 151)
II   a. clothier
     b. Ludgeri
III   a. 1515, 32, 1536–38?
IV   a. Catholic

130) STÖVE, Jakob, II
I   b. Jakob, I (no. 129) and Greta
     c. 1. Katherina Tosse
       2. N. Langermann
     d. from 1st. marriage:
       1/ Jakob, III (no. 131)
       2/ Rotger, proprietor of the Stadtkeller = Gertrud Buthmann
II   a. clothier
     c. assessed 1 daler in 1568 Lamberti tax (*QFGSM* IX, 52)

III   a. 1585–87 Ziegelherr, 1588 Kapellenherr
       c. Mesterlude 1583–84, 96 (Krumbholtz, 44)
       d. Roggenherr 1579–99

131) STÖVE, Jakob, III
I   a. 1545–1617 (Test. II, no. 705)
    b. Jakob, II (no. 130) and Katherina Tosse
    c. Anna v. Oeseden, daughter of Heinrich and Elsa Wedemhove (Test. I, no. 416)
    d. 1/ Katherina (+1622), unmarried
       2/ Anna = 1. Arnold Langerich
              = 2. Bernd Greving
       3/ Elizabeth = 1. Heinrich Loge
                 = 2. Johann Francke, lawyer
       4/ Johann, clothier, oxen merchant, and magistrate in 1635 = Klara Rodde
       5/ Heinrich, clothier, magistrate 1622–34 = 1. Klara Tzwyvel
                                 = 2. Katherina Laeke
II   a. clothier, guild master
    b. Lamberti, Roggenmarkt, opposite the mint
    c. his house was worth 1,400 dalers in 1617
III   a. 1597 Kapellenherr, 1598–1600 Kinderhausherr, 1601–04 Sterbherr, 1605–10 Richtherr, 1611–12 Gruetherr, 1613 Richtherr, 1615–17 Sterbherr
      d. provisor of Saint Lambert's 1596 (*QFGSM* IX, 54)
VI   his account book has been published by Eduard Schulte, "Danziger Kontorbuch" in *Hansische Geschichtsblätter* 62 (1937), pp. 40–72

132) TIMMERSCHEIDT, Heinrich
I   a. 1568–1638
    b. Bernd (+1611), notary and court clerk, and Margaretha Mumme (+1626)
    c. Katherina Droste (1576–1654), daughter of Johann Droste, secretary to the prince-bishop and Katherina von Münster
    d. none ?
    f. 1/ Franz, vicar in Speyer
       2/ Bernd, notary, = Gertrud Kemner; their son Johann (+1677) was Bürgermeister in 1661
       3/ Walmoda = Bernd Uphaus, magistrate
II   a. lawyer
III   a. 1611 Ziegelherr, 1630–31 Stuhlherr, 1632–35 Richtherr, 1636 Stuhlherr
    b. KG Aegidii 1607, 10, 14, 19, 25
V   b. Licentiat of Law

133) TINNEN, Bernhard von der   patrician
I   a. +1543
    b. Johann, Bürgermeister 1500–09, and Greta Kerckerinck
    c. Nese v. Bernsfeld, daughter of Gerhard and Jutta v. Hövel

  d. 1/ Margaretha = Heinrich Steveninck
   2/ Gertrud = Lubbert Steveninck
   3/ Christine, in Aegidii cloister
   4/ Dietrich, canon of Saint Ludger's
   5/ Bernd, in Stromberg = 1. Patronella Krakerugge
              = 2. Agnes Aschebrock
   6/ Gerhard, in Livonia
   7/ Johann = Anna von Wendt

II a. merchant ?
III a. 1509, 16, 22, 27, 31, 1536–40, 1541 Bürgermeister; he left Münster in
    1532 when Lutherans dominated city council
   e. paid taxes and raised feudal levy for episcopal army in 1534 (*GQBM*
    VIII, 11 & 101)
IV a. Catholic

134) TINNEN, Rudolf, zu Kaldenhof patrician
III a. 1618 Kapellenherr

135) TRAVELMANN, Bertold patrician
I   a. +1559 (Test. I, no. 446)
   b. Lubbert and Godela Bischopinck
   c. Jutta Warendorf (+1555), daughter of Bernd and N v. d. Tinnen
   d. 1/ Lubbert (no. 140)
   2/ Margaretha = Matthaeus Kerckerinck
   3/ two bastards: Bertold, pastor at Saint Jacob's and Hans in Livonia
III a. 1510, 13; 1527–31 Gruetherr, 1536–58 Bürgermeister
   e. paid taxes for episcopal army in 1534 (*GQBM* VIII, 11)
IV a. Catholic

136) TRAVELMANN, Christoph, zu Maser patrician
I   a. +1653
   b. Goddert (no. 138) and Elizabeth v. Heven
   c. Elizabeth Walzungen von Ackensbock, daughter of Heinrich and Anna
   Kerckerinck
   d. 1/ Christine
   2/ Anna Elizabeth
   3/ Goddert = Christine Raesfeld
II b. Martini, bei Hörstertor
III a. 1612, 15, 17, 19 Kinderhausherr, 1621 Stuhlherr, 1622–41 Kämmerer,
   1643–46, 1648–53 Weinherr

137) TRAVELMANN, Egbert, zu Ebbeling patrician
I   a. 1556–1611
   b. Lubbert (no. 140) and Richtmot Clevorn
   c. Anna von Caessem, daughter of Heinrich and Elizabeth Bischopinck
   d. 1/ Lubbert, magistrate 1625–47, = Katherina Anna von Remen
   2/ Richtmot
   3/ Godale = Hermann von Remen

III   a. 1588–90 Kapellenherr, 1591 Sterbherr, 1593–98 Stuhlherr, 1599–1603 Weinherr, 1604–09 Hospitalherr, 1610–11 Weinherr

138) TRAVELMANN, Goddert, zu Maser   patrician
I   a. 1545–91
    b. Egbert and Christine Kerckerinck
    c. Elizabeth von Heven, daughter of Christoph and Anna v. Remen
    d. 1/ Christoph (no. 136)
       2/ Goddert = Elizabeth Raesfeld
III   a. 1579–80 Kinderhausherr, 1581–86, 88–91 Stuhlherr; did not want to serve at first (RP, 1585 II/15, vol. 17, fols. 5–5v)

139) TRAVELMANN, Heinrich   patrician
I   a. +1557 (Test. I, no. 15)
    c. Anna = Lambert Buck (no. 25)
III   a. 1518–19, 23–26, 154?-54 Richtherr

140) TRAVELMANN, Lubbert, zu Ebbeling   patrician
I   a. +1583
    b. Bertold (no. 135) and Jutta Warendorf
    c. 1. Richtmot Clevorn, daughter of Egbert and Anna Bürse
       2. Matta Schenckinck, daughter of Hermann (no. 118) and Mechtild Buck
    d. from 1st. marriage:
       1/ Bertold, in Hamburg
       2/ Jutta = Johann Kerckerinck
       3/ Egbert (no. 137)
       from 2nd. marriage:
       1/ Godela = Baldewin Warendorf
       2/ Lübberla
       3/ Richtmot = Bernd Droste zu Hülshof
       4/ Godeka
       5/ Matta = Rudolf v. Caessem
II   c. assessed 5 dalers in 1568 Lamberti tax (QFGSM IX, 53)
III   a. 1567–69 Kapellenherr, 1579–82 Hospitalherr, 1576 Stuhlherr

141) TÜNNEKEN, Anton
I   b. Gert?
II   a. rentier (SR Aegidii, 1539, vol. 1, fol. 15)
III   a. 1561 Kinderhausherr
IV   a. Catholic

142) VENDT, Heinrich
I   a. 1521–1609
    b. Hermann (+1542), brewer and innkeeper, and Anna Bordeman
    c. Klara Wedemhove (+1599), daughter of Hermann and Neisa Ossenbrügge (StdAM, AXVII, 53a Test. I, no. 247)
    d. 1/ Hermann, no children

2/ Anna = Heinrich Frie (no. 49); their first son took the name Frie-Vendt to continue the family name (no. 50)

3/ Agnes = Goddert Volbert, son of no. 144

f. 1/ Dr. Hermann, lawyer and learned councillor in the episcopal government, = Gertrud Rotgers (StAM, MSS. I, 37. fols. 58–73)

2/ Margaretha = Jobst Holthaus (their son was Lambert, no. 70)

II   a. lawyer

b. Aegidii, Aegidiistrasse

c. assessed 5 dalers for house in 1568 Lamberti tax (*QFGSM* IX, 50)

III   a. 1561–63, 65, 67, 79–81, 88–91, 93–96, 1598–1604 Bürgermeister, 1568–69, 1605–09 Weinherr, represented Münster in Hansa Drittelstag: 1557 and 1567 in Cologne, 1567 in Emmerich

d. provisor of Aegidii 1575, 1604

IV   a. Catholic

b. strong supporter of the Jesuits, leader of the pro-clerical faction on the city council

c. 1591 Aegidii poorhouse

V   a. Poitiers 1551

b. Doctorate of Law

143) VERENDORP, Johann

I   a. 1519–92 (Test. I, no. 41)

b. Johann (+1540) (Test. I, no. 392)

c. Margaretha Plate

d. none

e. Johann von Vreden, son of Hermann

II   a. shopkeeper, guild master (StdAM, AII, 20, RP, 1564, vol. 1, fol. 7v)

b. Martini, am Hörsterberg

c. assessed 2.5 dalers in 1568 Lamberti tax (*QFGSM* IX, 50); total wealth ca. 4,000 dalers

III   a. 1574 Ziegelherr, 1576, 79–82 Bierherr, 1584 Hospitalherr, 1586–92 Gruetherr

b. KG Martini 1559, 62, 65, 67, 70

c. Mesterlude, 1561, 64 (Krumbholtz, 42)

IV   a. Catholic

c. 1592 orphanage zu Wegesende

144) VOLBERT, Johann

I   a. 1522–?

b. Egbert, a "rich brewer" and Anna (SR Aegidii 1539, vol. 1, fol. 16v)

c. Anna Rodde, daughter of Goddert (no. 116) and Gertrud Schmitjohan

d. 1/ Anna (+1588) = Dr. jur. Goddert Torck

2/ Goddert = Agnes Vendt (Test. I, no. 523) daughter of Heinrich (no. 142)

II   a. clothier; partner of Johann Langermann (no. 86)

III   a. 1565–66 Ziegelherr, 1567–69, 71, 86 Sterbherr, 1572, 76–77, 82–85 Gruetherr, 1574, 79–81 Richtherr

145) VOSS, Bertold
I   c. Elsa
        d. Elsa = Evert Werninck, shopkeeper
II   a. furrier
        b. Aegidii, Rothenburg
III   a. 1557–61
        b. KG Aegidii 1554, 55, 65, 67, 70
        c. Mesterlude 1555 (Krumbholtz, 41)
        d. provisor of Aegidii 1549, 51

146) WARENDORP, Boldewin, zu Nevinghof   patrician
I   a. +1621
        b. Johann (no. 148) and Elizabeth v. Knehem
        c. Gudula Alheid v. Bael
II   c. see no. 148
III   a. 1581, 85–86, 88–91 Kinderhausherr, 1593–97 Gruetherr, 1598–1600
        Kämmerer, 1601 Hospitalherr, 1602–04 Gruetherr, 1605–21
        Kämmerer; did not want to serve at first (RP, 1581 V/6, vol. 13, fols.
        30–30v)

147) WARENDORP, Heinrich   patrician
I   b. Heinrich, Bürgermeister 1464–66, 82 (Aders, WZ 110, 68)
        f. Johann (no. 148)
III   a. 1522, 1547–54 (Aders, 73; Kerssenbroch, 949)
        b. elector of KG in 1555
        e. paid taxes and raised feudal levy for episcopal army in 1534 together
        with his brother Johann (GQBM VIII, 16 & 93)
IV   a. Catholic

148) WARENDORP, Johann, zu Nevkinghof   patrician
I   b. Heinrich, Bürgermeister 1464–66, 82 (Aders)
        c. Elizabeth von Knehem (Test. I, no. 415)
        d. 1/ Hermann (+before 1576)
           2/ Boldewin (no. 146)
           3/ 6 daughters, of whom 4 became nuns
II   b. Lamberti, Salzstrasse
        c. house on Salzstr., house "Nevkinghof," 2 fields at Korkamp, 2 gardens
        outside Mauritz and Servatii Gates; total wealth over 4,000 dalers
III   a. 1536–?
        e. see no. 147
IV   a. Catholic

149) WEDEMHOVE, Christian
I   a. 1530–95 (Test. I, no. 427)
        b. Hermann and Neisa Ossenbrügge
        c. Gertrud Jonas (+1611), daughter of Hermann (no. 74) & Gertrud Blo-
        men (Test. II, no. 242)
        d. 1/ Anna = Bernd Bonse, shopkeeper

     2/ Agnes = Gograf Bernd Huge

     3/ Johann (no. 151)

     4/ Katherina = Lic. Gerhard Kronenberg, assessor at Chamber and Ecclesiastical Courts

     5/ Klara = Lic. Anton Hontemb, assessor at Ecclesiastical Court and syndic of cathedral chapter

     6/ Christian, clothier, KG Ludgeri 1602, 12 = Elizabeth Huge

     7/ Gertrud = Bernd van Oeseden (no. 103)

     8/ Hermann, student in Cologne, nominated to the pastorate at Venne by city council, died of the plague

   f. 1/ Johann (no. 150) = Katherina Pael

     2/ Maria = Wilbrand Plönies (no. 113)

     3/ Anna = Heinrich v. Oeseden

     4/ Klara = Heinrich Vendt (no. 142)

     5/ Margaretha = Wilhelm v. Oeseden

II   a. clothier

     b. Lamberti, Prinzipalmarkt

     c. assessed 3 dalers in 1568 Lamberti tax, house worth 1,400 dalers in 1595 (*QFGSM* IX, 50), house "Ruhr" outside Münster, 2 camps, total wealth ca. 3,000 dalers

III   a. 1582–85 Ziegelherr, 1586, 88–90 Sterbherr, 1591–95 Gruetherr

     b. KG Ludgeri 1565, 70, 75, 79

     c. Mesterlude 1566–76, Alderman 1577–81 (Krumbholtz 30*ff., 42ff.)

     d. provisor of Saint Lambert's 1568–69, 71, 74 (*QFGSM* IX, 47; PfA Lamberti, Urk. 39, 42)

IV   a. Catholic

150) WEDEMHOVE, Johann

I   a. +1584

     b. Hermann and Neisa Ossenbrügge

     c. Katherina Pael, daughter of Bernd and Katherina Dreier

     d. 1/ Hermann (+1586) = Anna Höfflinger, daughter of Christoph (no. 66) and Ursula Joddeveld (Test. I, no. 417)

     2/ Heinrich, magistrate in Lübeck

     3/ Johann (+1603) = Margaretha zur Heide (Test. II, no. 38)

     4/ Agnes (+1605) = Werner Langermann

     5/ Anna = Bernd v. Detten (no. 36)

     6/ Katherina = Johann Grave

   f. see no. 149

II   a. clothier

     b. Lamberti, Prinzipalmarkt

     c. assessed 5 dalers for several houses in 1568 Lamberti tax (*QFGSM* IX, 50)

III   a. 1556–64? 1565–66 Sterbherr, 1567–69, 71–81 Gruetherr

     d. 1556–65 provisor of Speckproven at Saint Lambert's

IV   a. Catholic

151) WEDEMHOVE, Johann
I   a. 1566–1613
    b. Christian (no. 149) and Gertrud Jonas
    c. 1591 with Elizabeth Erckelenz, daughter of Veit E. secretary of the Münster chancery, protonotary of the Chamber Court, and KG Lamberti 1580, 92
    d. 1/ Christian
       2/ Gertrud
       3/ other children died young
II   a. clothier, left his business in 1610
III a. 1610 Ziegelherr, 1611–13 Bierherr
    b. KG Ludgeri 1603, 05, 09, Lamberti 1607
    c. Mesterlude 1596, 1600–01
IV a. Catholic
VI composer of the family chronicle (*Westfalen* 40)

152) WERNIKE, Johann
I   a. 1550–1615
    c. Anna van Guelich (+1616), daughter of Arnold (no. 56) and Klara Elverfeld
    d. 1/ Hermann, canon at Saint Martin's
       2/ Arnold, wine merchant
       3/ Gertrud = Johann van Detten
       4/ Klara = Heinrich Deiterman
       5/ Johann, guild master of bakers, magistrate 1628–45
II   a. baker
    b. Martini, am Hörstertor
III a. 1601–04 Ziegelherr, 1605–10 Kapellenherr
    b. KG Martini 1587, 89, 91, 94, 96, 98

153) WYCK (Wieck), Christian van der   patrician
I   a. 1497–1576
    b. Bernhard, II and Anna Kerckerinck
    c. Christina von Freytag
    d. 1/ Melchior, Dr. jur., assessor at Reichskammergericht, = Anna v. Aldenbocken
       2/ bastard Konrad, notary = Maria Meyering
    f. 1/ Thomas (no. 154)
       2/ Anna, nun
       3/ Wendela
       4/ Bernhard, elector of KG in 1555
       5/ Agatha
       6/ Engelbert
       7/ Franz, Lic., bailiff at Bocholt
II   b. Lamberti, Alter Steinweg
    c. assessed 5 dalers for houses in 1568 Lamberti tax (*QFGSM* IX, 52); held fiefs from the bishop and from Überwasser Convent

III a. 1559–60 Bürgermeister, syndic of the city, represented Münster in 1562 Hansatag in Lübeck, and Drittelstage in Cologne, 1556, 57, 61, and Wesel 1564

V b. Doctorate of Law

VI see W. Moorrees's genealogical study

154) WYCK, Thomas van der   patrician

I a. +1559

   b. Bernhard, II and Anna Kerckerinck

   c. Katherina Droste, daughter of Johann D. zu Vehoff

   d. 1/ Bernhard IV

      2/ Gertrud, nun

      3/ Thomas, canon at Buschof

      4/ Anna, nun at Rengering

      5/ Katherina, nun at Aegidii

      6/ Christian II

   f. see no. 153

II c. house "Rüschhaus," later house "Vehoff"; held fiefs from Überwasser cloister

III a. 1545–54 (StdAM, AII, 1, fol. 9v and Kerssenbroch, 949)

   b. elector of KG in 1555

   e. paid taxes for the episcopal army in 1534 (*QFGSM* VIII, 11)

IV a. Catholic

155) WILCKINGHOFF, Andreas

I a. +1609

   c. Anna Holtebur

   d. 1/ Gertrud = Heinrich Elbrecht

      2/ Werner

      3/ Johann, notary = Katherina Crane

      4/ Katherina = Bernhard Greving, lawyer

II a. goldsmith, joined guild in 1583 guild master in 1598 (Krumbholtz, 244)

   b. Lamberti, Salzstrasse

III a. 1601 Ziegelherr, 1602–04 Kapellenherr, 1605–08 Sterbherr, 1609 Stuhlherr

   b. KG Ludgeri 1584, 91, 95, 97, 99

IV a. Lutheran (see appendix 4, no. 35)

APPENDIX TWO

The Jesuits in Münster, 1588–1618

The Jesuits are grouped into different ranks according to their service in Münster before 1618; thus, someone who was a novice in Münster and went on to become magister or priest after 1618 would be placed under category D and not B or C. For Jesuits whose places of origin correspond to names of citizens in Münster, I have indicated their possible ties to Münster thus: "Münsteraner?" The years given refer to years in which they were named in the sources and do not imply definitive tenures in Münster.

SOURCES

(1) LASJ = Litterae Annuae Societatis Jesu
(2) Comp. = "Compendium Historiae Collegii Monasteriensis Societatis Jesu, 1588–1618," StAM, FM, SFG, I. Loc. 8, no. 1a
(3) Duhr = Bernhard Duhr, *Geschichte der Jesuiten in den Ländern deutscher Zunge,* vols. 1 & 2
(4) ARSJ, Rh. Inf. = Litterae Annuae of the College of Münster (manuscripts), Archivum Romanum Societatis Jesu, Provincia Rhenana Inferiora 48
(5) Sökeland = Bernhard Sökeland, *Geschichte des Münsterschen Gymnasium von dem Übergang desselben an die Jesuiten im Jahre 1588 bis 1630* (Münster, 1826)
(6) SFG = "Testamente, Schenkungen der Jesuitenpatrum," StAM, FM, SFG, II. Loc. 6
(7) Hist Coll. Mon. = "Historia Collegii Monasteriensis Westphaliae," StAM, MSS. VII, 1026, 1
(8) Test. I & II = StdAM, B, Testamente I (sixteenth century) II (seventeenth century)

A. RECTORS

1588–1595 PETER MICHAEL, alias BRILLMACHER (1542–95). Native of Cologne, entered Society in 1573. Confessor to Duke Johann Wilhelm of Jülich-Cleve before serving as rector in Münster (Sökeland, 86–88; Duhr, I, 149–54; ARSJ, Rh. Inf. 48, 1595, fol. 49)
1595–1601 GISBET NIERBACH. Later rector of Jesuit College in Bonn 1604–06 (Duhr, II:1, 125, n. 3)
1601–1605 JOHANN COPPER. Later provincial of the Lower Rhine Province (SFG, nos. 20 & 72; Comp., fol.32v). 1608–16, rector of College in Cologne;

1616–24, provincial of the Lower Rhine Province; 1624–26, rector of College in Speyer; 1626–30, provincial of Upper Rhine Province (Duhr, I, 17, n. 3; 22, n. 5; 172, n. 1; 143, n. 2)

1605–1617 HERMANN BOSENDORF, Münsteraner, (1566–1623). Entered Society in 1588. His parents were Matthew B. and Gertrude Kerckerinck, sister of Freigraf Johann Kerckerinck, patrician. Served in Mainz before 1603 (Comp., fol. 28v); after 1617, he was rector of the university at Mainz and Provincial of the Lower Rhine Province (Sökeland, 89–90; SFG, III. Loc. I, no. 3)

B. PRIESTS

ARWILER, Reinert. 1588 (Hist. Coll. Mon. , fol. 9v)

ASCHENDORF, Wilhelm. Born in Telgte, entered Society in 1605, consecrated in 1626. Served as cathedral preacher in Münster, Trier, Osnabrück, and Paderborn, died in 1633 (Sökeland, 91f., Comp., fol. 52)

BAUMEISTER, Johann. Cologne 1613, Münster 1615, Fulda 1616 (Duhr, II:1, 23; Comp., fols. 76v, 80v)

CLEVER, Adolf. Münsteraner? Münster 1617 (Comp. fol. 87v) 1624 rector of College in Heiligenstadt; 1634, rector of College in Bamberg (Duhr, II:1, 155, n. 3; 169, n. 1)

DAMBROCH, N. 1616 (Comp., fol. 79v)

DRUFFEL, Otto. 1615 (Comp., fol. 76v)

DUERING, Johann. 1605–? (Comp., fol. 32; LASJ 1605, 323); studied at the Collegium Germanicum (LASJ 1612, 323)

ELVERICH, Heinrich. Born in Emmerich, entered Society in 1602, sent from Münster to Cologne in 1618, died in 1636 (Sökeland, 92f.)

FULLER, Johann. 1605–18 in Münster; his father Johann senior was secretary of the Paderborn cathedral chapter (SFG, no. 26; Comp., fol. 34)

GISEBOL, Hubert. Sent from Münster to Vechta in 1616; 1630s in Fulda (Comp., fol. 81v; Duhr, II:1, 410)

HAISIUS, Peter. From Belgium, 1588 in Münster (Hist. Coll. Mon., fol. 10v)

HAMBACH, Franz. Accompanied Rector Peter Michael to Münster 1588 (Duhr, I, 146)

HÖFFLINGER, Balthasar. Münsteraner; his parents were Christoph H., magistrate, and Ursula Joddeveld (see appendix 1, no. 66); entered Society before 1599 and served most of his life in Münster (SFG, no. 37; StdAM Test. I, no. 113)

HONGER, Konrad. Münster 1588 (Hist. Coll. Mon., fol. 9v)

HUMMEL, Rudolf. Münsteraner, entered Society in 1606; magister in 1613, consecrated in 1616? (SFG, no. 44; Comp., fols. 36, 65v); rector of College in Siegen, 1626–29 (Duhr, II:1, 98, n. 3)

LEMMIG, Gottfried. Münster 1615; sent to Fulda in 1616; rector of Jesuit College in Fulda, 1617–22 (Comp., fols. 74v, 80v; Duhr, II:1, 160, n. 5)

LOTZ (Lotsius), Johann. From 1604 in Münster; rector of College in Emmerich, 1617–24 (Comp., fol. 30; Duhr, II:1, 71, n. 5)

MANGOLDT, Laurenz. 1607 (Comp., fol. 40)

MORENHOVE, Reinert. Active in Münster from the founding of the College until his death in 1616; entered the Society in 1579 (Comp., fol. 80; ARSJ, Rh. Inf. 48 1616, fol. 203v)

OTTEN, Konrad. Münster 1613; missionary in Meppen, 1615 (Comp., fol. 62; Duhr, II:1, 60)

POLET, Nicolaus. From Paderborn; Münster 1588 (Hist. Coll. Mon., fol. 9)

PRECKWIN, Heinrich. Münsteraner; his parents were Heinrich P. and Elsa Buerman (Test. II, no. 1419, fols. 89–89v); magister in 1604, priest in 1613 (Comp., fol. 62; SFG, no. 70)

RAESFELD, Nicolaus. Münsteraner; his parents were the printer Lambert R. and Anna Dorhoff. Entered Society in 1615 (Comp., fol. 75; SFG, no. 72)

RISSEN, Georg. Münster 1607–15? Meppen 1615–? (Comp., fol. 39; Duhr, II:1, 60f.)

ROTTHAUSEN, Heinrich. Münster 1607–18; frequent missions to Hamburg; rector of College in Hildesheim, 1618–20; professor at Paderborn College after 1621 (Comp., fols. 39, 40; Duhr, II:1, 34, n. 1; 136, 401, 587)

RUST, Peter. 1613 (Comp., fol. 65v)

RYSWICK, Jakob. Native of Neumagen; preacher in Münster College, 1588–1601; thereafter, he served as confessor to Count Johann von Rietberg and worked in the county and in East Friesland (Sökeland, 62, 89; Duhr, II:1, 23, 46, 62; Hist. Coll. Mon., fol. 9v)

RYSWICK, Theodor. Worked in Emmerich, Kleve, and Xanten, 1606–10; Münster, 1615; Meppen, after 1615 (Comp., fol. 76v; Duhr, II:1, 57, 65, 69–70, 72; II:2, 37f., 189)

SANDER, Walter. From Cologne; Münster 1588–1612; sent in 1612 to Hildesheim (Hist. Coll. Mon., fol. 9; Comp., fol. 59v)

TACHSONIUS, Johann. Münster 1611; Düsseldorf, 1622 (Comp., fol. 52; Duhr, II:1, 82)

TOXITES, Melchior. Born 1557 in Cologne; Münster 1588–90; mission to Halberstadt, 1590–91; Fulda, 1594 (Hist. Coll. Mon., fol. 9; Sökeland, 62; Duhr, I, 418, 427–28, 459)

UPHAUS, Heinrich. Münster 1613–25; missions to Meppen, 1613 to Warendorf, 1625; superior of Jesuit house in Osnabrück, 1625–26 (Comp., fol. 65; Duhr, II:1, 55, 57, 85, 89, n. 7)

WACHTENDONCK, Friedrich. From Westphalian nobility; Münster 1615; sent to Emsland; active in Paderborn, 1601–1630s (Comp., fol. 73v; Duhr, II:1, 38, 43, 402–03)

WITTFELD, Peter. Münsteraner? His kinsmen were a brother Bernhard and a brother-in-law Heinrich Stücker; he was possibly the son of the city syndic Lic. Heinrich Wittfeld. Entered Society in 1610; consecrated in 1613 (Comp., fols. 48v, 63; SFG, no. 105)

ZUM KLEY, Sebastian. Münsteraner; entered Society in 1596; related to the Modersohns, a rich butcher family (SFG, no. 110)

C. MAGISTERS AND COADJUTORS

ALDENHOVE, Johann. 1614 magister; sent to Mainz (Comp., fol. 70v)

ALERDINCK, Bernd. Münsteraner; entered Society in March 1593; his parents were Hermann A. and Metten Mersmann; served in Paderborn, 1620–22 (SFG, no. 2; Duhr, II:1, 401, II:2, 146)

AVANT, Nicolaus. 1610–11, magister (Comp., fols. 48v, 52)

BIKSE, Johann. 1613 (Comp., fol. 65v)

BORCKELVE, N. Native of Paderborn; entered Society in 1617 (Comp., fol. 87)

BROCKIN, Egbert. 1606 (Comp., fol. 34v)

BRAND, Kaspar. Münster 1614–? Sent to Minden to help restore Catholicism in 1629 (Comp., fols. 70v, 81v; Duhr, II:1, 126f.)

BUNGART, Heinrich. Sent to Cologne in 1618 (Comp., fol. 89)

CASSING, Nicolaus. Münster 1617 (Comp., fol. 87v)

CLUTE (Cloeth), Gottfried. Münsteraner; from magisterial family; his father was Dr. Christoph Clute (+1603) and his stepmother was Anna Ubelgunne (Test. II, no. 793); he served as magister in Münster in 1608 but was soon dismissed from the Society because of poor health; died in 1610 as a student of theology in Mainz (SFG, no. 21; Comp., fol. 44v; see also appendix 1, no. 34)

DIKIRCH, Heinrich. 1606 (Comp., fol. 34v)

FABER, Nithard. 1610–11, magister (Comp., fols. 48v, 52)

FRENCKING, Johann. Native of Horstmar; novice in 1606; magister in 1613; rector of College in Hildesheim, 1630–34; at Paderborn College, 1628, 1636 (Comp., fols. 36, 65v; Duhr, II:1, 34. n. 1; 43, n. 4)

HAKE, Johann. Born in Haselünne; entered Society in 1617; sent to Trier (Comp., fol. 87)

HANTRAN, Wilhelm. 1610–11, magister (Comp., fols. 48v, 52)

HAUSBRANDT, Johann. Münster 1616; Halberstadt, 1639; rector of College in Koblenz, 1646–50 (Comp., fol. 82; Duhr, II:1, 31, n. 13, 37)

HEERDE, Johann. Münsteraner, from magisterial family; he served as magister in Münster in 1608 (Comp., fol. 44v); subsequent work probably in Trier and Düsseldorf (SFG, no. 32)

HEIMANN, Heinrich. 1610–11, magister (Comp., fols. 48v, 52)

HERTING, Johann. Born in Grossendorf near Fulda (1564–1614); entered Society in 1583; active in Münster for many years; died in Molsheim (Sökeland, 88f.)

HOLTAPPEL, Albert. Münsteraner, from magisterial family; magister in 1615; sent in 1627 to begin a new congregation in Coesfeld (Comp., fol. 76v; Duhr, II:1, 103)

HOVEL, Cornelius. Münsteraner? Magister in 1617 (Comp., fol. 87v)

HUGE, Hermann. Münsteraner, his parents were the merchant Bernhard Huge and Margaretha zur Lippe. A canon at Xanten, he entered the Society in 1607 and became priest in 1621 (Comp., fol. 38v; SFG, no. 43; see also StdAM, AII, 20, RP Nov. 21, 1603, vol. 35. fols. 159–159v)

HULS, Theodor. 1611 magister (Comp., fol. 52)

KALCKOVEN, Matthaeus. Magister 1616; superior of Jesuits in Stade 1629–32; superior of Jesuits in Siegen and Minden 1632; rector of College in Hildesheim, 1643–44 (Comp., fol. 82; Duhr, II:1, 34, n. 1, 98, n. 3, 128, n. 1, 130, n. 1)

KESTEN, Johann. 1616 (Comp., fol. 82)

KIRCHNER, Felix. 1616–17 (Comp., fols. 82, 87v)

KNEHEM, Caspar. He probably belonged to a noble family; related to Joanne von Knehem, canoness of Saint Mary in Cologne (see appendix 3, no. 11); a cousin was Nasa Timmermann; Münster 1605 (Comp., fol. 33; Test. II, no. 40, fol. 217v)

KÖRLER, Gottfried. Münsteraner, son of magistrate and wine merchant Johann; entered Society in 1617 and was sent to Trier (Comp., fol. 87; SFG, no. 51, fol. 56; see also appendix 1, no. 83)

LANDARTT, N. 1607 (Comp., fol. 40)

MANGETHIR, Joseph. Native of Lorraine; died 1611 in Münster (Comp., fols. 48v, 52v–53; LASJ 1611, 551)

MARQUERDING, Arnold. 1614 coadjutor (Comp., fol. 70v)

MISSING (Messing), Johann. Born in Senden, just outside of Münster; his parents were the notary Johann M. and Elizabeth Lennep. Entered Society in 1617; sent to Trier (Comp., fol. 87; SFG, II. Loc. 9, no. 32; Test. II, no. 1505)

MICHAEL, Heinrich. 1611 magister (Comp., fol. 52)

MODERSOHN, Heinrich. Münsteraner; the Modersohns were leading butcher families and sat on the city council. Magister, 1617–18; active in Heiligenstadt (Comp., fol. 89)

MÜLLER, Johann. 1610 (Comp., fol. 48v)

NUNNINCK, Hermann. Münsteraner; entered Society in 1607; magister in 1613 (Comp., fols. 38v, 65v)

OTTERSTEDT, Gottfried. Münsteraner; from leading guild family. Entered Society in 1617; sent to Trier; Aachen, 1638; provincial of the Lower Rhine Province, 1646–50 (Comp., fol. 87; Duhr, II:1, 17, n. 3; 80, n. 3)

RATING (Ratinger), Konrad. Native of Erfurt; Münster, 1588–? Rector of College in Trier, 1597 (Sökeland, 62; Hist. Coll. Mon., fol. 10v; Duhr, I, 99, n. 4)

SCHEIPER, Hermann. Münsteraner; entered Society in 1617 (Comp., fol. 87)

SCHEVER, Theodor. 1606 coadjutor (Comp., fol. 34v)

SCHLUNDER, Georg. Native of Werl; Münster, 1596–? (SFG, no. 87)

SCHOLBROCK, Heinrich. Münsteraner, his parents were Bernd S., wine merchant and magistrate, and Katherina Körler; dismissed from Society in 1608 because of poor health; later canon at Saint Ludger's (Comp., fol. 44v; see also appendix 1, no. 120)

SCHÜLTMANN, Gerhard. Münsteraner, 1614 magister (Comp., fol. 70v)

SILLING, Theodor. Münsteraner, his mother was Veronica. 1606, coadjutor; gave his inheritance to Münster College in 1625 (Comp., fol. 34v; SFG, no. 87)

STADTBROCH, N. 1607 magister (Comp., fol. 40)

STEIL, Johann. Native of Nuremberg; Münster, 1604–? Dismissed from Society and became parish priest in Coesfeld; he continued to collaborate with the Jesuits in re-catholicizing Coesfeld (Comp., fol. 30; Duhr II:1, 102f.; see also Offenberg, II, 33)

THEBEN, Johann. Münsteraner, his parents were Georg T. and Anna Palsering; Münster, 1614–15 (Test. II, no. 1740)

WIRSING, Sebestian. 1588 (Hist. Coll. Mon., fol. 9v)

ZOIA, Albert. 1610 coadjutor; later served in Landshut (Comp., fol. 48v; Duhr, II:1, 429)

D. NOVICES

BILLIUS, Peter. Münsteraner; 1607 (Comp., fol. 38v)

BOENING, Albert. 1614 (Comp., fol. 70v)

FLECK, Johann. Accepted as novice in 1613; sent to Paderborn in 1617 (Comp., fols. 75, 84)

HALLENHORST, Johann. 1616 (Comp., fol. 83)

HALSEN, Theodor. 1616, sent to Paderborn (Comp., fol. 81v)

HARBUN, N. 1617, sent to Paderborn (Comp., fol. 84)

HULSO, Albert. 1617, sent to Paderborn; 1625–26, magister in Münster (Comp., fol. 84; Duhr, II:1, 589)

LANENLOTT, Bernhard. 1613 (Comp., fol. 64)

LANENLOTT, Hermann (alias Witton). Münsteraner? Entered Society in 1613 and served as magister in Münster, 1624 (Comp., fols. 64, 75; SFG, no. 54)

LENNEP, Christian. Münsteraner, his parents were Johann L., Guild Alderman and magistrate, and Katherina Heideman. Entered Society in 1605; rector of College in Paderborn, 1625–32; rector of College in Münster, 1636–42 (Comp., fol. 37v; Duhr, II:1, 43, n. 4, 52, n. 7; see also appendix 1, no. 88)

LIEBET, Jakob. Münsteraner; novice in 1607; Fulda, 1626; rector of College in Aschaffenburg, 1636–38 (Comp., fol. 38v; Duhr, II:1, 151, 624)

MATTENKLOET, Laurenz. Münster, 1617–35 (Comp., fol. 85; SFG, no. 57)

MEYNERS, Bernhard. 1613 (Comp., fol. 64)

MODERSOHN, Philip. Münsteraner; sent as novice to Paderborn in 1616 (Comp., fol. 81v)

MOLL, Thomas. 1614 (Comp., fol. 70v)

OSTHOFF, Werner. Sent as novice to Münster in 1617 (Comp., fol. 85)

REXING, Joseph. 1616, sent to Paderborn (Comp., fol. 81v)

ROTMANN, Paul. 1613 (Comp., fol. 64)

SCHOLVER, Ernst. 1615, magister, 1618 (Comp., fol. 73, 88v)

STEINWEG, Johann. 1614; rector of College in Trier, 1642–46 (Comp., fol. 70v; Duhr, II:1, 28, n. 1)

STILLE, Bernhard. Münsteraner, his brothers were Heinrich and Jakob; 1614 (Test. II, no. 1500; Comp., fol. 70v)

VOGELSANG, Johann. 1618 (Comp., fol. 89)

WERNER, Johann. Münster, 1618–38 (Comp., fol. 88v; SFG, no. 97)

WERNIKE, Hermann. Münsteraner, son of the baker and magistrate Johann W. (see appendix 1, no. 152) and Anna v. Guelich; dismissed in 1609 because of epilepsy and later canon at Saint Martin's (Comp., fol. 48)

APPENDIX THREE

Benefactors of the Münster Jesuits, 1588–1618

Documents of donations are deposited in the former archive of the Jesuit College, StAM, FM, SFG, II Loc. 7–III Loc. 1; no individual signatures are given below. Where other sources of documentation are available, they are indicated. The first entry after the name of the donor is the amount of bequest or gift; the second describes the position of the donor where information is available; the third entry identifies the sources other than the archival deposit indicated above. The abbreviations used here are the same as in appendix 1. An asterisk (*) marks those who had Jesuit kinsmen.

A. THE CLERGY

Women

1) BERSWORDT, Elizabeth von der
   i/ 1,000 dalers
   ii/ nun at Überwasser and daughter of Bürgermeister
   Johann (appendix 1, no. 7)
   iii/ Test. II, no. 612
2) BERSWORDT, Maria von der
   i/ 1,900 d.
   ii/ nun at Marienfeld, sister of no. 1
   iii/ Test. II, no. 913.
3) BODDING, Gertrud
   i/ 260 d.
4) BUCK, N
   i/ 30 d. ii/ patrician iii/ Comp., fol. 25
5) FRIE, Elizabeth
   i/ 1,720 d.
   ii/ daughter of Jobst F. zu Bödding and Anna Boland (no. 55)
   iii/ Comp., fol. 39
6) GRON, Catherina
   i/ 50 d. iii/ Comp., fol. 61v
7) HAMELHOLTE, Anna
   i/ 300 d. ii/ brother Johann H., goldsmith?
8) HAMM, Sibylla von
   i/ 10 d. iii/ Comp., fol. 58

9) HEERDE,* Klara
   i/ 100 d.
   ii/ daughter of Bürgermeister Hermann Heerde (appendix 1, no. 58)
   iii/ Comp., fol. 28
10) HERDING, Elizabeth
    i/ 1,700 d.
    ii/ nun at Marienfeld and daughter of magistrate
    Hermann H. & Anna Clute (appendix 1, no. 62)
11) VON KNEHEM,* Joanne
    i/ 100 d. ii/ canoness of Saint Mary in Cologne
    iii/ Comp., fol. 60v
12) MISSING,* Elizabeth
    i/ 1,800+ d.
    ii/ daughter of notary Johann Missing senior (no. 64)
    iii/ Comp., fols. 44v, 64, 80v
13) VON MOTTE, Maria Klara
    i/ 100 d.
    ii/ noblewoman; abbess of Benedictine convent in Essen
14) VON PLETTENBERG, Anna
    i/ ? ii/ noblewoman iii/ Comp., fol. 68
15) SCHENCKINCK, Anna
    i/ 50 d. ii/ patrician iii/ Comp., fols. 65, 79
16) SCHEDELICH, N
    i/ 50 d. ii/ noblewoman iii/ Comp., fol. 53v
17) SCHOLVER, Anna
    i/ 50 d.
    ii/ daughter of Münster Chancellor Dr. Scholver?
    iii/ Comp., fols. 59v, 79, 83–83v
18) SWARTZ, Catherina
    i/ 100+ d. ii/ noblewoman
    iii/ Comp., fols. 18, 32, 43, 58
19) WESTENDORP, Ursula
    i/ all her possessions
    ii/ her brother Lambert was physician to the prince
    of Arburg in the Spanish army

Men

20) ARRESDORFF, Nicolaus
    i/ 100 d.
    ii/ Franciscan, pastor at Saint Lambert's, suffragan bishop
    iii/ Comp., fol. 88
21) VON ASCHEBROCK, Werner
    i/ ? ii/ cathedral canon at Münster
    iii/ Comp., fol. 51v
22) BIDDERWANT, Hermann
    i/ 300 d. ii/ vicar at Münster Cathedral

23) BRABECK, Engelbert
   i/ 1,100 d. ii/ cathedral canon at Münster
   iii/ Comp., fol. 59
24) BUCKELTHE, Heinrich
   i/ 60 d. ii/ priest
25) VON BÜREN, Arnold
   i/ 50 d. ii/ cathedral canon at Münster
   iii/ Comp., fol. 43
26) Cappenberg Cloister, prefect of
   i/ 100 d. iii/ Comp., fol. 9
27) VAN DETTEN, Johann
   i/ 2,000 d.
   ii/ canon of Old Cathedral, son of magistrate Bernd van Detten senior (appendix 1, no. 35)
   iii/ Comp., fol. 88
28) DROSTE, Everwin
   i/ 50 d. ii/ dean of Saint Martin's
29) DROSTE, Franz
   i/ 1,150 d. ii/ son of no. 28, priest
   iii/ Comp., fol. 34
30) FABRITIUS, Matthaeus
   i/ 600 d. ii/ pastor at Osnabrück Cathedral
   iii/ Comp., fol. 61
31) GERLACH, Conrad
   i/ ? iii/ Comp., fol. 72.
32) Iburg Cloister, abbot of
   i/ 50 d. iii/ Comp., fol. 9
33) LEDEBUIR, N
   i/ ? ii/ cathedral canon at Osnabrück
   iii/ Litt. Ann., 1588ff.
34) LUDEKING, Ludolph
   i/ 16 d. ii/ dean of Überwasser
35) MISSING,* Christopher
   i/ 1,100 d. ii/ son of no. 64
36) MOWEN, Bernd
   i/ 100 d. ii/ vicar at Saint Martin's
   iii/ Comp., fol. 36
37) SCHENCKINCK, N
   i/ 21 d. ii/ patrician iii/ Comp., fols. 51, 53
38) SCHMISINCK, Bernd
   i/ 50 d. ii/ cathedral canon at Münster
39) SCHOLBROCK, Heinrich (see also appendix 2)
   i/ ? ii/ canon at Saint Ludger's iii/ Comp., fol. 70v
40) TIMPE, Matthaeus
   i/ 2,200 d. ii/ rector of Collegium Dettensiam
41) TRAVELMANN, Bernd
   i/ 20 d. ii/ patrician and canon at Saint Ludger's

42) ZUM SANDE, Georg
i/ 150 d. ii/ chaplain at Saint Lambert's
iii/ Comp., fol. 84v

B. THE LAITY

Nobility

43) GRONHUISS, N
i/ 300 d. iii/ Comp., fol. 49
44) BILLERBECK, the lord of
i/ 1,000 d. iii/ Comp., fol. 89
45) HAITZFELD, Melchior
i/ 20 d.
46) KETTELER, Konrad
i/ 150 d. iii/ Test. I, no. 385; Comp., fol. 57
47) OSTHOFF, Hermann
i/ 625 d. iii/ Comp., fols. 46. 55v, 60
48) OVERLACKER, N
i/ 100 d. ii/ commander iii/ Comp., fol. 61v
49) VON DER RECK, N
i/ 100 d. iii/ Comp., fol. 8v
50) RIETBERG, the count of
i/ 200 d. iii/ Litt. Ann., 1601, 619
51) SCHEDELICH, Alheid
i/ 50 d. iii/ Test. II, no. 72
52) VELEN, Gertrud
i/ 100 d. iii/ Comp., fol. 34v
53) WOLFF, Bernharda
i/ 100 d.
ii/ widow of Dietrich von Galen and mother of the future prince-bishop Christoph Bernhard
iii/ Comp., fol. 61v; Test. II, no. 439

The Civic Elite

54) BERSWORDT, Johann v. d.
i/ 100 d.
ii/ Bürgermeister Münster (see appendix 1, no. 7)
iii/ Comp., fol. 9v
55) BOLAND, Anna
i/ 10 d.
ii/ widow of Jobst Frie, mother of no. 5
iii/ Comp., fol. 71v
56) EVERHARD, Dr.
i/ 40 d. iii/ Comp., fol. 17v
57) FRIE, Anna

i/ 500 d.

ii/ wife of Wolter Plönies, son of Hillbrand (see appendix 1, no. 109)

iii/ Comp., fols. 57v, 70v

58) HÖFFLINGER,* Christoph

i/ 1,000 d.

ii/ magistrate (appendix 1, no. 66)

iii/ Test. I, no. 113

59) KERCKERINCK,* Gertrud

i/ 1,420 d.

ii/ widow of Matthaeus and mother of Hermann Bosendorf, S.J. (see appendix 2)

60) KERCKERINCK, Johann zu Angelmodde

i/ 40 d.

ii/ patrician and magistrate (appendix 1, no. 78)

iii/ Comp., fol. 54

61) KERCKERINCK, Matthaeus zu Stapel

i/ 50 d. ii/ patrician

62) KLEINSORGEN, Gerhard

i/ 50 d. ii/ judge in Werl

63) KLEINSORGEN, Ursula

i/ 200 d.

ii/ wife of Herbolt v. Giessmar, Bürgermeister of Wartburg

64) MISSING,* Johann senior

i/ ?

ii/ notary and father of nos. 12 & 35

iii/ Test. II, no. 1505

65) MODERSOHN, N., widow of

i/ 125 d. iii/ Comp., fol. 47

66) PLÖNIES, Engela

i/ 100 d. iii/ Comp., fol. 55

67) RAHM,* Margaretha

i/ all her properties

68) SANDER, Theodor

i/ 200 d.

ii/ assessor at Ecclesiastical Court and magistrate in 1632

iii/ Comp., fol. 63v

69) SCHOLVER, Theodor, and wife

i/ 120 d.

ii/ chancellor of Münster territorial government

iii/ Comp., fols. 29v, 57v

70) SMITHUES, N., widow of

i/ 50 d. iii/ Comp., fol. 57v

71) VENDT, Heinrich

i/ 220 d.

ii/ Bürgermeister Münster (appendix 1, no. 142)

iii/ Comp., fols. 20v, 22, 28v

72) VOSS, Hermann, and wife Elizabeth Vinhagen
   i/ 35 d. ii/ lawyer iii/ Test. II, no. 730
73) VOSS, Katherina
   i/ 100 d. iii/ Test. II, no. 1932
74) WITTFELD, Heinrich
   i/ 40 d. ii/ syndic of the city of Münster
   iii/ Comp., fol. 48
75) WITTFELD, Johann
   i/ 9 d. ii/ from Coesfeld iii/ Comp., fol. 59v

Bürgers

76) BIERS, Swer
   i/ 50 d.
77) BODDING, Elsa
   i/ 10 d. iii/ Comp., fols. 60v, 88
78) DREIHAUSE, Anna
   i/ 50 d. ii/ wife of goldsmith Heinrich Isermann
   iii/ Test. II, no. 683
79) FRANCKE, Johann
   i/ 50 d. ii/ notary iii/ Test. II, no. 1457
80) GRONINGEN, Anna von
   i/ 200 d. iii/ Comp., fol. 58v
81) HOYMAN, Katherina
   i/ 5 d. iii/ Test. I, no. 387
82) KNEHEM,★ N. widow of
   i/ ? iii/ Comp., fol. 33
83) LIPPE, Johann zu
   i/ 50 d. iii/ Comp., fol. 34v
84) OLDEN, Catherina van
   i/ 100 d. iii/ Comp., fol. 60
85) PALSERING,★ Anna
   i/ ? ii/ widow of Georg Theben, son Jesuit
   iii/ Test. II, no. 1740
86) PERESELIUS, Adrian
   i/ 100 d.
87) PRECKWIN,★ Heinrich
   i/ 500 d. ii/ son Jesuit iii/ Test. II, no. 1419
88) REIMENSNEIDER, Elizabeth
   i/ 100 d. iii/ Comp., fol. 68
89) RHEME, N, widow of
   i/ ? iii/ Comp., fol. 55v
90) RUPE, Judith
   i/ 25 d. iii/ Comp., fol. 66v
91) SCHLOET, Christopher zum, and Elizabeth Kemner
   i/ 200 d. iii/ Test. II, no. 34

92) STILLE,* Heinrich
   i/ ? iii/ Test. II, no. 1500
93) STÜCKER, woman
   i/ 100 d.
94) TEGEDER, N, Lic.
   i/ 20 d. iii/ Comp., fol. 68
95) TIMMERMANN, Nasa*
   i/ ? ii/ widow of Jobst Dininckhove
   iii/ Test. II, no. 40
96) TIMPE, Catherina
   i/ 1,400 d. ii/ sister of no. 40

OTHERS

97) RECKLINGHAUSEN, city council of
   i/ ? iii/ Comp., fol. 14

APPENDIX FOUR

Protestants in Münster, 1560–1620

A. LUTHERANS AND CALVINISTS

1) BEIFANG, Johann Lic. (1562–1620)
   Family: father, Freigraf in Burgsteinfurt; wife, Gertrud Ozens, a Münsteraner, marriage and citizenship in 1602 (Hövel, *BB*, No. 1072)
   Office: see appendix 1, no. 5
   Denounced by the parish clergy for having never communicated (*QFSGM* IX, p. 37); called Calvinist by the Jesuits (Comp., fol. 38v)

2) BERNING, Peter
   Family: father Heinrich and mother Alheit Hundestegge; wife, Richtmot Potken, daughter of furrier and Guild Alderman Johann P.
   Office: see appendix 1, no. 6
   Denounced by Jesuits as Lutheran (Comp., fols. 71v, 78v)

3) BLOCCIUS, Johann
   Schoolmaster at the Saint Martin's parish school
   Dismissed by the clergy for his Protestant beliefs (RP, 1582 IV 5, vol. 14, fols. 16v–17v)

4) BLOCK, Johann Lic. (1562–1610)
   Family: father, Johann, emigrated from Horstmar (Hövel, *BB*, no. 78); wife, Elske Hesseling from Warendorf, marriage in 1597 (*BB*, no. 1377)
   Office: see appendix 1, no. 17
   Denounced by the parish clergy for having never communicated (*QFGSM*, IX, p. 37); Calvinist

5) BOGGEL, Wilbrand (+1606)
   Occupation: shopkeeper
   Burial forbidden by Lamberti pastor (RP, 1606 IX 3, vol. 38, fols. 178v–179)

6) BOLAND, Goddert (Gottfried)
   Family: parents Johann B. and Alheid; wife, Margaretha Herding
   Office: see appendix 1, no. 21
   Denounced by Jesuits as Lutheran (Comp., fols. 71v, 78v)

7) BUERMEISTER, Ludolf
   Occupation: clothier
   Citizenship: 1597 "Bürgerkind" (Hövel, *BB*, no. 1365)
   Office: see appendix 1, no. 27
   Reported by the Jesuits as a leading Protestant (Comp., fol. 34)

8) BURMAN, Bernhard (+1621)

Occupation: guildmaster of shopkeepers
Office: see appendix 1, no. 28
Denounced by the parish clergy for having never communicated (*QFGSM* IX, p. 37)

9) BURMAN, Hermann (+1616)
Occupation: tailor journeyman
Burial forbidden by Martini clergy (RP, 1616 III 5, vol. 48, fol. 70)

10) CAPELLAEN, Bernd (+1587)
Schoolmaster at the gymnasium
Burial forbidden by Martini clergy (RP, 1587 XI 16, vol. 19, fol. 94)

11) DICKMANN, Heinrich
Occupation: guild master of the shopkeepers
Family: from Burgsteinfurt; wife, 1st: Elsa Forckenbeck (1586) (Hövel, *BB*, no. 671), 2nd: Anna Wilckinghoff, daughter of Andreas W. ?, 3rd: Catherina Hesseling (StdAM, AII, 5, 1608 I 10)
Office: see appendix 1, no. 37
Denounced by the clergy for having never communicated (*QFGSM* IX, p. 37); called Calvinist by the Jesuits (Comp., fol. 78v)

12) DOCHT, Werner (+1588)
Burial forbidden by the Martini clergy (RP, 1588 II 19, vol. 20, fol. 7)

13) FORCKENBECK, Heinrich (+1613)
Occupation: shopkeeper, joined guild in 1590 (Krumbholtz, p. 256)
Family: father, Aleke, immigrant from Deventer.
Office: KG Martini 1604
He served as witness for Katherina Hesseling of Warendorf, who obtained citizenship through marrying the guild Alderman Heinrich Dickmann (no. 11) in 1608 (Hövel, *BB*, no. 1900); the Forckenbecks, Dickmanns, and Stoltenkamps were related (Lahrkamp, *Geburtsbriefe*, no. 211)
Burial forbidden by the Lamberti clergy (RP, 1613 XI 12, vol. 45, fol. 456)

14) GREVINCK, [Johann?]
Occupation: fuller (Lahrkamp, *Geburtsbriefe*, no. 190)
Relative or close friend of Andreas Wilckinghoff and the Stoltenkamps (Hövel, *BB*, no. 596)
Denounced by the Jesuits as one of the instigators of the 1608 anti-Jesuit carnival (Comp., fol. 40v)

15) HOLTERMANN, Dietrich (+1605)
Journeyman from Nuremberg
Burial forbidden by Lamberti clergy (RP, 1605 XI 24/25, vol. 37, fols. 154v, 156–57)

16) HESSE, Christopher
Family: from Bremen, a clothmaker; he and his wife Anna Brantz came to Münster in 1580 (Hövel, *BB*, no. 449)
Occupation: guild master of furriers
Office: guild Alderman 1607; KG Lamberti 1602, 15, 21
Reportedly seen in the company of some Anabaptists in 1594 (RP, 1594 VIII 19, vol. 26, fol. 58v); denounced by the Jesuits as one of the ringleaders of the

1608 anti-Jesuit carnival (Comp., fol. 40v); denounced by the parish clergy for having never communicated (*QFGSM* IX, p. 37); Calvinist

17) HÖBELINCK, [Johann?]

Citizenship: 1603 (Hövel, *BB*, no. 1723)

Reported to have been a Calvinist merchant who defaulted on loans amounting to 23,000 dalers in 1611 (Comp., fol. 55v)

18) KÖPPELIN, Peter

Occupation: master of the city mint

Office: KG Lamberti 1592, 96, 99

One of the citizens who buried the Protestant procurator Dietrich Seveker (see no. 26) (Röchell, p. 129)

Burnt in 1599 for minting false coins (RP, 1599 XII 2, vol. 31, fols. 107v and 108a)

19) KÖRDING, Dietrich

Occupation: joined shopkeepers' guild in 1562 (Krumbholtz, p. 255); guild master in 1566

Office: KG Lamberti 1562, Martini 1574

Questioned by the city council for challenging the clergy to give Lutheran sermons (RP, 1566 IX 19, vol. 3, fols. 39v-41)

20) LAEKE, HANS (1550-161?)

Occupation: sculptor

Office: see appendix 1, no. 84

Denounced by the parish clergy for having never communicated (*QFGSM* IX, p. 37); called Calvinist by the Jesuits (Comp., fol. 52v)

21) MEINERTZ, Heinrich

Occupation: fuller

Office: see appendix 1, no. 90

Denounced by the parish clergy for having never communicated (*QFGSM* IX, p. 37)

22) NIEHUIS (Neuhaus), Johann

Schoolmaster at Saint Ludger's parish school

Questioned by the city council for using Lutheran texts (RP, 1571 XII 3, vol. 7, fol. 31v)

23) NIEHUIS (Neuhaus), Wilhelm (+1604)

Family: from Deventer, married Lobach's widow and obtained citizenship in 1572 (Hövel, *BB*, no. 183)

Occupation: clothier

Office: KG Ludgeri 1590, 94

His factors were fined by the magistrates for unloading wares on Sunday during church service (RP, 1599 VIII 2, vol. 31, fol. 75)

Described as Calvinist by the Jesuits (Comp., fol. 29v)

Burial forbidden by the Lamberti clergy (RP, 1604 III 25/26, vol. 36, fols. 22v-23v)

24) NUESEN, Roger

Burial forbidden by the clergy (RP, 1615 VII 20, vol. 47, fol. 261)

25) SCHWARTARNDT, Heinrich

Occupation: guild master of the bakers

Office: KG Ludgeri 1557, 68, Lamberti 1563, 70, 75, 78
See no. 16

26) SEVEKER, Dietrich (+1597)
Family: wife, Henrika Beckers
Occupation: procurator at the Chamber Court
Burial forbidden by Überwasser clergy (Röchell, *Chronik* pp. 128–29; RP, 1597 I 24, vol. 29, fol. 3v)

27) STEINHOFF, Melchior (+1606)
Family: father, Gert S., guild master of the tailors (Hövel, *BB*, no. 217); wife Christina Stummel married Bürgermeister Johann Köttich of Burgsteinfurt after Melchior's death (Test. II, no. 980)
Occupation: glassmaker, joined guild in 1587 (Krumbholtz, p. 349)
Office: see appendix 1, no. 124
Burial forbidden by Martini clergy (RP, 1606 XII 7, vol. 38, fol. 255v)

28) STEVENINCK zu Wilkinghegge, Everwin, widow of (Margaretha von Ledebur?)
Burial forbidden by Überwasser clergy (RP, 1611 IX 10/12, vol. 43, fols. 173–174v, 176; Cf. appendix 1, no. 126)

29) STOLTENKAMP, Severin (1608)
Occupation: guild master of the fullers
Office: KG Martini 1608
Denounced by the parish clergy for having never communicated (*QFGSM* IX, p. 37); burial forbidden by Martini clergy

30) TOM RING, Ludger, the younger
Occupation: painter
Family: father, Ludger tom Ring senior
Emigrated to Lutheran Brunswick (Geisberg, "tom Ring")

31) UDING, Wilhelm (+1613)
Occupation: peddler (Höcker)
Family: from Milinck near Duffel; acquired citizenship through marriage to Anna Pickers (Hövel, *BB*, no. 1503)
Burial forbidden by clergy (RP, 1613 II 5, vol. 45, fol. 63)

32) VARWICK, Peter
One of the burghers who buried Dietrich Seveker (see nos. 16, 24; Röchell, *Chronik,* p. 129)

33) VOSS, Bernd (+1606)
Occupation: furrier
Denounced as Calvinist by the Jesuits (Comp., fol. 35)
Burial forbidden by the Lamberti clergy (RP, 1606 VI 20, vol. 38, fols. 107v–108)

34) WERMELINCK, ―――――――
Denounced by the Jesuits as one of the ringleaders of the 1608 anti-Jesuit carnival (Comp., fol. 40v)

35) WILCKINGHOFF, Andreas (+1612)
Occupation: guild master of the goldsmiths; entered guild in 1583 (Krumbholtz, p. 244)
Office: see appendix 1, no. 155

He was a friend of Heinrich Grevinck, with whom he often served as guarantor for new citizens (Hövel, *BB*, nos. 594, 596); in 1611, he acted as witness for the nobleman Dietrich Morrien and family, who acquired citizenship in Münster (the Morriens were a Calvinist noble family (Hövel, *BB*, no. 2164); denounced by the parish clergy for having never communicated (*QFGSM* IX, p. 37) and by the Jesuits as one of the ringleaders of the 1608 anti-Jesuit carnival (Comp., fol. 40v); burial forbidden by the Lamberti clergy (RP, 1612 XI 21, vol. 44, fol. 403)

36) WIRTZ, Wilhelm
A servant from Hamm who died in Münster; burial forbidden by the Lamberti clergy (RP, 1609 XII 3, vol. 41, fol. 274v)

37) WÖSTMAN, David
The Franciscans refused to bury his child because he did not go to confession and communion (RP, 1610 V 7, vol. 42, fols. 82–83)

B. ANABAPTISTS (MENNONITES)

38) BECKE, Hermann zur, and wife
They received an Anabaptist from Zupthen; burial forbidden by Martini clergy (RP, 1606 II 13, vol. 38, fols. 9–10)

39) DRICKMAN, Johann, and family
Occupation: baker
Rumored to be an Anabaptist because he refused to perform watch duties. He publicly abjured Anabaptism in order to remain in Münster (RP, 1597 I/10, II/7, III/27, IV/9; vol. 28, fol. 65v and vol. 29, fols. 6–7, 16v, 17v–18)

40) GRESSHOEFF, Adam, and family
Occupation: hawker (Heggekramer)
Exiled by the city council (RP, 1585 III/29, V/10, VIII/30, vol. 17, fols. 13, 22, 33v)

41) KNÖST, Heinrich, and family
Occupation: hawker
Exiled by the city council (see reference for nos. 37, 38, and RP 1586, II/3, VII/28, vol. 18, fols. 4 & 29)

42) NIPPERS, Elsa
(See reference for nos. 38 and 39)

43) NOTTELMAN, _____
(see references for nos. 37–39)

44) PUNIENCK, Dietrich and wife
She refused to have her baby baptized (RP, 1594 VIII 19, vol. 26, fol. 58v)

45) SPEDER, Salpeter
Arrested and exiled by the magistrates (RP, 1582 IV 27, vol. 14, fol. 19v)

SOURCES

MANUSCRIPT SOURCES

Stadtarchiv Münster

Verwaltungsarchiv (A)

AII 01, vol. 3: Ratswahl, 1600–1802
AII 1, 1a, 3, 4, 5a, 5b, 5c, 6, 7: Urkunden
AII 16–17: Ratsangelegenheiten, 1350–1531, 1555–1660
AII 19a: Ratsbeschlüsse, 1536–43
AII 20: Ratsprotokolle, 1564–1618
AVI 10: Verordnungen über das Brauen, 1537–1661
AVI 12–13: Korn- und Brotpreise, 1536–40, 1559–1618
AVIII 133: Accisen-Rechnungen, Wein, 1600–06
AVIII 153: Accisen-Rechnungen, Getränk/Wein, 1542–45, 1592–99
AVIII 188: Gruetamtsrechnungen, 1533–1618
AVIII 259: Schatzungsregister, 1539–50, 1603
AVIII 277: Kämmerei-Rechnungen, 1541–1620
AIX 76: Schoehaus-Protokolle, 1569–1614
AXIII 28, 39, 39a, 42b, 43, 43b, 47, 48, 48a, 51, 52, 58, 183, 365, 426, 436:
    Kultus-, Kirchen und Schulsachen
AXIV: Wiedertäufer 45a; Spanisch-Holländischer Krieg 48, 66, 68, 69

Gerichtsarchiv (B)

Testamente I, sixteenth century, 19 volumes and loose pergaments
Testamente II, seventeenth century, 51 volumes and loose pergaments

Stiftungsarchiv (C)

Almosenkorb Ludgeri
Speckpfründe Ludgeri
Armenkleidung Lamberti
Speckpfründe Lamberti
Lamberti Elende
Aegidii Elende
Martini Elende
Überwasser Elende
Almosenkorb Überwasser

Manuscripts

No. 4: Chronik des Minoritenklosters
No. 32a: Catalogus Librorum Saint Mauritz
No. 53: Ratswahlbuch
No. 61: Korntaxen, 1559–1836
No. 79: Saint Georgs-Bruderschaft
No. 120: Rechnungsbuch Johann Herdings, 1546–72
No. 139: Saint Anne Bruderschaft-Protokolle
No number: Ratslisten, two volumes

Staatsarchiv Münster

Fürstentum Münster

Studienfonds Münster Gymnasium
(archive of the former Jesuit College):
  Kasten I, Loc. 5–10
  Kasten II, Loc. 1, 6–9
  Kasten III, Loc. 1–6c, 8a–9c, 11b–12, 13b, 14b–c,
  15a, 17, 18d, 22a

Saint Aegidii: Urkunden: 256, 256a, 261a, 267b–c, 271d, 278d,
  280a, 281e, 283a, 287b, 292, 293b–d,
  298a, 301a, 303a, 303c, 308, 310a–b,
  312a–e, 327a–e, 328
Register: Einkünfte 2
Register B: Zehnte 65, 69, 75

Minoriten-Münster: Urkunden: 5a, 8a, 11

Altertumsverein Münster

Manuscripts: 14, 24, 86, 110, 133

Manuscripts

MSS. I, 37–39: Landesregierungen, Bestallungsbücher
MSS. I, 273: Almae Confraternitatis Chordigerorum S. P. Francisci
MSS. VII, 1026: Historia et Litterae Annuae Collegii
  Monasteriensis Westphaliae
MSS. VII, 1034: Liber Sodalitatis Civicae Monasteriensis

Bistums- und Diözesanarchiv Münster

Pfarrarchiv Saint Lamberti Münster

Urkunden: 20–21, 23, 25, 30, 32, 35, 37, 39, 44–45, 49, 61
Akten (unsorted): Karton 16–17 (Rechnungswesen)
  Karton 51 (Kirche)
  Karton 60 (Friedhof)
  Karton 64–65 (Pastorat)

Karton 71, 71a, 72, 73, 81 (Burse)
Karton 112 (Bruderschaften u. Vereine)

Pfarrarchiv Saint Ludgeri Münster

Akten (unsorted): Karton 17 (Kirchenvorstand)
Karton 23 (Prozesse)
Karton 19, 47–48 (Rechnungswesen)
Karton 35 (Armenwesen)
Karton 41 (Vikarien)

Pfarrarchiv Saint Martini Münster

Urkunden: U19–20, 23, 25–26, 28, 30, 33–36,
39–41, 43, A21, 49, 123, 159, 174
Akten: A18–19 (Kirche)
A54 (Kirchenvermögen)
A60, 61, 64 (Kirchenrechnungen)
A101a (Kapitel)
A113 (Vikarienburse)

Pfarrarchiv Saint Aegidii Münster

Urkunden: 163–193, 198a, 201–202, 205–206a,
209, 212–213, 215–216, 221, 223, 225a,
230, 232, 233, 235, 236a, 241, 243,
243a, 245, 247, 249–251, 256, 260, 267a
Akten: A8, 21, 27 (Kirche)
A1 (Pfarre)
A75 (Kaplaneien)
A97, 100, 103–08 (Eleemosyne)
A34–38 (Kirche)

Manuscripts

No. 180: Spicilegium Ecclesiasticum

Archivum Romanum Societatis Jesu

Provincia Rhenana Inferiora 48:

Litterae Annuae Collegii Monasteriensis, 1593–1595,
1597–1600, 1604–1605, 1610, 1615–1616

PRINTED SOURCES

Aders, Günther. "Das verschollene älteste Bürgerbuch der Stadt Münster." *WZ* 110 (1960), pp. 29–96.

Aders, Günther and Helmut Richtering, eds. *Gerichte des Alten Reiches. Teil I: Reichskammergericht A-K. Teil II: Reichskammergericht L-Z. Reichshofrat. Teil III: Register* (= Das Staatsarchiv Münster und seine Bestände). Münster, 1966–73.

Alberts, W. Jappe. *Kämmereirechungen der Stadt Münster über die Jahre 1447, 1448 und 1458.* Groningen, 1960.

Brandt, Ahasver von, ed. *Regesten der Lübecker Bürgertestamente des Mittelalters. I: 1278–1350. II: 1351–1363.* Lübeck, 1964/1973.

Brilling, Bernhard and Helmut Richtering, eds. *Westfalia Judaica. Urkunden und Regesten zur Geschichte der Juden in Westfalen und Lippe. I: 1005–1350.* Stuttgart, 1967.

Bücker, Hermann. "Das Lobgedicht des Johannes Murmellius auf die Stadt Münster und ihren Gelehrtenkreis" *WZ* 111 (1961), pp. 51–74.

———, ed. *Werner Rolevinck, de laude antiquae Saxoniae nunc Westphaliae dictae.* Münster, 1953.

Cornelius, Carl A., ed. *Berichte der Augenzeugen über das münsterische Wiedertäuferreich* (= GQBM II). Münster, 1853.

Darpe, Franz, ed. *Die ältesten Verzeichnisse der Einkünfte des Münsterschen Domkapitels* (= CTW II). Münster, 1886/1960.

———, ed. *Die Heberegister des Klosters Überwasser und des Stiftes St. Mauritz* (= CTW III). Münster, 1888/1964.

———, ed. *Verzeichnisse der Güter, Einkünfte und Einnahmen des Aegidii-Klosters, der Kapitel an St. Ludgeri und Martini sowie der St. Georgs-Kommende in Münster . . .* (= CTW V), Münster, 1900/1958.

Dorpius, Heinrich., *Warhafftige Historie, wie das Evangelium zu Münster angefangen und darnach durch die Wydderteuffer verstöret, wider auffgehört hat. Darzu die gantze handlung der selbigen buben vom anfang bis zum ende, beydes in geistlichen und weltlichen stücken fleyssig beschriben.* [Wittenberg], 1536.

Festum Liberationis nostrae ab impiissimo Cathabaptistarum impetu et tumultu, de mirabilii victoria, et anniversario festo contra furiosos Anabaptistas postridie natalis Ioannis Baptiste solenniter observando. Münster, 1545.

Ficker, Julius, ed. *Die Münsterischen Chroniken des Mittelalters* (= GQBM I). Münster, 1851.

Hartig, Joachim, ed. *Die Register der Willkommenschatzung von 1498 und 1499 im Fürstbistum Münster. Teil 1: die Quellen.* Münster, 1976.

Historia der Belegerung und Eroberung der Statt Münster. Anno 1535. N. p., 1535.

Hövel, Ernst, ed. "Ein Beitrag zur Geschichte der wiedertäuferischen Bewegung nach 1535." *QFGSM* IV, Münster, 1931, pp. 339–52.

———, ed. *Das Bürgerbuch der Stadt Münster 1538 bis 1660* (= QFGSM VIII), Münster, 1936.

Hüsing, Augustin, ed. *Der Kampf um die katholische Religion im Bisthum Münster nach Vertreibung der Wiedertäufer 1535–1585. Aktenstücke und Erläuterungen.* Münster, 1883.

Immenkötter, Herbert, ed. *Die Protokolle des geistlichen Rates in Münster (1601–1612).* Münster, 1972.

Jäger-von Hoesslin, Franziska. *Die Korrespondenz der Kurfürsten von Köln aus dem Hause Wittelsbach (1583–1761) mit ihren bayerischen Verwandten. Nach den Unterlagen im Bayerischen Hauptstaatsarchiv München,* Düsseldorf, 1978.

Janssen, Johannes, ed. *Die Münsterischen Chroniken von Röchell, Stevermann, und Corfey* (= GQBM III). Münster, 1856.

Keller, Ludwig, ed. *Die Gegenreformation in Westfalen und am Niederrhein. Aktenstücke und Erläuterungen. I: 1555–1585. II: 1585–1609. III: 1609–1623,* (= Publikationen aus den Königlichen Preussischen Staatsarchiven, 9, 33, 62). Leipzig, 1881/1887/1895.

Kerssenbroch, Hermann von. *Anabaptistici Furoris Monasterium inclitam Westphaliae Metropolim evertentis historica narratio.* Ed. Heinrich Detmer. 2 vol. (= GQBM V). Münster, 1899/1900.

Ketteler, Josef, ed. "Katalog der münsterischen Notare und Prokuratoren." *Beiträge zur Westfälischen Familienforschung* 20 (1962).

Kirchhoff, Karl-Heinz, ed. "Eine münsterische Bürgerliste des Jahres 1535." *WZ* 111 (1961), pp. 75–94.

Klocke, Friedrich, ed. "Nachrichten aus dem untergegangenen ältesten Ratswahlbuch (1354–1531)." *QFSGM* III (1927), pp. 107–16.

Kohl, Wilhelm, ed. *Das Bistum Münster I: Die Schwesternhäuser nach der Augustinerregel* (= Germania Sacra, n.f. 3: die Bistümer der Kirchenprovinz Köln). Berlin, 1968.

————, ed. "Die Notariatsmatrikel des Fürstbistums Münster." *Beiträge zur Westfälischen Familienforschung* 20 (1962).

————, ed. "Urkundenregesten und Einkünfteregister des Aegidii-Klosters (1184–1533)." *QFGSM,* n.f. III, Münster, 1966, pp. 7–285.

Krumbholtz, Robert, ed. *Die Gewerbe der Stadt Münster bis zum Jahre 1661* (= Publikationen aus dem Königlichen Preussichen Staatsarchiven, 70). Leipzig, 1898.

Lahrkamp, Helmut, ed. *Die Geburtsbriefe der Stadt Münster 1548–1809* (= QFGSM, n.f. IV). Münster, 1968.

————, ed. *Münsters Bevölkerung um 1685* (= QFGSM, n.f. VI). Münster, 1972.

————, ed. *Städtmünsterische Akten und Vermischtes.* Münster, 1964.

Laube, Adolf and Hans W. Seiffert, eds. *Flugschriften der Reformationszeit.* Berlin, 1975.

Legge, Theodor, ed. *Flug- und Streitschriften der Reformationszeit in Westfalen (1523–1583).* Münster, 1933.

Die Matrikel der deutschen Nation in Perugia (1579–1727), ed. Fritz Weigle. Tübingen, 1956.

Die Matrikel der deutschen Nation in Siena (1573–1738), 2 vols., ed. Friz Weigle, Tübingen, 1962.

Die Matrikel der Universität Basel, 2 vols., eds. Hans Georg Wacknernagel et al. Basel, 1956.

Die Matrikel der Universität Freiburg i. Br. 1460–1656, 2 vols., ed. Hermann Mayer. Freiburg, 1910.

Die Matrikel der Universität Köln. I: 1476–1559. II: 1560–1779. ed. Historisches Archiv der Stadt Köln, Bonn, 1919, Cologne, 1982.

Müller, Ernst, ed. *Die Abrechnung des Johannes Hageboke über die Kosten der Belagerung der Stadt Münster 1534–35 . . .* (= GQBM VIII), Münster, 1937.

Niesert, Joseph, ed. *Beiträge zur Buchdruckergeschichte Münsters oder Verzeichnis der vom Jahr 1486–1700 zu Münster gedruckten Bücher.* Coesfeld, 1828. (Supplementary volume appeared in 1834.)

————, ed. *Münsterische Urkundensammlung. I: Urkunden zur Geschichte der münsterischen Wiedertäufer.* Coesfeld, 1826.

Nuntiaturberichte aus Deutschland 1585–90. I. Abt. Die Kölner Nuntiatur. I. Hälfte. Edited by Stephan Ehses and Aloys Meister. Paderborn, 1895.

Pachtler, G. M., ed. *Ratio Studiorum et Institutiones Scholasticae Societatis Jesu.* 4 vols., Berlin, 1887–94.

Philippi, Friedrich, ed. *Landrechte des Münsterlandes.* Münster, 1907.

Richtering, Helmut, ed. "Die Familienchronik des Johann Wedemhove von 1610." *Westfalen* 40 (1962), pp. 133–49.

————, ed. *Gerichte des Alten Reiches,* 3 vols., Münster, 1973.

Ruperti, Michael. *Catechismus und Betböklin mit heylsamen Betrachtunge und Gebetlin vermehret und gebettert . . . dorch Michaelem Rupertum Werlensem Decken unser lieven frauwen Kercken tho Oeverwater binnen Münster.* Münster: Lambert Raesfeld, 1596.

Scholz, Klaus, ed. *Die Urkunden des Kollegiatstifts Alter Dom in Münster 1129– 1534.* Münster, 1978.

Schulte, Eduard, ed. "Kleine Listen zur Personengeschichte des 16. und 17. Jahrhunderts." *QFGSM* III, Münster, 1927, pp. 39–54.

————, ed. "Die Kurgenossen des Rates 1520–1802," *QFGSM* III, Münster, 1927, pp. 117–204.

————, ed. "Eine Londoner Liste von Münsterschen Erbmännern," *QFGSM* IV, Münster, 1931, pp. 325–38.

Schulze, Rudolf, ed. "Klosterchronik Überwasser während der Wirren 1531– 33," *QFGSM* II, Münster, 1924–26, pp. 149–66.

Schwarz, Wilhelm, ed. *Die Akten der Visitation des Bistums Münster aus der Zeit Johanns von Hoya (1571–73)* (= GQBM VII). Münster, 1912.

Society of Jesus. *Litterae Annuae Societatis Jesu 1588.* Rome, 1590.

————. *LASJ 1589.* Rome, 1591.

————. *LASJ 1594–95.* Naples, 1594.

————. *LASJ 1596.* Naples, 1605.

————. *LASJ 1597.* Naples, 1607.

————. *LASJ 1598.* Lyons, 1607.

————. *LASJ 1600.* Antwerp, 1618.

————. *LASJ 1601.* Antwerp, 1618.

————. *LASJ 1602.* Antwerp, 1618.

————. *LASJ 1605.* Dillingen, 1609.

————. *LASJ 1611.* Dillingen, 1611.

————. *LASJ 1611.* Lyons, 1619.

————. *LASJ 1613–14.* Lyons, 1619.

Steinbicker, Clemens, ed. "Die Liebfrauen-Bruderschaft an der Pfarr- und Kloster- Kirche Saint Aegidii (1441–1941)." *QFGSM* n.f. III, pp. 287–382. Münster, 1966.

Stupperich, Robert, ed. *Die Schriften Bernhard Rothmanns.* Münster, 1970.

————, ed. *Strassburg und Münster im Kampf um den rechten Glauben 1532–1534* (= Martini Buceri Opera Omnia Series I: Deutsche Schriften 5). Gütersloh, 1978.

Stürmer, Michael, ed. *Herbst des Alten Handwerks. Zur Sozialgeschichte des 18. Jahrhunderts*. Munich, 1979.

Symann, Ernst, ed. "Liber Tutorum et Curatorum, I. Teil: 1548–1599." *QFGSM* II, Münster, 1924/26, pp. 31–92.

Tibus, Adolph. *Die Jakobipfarre von 1508–1523*. Münster, 1885.

Timpius (Timpe), Matthaeus. *Der Ceremonien warumb/ das ist Lautere unnd klare ursachen und ausslegungen der furnemmsten Ceremonien/ welche auss einsprechung des Heiligen Geists bey dem Heiligen Gottesdienst inn der gantzen Heiligen christenheit von alters her gleichförmig und einhellig gebrauchet werden, sampt etlichen ungereimpten/ widerspennigen Ceremonien und Geberden der Sectischen*. Münster: Lambert Raesfeld, 1609.

————. *Erhebliche und wichtige Ursachen/ warumb weise und fürsichtige Leuth/ auss gottseligem eiffer/ bey sich beschlossen haben/ von dem so Gott ihnen gnadiglich verliehen/ hülff zu thun/ dass man in der wollöblichen Statt Münster/ welche die Hauptstatt ist inn Westphalen oder alten Saxen/ anfange eine hochberühmbte Universitet oder Academiam zu fundieren unnd zu stifften: und warumb billich alle Vaterlands liebende hertzen zu solchem hochpreisslichen Werck unnd frewdenreichen anfang behülfflich seyn sollen*. Münster: Lambert Raesfeld, 1612.

————. *Ernewerte Welt/ das ist: Heylsamer rath das H. Römisch Reich/ ja das gantze H. Christenthumb/ zu vorigen reichthumben/ gewalt/ zier/ und wolstandt widerumb zu bringen. Auss H. Biblischer Schrift/ hochgelehrten Theologen/ unnd dess H. Römischen Reichs Ordnungen/ Satzungen und Abschieden/ dem alten Christenthumb fürnemblich Teutschen Nation zu ehren/ auffnemmen und gedeyen zusammen getragen*. Münster: Lambert Raesfeld, 1610.

————. *Kinderzucht/ oder Kürtzer Bericht von der Eltern sorg unnd fürsichtigkeit in aufferziehung unnd unterrichtung ihrer Kinder*. Münster: Lambert Raesfeld, 1597.

————. *Leich- Trost- und Busspredigen auch Anweisung wie dieselbigen in Auslegung Sonn- und Freyrtag- Evangelien gebraucht werden konnen . . .* Münster: Kambert Raesfeld, 1613.

————. *Lustgarten der Jungfrauwen/ oder: sechs und zwenzig Paradeissgärtlin und Predigten/ von grossen Wirde/ Schönheit/ und nutzbarkeit der Jungfrauwschaft von vielen mitteln dieses unvergleichliches Perlin unverletzt zubewahren/ und sich wider das unverschambte Lasten der unzucht zubewapnen, von den fürnembsten Tugenten mit welchen sich die Jungfrauwen ausssbutzen müssen, und endtlich von vielen fürtrefflichen gaaben und gnaden dess geistliche Ordenstands*. Münster: Lambert Raesfeld, 1611.

————. *Newen Jahrspredigen/ oder: Deutliche Anweisung/ wie die Seelsorger (welche hiemit grösserer Mühe unnd Arbeit überhebt werden) auss H. Schrifft und der gantzen Welt Creaturen/ als auss zweyen grossen Kisten/ nach uraltem Löblichen Gebrauch/ am Newen Jahrstag/ allen Ständen Ihrer zubehör/ besondere Geistliche Geschenck zum Newen Jahr ausstheilen sollen sampt/ sehr nothwendigen Reguln dess Lebens/ in welchen ein jeglicher Christ/ wess Standts oder Würden er sit/ als in einem Spiegel erlernen kan/ wie er sich nach Gottes Wort/ in seinem Ampt unnd Beruff unverweisslich verhalten soll*. Münster: Bernhard Raesfeld, 1649.

————. *Processionpredigten/ oder: Deutliche Anweisung/ wie die Seelsorger zur Zeit der H. Bettfahrten/ Creutzgäng und Processionen/ bevor ab an S. Marcus Tag/ in der*

H. Car unnd Creutzwochen/ unnd am Hohen Fest des H. Fronleichnams Christi/ das Gemeine Volck lehren unnd underweisen sollen/ wie die abwendung der Thewrung/ des Krieges/ der weit umb sich fressenden Kranckheiten/ und aller anderen Trübseligkeiten von Gott zu erhalten sey. Münster: Bernhard Raesfeld, 1632.

———. *Speculum Magnum Episcoporum, Canonicorum Sacerdotum et aliorum Clericorum omnium tam Secularium quam Religiosorum, ex admirandis Pontificum, Episcoporum, Sacerdotum, aliorumque Ecclesiasticorum dictis et factis in gratiam Concionatorum et Eloquentiae Studiosorum per locos communes iuxta Alphabeti seriem digestis.* Mainz: Lambert Raesfeld, 1614.

———. *Spiegel der Eheleuth/ oder Kurtzer Bericht/ wie die Prediger nicht allein in ihrer Braut- und hochzeitlichen/ sondern auch Predigen die Eheleut von ihrem Ampt und schuldiger Pflicht/ oder wie ihr Standt nach Gottes Ordnung/ Willen und Befehl anzufangen/ unnd in guten Frieden/ Ruhe/ und Einigkeit/ zuhalten sey/ underweisen sollen.* Münster: Bernhard Raesfeld, 1632.

———. *Theatrum Historicum, continens Vindictas Divinas, et Praemia Christianorum Virtutum.* Münster: Michael Dalius, 1625.

———. *Tractatus tres spirituales.* Mainz: Lambert Raesfeld et Peter Henning, 1614.

Utsch, Karl, ed. "Die Kultusabteilung des Stadtarchivs Münster. Urkunden und Regesten." *QFGSM* IX, Münster, 1937, pp. 3–64.

Weinsberg, Hermann von. *Das Buch Weinsberg. Aus dem Leben eines Kölner Ratsherrn.* ed. Johann J. Hässlin. Munich, 1964.

SECONDARY WORKS

Abel, Wilhelm. *Massenarmut und Hungerkrisen im vorindustriellen Deutschland.* Göttingen, 1977.

Aboucaya, Claude. *Le Testament lyonnais de la fin du XVe au milieu du XVIIIe siècle.* Paris, 1961.

Abray, L. Jane. "The Long Reformation: Magistrates, Clergy, and People in Strasbourg." Ph.D. diss., Yale University, 1978.

800 Jahre Sankt Ludgeri Münster. Münster, 1973.

Aders, Günther. "Der Domdechant Arnold von Büren (+1614) und seine Nachkommen. Zugleich ein Beitrag zur Verfassungsgeschichte der Zünfte in Münster." *Westfalen* 40 (1962), pp. 123–32.

Alberts, W. Jappe. "Die Beziehungen zwischen Geldern und Münster im 14. und 15. Jahrhundert." *WF* 9 (1956), pp. 83–95.

Andreas, Willy. *Deutschland vor der Reformation.* Stuttgart, 1959.

Ariès, Philip. *The Hour of Our Death.* translated by Helen Weaver. New York, 1981.

Aschoff, Diethard. "Die Juden in Westfalen zwischen Schwarzem Tod und Reformation (1350–1530)." *WF* 30 (1980), pp. 78–106.

———. "Das münsterländische Judentum bis zum Ende des 30jährigen Krieges." *Theokratia* 3 (1979), pp. 125–84.

———. "Die Stadt Münster und die Juden im letzten Jahrhundert der städtischen Unabhängigkeit (1562–1662)." *WF* 27 (1975), pp. 84–113.

Aubin, Hermann, and Wolfgang Zorn, eds. *Handbuch der deutschen Wirtschafts- und Sozialgeschichte,* vol. 1. Stuttgart, 1971.

Ausstellung des Landesmuseums des Provinz Westfalen Juli/September 1924 (Katalog): Die Werke der Münsterschen Malerfamilie tom Ring. Münster, 1924.

Bächtold-Stäubli, Hanns, and E. Hoffmann-Krayer, eds. *Handwörterbuch des Deutschen Aberglaubens.* Berlin/Leipzig, 1927.

Bahlmann, August. *Das Kloster Rosenthal.* Münster, 1857.

Bahlmann, Paul. "Zur Geschichte der Juden im Münsterlande." *Zeitschrift für Kulturgeschichte* 2 (1895), pp. 380–409.

———. *Jesuiten-Dramen der niederrheinischen Ordensprovinz.* Leipzig, 1896.

———. "Matthaeus Tympe." *ADB* 39, pp. 53–55.

———. "Mönstersche Inquisitio." *WZ* 47 (1889), pp. 98–120.

Baron, Hans. "Franciscan Poverty and Civic Wealth as Factors in the Rise of Humanistic Thought." *Speculum* 13 (1938), pp. 1–37.

Baumer, Clemens. "Neue Beiträge zur Bibliographie des münsterischen Humanisten Murmellius und zur münsterischen Druckergeschichte." *WZ* 40 (1882), pp. 164–72.

Becker, Marvin B. "Florentine Politics and the Diffusion of Heresy in the Trecento: A Socioeconomic Inquiry." *Speculum* 34 (1959), pp. 60–74.

Benedict, Philip. *Rouen during the Wars of Religion.* Cambridge, 1981.

Bensing, Manfred. *Thomas Müntzer und der Thüringer Aufstand 1525.* Berlin, 1966.

Benzing, Josef. *Die Buchdrucker des 16. und 17. Jahrhunderts im deutschen Sprachgebiet.* Wiesbaden, 1963.

Bercé, Yves-Marie. *Fête et révolte: Des Mentalités populaires du XVIe au XVIIIe siècle.* Paris, 1976.

Berres, Johann Jacob. *Münster und seine handelspolitischen Beziehungen zur deutschen Hanse.* Münster, 1919.

Bireley, Robert. *Maximilian von Bayern, Adam Contzen S.J. und die Gegenreformation in Deutschland 1624–1635.* Göttingen, 1975.

———. *Religion and Politics in the Age of the Counterreformation: Emperor Ferdinand II, William Lamormaini, S.J., and the Formation of Imperial Policy.* Chapel Hill, 1981.

Blockmans, W. P., and W. Prevenier. "Armoede in de Nederlanden van de 14e tot het midden van de 16 eeuw: bronnen en problemen." *Tijdschrift voor Geschiedenis* 88 (1975), pp. 501–38.

Bockholt, Bernhard. *Die Orden des heiligen Franziskus in Münster.* Münster, 1917.

Bolton, Brenda M. "Mulieres Sanctae." In Susan M. Stuard, ed. *Women in Medieval Society.* Philadelphia, 1976.

Bömer, Alois. "Dietrich Tzwyvel," *Westfälische Lebensbilder.* Hauptreihe II:1. Münster, 1931. Pp. 15–29.

———. "Der münsterische Buchdruck in dem ersten Viertel des 16. Jahrhunderts." *Westfalen* 10 (1919), pp. 1–48.

———. "Der münsterische Buchdruck vom zweiten Viertel bis zum Ende des 16. Jahrhunderts." *Westfalen* 12 (1924–25), pp. 25–76.

Boogerd, L. van den. *Het Jezuietendrama in de Nederlanden*. Groningen, 1961.

Borchling, Konrad, and Bruno Claussen. *Niederdeutsche Bibliographie. Gesamtverzeichnis der niederdeutschen Drucke bis zum Jahre 1800*. 3 vols. Neumünster, 1931–57.

Börsting, Heinrich. *Geschichte des Bistums Münster*. Bielefeld, 1951.

Börsting, Heinrich, and Alois Schröer. *Handbuch des Bistums Münster*. 2 vols. Münster, 1946.

Bossy, John. "The Counter-Reformation and the People of Catholic Europe." *P & P* 47 (1970), pp. 51–70.

Böttcher, Kurt. *Das Vordringen der hochdeutschen Sprache in den Urkunden des niederdeutschen Gebietes vom 13. bis 16. Jahrhundert*. Berlin, 1916.

————. "Das Vordringen der hochdeutschen Sprache in den Urkunden des niederdeutschen Gebietes vom 13. bis 16. Jahrhundert." *Zeitschrift für Deutsche Mundarten* (1921), pp. 62–67.

Bouwsma, William J. *Venice and the Defense of Republican Liberty*. Berkeley, 1968.

Boxer, Charles R. *The Church Militant and Iberian Expansion, 1440–1770*. Baltimore, 1978.

Brady, Thomas A. *Ruling Class, Regime and Reformation at Strasbourg, 1520–1555*. Leiden, 1978.

Brandt, Ahasver von. *Mittelalterliche Bürgertestamente. Neuerschlossene Quellen zur Geschichte der materiellen und geistigen Kultur*. Heidelberg, 1973.

Brecht, Martin. "Luthertum als politische und soziale Kraft in den Städten." In Franz Petri, ed. *Kirche und gesellschaftlicher Wandel in deutschen und niederländischen Städten in der werdenden Neuzeit*. Cologne, 1980.

Brendler, Gerhard. *Das Täuferreich zu Münster 1534/35*. Berlin, 1966.

Breuer, Dieter. "Zensur und Literaturpolitik in den deutschen Territorialstaaten des 17. Jahrhunderts am Beispiel Bayerns." In Albrecht Schöne, ed. *Stadt-Schule-Universität. Buchwesen und die deutsche Literatur im 17. Jahrhundert*. Munich, 1976. Pp. 470–91, 571ff.

Brockpähler, R. "Der 'Gute Montag' der Bäckergilde Münster, Sage und historische Wirklichkeit." *RWZfVK* 28 (1976–77), pp. 197–99.

Burke, Peter. *Popular Culture in Early Modern Europe*. New York, 1978.

Chaunu, Pierre. *La mort à Paris: XVIe, XVIIe, XVIIIe siècles*. Paris, 1978.

Chrisman, Miriam. "The Urban Poor in the Sixteenth Century: The Case of Strasbourg." In Miriam Chrisman and Otto Gruendler, eds. *Social Groups and Religious Ideas in the Sixteenth Century*. Kalamazoo, Michigan, 1978.

Cohn, Henry. "Anticlericalism in the German Peasants' War, 1525." *P & P* 83 (1979), pp. 3–31.

Cornelius, Carl A. *Geschichte des Münsterischen Aufruhrs*. 3 vols., Leipzig, 1855/60.

Cox, H. L. "Prozessionsbrauchtum des späten Mittelalters und der frühen Neuzeit im Spiegel obrigkeitlicher Verordnungen in Kurköln und den vereinigten Herzogtümern." *RWZfVK* 22 (1976), pp. 51–85.

Dahm, Georg. "Zur Rezeption des Römisch-italienischen Rechtes." *HZ* 167 (1943), pp. 229–58.

Danckert, Werner. *Uneheliche Leute. Die verfemten Berufe*. Bern, 1963.

Davis, Natalie Z. *Society and Culture in Early Modern France.* Stanford, 1975.

Decker, Rainer. *Bürgermeister und Ratsherren in Paderborn vom 13. bis zum 17. Jahrhundert.* Paderborn, 1977.

———. "Die Hexenverfolgungen im Hochstift Paderborn." *WZ* 128 (1978), pp. 315–56.

Decker-Hauff, Hansmartin. "Untersuchungen zur Struktur der protestantischen Geistlichkeit südwestdeutscher Reichsstädte." In Erich Maschke and Jürgen Sydow, eds. *Gesellschaftliche Unterschichten in den südwestdeutschen Städten.* Stuttgart, 1967. Pp. 167–69.

Delumeau, Jean. *Le Catholicisme entre Luther et Voltaire.* Paris, 1971.

Demandt, Dieter, and Hans-Christoph Rublack. *Stadt und Kirche in Kitzingen.* Stuttgart, 1978.

Deppermann, Klaus. *Melchior Hoffmann: soziale Unruhen und apokalyptische Visionen im Zeitalter der Reformation.* Göttingen, 1979.

Detmer, Heinrich. *Bilder aus den religiösen und sozialen Unruhen in Münster während des 16. Jahrhunderts, II: Bernhard Rothmann.* Münster, 1904.

Dirlmeier, Ulf. *Untersuchungen zu Einkommensverhältnissen und Lebenshaltungskosten in oberdeutschen Städten des Spätmittelalters (Mitte 14. bis Anfang 16. Jahrhunderts).* Heidelberg, 1978.

Dobelmann, Werner. *Kirchspiel und Stift Saint Mauritz in Münster. Ursprung und Werdegang eines Stadtviertels und seines Vorlandes.* Münster, 1971.

Dollinger, Philippe. *Die Hanse.* Rev. German ed. Stuttgart, 1966.

Duggan, Lawrence. *Bishop and Chapter: The Governance of the Bishopric of Speyer to 1552.* New Brunswick, 1978.

Duhr, Bernhard. *Geschichte der Jesuiten in den Ländern deutscher Zunge.* 4 vols. in 5. Freiburg, 1907–28.

———. *Die Studienordnung der Gesellschaft Jesu.* Freiburg, 1896.

Eggers, Hans. *Deutsche Sprachgeschichte. III. Das Frühneuhochdeutsche.* Hamburg, 1969.

Ehbrecht, Wilfried. "Bürgertum und Obrigkeit in den hansischen Städten des Spätmittelalters." In Wilhelm Rausch, ed. *Die Stadt am Ausgang des Mittelalters.* Linz, 1974. Pp. 275–94.

———. "Hanse und spätmittelalterliche Bürgerkämpfe in Niedersachen und Westfalen." *Niedersächsisches Jahrbuch für Landesgeschichte* 48 (1976).

———. "Köln-Osnabrück-Stralsund. Rat und Bürgerschaft hansischer Städte zwischen religiöser Erneuerung und Bauernkrieg." In Franz Petri, ed. *Kirche und gesellschaftlicher Wandel* . . . . Pp. 23–64.

———. "Verhaltensformen der Hanse bei spätmittelalterlichen Bürgerkämpfen in Westfalen." *WF* 26 (1974), pp. 46–59.

———. "Zu Ordnung und Selbstverständnis städtischer Gesellschaft im späten Mittelalter." *Blätter für deutsche Landesgeschichte* 110 (1974), pp. 83–103.

Eisenstein, Elizabeth. *The Printing Press as an Agent of Change: Communications and Cultural Transformations in Early Modern Europe,* 2 vols. Cambridge, 1979.

Endres, Rudolf. "Zünfte und Unterschichten als Elemente der Instabilität in den Städten." In Peter Blickle, ed. *Revolte und Revolution in Europa* (= Historische Zeitschrift, n.f., Beiheft). Munich, 1975. Pp. 151–70.

Endriss, Albrecht. "Phasen der Konfessionsbildung—Aufgezeigt am Beispiel der Reichsstadt Wimpfen im Zeitraum von 1523 bis 1635." In Horst Rabe et al., eds. *Festgabe für Ernst Walter Zeeden.* Münster, 1976, pp. 289–326.

Engel, Gustav. *Politische Geschichte Westfalens.* Cologne, 1969.

Ennen, Edith, and Franz Irsigler. "Die frühneuzeitliche Stadt." *WF* 24 (1972), pp. 5–63.

Erhard, Heinrich A. *Geschichte Münsters.* Münster, 1837.

Evans, Robert J. W. *Rudolf II and His World.* Oxford, 1973.

Evennett, H. Outram. *The Spirit of the Counter-Reformation.* Cambridge, 1968.

Fahne, A. *Geschichte der Westphälischen Geschlechter.* Cologne, 1858

———. *Die Herren und Freiherren von Hövel.* 3 vols. in 4. Cologne, 1860.

Falk, Franz. *Die deutschen Sterbebüchlein von der ältesten Zeit des Buchdruckes bis zum Jahre 1520.* Cologne, 1890. Reprint Amsterdam, 1969.

Febvre, Lucien, and Henri-Jean Martin. *The Coming of the Book: The Impact of Printing 1450–1800.* Translated by David Gerard. London, 1976.

Flemming, Willi. *Geschichte des Jesuitentheaters in den Ländern Deutscher Zunge.* Berlin, 1923.

Franz, Günther, ed. *Beamtentum und Pfarrerstand 1400–1800.* Limburg/Lahn, 1972.

———. *Der Deutsche Bauernkrieg,* 10th rev. ed. Darmstadt, 1975.

Franzen, August. *Der Wiederaufbau des kirchlichen Lebens im Erzbistum Köln unter Ferdinand von Bayern, Erzbischöf von Köln 1612–1650.* Münster, 1941.

Freed, John. *The Friars and German Society in the Thirteenth Century.* Cambridge, Mass., 1977.

Friedrichs, Christopher R. *Urban Society in an Age of War: Nördlingen, 1580–1720.* Princeton, 1979.

Geisberg, Max, *Die Stadt Münster,* 6 vols. (= Bau- und Kunstdenkmäler von Westfalen, 41). Münster, 1932–41.

———. "Die tom Rings." *Westfälische Lebensbilder* II:1, Münster, 1931, pp. 30–50.

Gimpel, Klaus. "Das Gast- und Irrenhaus in Münster," *Historia Hospitalium. Zeitschrift der deutschen Gesellschaft für Krankenhausgeschichte* 14 (1981).

———. "Patriotische Einflüsse im münsterischen Gute Montags-Brauch des 19. Jahrhunderts." *WF* 28 (1976–77), pp. 197–99.

Grewe, Josef. *Das Braugewerbe der Stadt Münster.* Leipzig, 1907.

Greyerz, Kaspar von. *The Late City Reformation in Germany: The Case of Colmar, 1522–1628.* Wiesbaden, 1980.

Grundmann, Herbert. *Religiöse Bewegungen im Mittelalter.* 2nd rev. ed. Hildesheim, 1961.

Haller, Betram. "Köln und die Anfänge des Buchdrucks in Westfalen." *Köln Westfalen 1180–1980. Landesgeschichte zwischen Rhein und Weser* (catalogue of the exhibition in the Landesmuseum Münster, Oct. 26, 1980, to Jan. 18, 1981). Ed. Landschaftsverband Westfalen-Lippe. Vol. 1. Lengerich, 1980. Pp. 441–44.

Harding, Robert. "Revolution and Reform in the Holy League: Angers, Rennes, Nantes." *JMH* 53 (1981), pp. 379–416.

Hartung, Fritz. *Deutsche Verfassungsgeschichte vom 15. Jahrhundert bis zur Gegenwart.* 9th ed. Stuttgart, 1969.

Hengst, Karl. *Kirchliche Reformen im Fürstbistum Paderborn unter Dietrich von Fürstenberg (1585–1618)*. Paderborn, 1974.

Herzog, Ulrich. *Untersuchungen zur Geschichte des Domkapitels in Münster und seines Besitzes im Mittelalter*. Göttingen, 1961.

Hölker, Karl. *Die Maler Familie tom Ring* (= Beiträge zur Westfälischen Kunstgeschichte 8). Münster, 1927.

Hömberg, Albert. *Westfälische Landesgeschichte*. Münster, 1967.

———. *Wirtschaftsgeschichte Westfalens*. Münster, 1968.

Honselmann, Klemens, "Der Kampf um Paderborn 1604 und die Geschichtsschreibung," *WZ* 118 (1968), pp. 229–338.

Hsia, R. Po-chia, "Civic Wills as Sources for the Study of Piety in Münster, 1530–1618," *SCJ* 14 (1983).

———. "Die neue Form der Ratswahl in Münster 1554/55," *WZ* 131/132 (1981/82), pp. 197–204.

Huizinga, Johann. *The Waning of the Middle Ages*. New York, 1954.

Hülsbusch, Werner, ed. *800 Jahre Saint Martini Münster*. Münster, 1980.

Humborg, Ludwig. *Die Hexenprozesse in der Stadt Münster*. Münster, 1914.

Humburg, Norbert. *Städtisches Fastnachtbrauchtum in West- und Ostfalen. Die Entwicklung vom Mittelalter bis ins 19. Jahrhundert*. Münster, 1976.

Hüsing, Augustin. "Die alten Bruderschaften in der Stadt Münster." *WZ* 61 (1903), pp. 95–138.

Huyskens, Viktor. "Die Entstehung der Grossen Schützen-Bruderschaft zu Münster." *WZ* 62 (1904), pp. 241–45.

———. *Everwin von Droste, Dechant an der Kollegiatkirche Saint Martini zu Münster (1567–1604), und die Stiftsschule seiner Zeit. Teil I: Vom Leben und Wirken Everwin von Droste*. Münster, 1907. (Part One is the only part published.)

———. "Der Gute Montag." *WZ* 61 (1903), pp. 217–19.

———. *Zeiten der Pest in Münster während der zweiten Hälfte des 16. Jahrhunderts*. 2 parts. Münster, 1901/05.

———. "Zur Geschichte der Juden in Münster." *WZ* 57 (1899), pp. 124–35; 64 (1906), pp. 260–66.

Immenkötter, Herbert. "Die Auseinandersetzung des Domkapitels in Münster mit dem Geistlichen Rat." in Remigius Bäumer, ed. *Von Konstanz nach Trent. Beiträge zur Geschichte der Kirche und der Reformkonzilien bis zum Tridentinum. Festgabe für August Franzen*. Paderborn, 1972. Pp. 713–27.

Intorp, Leonhard. *Westfälische Barockpredigten in volkskundlicher Sicht*. Münster, 1964.

Jeannin, Pierre. *Les marchands au XVIe siècle*. Paris, 1969.

Jelsma, A. J. "De koning en de vrouwen: Münster 1534–35." *Gereformeerd Theologische Tijdschrift* 25 (1975), pp. 82–107.

Kellenbenz, Hermann. *Deutsche Wirtschaftsgeschichte*. Vol. 1. Munich, 1977.

———, ed. *Handbuch der europäischen Wirtschafts- und Sozialgeschichte*. Vol. 2. Stuttgart, 1980.

———. *The Rise of the European Economy: An Economic History of Continental Europe from the Fifteenth to the Eighteenth Century*. Translated by Gerhard Benecke. London, 1976.

Keller, Ludwig. "Die Wiederherstellung der katholischen Kirche nach den Wiedertäufer-Unruhen in Münster 1535–1537." *HZ* 47 (1882), pp. 429–56.

Ketteler, Joseph. *Das münstersche Geschlecht Herding.* Münster, 1926.

———. "Vom Geschlechterkreise des Münsterschen Honoratiorentums." *Mitteilungen der Westdeutschen Gesellschaft für Familienkunde* 5 (1928), pp. 422–30.

Keyser, Erich, ed. *Westfälisches Städtebuch.* Stuttgart, 1954.

Kiessling, Rolf. *Bürgerliche Gesellschaft und Kirche in Augsburg im Spätmittelalter.* Augsburg, 1971.

———. "Stadt-Land Beziehungen im Spätmittelalter. Überlegungen zur Problemstellung und Methode anhand neuerer Arbeiten vorwiegend zur süddeutschen Beispielen." *ZfBLG* 40 (1977), pp. 829–67.

Kirchhoff, Karl-Heinz. "Die Belagerung und Eroberung Münsters 1534/35. Militärische Massnahmen und politische Verhandlungen des Fürstbischofs Franz von Waldeck." *WZ* 112 (1962), pp. 77–170.

———. "Die Besetzung Warendorfs." *Westfalen* 40 (1962), pp. 117–22.

———. "Das Ende der lutherischen Bewegung in Coesfeld und Dülmen." *JbfWKG* 62 (1969), pp. 43–68.

———. "Die Erbmänner und ihre Höfe in Münster," *WZ* 116 (1966), pp. 3–26.

———. "Exekutivorgane und Rechtspraxis der Täuferverfolgung in Münsterland 1533–1546." *WF* 16 (1963), pp. 161–80.

———. "Gab es eine friedliche Täufergemeinde in Münster 1534?" *JbfWKG* 55/56 (1962–63), pp. 7–21.

———. "Kerssenbroch oder Vruchter. Wer schrieb 1534 das Bichtbok, die Kampfschrift gegen Reformation und Täufertum in Münster?" *JbfWKZ* 68 (1975), pp. 39–50.

———. "Kleine Beiträge zur münsterländischen Volkskunde um 1535," *RWZfVK* 8 (1961), pp. 92–105.

———. "Landräte im Stift Münster. Erscheinungsformen der landständischen Mitregierung im 16. Jahrhundert." *WF* 18 (1965), pp. 181–90.

———. "Die landständischen Schatzungen des Stifts Münster im 16. Jahrhundert." *WF* 14 (1961), pp. 117–32.

———. *Die Täufer in Münster 1534/35. Untersuchungen zum Umfang und zur Sozialstruktur der Bewegung.* Münster, 1973.

———. "Die Täufer in Münster. Verbreitung und Verfolgung des Täufertums im Stift Münster 1533–1550." *WZ* 113 (1963), pp. 1–109.

———. "Die Unruhen in Münster/Westfalen 1450–57." In Wilfried Ehbrecht, ed. *Städtische Führungsgruppen und Gemeinde in der werdenden Neuzeit.* Cologne, 1979.

———. "Wer war Heinricus Dorpius Monasteriensis?" *JbfWKG* 53/54 (1960/61), pp. 173–79.

———. "Wolter Westerhues (1497–1548), ein Glockengiesser in Westfalen." *WZ* 129 (1979), pp. 69–88.

———. "Zwinger und Neuwerk. Beiträge zur Geschichte der Befestigung der Stadt Münster im ausgehenden Mittelalter." *QFGSM,* n.f. V, Münster, 197?, pp. 55–94.

Kirschner, Julius. "The Moral Problem of Discounting Genoese Paghe 1450–1550." *Archivum Fratrum Praedicatorum* 47 (1977), pp. 109–67.

———. "The Moral Theology of Public Finance: A Study and Edition of Nicolaus de Anglia's 'Quaestio Disputata' on the Public Debt of Venice." *Archivum Fratrum Praedicatorum* 40 (1970), pp. 42–72.

Klocke, Friedrich von. *Das Patriziatsproblem und die Werler Erbsälzer*. Münster, 1965.

Klümper, T. *Landesherr und Städte im Fürstbistum Münster unter Ernst und Ferdinand von Bayern (1585–1650)*. Emsdetten, 1940.

Knemeyer, Franz-Ludwig. "Das Notariat im Fürstbistum Münster." *WZ* 114 (1964), pp. 1–142.

Koch, A. C. F. "The Reformation at Deventer in 1579–1580: Size and Social Structure of the Catholic Section of the Population during the Religious Peace." *Acta Historica Neerlandica* 6 (1973), pp. 27–66.

Koenigsberger, Helmut G. *Estates and Revolutions: Essays in Early Modern History*. Ithaca, 1971.

Kohl, Wilhelm. *Christoph Bernhard von Galen*. Münster, 1964.

———. "Die Durchsetzung der tridentinischen Reform im Domkapitel zu Münster." In Remigius Bäumer, ed. *Reformatio Ecclesiae: Beiträge zur kirchlichen Reformbemühungen von der Alten Kirche bis zur Neuzeit. Festgabe für Erwin Iserloh*. Paderborn, 1980. Pp. 729–47.

———. "Johann von Hoya (1529–1574)," *Westfälische Lebensbilder* 10 (1970), pp. 1–18.

Köhler, Hans-Joachim, ed. *Flugschriften als Massenmedium der Reformationszeit*. Stuttgart, 1981.

König, Joseph. *Geschichtliche Nachrichten über das Gymnasium zu Münster in Westfalen seit Stiftung desselben durch Karl den Grossen bis auf die Jesuiten 791–1592*. Münster, 1821.

Königliches Paulinisches Gymnasium zu Münster. Festschrift zur Feier der Einweihung des neuen Gymnasialgebäudes am 27. IV 1898. Münster, 1898.

Kraus, Jürgen. *Das Militärwesen der Reichsstadt Augsburg 1548–1806. Vergleichende Untersuchungen über städtische Militäreinrichtungen in Deutschland 16. – 18. Jahrhundert*. Augsburg, 1980.

Krins, Franz. *Nachbarschaften im westfälischen Münsterland*. Münster, 1952.

Krippenberg, G. "Das Patriziergeschlecht der Berswordt und Dortmund." *Beiträge zur Geschichte Dortmunds und der Grafschaft Mark* 52 (1955).

Lahrkamp, Helmut. "Alte Geschäftsbücher als Quellen zur lokalen Wirtschaftsgeschichte Münsters." *QFGSM*, n.f. V, Münster, 1970, pp. 290–93.

———. "Galens städtische Widersacher. Streiflichter zur Erhellung der münsterischen Opposition gegen den Fürstbischof Christoph Bernhard." *Westfalen* 51 (1973), pp. 238–53.

———. "Münsterische Reichskammergerichtsnotare 1549/1651." *QFGSM*, n.f. V, Münster, 1970, pp. 263–70.

———. "Münsters wirtschaftliche Führungsschichten." *QFGSM*, n.f. V, Münster, 1970, pp. 1–54.

———. "Das Patriziat in Münster." In Hellmuth Rössler, ed. *Deutsches Patriziat 1430–1740*. Limburg/Lahn, 1968. Pp. 195–208.

———. "Rückwirkungen der Türkenkriege auf Münster 1560–1685," *WZ* 129 (1979), pp. 89–108.

———. "Vom Patronatsrecht des münsterschen Rates." In Max Bierbaum, ed. *Studia Westfalica. Beiträge zur Kirchengeschichte und religiösen Volkskunde Westfalens. Festschrift für Alois Schröer*. Münster, 1973. Pp. 214–39.

Lanzinner, Maximilian. *Fürst, Räte und Landstände: Die Entstehung der Zentralbehörden in Bayern 1511–1598*, Göttingen, 1980.

Le Goff, Jacques. "Ordres mendients et urbanisation dans la France medievale." *Annales E.S.C.* (1970), pp. 924–46.

Le Roy Ladurie, Emmanuel. *Carnival in Romans*. Translated by Mary Feeney. New York, 1979.

Lethmate, Franz. *Die Bevölkerung Münster i. W. in der zweiten Hälfte des 16. Jahrhunderts*. Münster, 1912.

Lexikon für Theologie und Kirche. Edited by Josef Höfer and Karl Rahner. 2nd rev. ed. Freiburg, 1965.

Lieberich, Heinz. "Die gelehrten Räte. Staat und Juristen in Baiern in der Frühzeit der Rezeption." *ZfBLG* 27 (1964), pp. 120–89.

List, Günther. *Chiliastische Utopie und Radikale Reformation. Die Erneuerung der Idee vom Tausendjährigen Reich im 16. Jahrhundert*. Munich, 1973.

Löffler, Peter. *Studien zum Totenbrauchtum in den Gilden, Bruderschaften und Nachbarschaften Westfalens vom Ende des 15. bis zum Ende des 19. Jahrhunderts*. Münster, 1975.

Looz-Corswarem, Clemens von. "Die Kölner Artikelserie von 1525. Hintergründe und Verlauf des Aufruhrs von 1525 in Köln." In Franz Petri, ed. *Kirche und gesellschaftlicher Wandel*. . . . Pp. 65–154.

Lucas, B. *Der Buchdrucker Lambert Raesfeldt. Ein Beitrag zur Buchdruckereigeschichte Münsters im 16. und 17. Jahrhundert*. Münster, 1929.

Lüdicke, Reinhard. "Die landesherrlichen Zentralbehörden im Bistum Münster. Ihre Entstehung und Entwicklung bis 1650." *WZ* 59 (1901), pp. 1–169.

Lutz, Robert H. *Wer war der gemeine Mann? Der dritte Stand in der Krise des Spätmittelalters*. Munich, 1979.

Marré, Heinrich. *Die Wehrverfassung der Stadt Münster von den Wiedertäuferunruhen bis zur Regierungszeit Christoph Bernhards von Galen (1536–1650)*. Münster, 1913.

Maschke, Erich. "Deutsche Städte am Ausgang des Mittelalters." In Wilhelm Rausch, ed. *Die Stadt am Ausgang des Mittelalters*. Linz, 1974. Pp. 1–44.

———. *Die Familie in der deutschen Stadt des späten Mittelalters*. Heidelberg, 1980.

Maschke, Erich, and Jürgen Sydow, eds. *Gesellschaftliche Unterschichten in den südwestdeutschen Städten*. Stuttgart, 1967.

———. eds. *Städtische Mittelschichten*. Stuttgart, 1972.

———. eds. *Stadt und Umland*. Stuttgart, 1974.

Meckstroth, Ursula. "Das Verhältnis der Stadt Münster zu ihrem Landesherrn bis zum Ende der Stiftsfehde (1457)." *QFGSM*, n.f. II, Münster, 1962, pp. 3–196.

Mellink, Albert F. *Amsterdam en de Wederdopers in de zestiende Eeuw*. Nijmegen, 1978.

———. "Das niederländisch-westfälische Täufertum im 16. Jahrhundert." In Hans-Jürgen Görtz, ed. *Umstrittenes Täufertum 1525–1975*. Göttingen, 1975. Pp. 206–22.

———. *De Wederdopers in de Noordelijke Nederlanden 1531–1544*. Groningen, 1953.

Meyn, Matthias. *Die Reichsstadt Frankfurt vor dem Bürgeraufstand von 1612 bis 1614. Struktur und Krise*. Frankfurt, 1980.

Midelfort, H. C. Eric. "Madness and the Problems of Psychological History in the Sixteenth Century." *SCJ* 12 (1981), pp. 5–12.

———. *Witchhunting in Southwestern Germany, 1562–1684: The Social and Intellectual Foundations*. Stanford, 1972.

Miskimin, Harry A. *The Economy of Later Renaissance Europe, 1460–1600*. Cambridge, 1977.

———. "The Legacies of London: 1259–1330." In H. A. Miskimin et al., eds. *The Medieval City*. New Haven, 1977.

Moeller, Bernd. *Imperial Cities and the Reformation*. Translated by H. C. Erik Midelfort and Mark Edwards. Philadelphia, 1972.

———. "Kleriker als Bürger." in *Festschrift für Hermann Heimpel*, vol. 2, ed. Max-Planck-Institut für Geschichte. Göttingen, 1972. Pp. 195–224.

———. *Pfarrer als Bürger*. Göttingen, 1972.

———. "Probleme des kirchlichen Lebens in Deutschland vor der Reformation." In Raymund Kottje and Joseph Staber, eds. *Probleme der Kirchenspaltung im 16. Jahrhundert*. Regensburg, 1970. Pp. 13–32.

———, ed. *Stadt und Kirche im 16. Jahrhundert*. Gütersloh, 1978.

Mollat, Michel, ed. *Études sur l'histoire de la pauvreté*. 2 vols. Paris, 1974.

———. *Les pauvres au moyen âge*. Paris, 1978.

Mols, Roger. *Introduction à la demographie historique des villes d'Europe du XIVe au XVIIIe siècle*. 3 vols. Louvain, 1956.

Mommsen, Wolfgang J., et al., eds. *Stadtbürgertum und Adel in der Reformation. Studien zur Sozialgeschichte der Reformation in England und Deutschland*. Stuttgart, 1979.

Moorrees, W. *Het Münstersche Geslacht van der Wyck*. The Hague, 1911.

Moser, Hugo. *Deutsche Sprachgeschichte*. Stuttgart, 1950.

Mousnier, Roland. *L'Assassinat d'Henri IV*. Paris, 1964.

Muchembled, Robert. *Culture populaire et culture des élites dans la France moderne (XVe–XVIIIe siècles)*. Paris, 1978.

Müller, Eugen. *Die St.-Catherinen-Bruderschaft zu Münster 1330–1930*. Münster, 1930.

Müller, Johannes. *Das Jesuitendrama in den Ländern Deutscher Zunge vom Anfang (1555) bis zum Hochbarock (1665)*. 2 vols. Augsburg, 1930.

Neuer-Landfried, Franziska. *Die Katholische Liga 1608–1620*. Kallmünz, 1968.

Nordhoff, J. B. *Denkwürdigkeiten aus dem Münsterischen Humanismus. Mit einer Anlage über das frühere Press- und Bücherwesen Westfalens*. Münster, 1874.

———. "Die Minoritenkirche zu Münster." *Organ für christliche Kunst* 18 (1868).

Oberman, Heiko A. *Werden und Wertung der Reformation.* Tübingen, 1977.

Offenberg, Heinrich. *Bilder und Skizzen aus Münsters Vergangenheit.* 2 parts. Münster, 1898/1902.

Osborn, Max. *Die Teufelliteratur des 16. Jahrhunderts.* Berlin, 1893.

Ozment, Steven, ed. *Reformation Europe: A Guide to Research.* Saint Louis, 1982.

———. *Reformation in the Cities.* New Haven, 1975.

———. "The Social History of the Reformation: What Can We learn from Pamphlets?" In Hans-Joachim Köhler, ed. *Flugschriften als Massenmedium der Reformationszeit.*

Pastor, Ludwig von. *The History of the Popes.* Vol. 24. London, 1933.

Perouas, Louis. *Le diocèse de la Rochelle de 1648 à 1724: Sociologie et pastorale.* Paris, 1964.

Petri, Franz, ed. *Bischofs- und Kathedralstädte des Mittelalters und der frühen Neuzeit.* Cologne, 1976.

———. "Karl V und die Städte im Nordwestraum während des Ringens um die politisch-kirchliche Ordnung in Deutschland." *JbfWKG* 71 (1978), pp. 19–30.

———, ed. *Kirche und gesellschaftlicher Wandel in deutschen und niederländischen Städten der werdenden Neuzeit.* Cologne, 1980.

———. "Mass und Bedeutung der reformatorischen Strömungen in den niederländischen Masslanden im 16. Jahrhundert." In Martin Greschat and J. F. G. Goeters, eds. *Reformation und Humanismus. Robert Stupperich zum 65. Geburtstag.* Witten, 1969. Pp. 212–24.

———. "Vom Verhältnis Westfalens zu den östlichen Niederlanden." *Westfalen* 34 (1956), pp. 161–68.

Petri, Franz, and W. Jappe Alberts. *Gemeinsame Probleme Deutsch-Niederländischen Landes- und Volksforschung.* Groningen, 1962.

Peuss, Busso. "Das Geld und Münzwesen der Stadt Münster i. W." *QFGSM* IV, Münster, 1931, pp. 1–90.

Philippi, Friedrich. "Das alte Herdingsche Haus in Münster." *Westfalen* 12 (1922), pp. 77–81.

Pick, R. "Dietrich Zwivel der Ältere." *Annalen des Historischen Vereins für den Niederrhein* 26/27 (1874), pp. 399–401.

Pieper, Paul. "Hermann tom Ring als Bildnismaler." *Westfalen* 34 (1956), pp. 72–101.

Pieper-Lippe, Margarete. *Westfälische Zunftsiegel.* Münster, 1963.

Pirenne, Henri. *The Medieval City.* Translated by Frank Halsey. Princeton, 1969.

Planitz, Hans. *Die Deutsche Stadt im Mittelalter.* Graz, 1954.

Plassmann, Joseph O. *Leben und Treiben der alten Münsterländer.* Münster, 1935.

Platt, Robert S. *A Geographical Study of the Dutch-German Border.* Münster, 1958.

Press, Volker. *Calvinismus und Territorialstaat. Regierung und Zentralbehörde der Kurpfalz.* Stuttgart, 1970.

———. *Kaiser Karl V, König Ferdinand und die Entstehung der Reichsritterschaft.* Wiesbaden, 1976.

———. "Stadt und territoriale Konfessionsbildung." In Franz Petri, ed. *Kirche und gesellschaftlicher Wandel.* Pp. 251–96.

Preuss, Hans. *Die Vorstellungen vom Antichrist im späteren Mittelalter, bei Luther und in der konfessionellen Polemik.* Leipzig, 1906.

Prinz, Joseph. "Johannes Münstermann. Zu einem Bildnis von Hermann tom Ring." *Westfalen* 40 (1962), pp. 300–07.

Pugh, Wilma J. "Catholics, Protestants, and Testamentary Charity in Seventeenth-Century Lyon and Nimes." *French Historical Studies* 11 (1980), pp. 479–504.

Pullan, Brian. *Rich and Poor in Renaissance Venice: The Social Institutions of a Catholic State.* Cambridge, Mass., 1971.

Püschel, Erich. "Untersuchungen über die Verbreitung einer epidemischen Krankheit in Westfalen. Der Englische Schweiss des Jahres 1529." *WF* 10 (1957), pp. 57–63.

Rapp, Francis. "Die soziale und wirtschaftliche Vorgeschichte des Bauernkrieges in Unterelsass." in Bernd Moeller, ed. *Bauernkriegstudien.* Gütersloh, 1975.

Rediger, Fritz. *Zur dramatischen Literatur der Paderborner Jesuiten.* Emsdetten, 1935.

Reichling, D. *Johannes Murmellius. Sein Leben und seine Werke. Nebst einem ausfürlichen bibliographischen Verzeichnis sämtlicher Schriften und einer Auswahl von Gedichten.* Freiburg, 1880. Reprinted Amsterdam, 1963.

Reincke, Heinrich. *Hamburg am Vorabend der Reformation.* Edited by Erich von Lehe. Hamburg, 1966.

Reissman, Martin. *Die Hamburgische Kaufmannschaft des 17. Jahrhunderts im sozialgeschichtlichen Sicht.* Hamburg, 1975.

Remling, Ludwig. "Bruderschaften in Franken. Kirchen- und sozialgeschichtliche Untersuchungen zum spätmittelalterlichen und frühneuzeitlichen Bruderschaftswesen," Ph.D. diss., University of Würzburg, 1981.

———. "Fastnacht und Gegenreformation in Münster: Diarien, Chroniken und Litterae Annuae der Jesuiten als Quellen." In *Jahrbuch für Volkskunde* (1982), pp. 51–77.

Riedenauer, Erwin. "Kaiser und Patriziat. Struktur und Funktion des reichsstädtischen Patriziats im Blickpunkt kaiserlicher Adelspolitik vom Karl IV bis Karl VI." *ZfBLG* 30 (1967), pp. 526–653.

———. "Kaiserliche Standeserhebungen für reichsstädtische Bürger 1519–1740. Ein statistischer Vorbericht zum Thema 'Kaiser und Patriziat.' " In Hellmuth Rössler, ed. *Deutsches Patriziat.*

Riering, Bernhard. "Das westliche Münsterland im hansischen Raum." In *Westfalen, Hanse, Ostseeraum.* Münster, 1955. Pp. 170–208.

Riewerts, Theodor. "Deutsches und Niederländisches bei Hermann tom Ring." *Westfalen* 23 (1938), pp. 276–87.

Ritter, Moritz. *Deutsche Geschichte im Zeitalter der Gegenreformation und der Dreissigjährigen Krieges.* 3 vols., Stuttgart, 1898–1908.

Rixen, Carl. *Geschichte und Organisation der Juden im ehemaligen Stift Münster.* Münster, 1906.

Robisheaux, Thomas. "Peasants and Pastors: Rural Youth Control and the Reformation in Hohenlohe, 1540–1680." *Social History* 6 (1981), pp. 281–300.

Roelker, Nancy. "The Appeal of Calvinism to French Noblewomen in the Sixteenth Century." *Journal of Interdisciplinary History* 2 (1972).

Rössler, Hellmuth, ed. *Deutscher Adel 1430–1555*. Darmstadt, 1965.

———, ed. *Deutsches Patriziat 1430–1740*. Limburg/Lahn, 1968.

Rondorf, J. *Die westfälischen Städte in ihrem Verhältnis zur Hanse bis zum Beginn des 16. Jahrhunderts*. Münster, 1905.

Roth, Karl. *Die Ministerialität der Bischöfe von Münster*. Münster, 1912.

Rothert, Hermann. *Westfälische Geschichte. II: Das Zeitalter der Glaubenskämpfe*. Gütersloh, 1949.

Rublack, Hans-Christoph. *Die Gescheiterte Reformation. Frühreformatorische und protestantische Bewegungen in süd- und westdeutschen geistlichen Residenzen*. Stuttgart, 1978.

Rupprich, Hans. *Die Deutsche Literatur vom späten Mittelalter bis zum Barock. II. Teil: Das Zeitalter der Reformation 1520–1570*. Munich, 1973.

Safley, Thomas M. "Marital Litigation in the Diocese of Constance, 1551–1620." *SCJ* 12 (1981), pp. 61–77.

Salmon, J. H. M. "The Paris Sixteenth, 1584–94: The Social Analysis of a Revolutionary Movement." *JMH* 44 (1972).

Die Sanct Georgs Bruderschaft zu Münster. Münster, 1896.

Schafmeister, Karl. *Herzog Ferdinand von Bayern Erzbischof von Köln, als Fürstbischof von Münster (1612–1659)*. Münster, 1912.

Schilling, Heinz. "Aufstandsbewegungen in der Stadtbürgerlichen Gesellschaft des Alten Reiches. Die Vorgeschichte des Münsteraner Täuferreichs, 1525–1534." *GG*, Bauernkrieg-Beiheft (1975), pp. 193–238.

———. "Bürgerkämpfe in Aachen zu Beginn des 17. Jahrhunderts: Konflikte im Rahmen der alteuropäischen Stadtgesellschaft oder im Umkreis der frühbürgerlichen Revolution?" *Zeitschrift für Historische Forschung* 1 (1974).

———. *Konfessionskonflikt und Staatsbildung. Eine Fallstudie über das Verhältnis von religiösem und sozialem Wandel in der Frühneuzeit am Beispiel der Grafschaft Lippe*. Gütersloh, 1981.

———. *Niederländische Exultanten im 16. Jahrhundert*. Gütersloh, 1972.

Schmidt, Heinrich. *Die Deutschen Städtechroniken als Spiegel des bürgerlichen Selbstverständnisses im Spätmittelalter*. Göttingen, 1958.

Schmitz-Kallenberg, Ludwig. *Monasticon Westfaliae. Verzeichnis der im Gebiet der Provinz Westfalen bis zum Jahre 1815 gegründeten Stiften, Klöster, und sonstigen Ordensniederlassungen. Münster, 1909.*

Schmülling, Wilhelm. "325 Jahre Marienwallfahrt Telgte." *RWZfVK* 25 (1979/80), pp. 283–87.

Scholz, Karl, "Einige Bemerkungen zu den Testamenten münsterischer Kanoniker," *Westfalen* 58 (1980), pp. 117–20.

Schöningh, Wolfgang. "Westfälische Einwanderer in Ostfriesland 1433 bis 1744." *WF* 20 (1967), pp. 5–57.

Schönstädt, Hans-Jürgen. *Antichrist, Weltheilsgeschehen und Gottes Werkzeug. Römische Kirche, Reformation und Luther im Spiegel des reformationsjubilaeums 1617*. Wiesbaden, 1978.

Schormann, Gerhard. *Hexenprozesse in Nordwestdeutschland*. Hildesheim, 1977.

Schreiber, Georg. "Deutsche Türkennot und Westfalen." *WF* 7 (1953/54), pp. 62–79.

Schröer, Alois. *Die Kirche in Westfalen vor der Reformation.* 2 vols. Münster, 1967.

———, ed. *Monasterium. Festschrift zum 700jährigen Weihgedächtnis des Paulus-Domes zu Münster.* Münster, 1966.

———. *Die Reformation in Westfalen. Der Glaubenskampf einer Landschaft.* Vol. 1. Münster, 1979.

———. "Das Tridentinum und Münster." in Georg Schreiber, ed. *Das Weltkonzil von Trient.* Vol. 2. Freiburg, 1951. Pp. 295–370.

Schulze, Rudolf. *Das adelige Frauen- (Kanonissen-) Stift der Hl. Maria (1040–1773) und die Pfarre Liebfrauen-Überwasser zu Münster Westfalen (1040). Ihre Verhältnisse und Schicksale.* 2nd rev. ed. Münster, 1952.

———, ed. *Das Gymnasium Paulinum zu Münster 797–1947.* Münster, 1948.

———. "Der niederländische Rechtsgelehrte Vigilius van Zuichem (1507–1577) als Bischöflich-Münsterischer Offizial und Dechant von Liebfrauen (Überwasser) zu Münster." *WZ* 101/102 (1953), pp. 183–230.

Schulze, Wilfried. *Reich und Türkengefahr im späten 16. Jahrhundert.* Munich, 1978.

Schwarz, Wilhelm E. "Studien zur Geschichte des Klosters der Augustinerinnen Marienthal genannt Niesing zu Münster." *WZ* 72 (1914), pp. 46–151.

Scribner, Robert W. *For the Sake of Simple Folk. Popular Propaganda for the German Reformation.* Cambridge, 1981.

———. "Reformation, Carnival, and the World Turned Upside-Down." *Social History* 3 (1978), pp. 303–29.

———. "Why Was There No Reformation in Cologne?" *Bulletin of the Institute of Historical Research* 49 (1976).

Die 600jährige St. Antonii Erzbruderschaft Münster i. Westfalen. Münster, 1969.

Seils, Ernst-Albert. *Die Staatslehre des Jesuiten Adam Contzen, Beichtvater Kurkürst Maximilian I. von Bayern.* Lübeck/Hamburg, 1968.

Sieber, Siegfried. "Nachbarschaften, Gilden, Zünfte und ihre Feste." *Archiv für Kulturgeschichte* 11 (1914), pp. 455–82.

Simon, Irmgard. "Fastnachtsbräuche in Westfalen." *RWZfVK* 6 (1959), pp. 56–69.

Sökeland, Bernhard. *Geschichte des Münsterschen Gymnasium von dem Übergange desselben an die Jesuiten im Jahre 1588 bis 1630.* Münster, 1826.

Spieckermann, Heinrich. *Beiträge zur Geschichte des Domkapitels zu Münster im Mittelalter.* Emsdetten, 1935.

Spindler, Max, ed. *Handbuch der Bayerischen Geschichte.* Vol. 2. Munich, 1966.

Stadt- und Marktkirche Saint Lamberti Münster (Westf.) Festschrift zur Feier der Wiedererrichtung am 31. Januar 1960. Münster, 1960.

Steinberg, S. H. *Five Hundred Years of Printing.* Rev. ed. Bristol, 1961.

Steinbicker, Clemens. "Das Beamtentum in den geistlichen Fürstentümern Norddeutschlands im Zeitraum von 1430–1740." In Günther Franz, ed. *Beamtentum und Pfarrstand 1400–1800.*

———. "Vom Geschlechterkreis der münsterischen Rats- und Bürgermeisterfamilie Timmerscheidt. Ein Beitrag zur Geschichte des münsterischen Honoratiorentums des 17. Jahrhunderts." *WZ* 111 (1961), pp. 95–117.

Stievermann, Dieter. *Städtewesen in Südwestfalen: Die Städte des Märkischen Sauerlandes im späten Mittelalter und in der frühen Neuzeit.* Stuttgart, 1978.

Störmann, Anton. *Die städtischen Gravamina gegen den Klerus am Ausgang des Mittelalters und in der Reformationszeit.* Münster, 1916.

Stoob, Heinz, ed. *Die Stadt. Gestalt und Wandel bis zum industriellen Zeitalter.* Cologne, 1976.

Stratenwerth, Heide. *Die Reformation in der Stadt Osnabrück.* Wiesbaden, 1971.

Strauss, Gerald. *The Lutheran House of Learning.* Baltimore, 1978.

———. *Nuremberg in the Sixteenth Century.* Bloomington, 1976.

Stüdeli, Bernhard E. J. *Minoritenniederlassungen und mittelalterliche Stadt.* Werl, 1969.

Studt, Bernhard, and Hans Olsen. *Hamburg. Die Geschichte einer Stadt.* Hamburg, 1951.

Stupperich, Robert. "Devotio moderna und reformatorische Frömmigkeit." *JbfWKG* 59/60 (1966/67), pp. 11–26.

———. "Dr. Johann von der Wyck. Ein münsterscher Staatsmann der Reformationszeit." *WZ* 123 (1973), pp. 9–50.

———. "Hessens Anteil an der Reformation in Westfalen." *Hessisches Jahrbuch für Landesgeschichte* 18 (1968), pp. 146–59.

———. "Wer war Henricus Dorpius Monasteriensis?" *JbfWKG* 51/52 (1958/59), pp. 150–60.

Szarota, Elida M. *Das Jesuitendrama im deutschen Sprachgebiet.* 2 vols. in 4. Munich, 1979/80.

Theuerkauf, Gerhard. *Land und Lehnswesen vom 14. bis zum 16. Jahrhundert. Ein Beitrag zur Verfassung des Hochstifts Münster und zum nordwestdeutschen Lehnrecht.* Cologne, 1961.

———. "Der niedere Adel in Westfalen." In Hellmuth Rössler, ed. *Deutscher Adel 1430–1555.* Darmstadt, 1965. Pp. 153–76.

Thomas, Keith. *Religion and the Decline of Magic.* New York, 1971.

———. "Women and the Civil War Sects." *P & P* 13 (1958).

Tibus, Adolph. *Geschichtliche Nachrichten über die Weihbischöfe von Münster.* Münster, 1862.

Tophoff, Theodor. "Die Gilden binnen Münster." *WZ* 35 (1877), pp. 3–157.

Trüdinger, Karl. *Stadt und Kirche im spätmittelalterlichen Würzburg.* Stuttgart, 1978.

Trusen, Wilfried. "Zum Rentenkauf im Spätmittelalter." In *Festschrift für Hermann Heimpel.* Vol. 2. Göttingen, 1972. Pp. 140–58.

Uthmann, Karl. *Sozialstruktur und Vermögensbildung in Hildesheim des 15. und 16. Jahrhunderts.* Bremen, 1957.

Valentin, Jean-Marie. *Le théâtre des jésuites dans les pays de langue allemande (1554–1680).* 3 vols. Bern, 1978.

Vann, James A., and Steven Rowan, eds. *The Old Reich: Essays on German Political Institutions, 1495–1806* (= Études presenteés à la Commission Internationale pour l'Histoire des Assemblies d'États 48). Brussels, 1974.

Verdenhalven, Fritz. *Alte Masse, Münzen und Gewichte aus dem deutschen Sprachgebiet.* Neustadt a.d. Aisch, 1968.

Vierkotten, Ursula. "Zur Geschichte des Apothekenwesens von Stadt und Fürstbistum Münster." *QFGSM*, n.f. V, Münster, 1970, pp. 95–208.

Vogler, Bernard. "Die Ausbildung des Konfessionsbewusstseins in den pfälzischen Territorien zwischen 1555 und 1619." In Horst Rabe et al., eds. *Festgabe für Ernst Walter Zeeden*. Münster, 1976. Pp. 281–88.

———. *Le clergé protestant rhenan au siècle de la réforme 1555–1619*. Paris, 1976.

Vogler, Günther. "Das Täuferreich zu Münster im Spiegel der Flugschriften." In Hans-Joachim Köhler, ed. *Flugschriften als Massenmedium der Reformationszeit*.

Vogt, H. "Der Bonner Dechant Johannes Hartmann." *Bonner Geschichtsblätter* 18 (1964), pp. 45–53.

Vovelle, Michel. *Pieté baroque et déchristianisation en Provence au XVIIIe siècle: Les attitudes devant la mort d'après les clauses des testaments*. Paris, 1973.

Waitz, Georg. *Lübeck unter Jürgen Wullenwever und die Europäische Politik*. 3 vols. Berlin, 1855–56.

Weidkuhn, Peter. "Fastnacht-Revolte-Revolution." *Zeitschrift für Religions- und Geistesgeschichte* 21 (1969).

Weskamp, Albert. *Das Heer der Liga in Westfalen zu Abwehr des Grafen von Mansfeld und des Herzogs Christian von Braunschweig (1622–23)*. Münster, 1891.

Weyrauch, Erdmann. *Konfessionelle Krise und soziale Stabilität. Das Interim in Strassburg (1548–1552)*. Stuttgart, 1978.

Williams, George. *The Radical Reformation*. Philadelphia, 1975.

Winterfeld, Luise von. *Geschichte der freien Reichs- und Hansestadt Dortmund*. Dortmund, 1934.

———. "Das westfälische Hansequartier." *Der Raum Westfalen* II:1, Münster, 1955, pp. 257–354.

Wormstall, Albert. "Das Schauspiel zu Münster im 16. und 17. Jahrhundert." *WZ* 56 (1898), pp. 75–85.

Zaretzky, Otto. "Unbeschriebene münsterischen Drucke aus dem ersten Viertel des 16. Jahrhundert." *Westfalen* 14 (1928), pp. 62–66.

Zeeden, Ernst W. *Deutschland im Zeitalter der Glaubenskämpfe*. Munich, 1977.

———. *Die Entstehung der Konfessionen. Grundlagen und Formen der Konfessionsbildung im Zeitalter der Glaubenskämpfe*. Munich, 1965.

———. "Grundlagen und Wege der Konfessionsbildung in Deutschland im Zeitalter der Glaubenskämpfe." *HZ* 185 (1958), pp. 249–99. Reprinted in his *Gegenreformation* (= Wege der Forschung 311). Darmstadt, 1973.

———. "Das Zeitalter der Glaubenskämpfe 1555–1648." In Herbert Grundmann, ed. *Gebhardt Handbuch der deutschen Geschichte*. Vol. 2, no. 2. Stuttgart, 1970.

Zeeden, Ernst W., and Hansgeorg Molitor, eds. *Die Visitation im Dienst der kirchlichen Reform*. 2nd rev. ed. Münster, 1977.

Zuhorn, Karl. "Die Beginen in Münster." *WZ* 91 (1935), pp. 1–149.

———. "Vom Münsterschen Bürgertum um die Mitte des XV. Jahrhundert." *WZ* 95 (1939), pp. 88–193.

INDEX

3 5282 00144 1669